Acclaim for
A NATURAL WOMAN

"Like her songs, King's autobiography soars on an almost impossible level of sincerity...[It] will win your heart."

—*New York Daily News*

"Weaving a tapestry of rich and royal hue, King's affecting memoir eases readers through her life...King's passionate engagement with all kinds of music, and her musical genius [flood] through these reflections."

—*Publishers Weekly* (starred review)

"[King's] story mirrors the story of rock music in the last half of the twentieth century. As they used to say on *American Bandstand*: I give it a 99—love the words, and it's easy to dance to."

—Mary Kay Andres, author of *Spring Fever,*
in the *Miami Herald*

"[A] candid, endearingly chatty memoir that traces King's rise from a precocious Brooklyn girl to one of the world's most beloved singer/songwriters."

—*USA Today*

"[Her] voice comes through strongly on every page of this memoir, an engaging assortment of recollections...refreshingly candid...A warm, winning read that showcases baby-boomer culture at its best."

—*Kirkus Reviews*

"Her book's humble granola-and-chardonnay prose is about as earnest as you'd expect from the songwriter behind 'You've Got a Friend.' But King's best melodies often have a dark edge, and it's detectable in her autobiography too."

—*New York Times Book Review*

"King does not tell the usual celebrity story of hardship, riches, overindulgence, downfall and rehab. A NATURAL WOMAN is a far more original—and sometimes, determinedly unglamorous—tale."
　　　　　　　　　　　　　　　　　　　　　—*Los Angeles Times*

"Written with the same friendly, chatty, warm, and open tone with which she stitched her album *Tapestry*. Her voice comes through as clearly in text as it does on her recordings. A NATURAL WOMAN helps fans find a new appreciation and better understanding of how close to home her confessional songs [really] were...A NATURAL WOMAN may be a solid, accessible guidebook on music theory and pop music history from a songwriter who helped frame it, but its stories also offer rare insight into a woman who has steadfastly guarded her privacy."
　　　　　　　　　　　　　　　　　　　　　—*Miami Herald*

"The title of Carole King's autobiography is a good fit for the humble, glamour-free portrait she paints of her seven decades... an enjoyable amble."
　　　　　　　　　　　　　　　　　　　　　—*Seattle Times*

"Chronicles King's extraordinary life, drawing readers into her musical world...Deeply personal, King's long-awaited memoir offers readers a front-row seat to the woman behind the legend."
　　　　　　　　　　　　　　　　　　　　　—*Washington Examiner*

"I couldn't get through this book without humming or singing some of Carole King's famous songs as I went along. To read the backstage version of her onstage life is to understand where the songs came from and have the chance to relive their creation with her, one of America's greatest tunesmiths and lyricists."
　　　　　　　　　　　　　　　　　　　　　—BookReporter.com

"A NATURAL WOMAN [is] as charming and winning as you'd hope."   —*Vanity Fair* Hollywood Blog

"Fascinating, and, at times, rather shocking."
                              —*Christian Science Monitor*

"A NATURAL WOMAN chronicles King's extraordinary life, drawing readers into her musical world, including her phenomenally successful Number 1 album *Tapestry* and into her journey as a performer, mother, wife, and present-day activist."
                              —SheKnows.com

A NATURAL WOMAN

a memoir

CAROLE KING

GRAND CENTRAL
PUBLISHING

NEW YORK   BOSTON

Grand Central Publishing
Hachette Book Group
1290 Avenue of the Americas
New York, NY 10104

www.HachetteBookGroup.com

Printed in the United States of America

LSC-C

Originally published in hardcover by Grand Central Publishing.

First trade edition: February 2013

Printing 9, 2022

Grand Central Publishing is a division of Hachette Book Group, Inc.
The Grand Central Publishing name and logo is a trademark of Hachette Book Group, Inc.

The Hachette Speakers Bureau provides a wide range of authors for speaking events. To find out more, go to www.hachettespeakersbureau.com or call (866) 376-6591.

The publisher is not responsible for websites (or their content) that are not owned by the publisher.

The Library of Congress has cataloged the hardcover edition as follows:

King, Carole, 1942–
    A natural woman : a memoir / Carole King. — 1st ed.
        p. cm.
    Includes bibliographical references and index.
    ISBN 978-1-4555-1261-4 (regular edition) — ISBN 978-1-4555-1547-9 (large print edition)   1. King, Carole, 1942–   2. Singers—United States—Biography. 3. Composers—United States—Biography.   4. Pianists—United States—Biography.   I. Title.
    ML410.K636A3 2012
    782.42166092—dc23
    [B]
                                                                    2011047070

ISBN 978-1-4555-1262-1 (pbk.)

Author's Note

Over the years many people have urged me to write a book about my life. Each time my answer was, "I'm too busy living my life to write about it." I was no less busy in 2000, when I was fifty-eight, but two years shy of sixty seemed as good a time as any to begin reflecting on the prior decades.

As I began to put together an outline, keeping track of all the bits and pieces was akin to herding cockroaches. Memories scurried out of sight as soon as they came to light, but I persevered. It was important to me to write this book myself, and it's taken me nearly twelve years to do it.

In order to arrive at some degree of objective truth, I undertook some research, and I interviewed friends, family, and colleagues about shared experiences. But my primary purpose in writing this memoir was to entertain readers and share what I remembered. If any dates or facts are inaccurate, I will greatly appreciate your understanding that this is not a historical treatise. It's a memoir.

Where the title of one of my albums is the same as that of a song within that album, the title of the album is always in italics. The song title appears in quotes.

AUTHOR'S NOTE

A *Natural Woman* includes stories to the best of my recollection about my life and my music, with occasional observations about how I perceived the cultural context for both. Just as I can only fit so many songs into one concert, I could only fit so many stories into this book. I hope you enjoy the ones I've chosen.

Carole King
Custer County, Idaho

Showtime 2005

Soundcheck isn't going well. There's a persistent hum in my monitor that no one seems to be able to fix. The lights are throwing a shadow from my microphone boom onto the keyboard, making it hard for me to see middle C. The piano bench is too low. It's not adjustable. A few minutes ago, when I turned around to take off my guitar, I banged the headstock into the side of the piano visible to the audience. My guitar is cracked where the headstock meets the neck, and there's a big ding on the piano.

But these are minor problems compared to the sensation I feel in my throat, the one I get when I'm about to lose my voice. How can I give my audience what they've come for if I don't have a voice?

My bandmates, Rudy Guess and Gary Burr, try to dispel my anxiety.

"Hey, it's okay," Gary volunteers. "Your voice will be there for the show."

Rudy adds, "Carole, don't worry about the guitar. It wasn't your fault."

Their consoling remarks only make me feel worse. I know why

1

the guitar bang happened. It was because I was in too much of a hurry.

My mood doesn't improve when John Vanderslice, our production manager, announces, "It's 6:55, doors open at 7:00, and you need to leave the stage right now."

"But, Slice, we didn't check our vocal balance or get a level on 'Earth Move'!"

Usually we play a chorus of "I Feel the Earth Move" in each new venue so the sound team can assess our likely maximum volume. Whatever level of "loud" we achieve, the sound guys know it goes to "louder" during the actual performance and prepare accordingly. But how can they prepare if they never got to hear where "loud" was?

"Sorry," Slice says, handing me my backpack and beckoning to the piano tuner in one fluid motion.

As I head backstage, my manager, Lorna Guess, intercepts me.

"Don't forget, you have a preshow with some radio contest winners," she reminds me. "Why don't you put this on?"

"This" is a lanyard with a hand-lettered laminated sign that says "Voice At Rest." It explains to others why I'm speaking only in hand signs and whispers, and at the same time reminds me not to speak unnecessarily.

It's unusual for me to meet radio contest winners before a show. Usually I try to conserve my energy for the concert and greet people afterwards. But we have a long bus ride tonight and need to leave immediately after the performance. Touring bands call it "play and wave."

I have less than an hour to meet, greet, eat, and primp. I'm hoping the crew will be able to buff out the ding on the piano, raise the piano bench, eliminate the shadow on the keyboard, and get rid of the hum. I shouldn't worry. In over thirty years of performing in concert I've never gone onstage and found a hum heard at soundcheck still there at showtime. But tonight I am not in harmony with the universe. This is not a good way to feel before a show.

Lorna brings me to the room known as Hospitality where the radio contest winners are. These lovely people are longtime fans. Each has a story. They respect the "Voice At Rest" sign and do all the talking. I listen attentively and sign albums. By the time I've met them all, it's 7:20. Showtime is 8:00.

Lorna walks me over to Catering. Gary and Rudy are at one table and some of the crew are at another. Lorna joins her husband (Rudy) while I stop at the crew table. From their wry jokes I learn that the air-conditioning on their bus hasn't been working for the past few days. It's midsummer in the Midwest. Ignoring my "Voice At Rest" sign, I ask if there's anything I can do to hasten the arrival of a replacement bus. They tell me it's already on the way. I tell them I couldn't function on tour without them. They brush aside my compliments and urge me to enjoy my dinner and not worry about the bus, hums, broken guitars, or their ability to adjust for "louder." Lorna signals me to stop talking. Like a flock of birds, the crew all get up at once to go back to work. Christian Walsh, the FOH (front-of-house) sound man, stops long enough to assure me that everything will be working perfectly by showtime. His upbeat mood makes me feel a little calmer as I walk to the buffet.

I sit down at the now vacated crew table with a plate of salad and just enough rice to sample the sauces from the meat and fish dishes. I always swear I won't eat the cheesecake, and then I always do. I think if I eat half a piece and go back for the other half I'm not really eating a whole piece. I eat quickly, and then I look at my watch: 7:35. Yikes! I hurry to my dressing room, brew a cup of Throat Coat tea, pull a couple of outfits from my wardrobe trunk, and wait for the steamer to heat up. I check my hair in the mirror.

It's frizzy. I daub some conditioner into my hands, add a splash of water, and scrunch the mixture into my hair. Much better.

The importance of hair: I'm feeling optimistic.

I steam my first-act trousers and my second-act blouse. Steaming my clothes grounds me. It gives me ownership of my preshow preparation. I take a sip of tea. It's too hot. I set the cup down and begin to put on my makeup. I've finally figured out how much I need for a concert. It's not much, and it doesn't take long to apply.

Two short raps on the door announce the arrival of Brandon Miller, guitar tech and all-around crew member. He's come for The Book, a loose-leaf notebook that contains each show's set list, charts, lyrics, notes about songs, and the names of local people to mention. I am the keeper of The Book at all times on tour except when Brandon is transporting it to and from the piano. Without The Book I would have to depend on my memory, which has fewer available gigabytes every year.

I begin to dress, simultaneously creating and observing my metamorphosis into the woman the audience has come to see. I'm wearing a black beaded top with a matching jacket over my "security" black pants—"security" because they always fit comfortably and look good no matter how much cheesecake I've just had. I quickly choose some accessories from the accumulation of costume jewelry that I've carried on tour since 1989. It runs the color gamut and is still serviceable, albeit by no one's standard except mine.

I look in the mirror. Ta-dah! It's 7:56, and I look exactly like Carole King. Slice knocks on the door and calls out, "Four minutes!" By the time I open the door and peer outside, Slice has already left to round everyone up for our circle. Tonight "everyone" includes Rudy, Gary, Lorna, and anyone else backstage who isn't doing an essential job at that moment. My own essential job will begin in what is now three minutes. As I wait for the others I wonder if I'll remember to turn on my light. The show is supposed to begin with me turning on the lamp atop my piano before I sit down to play—a gesture I created to set a welcoming tone and establish that we're in my living room.

Lorna arrives at my dressing room with Rudy, Gary, and Joe Cardosi, our tour manager and lighting director. Slice pops in long enough to make sure everyone's there, tells us they're holding until 8:15, then dashes away to make sure everything is in order. The rest of us form a huddle and make jokes and quips about topics ranging from politics and sports to music and fashion. Gary is wearing a long-sleeved black shirt with images of gray rats of various sizes. He calls it his rat shirt. Rudy says he's glad for the reprieve because he doesn't have his blue Beatle boots on yet. Gary reminds Rudy that he's not onstage for the first song. Joe tells me the name of the local baseball team in case I decide to play "Hard Rock Café." Then Rudy spontaneously hums a low note. We all join Rudy and let the note rise gradually in pitch and volume until it turns into a roar. We end with a shout and break the circle. Seconds later, Slice opens the door and says, "Showtime!"

The others resume their preshow tasks. Slice stays with me. I rely on him to keep me from having a *Spinal Tap* moment. He has taped white arrows marked STAGE on the floor, but the arrows aren't registering because I'm already thinking about the show. Did they fix the hum? Will I feel comfortable playing the replacement guitar? Will I remember to turn on my light? Will my voice hold up??

I follow Slice past a series of long concrete-block walls filled with performance photos of other artists who've appeared at this venue. Suddenly Slice gets a call on his cell saying he's urgently needed to solve a last-minute problem. He parks me by a wall, says, "Wait here!" and takes off. I look up and see photos of Bob Dylan, Barbra Streisand, Aerosmith, Jefferson Starship, Johnny

Cash, Reba McEntire, Joni Mitchell, Simon & Garfunkel, Earth, Wind & Fire, Crosby, Stills and Nash, David Bowie, U2, and the Rolling Stones.

I well up unexpectedly at the realization that I am one of a select cadre of people who do this thing that I'm minutes away from doing. All have walked these corridors before me, and many will walk them after me. How did *I* get here?

The wiseass answer would be: on a bus from the hotel. But as I see it, the journey started with my grandparents.

PART I

Chapter One

The Name of the Father

*I*n the first decade of the twentieth century a man and a woman from Poland, another man from Poland, and a woman from Russia undertook to cross a continent and an ocean with little more than a fierce determination to find a better life in America. They were my grandparents, and they found that better life in Brooklyn, New York. Had my grandparents not emigrated when they did, I might have been born Jewish in Eastern Europe during World War II, or I might not have been born at all. Instead, I was born in 1942 in New York City.

The story I heard was that when each of my grandparents landed on Ellis Island, an American immigration official wrote down his or her name. My paternal grandparents' surname, Glayman (pronounced GLYE-man), was written down as Klein, which means "small" in German. Though not German, my grandfather, David, was of small stature and, at four foot eight, his young wife, Mollie, was even shorter. Their DNA and the similar stature of my maternal grandparents would foreclose a prepubescent dream of at least one of their future American granddaughters. Predestined to reach a maximum adult height of five feet two inches, I would never grow up to become a tall, slender fashion model.

My name at birth was Carol Joan Klein. It would take me five decades to appreciate my surname and the history that came with it. Along the way I would add an "e" to Carol and acquire several more surnames.

Note to self: wanting to change your surname is not a good reason to get married.

My father's name was Sidney Klein. Everyone called him Sid. My mother's name was Eugenia Cammer. Everyone called her Genie. They met in an elevator at Brooklyn College in 1936. Dad was studying chemistry; Mom's majors were English and drama. They were married on October 6, 1937, after which my mother rechanneled her considerable ambition and intelligence into running a household on a weekly budget of fifteen dollars. My dad left college before graduating and worked briefly as a radio announcer, thereby setting the precedent of a Klein in front of a microphone. He didn't stay in that job very long. With job security on his mind during the Great Depression, he went into civil service and found his calling as a New York City firefighter.

My dad liked helping people and solving problems. He did both every time he pulled someone out of a burning building. My father's captain proudly described him to my mother as "always first on the nozzle," a revelation that brought little comfort to a fireman's wife. Though many of his colleagues died saving others, my dad lived for many years after his retirement. When I was very young, his shift at the firehouse kept him away from home for several days and nights at a time. I missed him, but the upside was that we were able to do things as a family on his days off. Sometimes we went to Coney Island, a short bus ride from our house, where Mommy and Daddy would sit on a bench nearby while I played in the cool, damp sand under the boardwalk. After a while

I'd climb up onto the splintery wood and let Mommy brush the sand off me. Then I'd skip along the boardwalk between Mommy and Daddy, holding both their hands, until we arrived at the stand where Daddy always gave me a nickel to buy a huge sugary mound of cotton candy.

But the thing I remember most about Coney Island is Daddy, Mommy, and me crowded into one of those primitive audio recording booths to record my voice on a black acetate disc so they could preserve the moment for posterity. That was my first recording experience. I no longer have that disc, but I still remember my three-year-old baby voice saying, "My name is Carol Joan Klein, and I live at 2466 East 24th Street in Brooklyn, New York."

I sang "Twinkle, Twinkle, Little Star." And then I began to cry.

Chapter Two

Almost Perfect

On December 7, 1941, a surprise attack on Pearl Harbor by the Japanese military effectively ended the debate about whether America should engage more actively in the war against Germany and Japan. I was born two months later in Manhattan on February 9, 1942.

Because firefighters were essential on the home front, my dad didn't serve in the military, but he, too, put his life on the line every day. My mother managed our family's money and took care of the semidetached two-family house in Brooklyn on which she and my father had put a down payment after I was born. My mother also took care of me, which I'm told was a full-time job. The rent they collected from the family upstairs was negligible. My father refused to go on relief and my mother refused to go into debt. To make the mortgage payments, my mother shopped with an eye for bargains for everything from food and clothing to laundry soap and tooth powder. She cooked, cleaned, and washed and hung my dad's sooty clothes on a clothesline with wooden clothespins that lent themselves to being painted and decorated with bits of cloth to look like tiny men and women. In the spring and summer, my mother tended her Victory Garden in our backyard. That's where one of my earliest musical memories took place.

It's still wartime. I'm three years old, and I'm supposed to be helping my mother in the garden, but on this sunny spring day I'm easily distracted by my desire to gambol around the yard and climb up on things on which I shouldn't be climbing. Our neighbors, Mrs. Butler and Mrs. Bursch, call out to my mother whenever they think I'm in danger, which is approximately every two minutes.

Mrs. Butler lives upstairs from Mrs. Bursch. They're always together. "Butler and Bursch" is how we think of the single unit the two women seem to have become. Mr. Butler and Mr. Bursch exist but are rarely seen. In good weather, Butler and Bursch sit on a bench across the street next to the public playground. On this occasion they sit on painted metal chairs on the back porch outside Bursch's kitchen while giving my mother a running commentary on my activities. Clods of freshly watered dirt squish between my bare toes as I cavort among the vegetables and help my mother pull weeds. I pirouette around the garden and sing along with my mother while the radio plays one of the popular songs of the day, "Bell Bottom Trousers (Coat of Navy Blue)." I'm too young to understand the meaning of the words, but I sing and dance to the catchy chorus with gusto while my mother alternates between singing and laughing.

When the song is over, Bursch exclaims to my mother, "Isn't she cute! Mark my words, Genie. Someday she'll be famous."

Butler is less optimistic. "I don't like those popular songs. I wish they'd play real music like Caruso sings."

The first piece of furniture in my parents' home was a piano. My mom had deeply disliked the piano lessons my grandmother forced her to take, but she appreciated them later when she found that she could earn fifty cents a lesson teaching piano to neighborhood children. And when she discovered my insatiable curiosity about music, she was able to pass her knowledge on to me. From the time I could stand on tiptoe to reach the piano keys, I was relentless in asking my mother to teach me the names of notes. The first note she taught me was D above middle C, which I played repeatedly in various rhythmic configurations.

D. D. D. D.
D.D.D.   D.D.D.
D...D-D...
D-D-D-D-D-D-D-D.

It was clear that she would have to teach me the rest of the notes just to get some relief.

Although my father's family had been too poor to afford music lessons, one of my Klein aunts had taught herself to pick out chords on a piano at a friend's home, and she could sing almost as beautifully as if she had been trained. Though my dad had "an ear for music," his entire repertoire on piano comprised both parts (one at a time) of the duet of "Heart and Soul," the melody of "Chopsticks," and a tune in F-sharp that didn't have a name but allowed him to utilize only the black keys as he rolled his fist up and down the piano to produce a melody. Whenever he played the little tune on the black keys, it never failed to delight me.

Neither my aunt nor my father could tell you the name of a note, but they could sing it back. After my mother taught me the names of all the notes, I could not only sing a note back, I could correctly identify it. Because my father didn't understand the difference between perfect pitch and relative pitch, he boasted to anyone within earshot of his little girl and a piano that Carol had perfect pitch.

Perfect pitch is when a note matches up consistently with that note in your memory. Whether you're asked to sing middle C, A, or E-flat, you will always sing it correctly. With relative pitch, you may not be able to sing or identify a note perfectly the first time, but once you know the first note, you can correctly sing and identify the rest of them. That's what I do.

Either way, my ability to identify notes impressed my dad, who enjoyed showing me off to his friends. Sometimes, when he and his firehouse buddies had a common day off, they gathered at our house with their wives. The men sat in the living room and told jokes while the women served and refilled the men's drinks in big green glasses with crackling ice cubes and replenished the little snack dishes that my mother brought out only when we had company. After a while, my father would casually migrate over to the piano and instruct me to stand on the opposite side of the room with my face to the wall so I couldn't see the piano. Then he'd begin. He always started with middle C.

"What note is that, Carol?" he'd ask, smiling at his friends as if he knew a secret that they didn't.

"Middle C," I'd answer.

"What note is *that?*"

"E-flat."

"How about *that* one?"

"B."

"And *this* one?"

"F-sharp."

With that, I turned away from the wall. My dad's smile was so broad that it encompassed the lower half of his face. I enjoyed making my father happy and getting the notes right—two separate thoughts that an astute psychologist might correctly interpret as one—but I didn't enjoy being shown off like a trained puppy. And yet those early "performances" were excellent training for my ear.

Even better were the many blissful hours I spent on my own matching up notes in my head with notes on the piano. I had begun making up songs when I was three. Perched precariously on Brooklyn and Manhattan telephone books atop the piano bench, I improvised words and melodies at the top of my lungs while my little fingers pounded out a rudimentary accompaniment on the piano. Using the most advanced form of recording then available in our household, my mother transcribed onto music paper a song I wrote called "Galloping."

My first real music lesson took place when I was four. My mother invited me to climb up and sit next to her on the piano bench. (By then I needed only the Brooklyn phone book.) She introduced me to music theory and elementary piano technique using a child-sized book with a bright red cover called *Teaching Little Fingers to Play,* by John Thompson. Here is one of the first songs I learned:

$$1 \quad 2 \quad 3 \quad 1 \quad 2 \quad 3 \quad 2 \quad 1 \quad 2 \quad 3 \quad 1 \quad 1$$
Here we go—up a row—to a birth-day par—ty

The numbers indicated the fingering—thumb being 1, index finger 2, and middle finger 3. In this song, 1, 2, and 3 corresponded with middle C, D, and E. I learned the difference between quarter notes ("here we") and a half note ("go"), where each note was written on or between the lines of the treble staff, and how each note made the journey from the page through my brain and fingers to the piano to produce its own unique tone. My mother never forced me to practice. She didn't have to. I wanted so much to master the popular songs that poured out of the radio that I played everything she taught me many times over, undoubtedly driving her to distraction even more than had my repetition of D.

My mother enrolled me in kindergarten when I was four. By the end of the school year I had demonstrated such an exceptional facility with words and numbers that my teachers promoted me directly to second grade. Skipping grades, a common practice in the 1940s, might have been good for my intellectual curiosity, but it was not good for my social development. From second grade on, I was two years younger than most of the kids in my class.

One afternoon, while my father was at his workbench in the basement, my mother was in the kitchen with me. The radio on the shelf above the kitchen table was playing quietly in the background. Between sips of milk and bites of Fig Newtons I was using a yellow pencil to copy random words from a newspaper into a composition book with a black-and-white marbled cover. My mother had just gone to get something from her sewing room at the other end of the house when something about Dinah Shore's voice on the radio singing "Shoo Fly Pie and Apple Pan Dowdy" made me set my pencil down. I climbed up on a chair, turned the radio up to full volume so I could hear it in the living room, and ran to the piano to see if I could play it. Hearing the radio suddenly blasting, my mom came running to see if I was all right. When she saw me sitting at the piano she walked into the kitchen, turned off the radio, came back and sat next to me on the bench, and taught me a few basic triads that were compatible with Sonny Burke's orchestral accompaniment. As she played the chords, we sang the melody and lyrics together.

Hearing my mom and me at the piano brought my dad upstairs. At first he sang along from the doorway, then he came over and sat on the opposite end of the bench from my mother with me in the middle. It was fascinating to watch my dad play the melody to "Heart and Soul" while my mom provided the two-handed accompaniment. Then they switched seats and parts. Seated between them, I couldn't resist making the duet a trio. Some of the chords to "Heart and Soul" were similar to the ones my mother had just taught me for "Shoo Fly Pie," and though I didn't have my parents' agility, the notes I played were harmonious enough to put smiles on all our faces.

It was a happy time. My mom and dad and I were a family. My parents loved each other. They loved me; I loved them; and we all loved music. My early childhood not only gave me a sense of security, it was enriched by a remarkable device that transmitted the latest popular songs and other forms of entertainment through a speaker by means of vacuum tubes, an amplifier, and the intersection of creativity with people's need for it.

Chapter Three

Over the Airwaves

At age five I loved the radio not only because it was the center of a pleasurable activity that drew my family together, but because it was the source of a wealth of words, sounds, stories, and music. When I was ill enough to stay home from school, I curled up under the covers and listened to the daytime soaps, for which the musical scores were usually composed live on the spot.

"*The Romance of Helen Trent!*" the announcer would say dramatically, immediately followed by the swell of an organ. The sense of continuity that I began to acquire after a few days of following the adventures of Lorenzo Jones, Ma Perkins, and Our Gal Sunday was lost as soon as I was well enough to go back to school. I might have been more motivated to malinger, but I knew my mother would know I was faking it, and anyway, I liked school.

After school I did arithmetic and sang along with Tony Pastor and His Orchestra to "Dance with a Dolly (with a Hole in Her Stocking)." Even without the music, the rhythm of the hook was catchier than Roy Campanella's baseball mitt.

The first radio I remember was a polished brown wooden box with knobs, push buttons, and evenly spaced horizontal ridges that

I now know were typical of art deco design. The radio sat on a painted white shelf in the kitchen that my dad had installed above our Formica table with its chrome frame. The crinkly pattern on the Formica looked as if someone had crumpled a big sheet of red paper and then flattened it out.

When my father came home from his shift at night he often found my mother cutting up celery and carrots to add to the pot of chicken soup simmering on our Welbilt stove. After tossing in vegetables and tasting the broth with an oversized soup spoon, my mother added salt, peppercorns, and a bay laurel leaf while my father emptied the pockets of the pants he had been wearing at the firehouse, leaving his wallet, keys, assorted coins, notes on scraps of paper in his handwriting, and a sooty handkerchief all a-tumble on the tabletop. When my mom reminded him that the soup was almost ready and that she and I were waiting to set the table, he moved his things to a small table in the foyer and went to wash his hands.

As we ate, my dad got all worked up listening to the news delivered by Edward R. Murrow or Lowell Thomas. Then he laughed at Baby Snooks and Jack Benny and was soothed by the music of Glenn Miller and His Orchestra, Tommy Dorsey and His Orchestra, and Jimmy Dorsey and His Orchestra. (Kudos to those bandleaders for acknowledging their musicians.)

My dad and I shared a liking for the mysteries on WOR, a Mutual Broadcasting Company radio station. We were avid fans of *The Shadow, The Lone Ranger, Inner Sanctum, The Green Hornet, Suspense,* and *Mr. Keen, Tracer of Lost Persons.*

Sometimes we went to movies and ball games, but radio was our preferred form of entertainment before TV took over our household and everyone else's. The large quantity and quality of radio programming in my formative years brought my parents and me into a world in which the aural cues we were given forced us to use our imagination to create our own visual reality. This would continue to be the case for many years until MTV took the imagination out of music by providing a definitive visual for each song.

But specific visuals were already being transmitted in 1948, when I was six. The networks were using Nielsen ratings to report who was watching what. I didn't need ratings to tell me who was watching what on East 24th Street. In those days, if a neighborhood was lucky, one family on the block owned a television. Though we had no more money or prescience than anyone else on our block, somehow we turned out to be that family.

On weeknights, after rushing through an early supper at home, up to six families from our block would squeeze into our living room and try to fit around our brand-new blond-wood console with a seven-inch black-and-white TV screen. During commercials the other kids and I munched noisily on handfuls of potato chips grabbed from large white plastic bowls. We slurped Pepsi-Cola from straws in paper cups and listened to the adults' comments about the show until the entertainment came back on. We were so absorbed that we never noticed how tinny the sound quality was.

After my little brother was born on December 4, 1948, other women emptied ashtrays and refilled bowls of potato chips while my mother changed Richard's diaper and fed him in the relative quiet of her sewing room. I helped when she asked me to, but when I had to choose between volunteering and watching television, the choice was clear.

On Monday nights we watched *I Love Lucy*. If you didn't see it you'd be left out of the conversation at school or work the next day. On Tuesday nights it was the *Texaco Star Theater*. Texaco would probably not have been pleased to know that we called the program "Milton Berle." Not "The Milton Berle Show." Just "Milton Berle."

"What are you doing Tuesday night?"

"Whattaya think we're doin', stupid? Watchin' Milton Berle!"

A nation united.

I don't remember whether the idea for me to move from a watcher to a performer was mine or my mother's. I do remember that in 1950 my mother took me to audition for *The Horn and Hardart Children's Hour* as part of a duo with a friend from school. Loretta Stone was ten and I was eight when we decided to perform together. Our act consisted of Loretta singing the high harmony to "If I Knew You Were Comin' I'd've Baked a Cake" while I sang the melody and accompanied us both on a ukulele. I didn't mind performing when I had someone onstage with me to share the attention, and I was eager to see if we could get on the show. I thought the audition went well, but the typical protocol for people conducting an audition was to reveal absolutely nothing until they were ready to tell you either, "You're hired," or "Don't call us, we'll call you."

With no reaction on which to hang hope or disappointment, I put it out of my mind until the afternoon I came home from school and found my mother looking exceptionally pleased. She could barely contain her delight as she blurted out that she had received a call from *The Children's Hour* saying that Loretta and I had been chosen to perform on the show.

"Mama, really? They want us??"

"Yes!" she said, holding out her arms for a hug. As I went to her I could see the tears of joy in her eyes. It was as if I had just given my mother the moon. I was happier for her than I was for myself until I told Loretta the news and heard her screaming over the phone. By the time she and her mother came over to hear the details in person, I, too, was in possession of the moon.

Our upcoming television appearance prompted me to adopt a professional name. "Carol Klein" didn't sound like a name that people would be excited to read out loud to each other as they perused *Hit Parader*. Though my name was alliterative, it didn't have the zing of, say, Patti Page. I decided upon Carol Kane, a name I used only once, for that show. (I hadn't yet heard of the comedic actress born with that name.)

The Children's Hour performance was broadcast live in front of an audience. I experienced some nervousness, but having Loretta with me to share the experience gave me enough confidence to get through the performance with joy. The audience's applause told us that we had connected, and I'm pretty sure we left the studio on a big puffy white cloud. We did another professional show called *The Amateur Hour*, hosted by Ted Mack, but it takes a lot of time and energy for the parents of a would-be child star to pursue that child's career. After that Loretta and I performed occasionally at school, but that was it.

In the early 1950s I had no idea of the impact television would have on society. I was simply enchanted. I watched devotedly as some of my favorite radio shows successfully crossed over to television. The characters of *The Jack Benny Program* looked exactly as I had imagined them. Another successful favorite was *You Bet Your Life*, starring Groucho Marx, with sidekicks George Fenneman and a toy duck modeled after Groucho with glasses and a mustache. Whenever a contestant said the secret word—as one of the contestants inevitably did—the duck would drop down from the rafters on a string with a cigar and a hundred dollars in its bill. Hearing them describe the duck drop on the radio when I was eight, I found the concept hilarious. Seeing the duck drop down on television when I was nine made me laugh so hard my stomach hurt.

In 1952, when junior high school comprised grades seven through nine, I entered seventh grade. I was ten. Most of my classmates were eleven or twelve. At ten, a disparity of two years can be a chasm. Not only was I smaller than other seventh graders, the physical changes of puberty weren't even in my thoughts, let alone my body. Every day at school I piped up with all the correct answers in class, which made me appear confident. But it wasn't cool for a girl to be smart, and I was intimidated by the apparent popularity of the older kids. I would have felt even more socially inferior had it not been for the entertainment and inspiration I drew from TV and radio. As those media outlets were growing up, so was I. Rather than supplanting radio, TV supplemented it. While TV lent itself more to variety shows, sports, and situation comedies, popular music was thriving on the radio. The top songs on the hit parade sailed out over the airwaves like sonic ships over a fair-weather sea, bringing cultural commonality to delighted listeners across America. Among the popular songs that year were Jo Stafford's "You Belong to Me," the Mills Brothers' "The Glow Worm," and Kay Starr's "Wheel of Fortune."

These and other songs on the hit parade were a lot more interesting to me than events of world importance that were unfolding at the periphery of my carefree innocence. Among them was an increasing awareness by white Americans of the separate and unequal status of Americans of color.

Chapter Four

Them and Us

At twelve I wasn't aware that the decade in which I was about to become a teenager was the Eisenhower fifties, *The Man in the Gray Flannel Suit* fifties, the postwar celebration-of-material-things fifties in which "swell" meant excellent and "gay" meant merry. I had no idea of the limited control people had of their destiny if they were anything other than a wealthy male white Anglo-Saxon Protestant. And the way women were depicted on television gave me the idea that society expected little more from a young girl than being attractive and helping men accomplish great things. If she got good grades in school and helped her mom around the house, so much the better.

From my father's comments as he listened to the news I inferred that politically there were two sides: "them" and "us." "We" were proud, patriotic Americans, but if you questioned anything the government did, you were "them." "We" stood for capitalism, freedom, and democracy. "They" stood for communism. The prevailing message was that America's enemy was the Soviet Union, whose goal it was to take over the world, country by country, until everyone in the entire world was a communist. I learned about the domino theory: if one country fell to communism, the rest would follow. As a Jewish child I had heard over and over how Hitler had annihilated six million Jews and nearly taken over the world in the forties until patriotic Americans and our allies in Europe defeated him. By the early fifties, communism had become the new enemy of patriotic Americans.

At twelve, I had trouble identifying the enemy. Hadn't the United States fought against Hitler on the same side as Soviet Russia? And what about the other "they"—Communist China? Which country was the worse bad guy? And why, if the Soviet Union and China were both communist, were they not getting along with each other? As my generation entered adolescence it was natural for us to see the adults in our lives as "them," but there was more going on than just a generational separation.

At first we didn't see any indication of revolution brewing under the blanket of conformity that lay across America, but seeds of racial integration were already taking root in film, theater, dance, and the visual arts. A momentous change occurred in major-league sports with the addition of a man of color—Jackie Robinson—to the lineup of the Brooklyn Dodgers in 1947. But the field with the most fertile soil for radical transformation and the greatest ability to capture the attention of young people was popular music.

Before the fifties, music written and performed by black Americans was listened to mostly by black Americans. The popularity of such recordings was tracked on rhythm and blues charts. Such music was largely absent from the popular music charts that typically reflected the taste of white mainstream listeners. A sampling of pop charts over the first half of the decade shows the first signs of black music crossing over. This crossover was a tangible measure of the increasing influence of R&B music on white teenagers—a trend that would continue into the twenty-first century with rural white teenagers rapping urban rhetoric over boombox beats.

In 1950, Teresa Brewer's "Music! Music! Music!" topped the charts. As were most artists on the pop charts that year, Miss Brewer was white.

In 1951, "Rocket 88," a paean to an Oldsmobile, reflected the enthusiasm of young people for cars. Written and performed by black Americans, the Jackie Brenston version shot to the top of the R&B charts, but it was the recording of "Rocket 88" by Bill Haley and the Saddlemen that connected with white audiences.

In 1952, Ruth Brown's "5-10-15 Hours" hit #1 on the R&B charts, but Miss Brown didn't break onto the pop charts until the following year with "(Mama) He Treats Your Daughter Mean."

In 1953, a young white man recorded his first demo in Memphis. With his good looks, shockingly sexy presentation, and parents' fears that their children would be incited by his pelvic movements to participate in wild orgies, Elvis Presley was uniquely positioned to make black music and dance popular with white teenagers.

In 1954, a group of black male singers known as the Penguins waddled up the R&B charts with "Earth Angel." (Let the record show that when I was thirteen "Earth Angel" accompanied my first kisses.) Though the Crew Cuts, a white group, released a cover the following year, it was the Penguins' version that inspired teenagers to form couples, dance, and make out. When both versions appeared in 1955 on the pop charts, the white group peaked at #3, five places above the black group.

In 1955, Bill Haley and the Comets' "Rock Around the Clock" held the #1 position on the pop charts for eight weeks. Initially I didn't know or care what color the group was, nor did any of the kids I knew. We just loved listening and dancing to that song.

Before "Rocket 88" was accredited by the Rock and Roll Hall of Fame in 1991 as "the first Rock and Roll song ever recorded," I had attributed that status to "Rock Around the Clock," a misperception undoubtedly enhanced by the inclusion of that song in a popular movie. To my knowledge, *The Blackboard Jungle* was one of the first films to cross-market a theme song. I believe "Rock Around the Clock" flew up the charts because teenagers like me saw the movie and ran out the next day to buy the single.

African Americans from my generation would likely cite a different song as a significant point of change, but for me it was unquestionably Bill Haley and the Comets' "Rock Around the Clock." That may not have been the first rock and roll song, but that 45 rpm single in 1955 divided my world into Before Rock and Roll and After Rock and Roll.

Before Rock and Roll, whenever I was upset about something, I had found comfort in going to the piano and playing whatever came out. I had needed more comfort than usual in the years between 1951 and 1955, when two events transformed my family and permanently realigned the planets in my emotional universe.

Chapter Five

The Planets Realign

The first event occurred in 1951 when I was almost nine, when my two-year-old brother was diagnosed as profoundly deaf and what was then called "severely retarded." My mother was working as a secretary in a New York City school. Knowing that she couldn't afford to hire someone to care for Richard at home nor quit work to do it herself, she made the agonizing decision to place him in a facility suitable for his needs.

The day my brother left, my mother didn't want me to experience the sights and sounds of his new environment, so she left me in the care of my grandmother and drove him to his new home by herself. Though my mother visited him frequently, I didn't see my brother for almost a year, when both our parents drove me out to see him on his birthday. My mother's plan was to take Richard to get some hot dogs and then go to a playground where he could ride on a little merry-go-round and go down the slide with me. Despite my mother's concerns, I didn't find any of the sights and sounds intimidating. It looked to me like a big school with a lot of buildings.

Richard had abilities as well as disabilities. He was very good at communicating his enjoyment of certain things, with cars and hot dogs high on the list. As soon as he saw us he giggled with happiness. Though he couldn't comprehend the concepts that characterized our relationships—mommy, daddy, sister, family—he knew we belonged to him. But we weren't the main attraction. From the moment he saw our car, Richard could not contain his enthusiasm. He ran to the car and jumped up and down until my father opened the door, then Richard climbed into the back seat. Once in, he kept jumping up and down until I entered from the other side, sat down next to him, and showed him by example that he needed to sit still. This was before seat belts were in common use.

As we drove toward the playground, my pleasure at seeing my brother was diminished when I caught sight of our dad's grim expression in the rearview mirror. And when my mom turned around to look at Richard, tears welled up in her eyes. Suddenly I started thinking about all the experiences my brother would miss. He wouldn't learn to pump his feet to make his swing go up and down next to mine in the playground across the street. He wouldn't sit at Ebbets Field with our father and me and learn the difference between a ball and a strike. Nor would he yell at an umpire who made a wrong call against our beloved Brooklyn Dodgers. He'd never run in and out of the waves with me at Brighton Beach while our mother watched from our blanket. And he would never hear a note of music.

I didn't realize how much I had missed my little brother. When he was still at home, each night as I drifted off to sleep I'd been comforted by the sound of his breathing through the thin wall between our rooms. I never felt resentful or competitive. As the older sibling, I had felt no lack of attention from my parents either before or after Richard was born. I didn't like living as an only child. I wanted my brother to be normal.

If Richard's going away was difficult for me, it had been far more distressing to my mother. A prevailing societal ignorance about his disability had led some of my mother's friends and close family members to express their wrongheaded opinion directly to her that having such a child was her fault and she should be ashamed of him. Seeing my mother struggle with such hurtful remarks, I wanted to help. But I didn't know how. To her everlasting credit, my mom was resolute in looking for joy in her son's existence, and she found it in his smallest accomplishments.

My father, too, was distressed, but his way of managing pain was to build a wall around it. That was probably why he didn't accompany my mother in bringing Richard to his new home, and after Richard left my father rarely spoke of him. From things I'd heard him say to my mother, I understood that he carried the additional burden of a father's failure to produce a healthy son, so I tried to be both son and daughter to him. As the only girl on the block I was already accustomed to playing ball with boys. Now I went to baseball games with my dad, asked him to show me how to use tools, and worked with him on household projects.

One positive outcome of my attempts to be both daughter and son was that my parents never told me, nor did I ever feel, that I couldn't do something because I was a girl. All possibilities were open to me. My way of dealing with Richard's condition was to strive for excellence in everything I undertook. As the child with all the advantages, I felt that I owed it to Richard and my parents to make up for what he couldn't do.

Later in Richard's life, when my mother was still able to travel, whenever she and I would visit him at the residence to which he had been transferred, he never failed to recognize us. I enjoyed renewing my bond with my brother, and he responded in all the ways of which he was capable. Still later, when I visited him alone or with one of my then adult children, I felt that same strong connection with Richard when he grabbed my hand and pulled me over to look at some little thing he found fascinating such as a doorknob or a box of Legos.

Richard had the "mischievous" gene. He wasn't so disabled that he didn't understand when he was told not to do something. The stimulus of being told "No!" through unambiguous verbal and nonverbal signals typically caused a response in which he did exactly the proscribed action while looking sidewise at the person who had just told him not to do it. I was proud of my brother's instinct to challenge authority and found his displays of spunk reassuring. Richard may have been deaf and intellectually disabled, but he was a Klein.

The second disruption of my universe occurred in 1953 when I was eleven. When my parents separated for the first time, I shouldn't have been surprised. I had borne witness to scenes in which they alternately yelled at each other and suddenly went silent in mid-conversation. Each time, the sight of them turning away from each other, thin-lipped, bottling up the hurt while trying to keep it from reaching their hearts, was more than I could bear. I didn't know which was worse, the shouting or the silence. As their only child who could potentially have had any influence on the situation, I took responsibility for fixing their problems. I said and did everything I could think of to bring them back together. I tried so hard, but the damage was irreparable. After separating, they divorced. I never got over that. Our home had once been happy. Now it was broken.

It wasn't until much later that I realized my brother's disability had probably been an underlying cause of our parents fighting. It's not difficult to see how my mother would have taken my father's withdrawal as a lack of support, with blame and accusations undoubtedly escalating from there. And yet as fervently as I wished that my mother and father would get back together, they must have had similar feelings some of the time. Over the next seven years they tried several times to reunite, and they even remarried each other, but every reconciliation was followed by another separation and, ultimately, their final divorce.

Some psychologists believe everyone has an underlying thought that drives them—a sentence repeated in a person's subconscious like a mantra. It might be, "Notice me!" or "Don't hurt me!" or "Nothing good ever happens, and if it does, it won't happen to me." When my mother and father started fighting, my mantra became "I just want everyone to be happy." I had put so much time and hope in being able to keep my parents together, but I couldn't do it. I was just a child.

The breakup of my family flung me on a quest for "home" that would take me through four marriages, two subsequent relationships, and a variety of places to live. The home I was looking for had a mommy, a daddy, and one or more children, all of whom loved each other very much. It would take me decades to figure out that "home" needed to exist inside me before I could find or create it externally.

But I didn't know that in the early fifties. Sometimes my emotions about things I couldn't talk about were so overwhelming that I went to the piano and played until I was exhausted. Other times I acted out by misbehaving in school. And sometimes I literally acted out by playing insolent girls in a succession of school and neighborhood plays, some of which were written and directed by my theatrically gifted mother. At one point I thought, Maybe if I become an actress it will make my mother feel better, and I can be someone other than myself. I didn't realize that I was adopting a dream of acclaim that had been handed down to me by two previous generations.

Chapter Six

The Thee-a-tuh

*M*y maternal grandmother, Sarah Besmosgin, was born in the final decade of the nineteenth century in a small village in Russia called Orsha (now part of Belarus). Her father, my great-grandfather Yitzrok, was a scholar, a prestigious occupation in the Jewish community that didn't bring in a single ruble of income. Sarah's mother, my great-grandmother Riva Leah (pronounced RIV-er LAY-uh), had to work as a baker to support her family. The job of delivering those baked goods to wealthy families fell to Riva Leah's eldest daughter. When twelve-year-old Sarah looked through a grand parlor window and saw a girl her own age playing a piano, that image became a symbol of the wealth and accomplishment to which she could never aspire. She resolved instead to become an *aishes chail* (rhymes with "gracious mile," has a guttural "ch"). Loosely translated, an *aishes chail* is "a woman of worth, a virtuous woman." To my grandmother it meant becoming the mother of a renowned classical pianist.

After emigrating to America, Sarah met Israel Benjamin Cammer—my Grandpa Bennie. They had two daughters, Eugenia and Gladys. Like many women of her generation, my grandmother understood that she was powerless out in the world, but inside the home she ruled with an iron will. Brushing aside the aspirations of her older daughter—my future mother—to write plays and participate in dramatic productions in school, my grandmother made my mother spend hours practicing the piano. Though my Grandma Sarah never attained her goal of becoming an *aishes chail* as she understood it, the benefits of her compulsory musical training would accrue to my mother later, when she would use it to write and direct musical theater productions. Benefits would also accrue, through my mother, to me. My mother reunited with her creative muse in college when she majored in English and drama and worked in summer stock as Eugenia Merrill. After I was born she had to quit summer stock, but she stayed active in theater by writing, directing, and acting in local productions.

My mother began taking me to Broadway plays and musicals when I was five. She absorbed everything and incorporated what she saw into her own productions. Combining nepotism, talent, and proximity, she cast my father as Nathan Detroit in what people who saw the show referred to for years afterward as "Genie's *wonderful* production of *Guys and Dolls*." I, too, absorbed everything. I kept the memory of those shows alive by listening to my mother's collection of original cast recordings. Along with *Guys and Dolls* her collection included *South Pacific, Oklahoma!, The King and I, Carousel, Peter Pan, My Fair Lady,* and, later, *West Side Story.* When I was thirteen my dad bought me a portable phonograph—a gray-flocked metal turntable in a blue metal case with a handle that made it easy for me to carry it to the girls-only sleepovers we called "pajama parties." Not long after I acquired the phonograph, my mother's albums grew legs, walked into my room, and jumped onto the turntable.

At first I was a little confused when my mom cast me in one of her original plays as a bratty girl called Nina. As my mother, she was constantly exhorting me to behave better. As my director, she encouraged me to behave as badly as I liked. Seeing my confusion, she said, "You may behave badly only when you're playing Nina." I had so much fun with that role that I began to think more seriously about becoming an actress. That notion continued to percolate until an opportunity arose for me to do something about it.

In the mid-fifties the High School of Performing Arts was located on West 46th Street. In the eighties it would be merged with the High School of Music and Art, relocated to Lincoln Center, and given the unwieldy name "The Fiorello H. LaGuardia High School of Music and Art and Performing Arts." LaGuardia Arts would continue its forebears' tradition as an alternative public high school, offering a rare opportunity for children whose families could not otherwise afford its highly specialized training in theater and visual arts.

In the fifties, some high schools in New York City were beginning to change from four years to three, that is, grades ten through twelve. Elementary schools went from kindergarten through sixth grade instead of K–8, which left grades seven through nine for junior high school. Middle schools would come later.

In September 1952, when I was ten, I entered seventh grade at Shell Bank Junior High School. Performing Arts was then a four-year high school to which students could be admitted from eighth grade and begin the fall semester in ninth, but P.A. also accepted students from ninth grade to become tenth-grade sophomores. I was eleven and a little more than halfway through eighth grade at Shell Bank when my guidance teacher announced that a limited number of New York City public school students would be selected to study drama the following year at the High School of Performing Arts. With my mother's support and encouragement, I applied for admission. I found two suitable monologues and practiced until

I could deliver them with confidence. I came home from the audition thinking I had performed well, but apparently the drama department judges disagreed.

At first I was crushed to learn that I would spend ninth grade at Shell Bank, but it turned out to be a blessing in disguise.

Chapter Seven

The Big Beat

*T*he music Alan Freed played on his nightly WINS radio program in 1954 was alarming parents from one end of Greater New York to the other. Some parents were unable to articulate precisely why they were fearful. Others heard their concerns expressed in hate-filled rants about the consequences of the crossover into "mainstream" (read: white) America of the songs, recordings, and dance moves of blacks. Such dire warnings played upon the already existing fears that malevolent forces outside their control would replace the values that the parents of kids my age had instilled in their offspring.

My introduction to Alan Freed's music came through a fellow student at Shell Bank. When I met Joel Zwick* in homeroom I was delighted to discover that he was only a month older than I. Our shared affinity for music and theater was evident as we cavorted around the stage of the school auditorium in colorful costumes in extravagant productions of light operas by Gilbert and Sullivan.

---

*Joel subsequently achieved success in TV, theater, and film as the director of *Laverne and Shirley, George Gershwin Alone,* and *My Big Fat Greek Wedding.*

I had so much fun performing in *The Mikado* as one of several Japanese schoolgirls dressed in kimonos and wigs. It made me happy to be part of the enchantment my classmates and I brought to our audience, which consisted principally of parents, friends, and teachers. I loved transporting the audience (and myself) to another time and another country. I delighted in pirouetting and moving my handheld fan in synchronized choreography with the other girls while we sang this song:

> *Three little maids who all unwary*
> *Come from a ladies' seminary*
> *Freed from its genius tutelary*
> *Three little maids from school*
> *Three little maaaaids—from school!*

In 1955, Alan Freed announced his Easter Jubilee, a musical revue at the Brooklyn Paramount Theater that would run for a week. When Joel invited me to go with him I accepted with enthusiasm. When the day came, we got on the train at Sheepshead Bay and found it packed with teenagers. I thought, These kids can't all be going to the Alan Freed show. But they were. Exiting the subway at Atlantic Avenue, we caught sight of and then became part of the teeming crowd forming outside the Brooklyn Paramount. The sense of anticipation rising in a hormonal crescendo was almost palpable.

Other than a friend of my dad's from the firehouse, I had rarely seen people of color in my neighborhood unless they were there to deliver furniture, clean houses, or perform other menial tasks. In April 1955, not only was Alan Freed's stage integrated, the audience was polychromatic. As Joel and I advanced slowly through the ticket line, the entry line, and up the aisle to our seats, it struck me that there were more black teenagers than I had ever seen.

Before I had a chance to reflect further, the band started playing. Backed by Count Basie's Orchestra (minus Count Basie), act after act came out to perform either their latest hit or the song that would soon become their latest hit.

The performance of a new song by one of Alan's acts, reinforced by repeated plays on his radio show, was usually followed by a marked increase in sales. One could infer that the power and influence of a disc jockey with a sizable audience might be a factor in his ownership, credits, or royalties in connection with the products he promoted. This may not have been the case with Alan Freed when he was listed as a cowriter on the Moonglows' "Sincerely," or when he owned or co-owned an act's record label. But in my teens I knew nothing of such practices, and had I been told that Alan was financially entangled with his artists, I wouldn't have cared. I only knew that thanks to Alan Freed I was becoming aware of a new kind of music that spoke to and for me. He had assembled a parade of talented performers such as the Penguins, the Moonglows, the Clovers, Danny Overbea, Red Prysock, LaVern Baker, Mickey "Guitar" Baker (no relation to LaVern), and B.B. King.

Alan called his music "the Big Beat." It was exactly the right name. The Big Beat was bigger, louder, and more sexually stirring than any music I'd heard before. It surely was not "Three little maaaaids—from school!"

During the show, as black and white teenagers danced in separate groups, each seemed to accept one another's presence in the same audience without animosity. It's possible that I'm remembering this racial harmony in 1955 through lenses turned rose-colored after more than fifty years, but I believe Alan Freed's shows heralded the movement of my generation toward racial integration not only of popular music, but of American society.

After the show I felt exhilarated and exhausted. Joining the stream of people leaving the theater, Joel and I found ourselves in the middle of a group milling around the stage door hoping to catch a glimpse of one of the performers. Suddenly the door opened and we were swept along with a group being ushered in. Through a space between two taller kids I saw LaVern Baker sashaying up the stairs past B.B. King and the Moonglows. I assumed Miss Baker was making her way to her dressing room, but years of experience since then have educated me to the probability that she had applied her makeup in front of a mirror shared with other performers, and that she had probably changed into her costume in the bathroom. Moving farther in, we saw Mickey Baker talking to a couple of the Penguins.

At that moment I knew I wanted to mean something to these people. I didn't want to *be* one of them. I just wanted them to know who I was and consider me worthy of respect. That ambition existed concurrently and in no way conflicted with my ambition to be an actress.

After that my fiscal priority became saving up to attend as many of Alan's revues as I could afford. I couldn't attend every show, but I always knew who was playing because Alan promoted his shows nightly on his radio program by touting the lineup and playing the music of those artists.

Over the next few years Alan presented many great acts, including Jerry Lee Lewis, Chuck Berry, Bo Diddley, Jackie Wilson, Fats Domino, Frankie Lymon and the Teenagers, the Cleftones, the Harptones, Joe Turner, Jo Ann Campbell, Mabel King, Shirley and Lee, and George Hamilton IV. He also introduced Screamin' Jay Hawkins (a forerunner of Alice Cooper, Black Sabbath, and Marilyn Manson). Jay's assertion of maniacally possessive love culminated in an agonizing shriek followed by a series of demonic groans and screams until he ended his turn onstage by collapsing into a coffin.

Alan had a particularly delightful treat in store for us at his

1957 Labor Day revue at the Brooklyn Paramount. I was in the audience when Little Richard burst onto the stage. He began to sing and play the piano with an eruption of energy that continued unabated for decades. Though I knew nothing about the gospel music that had informed him, Little Richard's powerful presence that night was suffuuuuused with the Spirit. It was a remarkable experience for this Jewish teenager to hear him sing nonsense syllables with the full capability of an astonishing vocal range that complemented the blazing rhythm coming out of his fingers. Had I considered myself a good writer of lyrics, I would have had to stop right there. I mean, what lyric could possibly say it better than this?

> *A-wop wop-a loo-mop a-wop bam boom*
> *Tutti frutti, aw rootie, tutti frutti, aw rootie*
> *Tutti frutti, aw rootie, tutti frutti, aw rootie*
> *Tutti frutti, aw rootie*
> *A-wop wop-a loo-mop a-wop bam boom*

Little Richard's music and presentation would influence artists and songwriters from James Brown and Elvis Presley to Smokey Robinson and Michael Jackson—all exceptional songwriters and performers who themselves would influence future generations.

Chapter Eight

Rhythm and Blues

*M*y mother had exposed me to music while I was still in her womb. After I arrived she played *Carmen* and other operas while my father was on duty at the firehouse. Her record collection included show tunes, pop songs, and works by such composers as Mozart, Beethoven, Brahms, Strauss, and Schubert. I loved "Papa" Haydn's *Surprise Symphony,* and my repeated, delighted exposure to Prokofiev's *Peter and the Wolf* taught me the sounds and personality characteristics of various orchestral instruments. But the music that set me on fire when I was thirteen resembled classical music about as much as a pride of lions resembles a sailboat.

As my generation entered adolescence in a decade largely run by uninspiring men, the music Alan Freed brought to us seemed heaven-sent. To many of our parents—thankfully not mine—that music came from the cauldrons of hell. The predictors of doom said, "If Alan Freed is allowed to stay on the air, his 'race music' will lead to miscegenation, free love, drugs, and anarchy!" They may have been on to something. There was no doubt that the records Alan played aroused a sexual awareness previously unacknowledged among my age group. His revues were a welcome wagon of freedoms of style, expression, dress, message, and sex. References to sex didn't need to be explicit. Sexuality was implicit in both music and lyrics. To begin with, "rock and roll" was a euphemism in black slang for sexual intercourse. Parse the lyric "Roll me all night long" from "Let the Good Times Roll" and you won't find a single objectionable word, but the meaning was unmistakable. And then there was that pulsing bass that drove the Big Beat.

Before adolescence I had been naïve about sex. Suddenly I was feeling the pounding bass notes and the throbbing drumbeats viscerally in ways and places I'd never felt before. My discovery of rock and roll coincided with my increasing awareness of the lower half of my body. No wonder I couldn't wait to stay up late and listen to Alan's presentation of the original rhythm and blues recordings. Some of those songs were introduced to Middle America by white artists. The Moonglows' version of "Sincerely" topped the R&B charts before the song became a pop hit by the McGuire Sisters. After Pat Boone's recording of "Ain't That a Shame" made it to #2 on the *Billboard* Hot 100, Alan's repeated spins sent Fats Domino's version to #16.

In the parlance of the period, records were called platters. The platters Alan played fed every cell of my body, mind, heart, and soul. The songs were simply written and simply recorded. The lyrics and the beat moved me. Though melody was present, it wasn't as important as the beat. The fact that a lot of the songs sounded as if they could have been written by a kid—as indeed many were—inspired me to think, If they can do it, maybe I can.

It wouldn't be easy. The music that had informed the songwriters on the records Alan played was a lot more gritty and diverse than the simple pop ditties, show tunes, and classical music to which I had been listening for most of my life. But I was determined to learn, and the timing in popular music and political history was favorable.

In the fifties, folk songs by the Weavers, Mitch Miller, and the Kingston Trio appeared on the pop charts, but folk would not become mainstream until the sixties when possession of a guitar, a pair of vocal cords, endless verses railing against the system, and a guitar case in which to receive spare change would be all a young man from as far from the pop scene as, say, Hibbing, Minnesota, would need to qualify as a folksinger.

Following its relatively strong influence on popular music in the thirties and forties, jazz became marginalized in the early fifties. Jazz musicians were mostly black men whose music was appreciated by a relatively small audience compared to pop. Some were lucky enough to dip into the more lucrative world of studio pop and earn extra "bread" during the day as sidemen, but they couldn't wait to jam with other musicians in a club until the wee hours. Jazz was a very different world from pop. Among other things, it was separate and unequal. With few exceptions, jazz players struggled economically, and marijuana, cocaine, and heroin were part of the culture. Sentences spoken in after-hours clubs were often as strung out as the speaker.

"Coooool, man. Reeeeeal cool."

As with jazz, the world of rhythm and blues was inhabited mostly by blacks at the low end of the national economic scale. In the late 1940s, names such as "race music" and "race records" were used in *Billboard* magazine to categorize the music emanating from black communities. Jerry Wexler, a journalist with *Billboard*, came up with "rhythm and blues" to replace the "race" tags. Wexler later explained that although the word "race" was commonly used by blacks to describe themselves as a "race man" or a "race woman," the appellation didn't feel right to him. He viewed the term "rhythm and blues" as more appropriate for enlightened times.

"Blues" referred to the traditional twelve-bar form with a I-IV-V chord progression. "Rhythm" derived from the strong 4/4 or 6/8 beat that drove most of the songs. With lyrics mostly about the lack of love, sex, cars, liquor, or money, it wasn't surprising that R&B's messages of adversity and alienation resonated with white teenagers.

Higher up on the economic scale, white artists dominated the popular music charts. There were some black pop artists, notably Nat King Cole, Johnny Mathis, and Harry Belafonte, but songs like Perry Como's "No Other Love" and Patti Page's "(How Much Is That) Doggie in the Window?" ("arf, arf") were typical of what I heard on pop radio. Though other genres existed, pop had the widest and whitest audience. But popular music was only one facet of the social context that informed my generation.

A strong undercurrent that would lead to the civil rights movement was already gathering momentum in the mid-fifties. At twelve and thirteen, I wasn't paying close attention because I was white and my preadolescent concerns had little to do with racial injustice. But glimpses of the news on television kept me aware of such things as the 1954 Supreme Court decision *Brown v. the Board of Education of Topeka*, which struck down the policy of "separate but equal" and required schools to integrate racially. And when newscasters reported the refusal in 1955 of a black woman named Rosa Parks to give up her seat on a bus in Alabama so a white man could sit in it, after which they reported the white authorities' reaction, I couldn't help but sympathize with the blacks' boycott of Montgomery buses.

Film was another field in which an early call to racial integration was being sounded. Sidney Poitier's performance as a student accused of threatening his teacher's wife in *The Blackboard Jungle* awakened moviegoers to the fact that a black actor could do more than sing, dance, roll his eyes, and serve white people. Notwithstanding, or possibly because of, the presence of Mr. Poitier, the film's appeal to white teenagers was tremendous. *The Blackboard*

Jungle was such a convincing portrayal of juvenile delinquency that it frightened complacent adults who thought such things couldn't happen in their neighborhood.

My friends and I danced the Lindy (in boy-girl couples) to "Rock Around the Clock" in newly finished basements lined with knotty pine in the homes of kids whose parents could afford such improvements. (Knowing what teenagers typically did in basements, initially I thought the spelling was "naughty pine.") Lindy stood for Lindy Hop, a joyous, bouncy dance that turned excessive adolescent energy into exhilaration. When we weren't doing the Lindy, we were holding each other (in boy-girl couples) and slow-dancing to "Earth Angel" by the Penguins or "Pledging My Love" by the late, great Johnny Ace, who of course wasn't late when he made the record.

I was fourteen when Elvis Presley burst into national prominence from rockabilly in 1956. I didn't realize then that Elvis was himself a form of racial integration. He was a white boy singing country music with an R&B influence and performing it with the visceral abandon of the blacks he'd observed around Memphis after his family moved there from Tupelo, Mississippi. With all the censors and sponsors controlling television in the fifties, I was glad it took the producers of *The Ed Sullivan Show* three appearances to decide to show Elvis only from the waist up. No one with eyes and ears, and certainly not this teenage girl, was unaware of Elvis's effect on popular culture. I liked his music, and he was undeniably teen-idol gorgeous, but I must confess that Elvis's music didn't influence me as strongly as the pop hits that preceded his breakthrough, or the R&B hits that followed.

I observed all these events from a place of self-centered adolescence. I didn't listen to the news or read a newspaper unless a teacher made me do it. I liked English and math but had no interest in social studies. Later in life, when I realized that we live social studies every day, I would find history, geography, politics, and current events fascinating. But in the mid-fifties, I was a Brooklyn teenager who liked to read, sing, play the piano, go to movies, whisper in class, dance the Lindy, and cuddle with boys.

Oh, and one more thing. I hadn't given up on acting.

Chapter Nine

Salad Days

They say if you want a career in theater, you gotta really want it. I must have really wanted it because when the opportunity presented itself to audition for Performing Arts a second time, I took it, and that time I was accepted.

I had been pulled so strongly to music in the intervening year that I was tempted to ask the judges to give my place to someone else so I could go to high school in Brooklyn with my friends. But several things kept me from doing that: first, I was confident that I could continue to be inspired by rock and roll and rhythm and blues while studying acting, with no loss of proficiency in either endeavor. Second, after failing the first time and then achieving admission, I was reluctant to turn my back on such an extraordinary opportunity. But perhaps the most compelling reason was that I knew that my studying drama at Performing Arts would make my mother happy.

I was thirteen in the summer of 1955 and already primed to enjoy the long vacation days. Knowing that I would start tenth grade with new classmates, I relished every bit of time I could spend with my friends from Shell Bank. Every morning we congregated at the Avenue X playground across the street from my house. In order to get in or out of the playground I had to pass the omnipresent Butler and Bursch on their park bench. I had to be extra careful that they didn't see me doing anything questionable or they would immediately report it to my mother. Really, my only such activity was smoking cigarettes, a habit I acquired to fit in and happily gave up fourteen years later. To earn money for cigarettes, movies, and other indulgences, my friends and I either did odd jobs for our parents, worked part-time in offices or stores, or babysat. When we weren't working, sometimes we took a bus to Brighton Beach, rubbed each other with suntan lotion, and displayed our budding bodies in the noonday sun. This was before we learned about the perils of exposure to the sun without an SPF number.

Hormones and pheromones mingled in the heat as we walked up and down such thoroughfares as the Coney Island Boardwalk, Sheepshead Bay Road, or Kings Highway. We did what teenagers typically do: the boys swaggered while the girls whispered and giggled. We also visualized ourselves wearing the fall clothes already on display in the store windows, but with barely enough money to share a banana split between us and still have bus fare home, we couldn't afford to buy any of the cute outfits. Instead I settled for a box of handkerchiefs with the initial "C" embroidered on each handkerchief alternately in pink, blue, or yellow.

The summer of '55 was a succession of salad days—a sweet, simple, peaceful time of golden youth and green innocence. There was nothing but the vine-ripe fruit of each delicious day and honeysuckle night. I thought, If every child on earth could experience just one such summer, it would be a much better world.

But as every school-age child learns, summers end.

Chapter Ten

To Manhattan and Back

$\mathcal{I}$ spent part of my first day at Performing Arts trying to avoid being jostled by overly excited students running up and down the stairs. It wasn't easy to figure out where all the rooms were, and when fifth period ended I wondered how I would get from one end of the school to the other in time for sixth period. I was enrolled in drama and dance classes taught by Uta Hagen and Martha Graham. Among the names I heard during the first roll call were Al Pacino and Rafael Campos. Other names reflected the careers in film and theater of some of my classmates' parents: Susan Strasberg, whose father was the acting teacher Lee Strasberg; Leticia Ferrer, daughter of Miss Hagen and the actor José Ferrer; and Frances Schwartz, daughter of the Yiddish theater actor Maurice Schwartz.

I began the semester thinking I could indulge my passion for popular music simultaneously with studying drama and taking the academic classes required of all New York State high school students, but the concentration demanded by the stimulating, sophisticated world of serious theater left little room for other pursuits. My fellow students were there because they wanted to act in movies (where the money was) and star in a Broadway show (where the prestige was). Their enthusiasm was infectious and I was highly motivated to do the rigorous work we were told was necessary to become a brilliant, celebrated, and (God willing!) financially successful actor.

My classmates and I learned to channel teenage angst into techniques that would inform a role or enhance an audition. At first I found the process fascinating, but as the semester progressed I became increasingly discouraged by the extraordinary effort it took to keep up with my fellow students. I excelled in academic studies, but as my teachers in the professional arena issued daily reminders of the hours of dedication required for success in each of their classes, my resolve began to waver.

The hours I spent commuting to and from Manhattan left me with no time to see my old friends, and the emotional exhaustion of the drama classes left me with no energy to see my new friends in a relaxed, teenage-kid-like setting, assuming any of them had such time to spend. We imitated adults in dress and manner. At fourteen I wore ensembles to school that included three-inch heels, a matching purse, and dangling earrings. I still wanted to be an actress and star in a Broadway show, but I felt that I was missing out on the everyday experiences an actress would need to portray normal people. They were also experiences a normal kid would have. I didn't know what "normal" was, but it didn't seem to exist for me at Performing Arts.

I didn't want to disappoint my parents by quitting, so I pulled myself together, resolved to make my experience at P.A. a good one, and applied myself with a renewed commitment to the three disciplines required to graduate in my chosen field. I found that the drama classes taught me to listen and tune in beyond people's words to the subtext of their underlying emotions and desires. In dance I learned to stretch and move my body. Not surprisingly, I enjoyed music the most. I expanded my knowledge of theory so quickly that my music teacher, Mr. Sachs, asked me to arrange "Beau Soir," a Debussy piece, for chorus, which meant writing vocal parts for soprano, alto, tenor, and bass (SATB). This had the consequence, doubtless unintended by Mr. Sachs, of preparing me to arrange vocals for popular songs.

When Mr. Sachs suggested I transfer from drama to music, I considered it. But the seeds of my discontent had grown into an unwieldy plant. I was tired of trying to flourish in a garden in which I no longer felt I belonged. In the second semester of my sophomore year I rejoined my former classmates at James Madison High School, where I remained until I graduated in June 1958. I've never regretted going to Performing Arts, and I've never regretted leaving. At the time I believed I was losing forever the chance to star in a movie or a Broadway show, but I was okay with that.

Chapter Eleven

Aspiring to Be Popular

My primary objective at Madison was to be attractive, well liked, and respected by the other kids, but the more I sought popularity, the more it eluded me. Heredity had made me small in stature and a year late in commencing puberty, and I was still two years younger than most of my classmates. The math was inescapable. In those socially crucial high school years, I was almost three years behind my peers in physical development.

I cried the day I overheard a boy refer to me as "cute." In those days it did not mean hot or attractive. "Cute" described a girl a boy thought of as a friend, not someone to date. As much as I didn't want to be the girl boys called for advice about how they could get the girl they really wanted, that was the purpose of virtually every call from a boy. With few friends and no siblings at home, I spent a lot of time alone. But my solitude had an unexpected benefit; it made me a good observer. When a girl is gossiping and discussing shades of nail polish with her friends, she's less available to pay attention to the world. Being alone gave me a chance to process what my senses took in without having to factor in other people's opinions.

There was no danger of my falling in with a bad crowd. There wasn't much of a bad crowd at my school. Sometimes the girls with more developed breasts and womanly shapes came to school with their hair curled in bobby pins under silk scarves. In addition to creating curls, this practice had a secondary purpose. It implied that the girl had a date after school with an older guy and didn't care if the boys at school saw her in a scarf. They dressed like Natalie Wood in *Rebel Without a Cause* and smoked in the school-yard. It's possible that they were dating juvenile delinquents, but at least the girls showed up for classes.

Most of my classmates and I came from working-class families in which one or both parents kept a close watch on our activities. We were expected to achieve academic excellence, and I met those expectations. Unfortunately, that was a recipe for failure for a girl hoping to be asked out on a date. No matter how much I tried to downplay my intellectual curiosity, boys never took me seriously, which meant that the most popular girls didn't take me seriously either. Or so I thought at the time.

Three decades later, a group of middle-aged men and women came backstage after one of my concerts to visit the middle-aged woman I had become. After they identified themselves as class-mates from Madison, I was incredulous when they told me that they had thought me one of the prettiest, most popular, and most envied girls in the class. My first impulse was to say, "I wish you had told me that then," but what I really wished was that I could have told myself these things at the time: You're pretty. You're smart. You're funny. You're just right the way you are. Be confi-dent. Be yourself. Like yourself. Don't worry, you'll date, and then you'll have different problems.

I didn't know those things when I was at Madison. All I could do was keep trying to find my place in the social realm. As it hap-pened, I wasn't the only teenager attracted to the liberal arts in search of peer acceptance and self-expression. A remarkable number of kids from my generation who attended high schools in Brooklyn went on to achieve success in music, film, TV, literature, journalism, theater, and the visual arts. Not only were we supported in such endeavors by our schools and families, but we were only a subway ride away from the array of opportunities awaiting us in New York City. It's no wonder we were drawn to the city in search of artistic and material success.

Alongside the culture of material success existed a subculture of alienated, antimaterialistic nonconformists, the literary core of which included Jack Kerouac, William Burroughs, and Allen Ginsberg on the East Coast, with Kenneth Rexroth, Gregory Corso, Michael McClure, and Philip Lamantia on the West Coast. There was some coast overlap: the first reading by Allen Ginsberg of his avant-garde poem *Howl* took place in 1955 in San Francisco, and Kerouac drank too much on both coasts. Other characters in the Beat generation included Ken Kesey and the Merry Pranksters, who would become a bridge between Beats and hippies.

I had no idea why it was called the Beat generation. Later I heard that Jack Kerouac coined the phrase in the late forties. Some said he used "beat" in the street sense of cheated or down and out. Others said "beat" was short for beatitude, but with its meaning of exalted happiness and serenity, beatitude seems unlikely—unless Kerouac was being ironic, which is entirely possible. Either way, the subculture became known as the Beat generation, and its members were "beatniks."

In 1957, when I was fifteen, the dominant style in the visual arts was abstract expressionism, exemplified by Jackson Pollock, Mark Rothko, Willem de Kooning, and Helen Frankenthaler. While visual artists created and displayed their work in Greenwich Village, jazz musicians such as Charlie Parker, Dizzy Gillespie, Miles Davis, John Coltrane, Tito Puente, Thelonious Monk, and

Charles Mingus could be heard at clubs such as the Village Vanguard or the Village Gate.

That year I sneaked off to Greenwich Village with some of the
more daring kids I knew. Unlike suburban kids, we didn't need a
car. We could get anywhere by bus or subway. Walking on Bleecker
Street I half expected to see a strung-out junkie on every corner.
Because everyone's parents had seen *Reefer Madness*,[*] I kept looking over my shoulder for my father, who I was certain would catch
me and ground me for a year. After boldly trying to get into the
jazz clubs, only to be turned away, we wound up in a coffee house
with no age restriction. There we listened to poetry readings in a
room full of people who looked like beatniks. Hanging out in the
Village made me feel "cool."

One night, notwithstanding my being fifteen and looking
twelve, the woman at the door admitted my friends and me to the
Vanguard. It was a propitious moment that expanded into a couple of hours of grace during which I witnessed two sets of jazz by
players I didn't know. The music was hot, cool, and mind-blowing.
After the Vanguard, my friends and I went to someone's apartment where they were smoking pot. Other than what I inhaled
secondhand, I didn't partake. I, too, had seen *Reefer Madness*. I was
convinced that smoking pot would lead me to harder drugs and I
would become a heroin addict. Luckily, nothing stronger than pot
was offered that night, and even if it had been, I've never been
tempted to try heroin in any form. At one point I wanted to leave
the apartment, but my friends wanted to stay, so I people-watched

---

[*]*Reefer Madness* was intended to alert young people and their parents to the deadly
dangers of smoking "marihuana." Among the unintended consequences were the
laughter of audiences in succeeding decades and the inclusion of the film's later title
(it was originally called *Tell Your Children*) in the lexicon of the twentieth century
as a synonym for greatly exaggerated antidrug propaganda.

and listened to music on the record player. By default, soon I became the one who selected the records. I found the music a lot more interesting than watching other people stoned on pot.

My parents' respect for the arts and the creativity they nurtured in me gave me a strong foundation from which to appreciate the music and art uniquely available in Greenwich Village, but their support most assuredly would not have included allowing me to go to the Village without adult supervision. After the night of the reefers I decided to stop risking a yearlong grounding. Instead I stayed in Brooklyn and prayed that a boy—any boy—would ask me out on a date.

Chapter Twelve

The Function of a Cosine

I had always been fearless about raising my hand to answer a teacher's question. Sometimes I gave a wrong answer, but my confidence in that sphere remained unshaken. But as a fifteen-year-old high school junior among seventeen-year-olds, when it came to winning the respect of my contemporaries my daily mantra went from "I just want everyone to be happy" to "What's wrong with me?"

Accepting a suggestion from my mother, I volunteered to contribute musically to the annual James Madison High School Sing. I found tremendous satisfaction in writing and arranging songs for the Sing, and I even performed some of the songs myself. But I really enjoyed teaching other students to sing what I had written. After the show, the applause lifted me to the point where I began to wonder what I could do next. Encouraged by teachers and classmates, I decided to start a singing group.

The Alan Freed shows had made me aware of the burgeoning number of street-corner groups, so called because they sometimes sang on street corners, subways, buses, or, depending on the size of the singers, anywhere they liked. They sang a cappella usually in four-part harmony. Similar groups were forming in high schools all over Brooklyn. One such group was the Tokens from Madison's rival Lincoln High School. After I heard Neil Sedaka and the Tokens perform "While I Dream" and "I Love My Baby," cowritten by Neil and Howard Greenfield, I began to compose in earnest. Most of my songs had decent melodies, but my lyrics weren't very good. It didn't matter. The street-corner benchmark left plenty of room for mediocre lyrics.

Arranging classical pieces at Performing Arts had given me enough confidence to arrange some pieces for Mr. Jacobs's chorus class. My arrangements were so well received that I decided to arrange some of my pop compositions for street-corner harmonies. Though the genres were considerably different, four-part harmony was four-part harmony. All I needed were a soprano, tenor, and bass. I would be the alto.

I recruited Iris Lipnick, Lenny Pullman, and Joel Zwick from Mr. Jacobs's class. Lipnick, Pullman, Zwick, and Klein didn't have quite the ring we were looking for, so we pulled a word from our trigonometry books and became the Cosines. It was a dreadful name, but it was ours. We worked on vocal arrangements, choreographed steps at my house after school, and then performed for free at dances and other school events. For some reason I've blocked out all memory of the names, melodies, and lyrics of most of our repertoire except one: "Leave, Schkeeve." My God! Of all the songs we sang, I can't believe that's the one I remember. We wrote that song as a group. I had no idea what a schkeeve was, but it rhymed with "leave," and that was all that mattered. Only a teenager with no social life would have put so much effort into arranging a song whose main lyric was "Leave, schkeeve / Bum doo-bee doo-wop."

In those days I wrote exclusively on piano. I was really excited about writing that arrangement. I've always loved wrapping layers around a melody. When arranging for voices with a band, usually I begin with a foundation consisting of melody, lyrics, and the chords and rhythm coming from my piano. Then I bring in the rhythm section: a drumbeat on a kit with three drums, several cymbals, and a pair of sticks, mallets, or brushes; a bass line that's pretty close to what my left hand plays on the piano; a rhythm guitar that complements my piano; and sometimes a lead guitar to add accents and fills to the mix of piano, rhythm guitar, bass, and drums. Then I add vocal harmonies. And if I'm lucky enough to have the use of an orchestra, I add a final layer of orchestral instruments.

At best, the aggregate is an aural design that adds to the emotion of a song. But there's a fine line: vocal and instrumental flourishes can make an arrangement more interesting, but they can also detract from the mood. As ambiance is to a room, mood is to a song. If you add too many lights and a pinball machine, the mood is lost. When my instinct is working well, it notifies me when I'm adding too many elements. When it's working *really* well, I feel as if the arrangement is writing itself through me. Though on occasion I've overarranged, in general my guiding principle is "less is more."

In the case of the Cosines, less didn't need to be more because we didn't have a lot of elements to begin with. Though most of my arrangements for the group were in the "doo-wop" style of the era, I arranged pop standards such as "Once in a While" and "Young and Foolish." I was an artist in sound as I filled my sonic canvas with the colors and textures of vocal harmonies, which is why I preferred writing and arranging over performing. When I did perform, my preference was still to have someone else up there with me to attract some of the attention. As with Loretta Stone, this was the case with the other three Cosines, whose dance steps and humorous antics in the foreground would keep the audience's eyes on them while I sang and played piano in the background. That seemed to work for our audiences, whose laughter, dancing, and applause made us feel terrific. As Madison's own singing group, we were a worthy rival for the Tokens and groups from other high schools.

I still wasn't being asked out on dates, but I was no longer lonely. I had finally found my niche in the social structure. With music as a path to peer recognition, I had become cool. But as rewarding as it was to perform with the Cosines, I wanted to hear my songs on the radio. In between homework, school activities, and household chores, I wrote prolifically and wondered if there was any way I could meet Alan Freed.

Chapter Thirteen

Atlantic and ABC-Paramount

I was still fifteen when I confided to my dad one afternoon that I wanted to play my songs for Alan Freed. My father sprang into action. All a New York City firefighter had to do was show his badge and he would be admitted as a V.I.P. anywhere in the city, from the finest restaurant to a museum, movie theater, or radio station WINS.

I don't know if Alan really thought I had talent or if he was just being nice to the fireman's kid, but he listened attentively to my songs, and he even took time to explain how the process worked. He told me to look in the phone book under "Record Companies," make an appointment, and play my songs live for the A&R man in charge of finding artists and repertoire (a fancy name for songs). Usually a label had its own publishing company. If an A&R man liked one of my songs, he might offer me a contract and an advance of twenty-five dollars. The contract was simple. The publishing company would own the copyright and receive all the publishing income. The writer would get a standard writer's mechanical and sheet music royalty minus the advance and the cost of recording a demo in one of the nearby demo studios such as Associated, Dick Charles, or Bell Sound. Alan chuckled when he said Atlantic Records didn't use an outside studio. "If Jerry and Ah-mond like a song," he said, "they'll set up a mic in their office and record a demo on the spot." That's what I thought he'd said: "Jerry and Ah-mond."

I would soon learn that Alan had said "Jerry and Ahmet," referring to Jerry Wexler and Ahmet Ertegun, partners in Atlantic Records whose sharp intuition and lifelong love of jazz, blues, and other black music would bring career longevity to both. In 1957, at forty and thirty-four, Jerry and Ahmet were zealous in their quest for men and women of exceptional talent who might contribute even further to Atlantic's success. They went to jazz clubs in big northern cities, churches in small southern towns, and bars wherever they found them. Their roster included Solomon Burke, Ruth Brown, Clyde McPhatter, and Ray Charles.

I didn't know any of that when I opened a Manhattan phone book to "Record Companies" that night and wrote down the address for Atlantic Records. All I knew was that Alan Freed had spoken the name, which made it as good a place as any to start. Rather than call for an appointment and risk rejection, I thought I would just go there and see if someone would listen to my songs. The next day, less than ten minutes after the last school bell had rung, I was on an express train from Kings Highway to Manhattan wearing a pink sweater set, a black felt skirt with a pink poodle on it, a ponytail, white bobby sox, and a pair of white sneakers. Along with my schoolbooks in one hand and sheet music in the other, I carried the belief that I was as good as anyone out there. I still had that feeling when I got off the BMT at 57th Street. Someone was going to get her songs recorded. Why not me?

The elevator in the building on West 56th Street must have been the slowest elevator in New York City. My family could have eaten an entire meal in Patsy's Restaurant before I reached my floor. On the way up I thought about my presentation. Since my dad's wire recordings were sonically, shall we say, not the best way to present a song, I had come prepared to play my songs in person. In those days every A&R man worth his salt had a recently tuned piano in his office. They were so eager to find new talent that most were willing to listen to young people playing live in their offices.

Finally I arrived at the door that said Atlantic Records. I turned the knob, walked in, and nearly bumped into a desk with a woman seated behind it. She might have been a secretary, a bookkeeper, or a receptionist. Probably she was all three. When she looked up and asked, "May I help you?" I answered with a question.

"Is anyone available to listen to my songs?"

Before she could decide between saying no or asking her bosses if they wanted to listen to a teenage girl who had just wandered in off the street, Jerry and Ahmet came out and escorted me to the piano in their office so quickly that I didn't have time to get nervous. Their shared office contained a piano and two catty-corner desks. A room next to theirs was both the office of Nesuhi Ertegun (Ahmet's brother) and the art department.

Ahmet and Jerry listened with interest as I played each song in turn, in response to their nods and words of encouragement. When I had finished playing the last song I looked at them expectantly.

"You got talent," Jerry declared.

Ahmet looked at Jerry and then at me.

"Yeah, man, very soulful. Come back and see us when you got more songs."

As I rode down in the slow elevator my shoulders sagged with disappointment because they hadn't offered me a contract or an advance, but by the time I got to the lobby my optimism had returned. After all, they hadn't said, "Don't call us, we'll call you." I took that as a triumph and walked to Seventh Avenue with my shoulders back and my head high. Anyway, there were other record companies.

The next afternoon, inspired by their chart-topping success with Paul Anka's "Diana," I called ABC-Paramount. The secretary who answered the phone said, "I'm sorry, we're not seeing any new artists." I had practically worn out my copy of "Diana," not only because I loved the song but also because I couldn't figure out what instrument had played the distinctive sound in the catchy instrumental hooks. That recording, by a Canadian only seven months older than I, was so popular that I was certain his A&R man would want to hear my songs. Even if they weren't seeing any new artists, surely they'd see *me*. I kept calling until a secretary named Betty Berlin gave me an appointment with her boss.

Don Costa had started out as a guitarist. He and Bucky Pizzarelli had played the dueling guitars on Vaughn Monroe's "Ghost Riders in the Sky." Later in his career Don would produce, arrange, and conduct for Trini Lopez, Kenny Rankin, Donny Osmond, Marv Johnson, Sammy Davis Jr., and Frank Sinatra. In 1957 Don was head of A&R at ABC-Paramount Records. His job included signing artists, choosing songs, producing, and arranging.

The day of my appointment I spent the entire subway ride to Times Square trying not to be nervous. By the time I entered the impressive reception area leading to ABC-Paramount's suite of offices at 1501 Broadway, I was bold and confident. I gave my name to the receptionist. She put down her *Vogue* magazine and called Mr. Costa's secretary. After confirming that I had an appointment, the receptionist pointed to a seating area, asked me to wait there, then resumed perusing her magazine. As the minutes ticked by, my confidence began to wane. How foolish of me to expect an important A&R man to be on time! When at last his secretary emerged, my self-assurance had all but vanished. Betty Berlin introduced herself to me, escorted me into Mr. Costa's office, presented me to him, and walked out.

Mr. Costa could not have been more affable. With a few pleasantries he made me feel that this meeting was no less important to him than a meeting with one of the label's top artists. Then we got down to business. He invited me to sit at the piano and said, "Let me hear what you've got."

The first song I played was "Leave, Schkeeve." As soon as I started playing, his attentive demeanor and my familiarity with the material restored my confidence. At the end of the song, he asked if I had another. I played five songs with no visible reaction or comment from Mr. Costa other than, "Do you have another song?" Finally I ran out of songs, and the outcome I least expected happened. Mr. Costa offered me a recording contract.

Oh my God, I thought. Is he seriously inviting me to be on the same label as Steve Lawrence, Eydie Gormé, Lloyd Price, and Paul Anka??

He was.

Moments before, I had been a high school student pulling pages of self-composed pop songs from a school notebook. Now a man with the power to make such decisions was offering me a recording contract with a major label. As I pondered the possibilities, I was brought back to reality by the recollection that I hadn't wanted to be a solo artist. I had come hoping to get my songs recorded, and if the subject of who would sing them came up, I was going to propose an audition for the Cosines. But when I explained all that to Mr. Costa, he said, "I don't see any reason to audition the group. You have more than enough talent to be a successful artist on your own."

Talk about conflicting emotions! I was ecstatic that he wanted to sign me and at the same time anxious about breaking the news to my fellow Cosines. How could I tell Iris, Joel, and Lenny that I had been offered a solo contract and the A&R man had no interest in hearing the rest of the group?

Mr. Costa signaled the end of our meeting by standing up and saying that ABC-Paramount's legal department would give me a contract on the way out for my parents to sign. He extended his hand and said, "I look forward to working with you."

Returning his handshake, I said, "I look forward to working with you, too, Mr. Costa."

"Call me Don," he said.

As I began to gather my books and my music, I remembered that I hadn't asked him about the sound on "Diana." When I did, he confided almost conspiratorially that it was a guitar and a saxophone playing in unison. I was thrilled to learn this, first, because I never would have figured it out on my own, and second, because he considered me worthy of sharing an arranger's trade secret.

Escorting me out of his office, he asked if I'd like to attend one of his recording sessions later that week.

Would I? Were Steve and Eydie married?

My providential day continued when I found both my parents in a period of reconciliation at home. When I burst in with the news and showed them the contract, they were as delighted as I was, and they were particularly proud that I had accomplished this entirely on my own. But they had some reservations. Their primary concern was making sure that the contract wouldn't keep me away from my studies. I assured them that it wouldn't. A lawyer friend of my father's came over after supper to review the contract. Once my parents determined that the only thing required of me was that I record a certain number of songs every year for the next three years at ABC-Paramount's option, for which the record company would pay me what the lawyer confirmed was a standard beginning artist's royalty after certain costs were recouped, all three of us signed the contract, thereby making official my status as a recording artist with ABC-Paramount Records, Inc. The perils of the "after certain costs are recouped" clause wouldn't become known to me during my term with ABC-Paramount. I would never sell enough units under that contract to recoup the cost of the coffee Mr. Costa—Don—drank at my first session.

If Lenny, Joel, and Iris were disappointed the next day when I told them I had been signed as a solo artist, they gave no sign of it. All three of my friends were generous in recognizing the offer as an exceptional opportunity, and they encouraged me to take full advantage of it. That afternoon, as I pushed my way onto a crowded Manhattan-bound express with the signed contract securely tucked among the pages of my loose-leaf notebook, recoupment was the farthest thing from my mind.

Chapter Fourteen

Conducting an Orchestra

On the day of the recording session to which I had been invited, the train could not go fast enough.

Don Costa was scheduled to record a full orchestra with top studio musicians, including Charlie Macey and Al Gorgoni on guitar and Buddy Saltzman on drums. When I arrived eight minutes before the session was scheduled to begin, most of the musicians were already in the studio. Making my way through the hallway to the control room, I passed a musician on a pay phone confirming the location of his next gig. Two others were standing near the coffee machine complaining about the producer of a session on which they had worked the previous day. Inside the studio, players were variously drinking coffee, chatting with the musician in the next chair, or eating a familiar New York breakfast sandwich: scrambled egg on an onion roll. While some instrumentalists were warming up or tuning up, others wouldn't even bother to pick up their instrument until they heard "A-one!" Pronounced "uh-one," that command tells English-speaking musicians that a countoff is beginning: "A-one! A-two! A-one-two-three-four...." If you ever need to quickly get the attention of a roomful of American musicians, "A-one!" will do it every time. Warning: do not use this command frivolously.

Don was in the control room when I entered. As soon as he saw me he stood up, greeted me, and introduced me to the engineers. Then he escorted me into the studio and presented me to the orchestra. Surely Don Costa had better things to do than delay a session to introduce a teenager to his colleagues, but he clearly enjoyed being a genial host in what was unquestionably his domain. When at last he stepped in front of the podium and picked up his baton, every musician came to attention with his or her instrument poised to play. I watched from a folding chair on the sidelines as Don began to go over the arrangement.

Fifteen minutes later they were still rehearsing when Don had to leave the studio for a few moments. Not wanting to see the orchestra lose momentum, I stepped up to the podium and picked up the baton. I don't know what made me think I could conduct an orchestra. I knew how to read music, but I had never read a score or performed the physical movements of conducting. Still, I had heard the orchestra run through the score several times, and I believed I knew the arrangement well enough to be able to move my arms in something approximating what I'd seen Don do. I lifted the baton, the players lifted their instruments, I counted off—"A-one! A-two! A-one-two-three-four"—and I was leading the orchestra.

If Don was flabbergasted when he returned and saw me at the podium, he never said a word. He let the players finish the song, helped me down, took the baton, resumed the rehearsal, and, after a final play-through, began recording. Watching and listening from my folding chair, I was oblivious to everything but the fact that I had just conducted an orchestra.

Chapter Fifteen

The Right Girl

*I*n the mid-fifties, the recording industry turned mostly on singles. The A side was a song that the record company believed would be a hit. The B side was usually considered filler, though never by the writers of that song, who were delighted to receive a check for the same amount of units sold as the writers of the A side.

I recorded four songs for ABC-Paramount with Don Costa producing and arranging. I played the piano and sang while other musicians played drums, bass, guitar, and saxophone. Don hired background vocalists for some of the records. The first single was "Baby Sittin'," backed with "Under the Stars." I wrote the music and lyrics for both. I shudder to recall.

> *Baby, baby, baby baby sittin', I'm-a*
> *Baby, baby, baby baby sittin', I'm-a*
> *Baby, baby, baby baby sittin'*
> *You know the baby I mean—he's seventeen*

And the B side was almost as repetitive:

Under the stars, we kissed good night
Under the stars, you held me tight
Under the stars and the moon above
Under the stars, we fell in love

The second single was "Goin' Wild," backed with "The Right Girl"—or maybe it was the other way around.

My lovin' baby's got a special rock & rollin' style
Every time we dance he really drives me wild
I'm goin' wild, I'm goin' wild
Goin' crazy goin' batty 'bout my rock & rollin' daddy
Goin' wild

If that doesn't convince you that I needed help with lyrics, consider these opening lines from "The Right Girl":

I know I-I am the right girl
The right girl for you-uh-oo-oo
And you-oo-oo are the right boy for me too-oo-oo
Uh-oo-oo . . .

Though I wasn't good at writing lyrics myself, I knew how important they could be in a pop song. Lyrics gave a singer the ability to express an emotional dimension beyond "La la la la"— not that there's anything wrong with "La la la la," or, for that matter, "Bum doo-bee doo-wop." Lyrics aimed at my generation didn't need to be good, but they needed to be relevant to the burning issues of a teenager's life. As far as I knew, the biggest concern of teenage girls in the fifties was, "Does he like me?"

Years later I would learn that the biggest concern for many

teenage girls in the fifties was the sexual and physical abuse they endured on a regular basis, often from someone in their family. Unaware of such abuse personally, I never even knew it existed because victims were too ashamed to speak of it. I was also unaware that some teenagers had feelings for others of the same gender. Even if I had been aware of such things, I wouldn't have known how to put them in a song. Instead I wrote about what I knew—the naïve yearning of a girl in puberty for love and devotion from a boy.

Because girls didn't ask boys out in those days, I was spared the risk of rejection. Since I couldn't ask a boy out directly, I had to be creative. Sometimes I used the "asking a question about homework" ploy to initiate a conversation that I hoped would end with the boy asking me out. Unfortunately I never got the invitation, only the answer.

I didn't know that boys, too, worried about rejection. If a guy wasn't on the football team, if he was short, overweight, wore glasses, had pimples, was brainy, or, God forbid, didn't smoke, he was definitely not cool. With every molecule of testosterone raging through his out-of-control body, a male teenager who didn't have the right look despaired of getting a girl to say yes to a date, let alone the ultimate yes. The right look was exemplified by pop idols such as Frankie Avalon and Fabian, who were wholesome, and movie actors James Dean and Marlon Brando, whose darkness of mood and image made them *beyond* cool. Under their influence boys wore cigarette packs in the rolled-up sleeves of their T-shirts, hooked their thumbs in their Garrison belts, and tried to look misunderstood.

If boys aspired to be as cool as James Dean, Natalie Wood embodied everything girls wanted to be. She played young, beautiful teenagers with bad-girl overtones. Her characters were sexy, romantic, and often tragic. Though I had explored forbidden things such as smoking cigarettes and sneaking off to Greenwich Village, no one considered me cool or a bad girl. I was so far from resembling Natalie Wood that it didn't even occur to me to try to be like her. Any hopes I might have had were dashed the day I heard a boy say my name in the stairwell below me.

"Carol Klein?" he said. "Aaah...she's okay, but I'd rather go out with that tall blonde with the big—"

"Ohhh, yeah!" his friend interrupted, moaning. "I go for *her*!!"

As I hastened back up the stairs I was feeling three things: the flush of embarrassment reddening my face, gratitude that no one had seen me, and the drive to develop other assets that would make me attractive enough to fulfill my biological destiny.

Chapter Sixteen

Graduation

*T*he release of my singles in 1958 went virtually unnoticed by the public. It probably didn't help that I wasn't out there promoting them, but I was just as happy to stay home and prepare for college. As much as I would have enjoyed having a hit single, I didn't want the peripatetic life of a performing artist any more than my parents wanted it for me. By then I was using the professional name I would use for the rest of my life. It had evolved in two steps. First I had added the "e" to Carol to distinguish myself from two other Carol Kleins in my school. Then, following a precedent established by Jewish entertainers before me who believed a non-ethnic name would improve their chances for success, I decided on King.

Tinkering with my name was more psychologically significant than the evolution implied. I was still seeking a change of identity. I was also trying to downplay my intelligence because brainy girls were considered less desirable, but playing dumb conflicted with my passion for learning. I loved knowing the answers, and I liked bringing home good grades. Though traditionally bestowed on men, education was important in my family. My grandparents were unusual among immigrants of their generation in sending both their daughters to college. It was then more common for a female high school graduate who wasn't already wearing an engagement ring to be sent to work until she found a rich husband, married him, and moved out. It was my grandmother who had insisted on college for my mother and my aunt. My compliant grandfather did his part by working hard, coming home, and facilitating Sarah's wishes.

That I would go to college was never in question, but I had yet to decide where. I considered Ohio State in Columbus, where my cousins lived, but if I enrolled as a resident in one of the five New York City colleges I could continue to live at home and tuition would be free. My older female relatives predicted that I would meet my future husband in college—as had my mother. Ideally, mine would be a premed student. Becoming the "Mrs." in "Dr. and Mrs. (insert Jewish name here)" was the highest achievement they could imagine for a young woman. But first I had to pass the rigorous exams called Regents that New York State required of every senior. I passed with high marks and received my diploma as a graduate of James Madison High School in June 1958. I was sixteen.

Though my parents were unflagging in support of my musical ambitions, they wisely counseled me to choose a career I could count on to earn a living. I figured I'd get a degree, become an elementary school teacher, get married, have four children, and write songs in my spare time. I was about to enroll in Brooklyn College when my parents, then reconciled, announced that we'd be moving to Rosedale, a suburban neighborhood in Queens.

Queens? I thought with dismay. What could there possibly be in Queens?

When I entered Queens College in the fall of 1958 I had no idea that Art Garfunkel and Paul Simon were anything other than fellow freshmen until I saw their photo in a magazine with a caption identifying Artie as "Tom" and Paul as "Jerry." Prior to ABC-Paramount's 1958 launch of my ill-fated singles, a small company called Big Records released a single by Tom and Jerry called "Hey Schoolgirl." Having made the top 50, it was considered a hit.

Paul and I soon became friends. Among the things we had in common were a similarity of age and a desire to stay involved in writing and recording popular music. Hoping to earn some extra cash, we began making demos together as the Cousins. Paul played bass and guitar, I played piano, and we both sang. Some songs were his, some were mine, and some were written by other people. The income was negligible, but we would have done it for nothing.

We were especially proud when part of an arrangement we created for a demo of a song by Mary Kalfin was used on a master release on Audicon Records. Though the single didn't make it past #69 in *Billboard*, the Passions' "Just to Be with You" is considered a doo-wop classic.

Paul and I never wrote a song together. When I asked Paul in 2006 why he thought that was, he said he'd never thought of himself as a collaborative songwriter and didn't think he was any good at writing lyrics until "The Sound of Silence" went to #1 in 1966.

I was still writing my own lyrics in 1958, but they weren't much improved from 1957. I needed a collaborative songwriter with better lyrical skills than mine.

Chapter Seventeen

Goffin and King

At fifteen, when I was a high school junior, I had come upon a drawing in *True Story* magazine of a young man with dark hair and dark eyes. It had so epitomized my ideal boyfriend that I cut it out and put it in my wallet. It was still there the day I met Gerry Goffin.

In the fall of 1958, when Gerry was nineteen and I was sixteen, he was a night student at Queens College. Since I was a day student, our schedules were unlikely to overlap. One afternoon, while studying for a test in the student union with my friend Dorothy, I was having trouble concentrating due to intense menstrual cramps. I was just putting away my books when the door opened and Gerry walked in. My heart stopped. He looked exactly like the drawing in my wallet.

As soon as my heart started beating again I received another surprise. Dorothy knew Gerry. She waved him over, introduced us, and told Gerry I wasn't feeling well. He offered to drive me home. On the way we stopped at a drugstore, where Gerry bought a pack of cigarettes and I bought some Midol. Back in the car, Gerry stripped the cellophane from the top of the pack, shook out a cigarette, and put it between his lips. After lighting the cigarette, he shook the match and tossed it out the window. I thought of my father's occupation and cringed inwardly but said nothing. Gerry started driving again. With the radio playing jazz, a conversation about music was quite natural. We had in common two genres that we liked—jazz and show tunes. When Gerry said there was one kind of music he didn't like, I asked, "What kind is that?"

"Rock and roll."

Oh, great.

Gerry elaborated by citing the opinions of people of high intellect and musical sophistication who considered rock and roll a temporary and inferior trend.

"A lyric's gotta have a deeper meaning with emotional impact," Gerry said in his thick Brooklyn accent. "'A wop wop-a loo-mop' doesn't meet those criteria."

I wanted to tell him how emotional the impact of Little Richard's music had been on me, but at that moment the boy who looked like my drawing could have persuaded me that the sun rose in the west.

Then Gerry revealed that he had written a book and lyrics for a musical he called *Babes in the Woods*, based on a novel, *The Young Lovers*, by Julian Halevy. Gerry was looking for someone to set his lyrics to music so he could bring the project to a Broadway producer and achieve his dream of making so much money that he would never again have to work at a nine-to-five job.

I waxed enthusiastic in telling Gerry how it felt to play a song for an A&R man and have him like it enough to record it. Gerry listened intently, finished his cigarette, and threw it out the window. I wanted to scream, "Don't do that!" but again, I said nothing. A couple of minutes later, he lit another cigarette with one hand while steering with the other. He looked so incredibly cool that I lost mine, which is probably what made me do what I did next.

"Actually," I volunteered, "Atlantic is looking for a song for Mickey and Sylvia."

Gerry took a deep drag on his cigarette, exhaled, and said, "Why don't we write something for them?"

I was taken aback. He had just spent twenty minutes conveying the low esteem in which he held rock and roll. When I asked why he wanted to write a song in a genre for which he had so little respect, he said he wanted to do it as an intellectual exercise, just to see if he could.

Seeing that we were only a block from my house, I rapidly recounted how I had first seen Mickey "Guitar" Baker backstage at the Alan Freed show.

"And then Mickey teamed up with a woman named Sylvia Robinson for a vocal duet on Atlantic Records, and then 'Love Is Strange' became a smash hit, and that's what we need to use as a model...Oh, look! Here we are!"

I introduced Gerry to my mother, then he and I went into the living room. After only two spins of "Love Is Strange," Gerry came up with an idea for the follow-up. "The Kid Brother" would be about a couple of teenagers trying to make out who were constantly interrupted by the girl's little brother. The punch line, to be half sung and half spoken by Mickey, was "Here's a quarter, kid. GET LOST!!"

We completed our first Goffin and King song in less than an hour.

Writing with Gerry was easy and comfortable. After we agreed that he would write lyrics for my rock and roll songs and I would write the music for *Babes in the Woods*, our next few writing sessions were devoted to the musical. But because pop songs had the potential to deliver a more immediate financial reward, we began writing more in that direction. Our work together in the fledgling discipline (or lack thereof) of rock and roll would become so lucrative that *Babes in the Woods* would be permanently relegated to the dusty attic of memory (or lack thereof).

The financial reward for our first effort was less than we had hoped. We brought "The Kid Brother" to Atlantic, and Jerry and Ahmet liked the song. Unfortunately Mickey and Sylvia had just broken up. Mickey and his new partner, Kitty Noble, recorded our song, but the capricious winds of fortune blew "The Kid Brother" in the opposite direction of "Love Is Strange." "The Kid Brother" was released as the B side of an A side called "Ooh Sha La La" that didn't do well. Nevertheless, we considered it a major accomplishment to have our first song recorded by Mickey Baker. We wrote more songs and occasionally sold one for a twenty-five-dollar advance—pocket change for a publisher, but a fortune to us.

Chapter Eighteen

Married, with Children

At first Gerry and I spent most of our time together writing songs. As our musical catalog grew in 1959, so did our romantic relationship. That summer we were married at my parents' home in Rosedale. The day after the wedding we moved to a one-room basement apartment on Bedford Avenue, a block away from the house at 2466 East 24th Street in which I had spent my childhood. The move was our honeymoon. While Gerry continued working as a chemist in downtown Brooklyn, I took a job as a secretary with a company in Manhattan that manufactured industrial chimneys. After work, using my grandmother's recipe and others from Leah Leonard's *Jewish Cookery*, I prepared supper for Gerry and me on a two-burner stove in the tiny alcove that served as a kitchen. With minimal exaggeration, Gerry used to tell people that our apartment was so small that he could turn the shower on with one hand while opening the refrigerator with the other.

After dinner, we wrote songs. Sometimes I took a day off to meet with publishers and record executives in the hope of receiving one of those twenty-five-dollar checks. We didn't get one often, but when we did the money was as welcome as a couple of fluffy matzoh balls in a bowl of chicken soup. It would be even more welcome the following year. I was pregnant. Working by day, writing by night, we were either in debt or breaking even—never ahead. We kept hoping for a hit that would free us from our day jobs, but one day my boss did that for me before we could afford to lose the income. My bouts of morning sickness when I was at work and my taking too many days off to meet with publishers may have impaired his confidence in my commitment to industrial chimneys.

I was on a song-selling mission the day I ran into Neil Sedaka on Broadway. When I told him Gerry and I were pushing our own songs, Neil suggested I meet with Don Kirshner and Al Nevins, with whose publishing company he and Howie Greenfield were signed. When I called to request an appointment, the secretary said her bosses could see me the next day. Gerry couldn't take time off from work, so I would attend the meeting alone. The next day I took the BMT to 49th Street. As I walked up Broadway, I was filled with so much anticipatory energy that I barely noticed the teeming street scene around me. Riding up in the elevator I reminded myself of my two objectives: getting us a publishing deal sufficient to get out of debt, and signing with a publisher with a track record of hits with top artists. Having already attained a #1 hit by Connie Francis with "Stupid Cupid," written by Neil and Howie, Aldon Music met the second requirement.

Aldon combined the first names of Al Nevins and Don Kirshner. Al had been one of the Three Suns, best known for their 1944 hit "Twilight Time." Al had financed the partnership, while Don had brought his close friendship with Bobby Darin and Connie Francis and an unerring ear for a hit. Arriving in Aldon's reception area I could hear a cacophony of male and female voices singing, several pianos playing different songs in different rooms, and two or three current hit records blaring, all at the same time. When I gave the secretary my name she escorted me into Al's office to meet her bosses. After introducing me, she left and shut the door behind her. My first impression of Al's office was that it must have been decorated by someone who designed brothels. It had red drapes, a red carpet, and a red piano that dominated the room. The piano had red-and-black stools and a lacquered black shelf around it with red coasters on which people could set their drinks. One could almost imagine the piano being announced in a basso profundo voice: The Red Pianohhhhh.

After I had answered a few preliminary questions such as "How do you know Neil and Howie?" Al invited me to sit at the piano and play some songs. Donnie was constantly in motion, alternately pacing, tapping his feet, and nodding his head slightly off rhythm. After each song, Al applauded enthusiastically, Donnie winked at me, then Donnie and Al looked conspiratorially at each other. After the fourth song, Al praised the music and the lyrics and Donnie complimented me on my "piano feel," by which I gathered he meant my pound-out-the-rhythm-as-hard-as-I-could style of accompaniment. Al was just saying he'd like to meet Gerry when Donnie looked at his watch, stood up, and said, "Gotta run, babe."

Moving toward the door, he added, "I gotta go meet Connie"— I assumed he meant Connie Francis—"but can ya come back tomorrow? Bring Gerry."

"Sure, no problem."

Donnie paused at the door long enough to say, "I like what you're doin'. Lemme hear some more songs," and then he was gone.

Al recapped more elegantly what Donnie had just said, then walked me out to have his secretary set up an appointment for Gerry and me for the next day.

I floated home. (Full disclosure: a Brooklyn-bound BMT train was involved.) When Gerry got home from work I told him how it went. He was skeptical but willing to take a day off to hear what they had to say.

At the conclusion of our meeting the following day, Donnie and Al offered Gerry and me a three-year publishing contract that would give us, as a team, an advance of $1,000 the first year, $2,000 the second year, and $3,000 the third year. In exchange for $6,000, to be deducted from our future royalties, Gerry and I would assign ownership of the copyrights of all the songs we would write under the term of the agreement to Aldon Music, Inc., "and/or their heirs and assigns." Any advances would be recouped from the writers' share of the publishing income. The publisher's share, equal to that of the writers, would go to Aldon and/or their heirs and assigns. At the time I had no idea what "heirs and assigns" were, but with extensions our agreement with Aldon would come to include all the songs that Gerry and I wrote separately or together from the time we signed with Aldon in 1959 until several years after the release of *Tapestry* in 1971.

We left that meeting feeling as if we had struck gold. To us, $6,000 was a huge sum of money, and that first check for $1,000 did get us out of debt. To Al and Donnie, $6,000 was a relatively small amount to invest in what was then fifty-six years of ownership and/or the right to transfer ownership of the copyright of any song written by Gerry and/or me during the term of the contract.

With our immediate financial concerns alleviated, we focused on the need to find a bigger apartment before the anticipated arrival of our baby in March. We moved to a ground floor two-bedroom apartment on Brown Street between Avenue Z and Voorhies Avenue in Brooklyn. That entire area had been cornfields when I was a child. Now it was filled with attached brick duplex houses in which a family could live on the upper two floors and cover their mortgage by renting out the ground-floor apartment. Gerry pejoratively called the neighborhood a "people farm," but I was thrilled to be living in four rooms instead of one.

In January 1960, I was a month shy of eighteen. The baby's due date was approaching, and all I knew about giving birth was that it would be painful. My main source of information was my mother, who was as helpful as she could be considering that her own experience had been limited to two births for which she had been medicated. Her own mother had practiced natural childbirth, though not by choice or name, but childbirth without drugs was no more an option for me in 1960 than it had been for my mother in the 1940s.

"When I was giving birth to you," she recalled, "the drugs they gave me made me groggy, but they didn't stop the pain." She hastened to add, "Don't feel bad. You were worth it, even if you did elbow me away the first time I held you...." I rolled my eyes and then we both smiled. It wasn't the first time I had heard that story.

Then her eyes clouded with sadness as she recounted the memory of my brother coming out purple and staying that way for what seemed to her like too long a time before he turned pink. At subsequent doctor visits, when she suspected that Richard had a hearing disability, she was told that his purple color could have been an indicator of oxygen deprivation, which she later came to believe had caused his disabilities.

My mother's recollections were not giving me a lot of confidence. As an apprehensive seventeen year old undertaking to learn exactly how childbirth worked and how much it would hurt, I wanted my mother to tell me how painless and uncomplicated her experiences had been. At the same time, I was grateful for her counsel. Had one of my daughters become pregnant at seventeen I would have said, "You're much too young to have a baby!" but then I would have risen to the occasion, as did my mother.

Though Gerry and I had originally planned to wait before having children, Gerry, too, rose to the occasion. When I went into labor, he helped me into the car very carefully and made sure I had everything I would need with me. Because it would be another decade before fathers were invited to participate in deliveries, Gerry was pacing and smoking in the fathers' waiting room when our daughter Louise Lynn Goffin was born on March 23, 1960. I was allowed to hold Louise for less than a minute before a nurse took her away to clean her up, swaddle her in a pink blanket, and tuck her in a bassinet in the nursery far from her germy mother. Another nurse brought Gerry to the hallway outside the nursery so he could view his new baby through a window. When at last my nurse allowed him in to see his wife and daughter during one of Louise's allotted visits to my room, Gerry was profoundly moved. He kept telling me how beautiful Louise was, how much he loved her, how much he loved me, and what a good father he was going to be.

Seeing Gerry's eyes shining with such a strong commitment to love his family and keep us safe, I fell in love with him all over again.

My mother, 1938 *From the
Collection of Eugenia Gingold*

Age 4 rowing
*From the Collection of
Eugenia Gingold*

Age 4 at the piano *From the
Collection of Eugenia Gingold*

Family portrait, age 5 *From the Collection of Eugenia Gingold*

Age 8 onstage *From the Collection of Eugenia Gingold*

With mother and brother
Richard, age 9 *From the
Collection of Eugenia Gingold*

With my parents, age 15 *From
the Collection of Eugenia Gingold*

Age 15 at James
Madison High
School *From the
Collection of Eugenia
Gingold*

Age 17 writing *From the*
Collection of Eugenia Gingold

With Gerry *From the*
Collection of Eugenia Gingold

Studio, 1957 *Michael Ochs*
Archives/Michael Ochs Archives/
Getty Images

Wedding,
1959 *From the Collection of Eugenia Gingold*

With Gerry, Louise, and baby Sherry *From the Collection of Eugenia Gingold*

With Little Eva, 1961 *From the Carole King Family Archives*

Gerry, 1961 *From the Carole King Family Archives*

Louise and Gerry in Brooklyn, New York, 1961 *From the Carole King Family Archives*

My dad after a fire, 1962
From the Collection of Eugenia Gingold

With Don Kirshner, Al Nevins, Little Eva, and Gerry, 1962 *Frank Driggs Collection/Archive Photos/Getty Images*

Studio with Paul Simon and Gerry *Michael Ochs Archives/Michael Ochs Archives/*
Getty Images

With Gerry in New
Jersey, 1965 *From
the Carole King Family
Archives*

Chapter Nineteen

Cubicles

As a child I had imagined, erroneously, that Tin Pan Alley was a physical alley next to the Brill Building. Both were symbols of music publishing in the twentieth century, which is probably why so many people think, erroneously, that Gerry and I wrote in the Brill Building. But we didn't. The Brill Building was at 1619 Broadway. The building that housed Aldon Music was 1650 Broadway. With a logic peculiar to Manhattan, the entrance to 1650 Broadway was on West 51st Street. (New York Real Estate 101: why use a street address when you can charge higher rent with a Broadway address?)

At first, when we drove to Aldon from Brooklyn, we parked in the outdoor parking lot across the street. We had to find another location when the one-story lot became a twenty-two-story Sheraton hotel. (New York Real Estate 102: why maintain a business on one level when you can make so much more money renting space on twenty-two floors?)

Crossing the street we invariably passed a man whom local vendors called "Larry Sick-Sick." Homeless and mentally ill, Larry was never far from the entrance to 1650. We never knew his last name, and someone other than he must have told us his first name, because we never heard him utter anything but the one word he hissed repeatedly whenever anyone walked by: "Sick-sick-sick-sick-sick-sick-sick!"

Another local character was Moondog, an imposing figure often seen outside the Warwick Hotel on Sixth Avenue and 54th Street. Sometimes he stood on the corner of Broadway and 51st Street. His form of mental illness compelled him to stand on a corner in the same upright position all day. He wore a blanket and big leather boots and held a long wooden staff. I never heard Moondog speak. In fact, I never saw him do anything other than stand upright with his long wooden staff through rain, snow, sleet, heat, and fine weather. Though I never saw Larry or Moondog soliciting money or food, some kindly souls must have made sure they had enough to eat. To most passersby, including young and naïve me, Moondog and Larry Sick-Sick were two among many odd citizens among the eight million residents of the Big Apple.

Aldon Music has been described as boot camp for songwriters. That it was. And yes, we did write in cubicles. The cubicles were the source of the cacophony I'd heard when I first visited the office. Each was barely big enough to contain an upright piano with a bench, a chair for the lyricist, and a small table with enough room for a legal pad, a pen, an ashtray, and a coffee cup. The proximity of each cubicle to the next added an "echo" factor. While I was playing the song on which Gerry and I were working, we heard only our song. As soon as I stopped playing we could hear the song on which the team in the next cubicle was working. Not surprisingly, with each of us trying to write the follow-up to an artist's current hit, everyone's song sounded similar to everyone else's. But only one would be chosen. Inevitably the insecurity of the writers and the competitive atmosphere fostered by Donnie spurred each team on to greater effort, which resulted in better songs. It wasn't only about writing a great song; it was about *winning*.

Though Gerry and I typically wrote together at home after dinner, sometimes he'd call in sick to his day job and we'd write in a cubicle while the secretaries fussed over Louise. Gerry, in particular, thrived on being where the action was. I didn't realize at the time that *we* were the action. By "we," I mean the Aldon songwriters. I don't believe any of us knew then how much influence we would have on popular music.

Vital to that influence were the musicians and background singers who performed on our demos. One night we were listening to a playback when Gerry happened to mention that we were looking for female background singers. The engineer suggested three young black women from Brooklyn known collectively as the Cookies. Dorothy Jones, Margaret Ross, and Earl-Jean McCree had a near-perfect vocal blend. After a number of our demos became masters and then hits, the Cookies were heard around the world. Among their hits were "Girls Grow Up Faster Than Boys," "Don't Say Nothin' Bad About My Baby," and, most famously, "Chains." Other records featuring Tony Orlando and Neil Sedaka on which the Cookies sang also became hits. Sometimes they were in the studio with Aldon writers from midmorning to the wee hours.

One night Gerry, Dorothy, Margaret, Earl-Jean, and I emerged from a demo session at 3 a.m. onto an almost deserted Broadway. Apart from a few hookers and johns, we seemed to be the only people around. While the Cookies and I waited for Gerry to get the car, we were approached by several different vehicles containing men inquiring about everything from a single to a five- or six-some. Thankfully, Gerry pulled up and whisked us all back to Brooklyn, leaving the potential johns to wonder what he had that they didn't.

What he had was a wife and a baby daughter to support. He also had a mother-in-law who lived too far away to babysit on a moment's notice. My participation in late-night demo sessions was possible only when Grandma Sarah, who lived nearby, could watch Louise. My grandmother couldn't understand how any-one could earn a living writing songs that appealed to teenagers, but that's exactly what Gerry and I were doing. Though now in his twenties, Gerry hadn't forgotten which three-letter word was foremost in the mind of every teen. It was s-e-x that kids thought about when they listened to lyrics about hearts full of love, hearts breaking, lovers longing, youth yearning, cars, stars, the moon, the sun, and that most innocent of all physical pastimes: dancing.

We wouldn't write a song about dancing until the following year, but sex was definitely the implied third character in our first big hit.

Chapter Twenty

Will You Love Me Tomorrow

Donnie was not without idiosyncrasies. He was deathly afraid to drive, and he refused to fly. It was rare to receive his full attention except when follow-ups or chart positions were a topic of discussion. And he constantly sought reassurance.

"Sheel, babe," he'd say to his wife, Sheila. "Look at this new carpet! Isn't it great?"

Then he'd turn to us: "Isn't my wife the greatest?"

And after playing a test pressing of Connie Francis's new recording of an Aldon song: "Doesn't Connie sound great? This is gonna be a *smash*!"

For Donnie, everything connected with him was "great." Ironically, that's what made Donnie great. His enthusiasm was so infectious that he got everyone within earshot all fired up about whatever he was fired up about, and what he was usually the most fired up about was convincing the artist or producer of a top 10 hit to record an Aldon song and release it as their next single, which Donnie called the "follow-up." When Donnie said, "Come on, guys, we gotta get that follow-up!" that was an unambiguous directive to head for the cubicles.

In 1960, the hottest girl group was arguably the Shirelles, four teenage girls whose then current hit was "Tonight's the Night." Donnie wanted that follow-up. Shifting into high gear, he summoned each writer or writing team into his office and addressed that writer or team as if she, he, or they were the *only* writer or team that could deliver his desired outcome.

"Now listen," he'd say. "The Shirelles are up. I'm gonna get the follow-up, and I want *you* to write it. Come on, babe," he exhorted, using the term with no regard for gender. "Do it for *me!*"

And we did. He made us want to do it—for *him*.

The next day each writer or team, in turn, went into Al's office to play Donnie the song they had written the night before. Al, who tended to leave the day-to-day business to Donnie, wasn't usually there. With Gerry at work, I waited with the other writers in the reception area. Hearing snippets of each new song coming through the door filled us alternately with confidence and anxiety.

Gerry and I competed the most fiercely against Barry Mann and Cynthia Weil. Each couple came to think of the other as "the other married songwriting team," and each couple was intimidated by how talented the other couple was. Whether in spite of that or because of it, we four have remained friends over many decades. What we shared was unique. We Aldon songwriters may have thought of ourselves as mortal enemies when it came to getting a follow-up, but we were a tightly knit brother- and sisterhood of friends, colleagues, peers, and, most of the time, allies.

Donnie chose Gerry's and my song for the Shirelles. The next hurdle was playing it for the people at Scepter Records. Their office was in the same building. As soon as Donnie hung up with Scepter, he gave me the go-ahead. Bypassing the elevator, I ran up the stairs with Gerry's handwritten lyric and played the song for Scepter's owner, Florence Greenberg, and Luther Dixon, the cowriter and producer of "Tonight's the Night." Florence and Luther liked the song and wanted to record it with the Shirelles right away, so I recorded the demo right there in their studio. It was a rudimentary presentation in which I sang the song live over my piano accompaniment and tried to sound like the Shirelles' lead singer, Shirley Owens. One of the other Shirelles—Doris Coley, Beverly Lee, or Micki Harris—told me later that when Shirley recorded the lead vocal, she was trying to sound like me sounding like her.

Within ten weeks after it was released on November 21, 1960, "Will You Love Me Tomorrow" climbed to #1 on *Billboard*'s popular music chart and stayed in the top 10 for seven weeks.

A lot of people think I wrote the lyrics for "Will You Love Me Tomorrow," because they express so eloquently the emotions of a teenage girl worried that her boyfriend won't love her anymore once she gives him her most precious one-time-only prize. Those lyrics were written by Gerry, whose understanding of human nature transcended gender. My contribution to "Will You Love Me Tomorrow" included writing the melody, playing piano in the studio, and arranging the string parts. Though I had previously written choral parts, I had never composed a string arrangement. But when Gerry suggested we use strings I was fearless in volunteering. I knew how to write and read music. I would work out the parts on the piano and refer to an arranger's handbook for transposition and range.

As I worked on the arrangement, Gerry sang ideas to me in a voice that many people considered unmusical, but I never did. Like a translator with a unique understanding of an arcane language, I was able to interpret the ideas Gerry was trying to get across. We had listened to hit records by the songwriting team of Jerry Leiber and Mike Stoller for artists ranging from Wilbert Harrison ("Kansas City") to the Coasters. We had also found inspiration in the work of Rodgers and Hammerstein and Aaron Copland. One of the most unusual arrangements we had ever heard was composed by Stanley Applebaum for Leiber and Stoller's production of "There Goes My Baby." Who but Leiber and Stoller would have thought to combine the voice of Ben E. King with cellos and timpani? That was visionary.

We, too, tried to be visionary. With "There Goes My Baby" as our model, I incorporated Gerry's ideas and my melodic lines into an arrangement meant to complement the voices of the Shirelles. I tried to make my charts look as professional as the ones I'd seen on the music stands at Don Costa's sessions by hand-copying the part for each instrument separately on music staff paper with a steel ruler and India ink. I wish I'd known that an arranger had only to scratch out a score in pencil and a team of copyists would work overnight to make the charts look the way they did on the music stands. After many hours handwriting more than fifteen charts, I was bleary-eyed. I looked at the clock. It was 4:45 a.m. I looked in on Louise and then went to bed.

The alarm rang entirely too soon. I dragged myself out of bed, brought Louise to my grandmother's, then took the BMT up to Scepter. Recording the rhythm track took less than an hour. Then the string players arrived. The first time I heard the cellos play the rhythmic figure at the beginning of "Will You Love Me Tomorrow," I was euphoric. To this day I can think of no greater musical joy than to hear a song or an arrangement come to life with instruments and voices. Some composers literally hear the sounds in their head as they write; Don Costa reportedly was such a composer. I had to wait until a session to hear what I wrote. As the musicians began to play the parts I had written for "Will You Love Me Tomorrow," I became giddy with excitement. My little black dots and squiggles on the page were coming out as beautiful music. The experience exceeded my wildest expectations.

I was eighteen.

The first time we heard "Will You Love Me Tomorrow" on the

radio we were in our 1956 Mercury Monterey. We didn't care that the speakers were low-fidelity. We knew how it was supposed to sound. The following week, "Will You Love Me Tomorrow" leaped onto the charts with what the industry called a bullet. Gerry and I had set a million as the number of singles sold that would trigger him quitting his day job. The day Donnie learned that the record had reached the million mark, he insisted on conveying the information personally to Gerry. He had his driver pick me up and then we drove to Gerry's workplace in Brooklyn. Upon hearing the news, Gerry walked away from his job and, as he said many years later, he hasn't had a real job since.

Though Gerry and I remained each other's primary collaborator, he began using his newly available daytime hours to write with other Aldon writers. One such collaboration with Barry Mann, "Who Put the Bomp," would become a hit single with Barry as the artist. I, too, collaborated with other writers, notably Cynthia Weil and Howie Greenfield. Aldon had become one of the hottest publishers in the business, but none of us stopped long enough to notice how successful the company was. We were too busy competing to be Donnie's "go-to" songwriters.

I never understood why some of Gerry's relatives persisted in referring to him as a "bum" even though he had been gainfully employed as a chemist. Quitting his day job only confirmed their opinion of him—until they realized that he was making more money than they were, at which point they took great pride in his success.

Now that we had reasonable financial security, with Gerry collaborating with other writers, I was hoping to lighten my workload and spend more time at home with Louise.

It didn't quite work out that way.

Chapter Twenty-One

Daughter Momentum

Division of labor in a family in the early sixties held that it was the man's responsibility to earn enough income to support his family while his wife handled household chores and child care— then considered "woman's work." Gerry was a loving husband and father who never failed to support his family, but he wasn't much help with chores or children. He might have been more helpful had I asked, but I didn't know enough to ask. I actually enjoyed two of my jobs (music and child care), and I really didn't mind folding laundry, ironing, or washing dishes, especially when I could time those tasks to coincide with reruns of *I Love Lucy*. Sometimes I did all three jobs simultaneously. When I held Louise, vacuumed, and commented on a lyric Gerry was working on from the comfort of his armchair, it never occurred to me that I had a right to expect my husband to participate equally in child care and housework. This would have been true even if I hadn't been earning half of our income.

I found child care at once challenging and joyous. It was challenging to be responsible for a little being with needs to be met ahead of mine, and utterly delightful to have this bright, beautiful, healthy little girl in my life. I loved learning the things I needed to know as a new mother and rediscovering things Louise learned as if I were learning them for the first time. This was equally true with our second daughter, Sherry Marlene Goffin, who arrived on March 3, 1962. But meeting the needs of *two* little beings made my role as a mother somewhat more complicated. I soon found myself saying things that all parents swear as children that they'll never say to their children. "Share your toys!" and "Stop that right now!" became part of my daily vocabulary along with "No bickering!" and "Because I said so!"

Propelled by daughter momentum, we acquired so much "stuff" that we were bursting out of our apartment. Gerry's wish to raise our girls in Manhattan was overridden by practicality. We found a house in a newly platted subdivision in West Orange, New Jersey, took out a mortgage, and moved to the suburbs.

That lighter workload I had envisioned for myself after Gerry quit his day job never materialized. I still had to drive to the city to play songs for artists and producers and sing and play on demos. The commute from New Jersey took at least an hour each way. And while it was possible to bring one child and her gear to the city, it was exponentially more difficult to bring two children and twice the gear.

In simpler times, when extended families lived near each other, older women helped younger women, stay-at-home sisters cared for nieces and nephews, and neighbors looked after each other's children. In the more mobile early sixties, working mothers had to hire outside help. While we were still living in Brooklyn, several babysitters had come and gone—including one who moved on to a different career. In New Jersey, my need to be in the city with Gerry several times a week made it essential that I find someone reliable to care for my girls. My prayers were answered when we found Willa Mae Phillips. With no biological children of her own, Willa Mae devoted her maternal energy to my children and remained a beloved member of our family from the time she came to work for us in New Jersey until her death in the mid-seventies. The memory of Willa Mae endures every time we repeat one of her down-home sayings. For example, after the entire family had torn the house apart for twenty minutes searching for car keys, a wristwatch, or a missing schoolbook, Willa Mae, having located the item in an obvious place, would hold it up triumphantly, saying, "If it'd been a snake, it would-a bit you."

There was no shortage of playmates on our suburban street. Willa Mae didn't drive—indeed, she emphatically refused to learn—but she could walk the girls to play dates. As Gerry and I crafted songs in our music room, Louise learned to write "L-U-L-U" on a chalkboard while Sherry and her playmates, under Willa Mae's watchful eye, delighted in the antics of Judy Garland and her funny-looking friends in *The Wizard of Oz* on the big television in the family room.

From earliest childhood Sherry saw the world with the eyes of truth and never hesitated to speak that truth. She could size up a situation, see through complicated explanations, double-talk, and misrepresentation (all euphemisms for the feces of a male bovine), and sum up in one sentence what others might be thinking but didn't dare say. My appreciation for this admirable quality would be sorely tested when Sherry became a teenager and said things I didn't want to hear.

"Mom, that haircut's been out of style for two years!"

Or, "Are you going to wear *that*??"

Writing songs for our daughters was something Gerry and I could do together to show them and the rest of the world how grateful we were for their presence in our lives. It was Sherry's candor that inspired Gerry to write a paean called "Child of Mine," on which we collaborated when Sherry was six.

I know you will be honest if you can't always be kind
Oh yes, sweet darlin'
So glad you are a child of mine

Later I would write the melody to a song called "Daughter of Light" for which Gerry wrote these words about Louise:

Daughter of light, you're a welcome sight
To a weary soul
Seeing you just lifts me out of the cold

Fast-forward to 1974, when I featured my Goffin daughters' vocal performances on *Really Rosie*, an album on which I collaborated with the noted children's author Maurice Sendak. Maurice is probably best known for his self-illustrated books *Where The Wild Things Are* and *In The Night Kitchen*. His *Nutshell Library* is a boxed set of four tiny books with poems that I set to music and recorded with Lou Adler. *Really Rosie* holds a special appeal for me first because I had the rare privilege of collaborating with Maurice, second because I acted the roles of Rosie and the narrator in a companion TV special, and third because that album is a permanent record of Sherry and Louise at twelve and fourteen.

I never imagined that in the eighties Louise would move to London and bring her beautiful spirit, musical talent, and successful career to fans on both sides of the Atlantic, or that Sherry would marry a New York–based studio musician and move to a suburban neighborhood where, after several years of driving her children to various activities and finding insufferable the music then designed to appeal to young children, she would create a collection of CDs that appealed to both children and parents. Sherry would make SugarBeats.com such a successful enterprise online that I would be inspired to start my own label, Rockingale Records.

However, before Sugar Beats or Rockingale, there was Dimension Records, started by Al and Donnie. Which brings me to the babysitter who changed careers.

Chapter Twenty-Two

The Loco-Motion

Before Willa Mae, while we were still living in Brooklyn, Gerry and I were rehearsing one day in 1961 with the Cookies. I was then pregnant with Sherry. Baby Louise was alternately being fussed over by the women, held by Gerry, or attended to by me. Hearing me say, not for the first time, that I really needed a dependable babysitter, Dorothy recommended a teenager she knew. At seventeen, Eva Narcissus Boyd was whip smart, cheerful, hardworking, and wonderful with Louise. Pop legend has it that Gerry and I heard her singing around the house and said, "Stop! We *must* record that voice!" The truth is, we knew Eva could sing when we hired her. With one of her older sisters covering child care, Eva often sang on our demos.

In 1962, Dee Dee Sharp had a #1 hit called "Mashed Potato Time" on a Philadelphia-based label called Cameo-Parkway. Gerry and I wrote "The Loco-Motion" with Dee Dee in mind and recorded the demo with Eva singing lead. But Cameo-Parkway was a self-contained hit factory. Dee Dee and her producers didn't want or need material from outside writers. If Cameo-Parkway's success hadn't already been enough motivation, their failure to consider a song that Donnie's golden ear had identified as a hit prompted Donnie to establish Dimension Records, on which he would release Aldon songs sung by artists under Aldon's control, with Aldon writers producing the records. It was Donnie who gave our babysitter her professional name: Little Eva. "The Loco-Motion" was Dimension's first release on June 8, 1962.

Donnie's instinct was literally on the money. It didn't take long for "The Loco-Motion" to reach #1, where it remained for seven weeks. Our catchy little dance tune would subsequently be recorded by a diverse assortment of artists over the next several decades, among them Grand Funk Railroad in the seventies and the Australian entertainer Kylie Minogue in the eighties.

Though "The Loco-Motion" alludes to dance movements, neither Gerry nor I had envisioned an actual dance. Eva had to invent one for personal appearances. Standing beside a locomotive for publicity photographs, with "The Loco-Motion" playing on loudspeakers, Eva moved her body that day in imitation of the arm that drives a locomotive, and a dance was born.

Eva's success had a downside for us—or, more accurately, for me. With Eva's career as our babysitter pretty much over, I was once again doing all three of my old jobs: songwriting, child care, and household management. The latter included (and this is only a partial list) cooking, dusting, vacuuming, cleaning the toilet, making beds, endless laundry, endless diapers, grocery shopping, picking up dry cleaning, and reconciling our monthly bank statements. When I interviewed potential replacements for Eva, I was very careful to communicate a requirement, second only to the ability to care for our children, that the applicant possess neither a good singing voice nor the desire to become a famous recording artist.

Donnie was so pleased with the success of "The Loco-Motion" that he put Gerry in charge of producing other artists. Soon

Dimension became a strong independent label, and Gerry was recognized as a talented producer with good instincts, a good ear, and the necessary perspective to keep everyone focused on the desired end product. When we wrote a song, Gerry often guided me toward the realization of a concept I didn't fully understand until later. Though we worked as a team in the studio, he was credited as the sole producer and paid accordingly. At the time, this seemed logical. Production credit was customarily given to the person in the control booth, and Gerry's contribution was essential. But I arranged and conducted. Sometimes I was a band member. Sometimes I sang background. And I often directed other singers with hand and body movements from a position close by in the studio. We both did what we did because we loved the work. But because I believed sole credit was important to my husband, it never even occurred to me to ask for a coproducer credit on any of the Dimension records.

Clearly I could have benefited from the women's liberation movement. But women's lib didn't fully come into its own until later in the sixties. I had no trouble valuing Gerry, but I didn't know how to value myself. And yet, as much as I valued Gerry, it would turn out not to be enough.

Chapter Twenty-Three

It Might as Well Rain Until September

Whenever I sang on a demo I usually tried to channel the vocal style of the artist for whom the song was intended. That's what I did on the demo of "It Might as Well Rain Until September," which Gerry and I had written for Bobby Vee. Even after Bobby recorded it, Donnie liked my demo so much that he released it on Dimension. I was no more interested in promoting the single than I'd been on previous labels, and I was unambiguous in communicating that to Donnie before he released the single. I had two small children at home in New Jersey, and I was unwilling to travel around the country to promote the record. At some point Donnie must have realized that I was more valuable to him at home writing for other artists, because he stopped pushing me to promote the single—with one exception. He wanted me to go to Philadelphia to appear on Dick Clark's *American Bandstand*.

"*Bandstand* can make or break a record," he said. "You *gotta* do it."

With Gerry supporting Donnie's position, I thought, They're right. I *gotta* do it.

That all-important appearance on *American Bandstand* consisted of me lip-synching to the record, shaking Dick Clark's hand, and hovering anxiously in the background while the *Bandstand* kids rated my single. One of their most frequently heard assessments of a record was "I give it a 99; I like the beat." Unfortunately, the *Bandstand* kids' evaluation of my record was 42 out of 100 and included comments such as "You can't dance to it," "It's too sad," and "I like the lyric, but I don't like the words."

Dick Clark had bestowed an inordinate amount of power upon this select cadre of Philadelphia high school students. Their opinions influenced a national audience in judging the creative endeavors of recording artists, producers, and songwriters. A thumbs-up or -down from these kids could begin or end a career. Riding the train back from Philadelphia, I felt terrible about the end of a career I didn't even want. In rhythm with the clackety wheels, I kept thinking, I'm *never* . . . gonna do this . . . again . . . *never* . . . do this . . . again . . . *never* . . . do this . . . again . . .

I was incredulous when, with no further promotion on my part, "It Might as Well Rain Until September" rose to the top 20 in *Billboard* and *Cashbox*.

Donnie was on a roll. His next release was our song "Chains," by the Cookies. He was confident that it would hit #1, and unlike me, the Cookies were able and willing to promote their single. They went on *Bandstand* and appeared on other radio and television shows with a history of bringing success to a decent song with a good beat that resonated with teenagers. "Chains" was a reasonably decent song with a good beat and a simple lyric. How could it not resonate with teenagers? And how could anyone go wrong with traditional twelve-bar blues? "Chains" featured the Cookies in three-part harmony and the sexy alto voice of Earl-Jean McCree singing solo in the bridge until she was joined by the other Cookies on the last word of the plaintive lyric, "But I can't break away from all of these chains!" With that they reprised the deceptively simple words of the refrain that brought us all back to that helpless feeling shared by everyone who's ever been hopelessly in love:

> *Chains*
> *My baby's got me locked up in chains*
> *And they ain't the kind that you can see-ee*
> *Wo-oh, these chains of lo-o-ove got a-hold on me . . . yeah!*

It's not difficult to understand Gerry's metaphor if you've ever been so deeply in love that all you can think of is the object of your desire, and even as you wish you could stop being obsessed with that person, you spend every sleeping moment dreaming about the one you love and every waking moment praying that he or she feels the same about you.

I just used an entire paragraph to convey an idea that Gerry was able to get across in three words: "chains of love." Even when his lyrics involved more frivolous subject matter, Gerry had a gift for tapping into what teenage listeners were feeling. If the arrangement, the beat, and the melody of "The Loco-Motion" sparked everyone's basic human impulse to dance and have fun, the lyric ignited it.

Not only was "Chains" fun to write, it was even more fun to watch it fly up the charts. I can't speak objectively about the merits of songs we wrote, but we definitely had a run of good luck in the sixties. The music we were writing resonated with young people from New York to Cambodia. This is not a random geographical reference. A woman who grew up in Phnom Penh told me years later that our music kept her from losing her sanity while Pol Pot was committing genocide in her country.

Gerry's and my level of success remained consistently high for a long time. Whether on Dimension or another label, rarely did a record that we had written or produced fail. When groups from the United Kingdom first began appearing on the American charts, Gerry and I were well represented. The Beatles recorded "Chains," the Hollies had a big hit with a Gerry Goffin–Russ Titelman collaboration titled "Yes I Will," and our demo of "I'm Into Something Good," featuring Earl-Jean McCree's lead vocal, led to a chart-topping American hit by a British band called Herman's Hermits.

Each week Gerry eagerly awaited the arrival of *Billboard* and *Cashbox*. It was a heady feeling in 1964 to see a new release of ours show up in the top 10 with a bullet. Rational adults a decade older than we were probably would have had trouble keeping so much success in perspective. At twenty-five and twenty-two, Gerry and I never considered the possibility that our success might not last forever.

Chapter Twenty-Four

Waddington Avenue

*M*emories often appear in my mind in the form of snapshots. It's almost as if I'm looking through a stack of photos, placing each in turn under the pile to keep them in order. The beauty of such images is that they evoke not just the visual but all my senses. My memory snapshots of the Goffin family in West Orange in the early sixties reawaken emotions I thought I had safely tucked away.

- Our Siberian husky, Lika (pronounced LIKE-uh), curled up in the only sunny spot on the floor of the family room. She sits up suddenly with ears alert in response to our doorbell that we had pretentiously and expensively modified to play "Will You Still Love Me Tomorrow." The ring is out of rhythm, with all the notes incorrectly timed as quarter notes: do do mi mi re re re do.
- Gerry shooting pool with a cigarette dangling from his mouth. He's barefoot on the indigo carpet in our damp, cool basement trying to find a place to line up a shot without being crowded by the river rock walls or the dark walnut door leading to our rarely used sauna.

- Willa Mae folding laundry in the family room on our mid-century modern brown-yellow-black-and-white couch while watching her soaps on a big-screen television in the walnut-paneled entertainment center.
- Louise in the family room holding my hand on a rainy day as we look through the sliding glass doors leading to the backyard. After identifying some familiar shapes in the patterns formed by the raindrops on the green plastic fence around the pool, we stand quietly together, enveloped in a feeling of peace.
- Willa Mae standing, ironing, and listening to soul and gospel music on her favorite radio station, WNJR.
- Sherry in her playpen mimicking the phrasing of the singers on WNJR while she explores the array of primary-colored Fisher-Price toys around her.
- Louise, Sherry, and me out for a walk on a crisp autumn day. We wave to the Salovich children next door as they clamber excitedly into their mother's car, then we continue walking toward the Trix-colored forest at the end of our street.

Our subdivision had been part of that forest until the developers cut down all the trees. Then homeowners like us who wanted trees had to pay a landscaper to bring new ones in.

- Louise and Sherry on the patio in the summer performing in plays with wildly imaginative plots written by Louise and Sherry and starring the authors.
- An exuberant Gerry carrying his radiantly happy wife around our backyard on his shoulders. After he puts me down we share a warm, loving hug.
- Sherry flying dangerously down the hill of our driveway on her bicycle to catch the Good Humor man. In addition

to ice cream I buy some punks that I hope will generate enough smoke to keep insects away. Sherry licks her drippy cone and tries to stay ahead of the melt.

- Louise and Sherry bursting through the door of our writing room at a crucial moment in the writing process. Without missing a beat I continue to play our black Baldwin Acrosonic spinet piano and say, "Not now! Mommy and Daddy are working!" The girls get the message and withdraw.

Working on a song is a situation around which I've never had trouble perceiving a clear boundary or conveying it in a way that brooks no interruption or argument.

- Gerry sitting on one of the two sofas in our writing room, scrawling lyrics on a yellow legal pad with a ballpoint pen. The ash grows long on his cigarette as it rests on the edge of a curved red-glass ashtray. The sofas, arranged in an L shape, are upholstered in an ornate black-and-white fabric. Matching drapes, red velvet wallpaper, large lamps with elaborate finials, black end tables, and a red carpet create an atmosphere reminiscent of Al Nevins's office.

My daughters' word for the décor in the red room was "hideous." I didn't take it personally. Gerry and I had delegated such decisions to a professional interior decorator who, with our attention focused on our children and our songwriting, had little difficulty obtaining our cursory approval of her selections. Lady Fortune must have liked the décor of our writing room because so many of the songs we composed in that room were recorded by leading producers with top artists and then flew up the charts.

Gerry and I were able to keep enough hits flowing out of our

Baldwin Acrosonic spinet piano to feel confident about being able to pay our mortgage. As our income rose, we employed a professional accountant. Depending on whether he reported good or bad news, Gerry's reaction was either to buy something extravagant such as a new car, or to say, "We gotta tighten our belts!" For Gerry, that meant cutting back on movies, theater, and lobster dinners at Rod's Restaurant on Northfield Avenue. For me it meant accommodating Gerry.

On the whole, I thought we were doing well. But Gerry did not enjoy living in the suburbs, an opinion he vigorously documented in a song called "Pleasant Valley Sunday." Sometimes we stayed in the city for dinner and a movie with Barry and Cynthia. Their Upper East Side apartment was within walking distance of a first-rate selection of movie theaters and restaurants. After the movie the four of us exercised our collective intellect over coffee by analyzing the film we'd just seen, for example, *David and Lisa*, *The Manchurian Candidate*, or *To Kill a Mockingbird*.

At the end of the evening, the Manns walked home while Gerry and I retrieved our car from a parking lot, drove west across Manhattan, traversed the Hudson River through the Lincoln Tunnel, then took Route 3 to the Garden State Parkway. Taking the exit for the Oranges, we drove west some more, until finally we arrived home. I say "we drove," but it was Gerry who drove while I slept. Gerry did not relish the drive for two reasons: he was making it effectively alone, and he would vastly have preferred going home to an apartment in the city.

One of the things that had sustained my parents and grandparents through two world wars and the Great Depression was the dream that someday their children and grandchildren would have a better life. Gerry and I were barely in our twenties when we achieved that dream. We were homeowners. We lived in a safe, attractive neighborhood in which we enjoyed the freedom to work, play, and raise our beautiful, healthy daughters in relative affluence. We didn't have to worry about a midnight knock on the door by soldiers in a tyrannical regime. We should have been deliriously happy, and indeed, I was happy. In my bubble of contentment, I thought my husband was happy, too. But Gerry was beginning to feel the winds of the societal storm brewing on both coasts. That storm would become a tempest with enough momentum to polarize families across America and around the world.

Chapter Twenty-Five

City of Angels

*H*aving achieved supremacy in New York, Donnie looked for new worlds to conquer. The next logical place was the West Coast. Hits by Hollywood artists such as Bobby Vee, the Everly Brothers, and Gene McDaniels were receiving quite a bit of airplay. Donnie's relationship with Liberty Records producer Snuff Garrett had already led to a string of top 10 hits for Aldon writers, including Bobby Vee's "Take Good Care of My Baby," by Gerry and me, and "Run to Him," by Gerry and Jack Keller.

Donnie's decision to open a West Coast office was astute and timely. His choice of Lou Adler to run it was equally shrewd. Lou's longtime relationships with West Coast artists and producers led to hits for Aldon writers with a diverse group of artists. Lou went to Nashville with the Everly Brothers to produce "Crying in the Rain," which I had written with Howie Greenfield.

The first time I heard "Crying in the Rain" on the radio I was driving home on Northfield Avenue. I was immediately transported back in time to relive my excitement at seeing the Everly Brothers at an Alan Freed show. I recalled the hours spent in my room singing the third part to the Everlys' distinctive dual harmonies on songs such as "Bye Bye Love" and "Wake Up Little Susie." Later I learned that I wasn't unique in this regard. Other fans were doing the same thing. People who couldn't carry a tune sang along with the duo and imagined themselves as the third Everly Brother. The Everlys' records were arguably an early form of karaoke; all the singer had to do was fill in the missing vocal. Suddenly I was crying. There I was, a housewife running errands in West Orange, New Jersey, hearing the Everly Brothers' recording of my song on the radio for the first time contemporaneously with millions of other people in the greater New York listening area.

With other producers and artists in L.A. clamoring for our demos and trying to recapture our sound and arrangements note for note on their masters, Donnie decided it was time to send Goffin and King to California.

In 1963 air travel was a lot less commonplace than it is today. Gerry was twenty-four and I twenty-one when we embarked on our first airplane trip, nonstop from New York to Los Angeles, out of what was then called Idlewild Airport.* With the prevailing westerly winds pushing hard against the plane, the flight took over six hours. I should have been more nervous about the idea of spending six hours in a heavier-than-air metal tube hurtling thousands of feet above the ground in the general direction of the Pacific Ocean, but I was too excited. Gerry, initially more nervous than I, quickly attained a more relaxed state of mind by imbibing the mixed drinks made with tiny bottles of liquor served by the attractive female flight attendant, then known as a stewardess. As we flew across the continent I watched cities turn to suburbs, then to farms and open spaces. Occasionally, spidery patterns of houses, streets, and roads indicated the presence of a town.

I had viewed images of the Rocky Mountains and the Grand

---

*Renamed John F. Kennedy International Airport (JFK) in December 1963.

Canyon in magazines, but seeing them in three dimensions from the perspective of an eagle I felt the power of nature on a grand scale. As the vast, diverse North American landscape unfolded below me, the beginning of my lifelong love for our home planet unfolded inside me. I've traveled across the country many times since then, both by air and on the ground, but I've never forgotten my first eagle's-eye view of America's magnificent natural landscape. That perspective would inform my later work to ensure that the remaining wild land in the Northern Rockies ecosystem is legally protected. Back then I saw vast empty landscapes. Since then so much more land has been developed, and so much less of it remains wild. When I tell members of the United States Congress that their grandchildren and great-grandchildren deserve to experience the remaining unspoiled land and wildlife on this earth as close as possible to the way it was thousands of years ago, I'm honoring a commitment I made on that first flight to Los Angeles.

Today when I step out of a terminal at Los Angeles International Airport I'm struck by the smell of exhaust fumes and the absence of sunlight under an overpass that wasn't there forty-odd years ago. Stepping out of the terminal in 1963, I was struck by how warm and bright the sun was. We had left New York in January and been miraculously transported into July. As I reached for my sunglasses I thought, *Now* I understand. Sunglasses aren't an affectation here; they're a necessity.

Climbing into the back seat of the stretch limo Lou had sent for us, I had the sensation of time moving more slowly than it did back east. This shouldn't have been surprising. Though we'd been flying for most of the day, it was barely past the crack of noon. We had the whole afternoon ahead of us. The limo glided out of the airport and headed east on Century Boulevard. When the driver told us we were only a half hour away from the Pacific Ocean I thought, Wow! It took us only six hours to be a continent away from the Atlantic Ocean. My grandparents' journey from Eastern Europe had taken six months!

The driver eased the limo into the unending stream of cars that filled every lane of the freeway. The northbound traffic looked like something out of a science-fiction movie, a creature composed of parallel streams of individual cars, each contributing mindlessly to the forward movement of the larger organism. Toward what goal? Fame? Money? Power? Sex? All of the above? At the time I didn't even know the questions, let alone the answers. In Beverly Hills rows of palm trees lining Sunset Boulevard reminded me of leggy starlets at a dance audition. Most houses were hidden, but some of the large estates displayed the owner's value of opulence over privacy. It wasn't until much later that I realized I hadn't seen even one person walking on the street.

Some things are trite because they're true. Sitting in the back of a chauffeured limousine being driven through Beverly Hills, I felt like the proverbial star of a Hollywood movie. By the time we reached West Hollywood I was certain that every house in the city had a pool, every man was as rich as Howard Hughes, and every woman as sexy as Marilyn Monroe. All I had to do was close my eyes and my heart's desire would be granted. When the limo pulled up to the apartment building where we would be staying, I had no idea how much my family's future would be determined by the City of Angels.

Chapter Twenty-Six

The British Invasion and Other
Signs of the Times

The world changed on my twenty-second birthday. It was February 9, 1964, when Gerry and I watched Ed Sullivan introduce the Beatles on his television show. I could barely hear the band over their screaming fans. By the time the Fab Four had finished their first number, teenage boys across America had resolved to let their hair grow and take up the guitar. The growing restlessness of young Americans was fertile soil for the seeds of dramatic sociological transformation planted by the lads from Liverpool. Irreverent answers in interviews with John Lennon, Paul McCartney, George Harrison, and Ringo Starr resulted in many young men realizing, Yeah! These guys look how *I* wanna look, and they're sayin' what I'm thinkin'! And as young men wanted to be the Beatles, young women wanted to...well, you know. But underlying the Beatles' sociological impact was their remarkable music. Their songs had catchy melodies, smart lyrics, imaginative harmonies, and energetic arrangements.

The day after the Beatles' appearance on *The Ed Sullivan Show,* the U.S. House of Representatives passed the Civil Rights Act of 1964. This might not have happened without the lobbying skills of President Lyndon B. Johnson, arguably the most powerful Caucasian American then working to ensure civil and voting rights for all Americans.

Gerry and I became involved in the civil rights movement in part because of our close connection with African American artists, but mostly because of our shared sense of outrage about racial injustice. We canvassed for the cause and gave money to support activists on the front lines in Mississippi and Alabama. When civil rights workers James Chaney, Michael Schwerner, and Andrew Goodman were murdered in Mississippi around the solstice of "Freedom Summer," we were saddened by the loss of all three, but the loss of Andy Goodman hit closest to home. We knew his mother, Carolyn.

President Johnson signed the Civil Rights Act on July 2, 1964, and the Wilderness Act on September 3, 1964. We viewed these as signs of progress. Other signs of the times included long hair, Renaissance clothing, East Indian print curtains, beanbag chairs, discotheques, pop art, hallucinogenics, and antiwar protests that would swell to such large numbers that President Johnson would announce on March 31, 1968, that he would not seek reelection.

In 1964 I was somewhat aware of current events, but I was more concerned about my husband's declared desire to expand his mind. I had no interest in doing that. Someone in our family needed to keep enough brain cells functioning to run our household. One of us needed to at least pretend to be an adult. I could do that by writing melodies to Gerry's increasingly socially conscious lyrics. After that, all I could do was hope those songs would be hits. There was a fair chance of that happening. As the antiwar movement grew stronger and Americans became increasingly polarized, protesters were romanticized in popular songs. A man's long hair, by which he self-identified as "hip," invited name-calling and worse from other men who proudly asserted their status as "straight" with the short hairstyle of a businessman or a Marine buzz cut. At the time "straight" was not associated with sexual orientation; it meant you were not a hippie. Women who wanted to be hip wore their hair long and straight, while the hairstyle of a straight woman might be a teased flip with bangs resembling that of an astronaut's wife. If a woman's hair was curly and she wanted to be hip, she either ironed her hair or wound it tightly around orange juice cans to remove all the curl. That was my category.

Other things besides hair revealed one's political inclination. "The Man" was a name hipsters used to refer to entrenched interests. You were either against The Man, or you *were* The Man. The slogan "If you're not part of the solution, you're part of the problem" galvanized young people to oppose the existing social order. In the music business, Bob Dylan and other folksingers with "message songs" began to eclipse the pop singers who had previously dominated the charts. Unfortunately for Gerry's and my livelihood, the marginalized artists included many who had been recording our songs. Groups from Great Britain such as the Rolling Stones, Gerry and the Pacemakers, and the Beatles climbed the charts in record numbers. Collectively referred to by the news media as "the British Invasion," most were self-sufficient. Sometimes they covered songs by American writers, but the British groups were successful in the United States primarily with their own material. They didn't need our songs. Without a small miracle, Gerry and I were not going to be able to maintain our comfortable lifestyle.

We got our miracle, and it wasn't small. It was exactly the size of the woman whose reign as the Queen of Soul would transcend several generations.

Chapter Twenty-Seven

A Natural Woman

The more Gerry and I traveled back and forth between coasts, the less happy I became about being away from our children so much. I thought we should look for opportunities closer to home. One of the most successful New York–based record companies was Atlantic Records. Jerry Wexler and Ahmet Ertegun had continued to be diligent in looking for songs for their R&B and soul artists whose strength lay more in performing than in writing. Ironically, their top artist, who wrote her own songs, would save our bacon by recording a song she didn't write.

One afternoon Gerry and I were walking down Broadway to retrieve our car when a long black limousine with dark windows pulled up alongside us. The rear window rolled down and revealed Jerry Wexler. He got right to the point.

"I'm looking for a really big hit for Aretha."

He didn't need to say her last name. Miss Franklin had already enjoyed several top 10 hits. We moved closer to the car to hear what else he had to say.

"How about writing a song called 'Natural Woman'?"

Gerry and I looked at each other. What a great title! We could do that. Wexler saw our look and nodded. Then he pressed the button to roll up his window, Gerry and I stepped back onto the sidewalk, and Wexler's face disappeared into the darkness. We watched the limo ease back into the flow of traffic down Broadway, then Gerry and I began walking again.

"Oh my God, he wants us to write for Aretha!"

"I think we can do it."

"Of course we can!"

"Yeah . . . I think I already got an idea."

With me bubbling over and Gerry thinking out loud in his thick Brooklyn accent, we continued to reaffirm our ability to deliver the requested song all the way to the lot where our car was parked.

Having a specific assignment that we had every reason to believe would lead to a cover by a top-selling artist was highly motivating. As soon as we came out on the Jersey side of the tunnel, Gerry put on WNJR to inspire the right musical mood. Arriving home, we parked in the driveway, went into the house, and found Willa Mae presiding over the children's after-dinner playtime. We spent some time with the girls, but we were chomping at the bit. We kissed them good night and headed up to the red room. I sat down at the piano, put my hands on the keys, and played a few chords. It was unbelievable how right they were, and we both knew it.

Four decades later Gerry remembered it this way in a phone call as we reminisced about writing this song:

"You sat down at the piano and out came some gospel chords in 6/8 tempo. Those chords were exactly where I thought the song should go. You made it really easy for me to come out with the lyrics. You made it effortless."

I don't know that I would have called it effortless. Our preparation and discussion on the way home had been an important part of the process. It put me in the right place to be a conduit for those chords. And then, once we had a verse and a chorus, effort was involved in thinking of a slightly different lyrical direction for the second verse that fit with the music already set up by the first verse. If Gerry thought my chords were exactly right, I was blown away by his lyrical imagery. A soul in the lost-and-found...a lover with a claim check...How did Gerry come up with these things??

The next day we recorded a piano-vocal demo and brought it to Jerry Wexler. He loved the song and said he'd get back to us after he played it for Ahmet and Aretha. As soon as we left, Wexler took our demo into the other room and played it for Ahmet, who also loved it. Then they had to play it for their engineer, Tom Dowd, the arranger, Arif Mardin, and then, of course, the song had to be approved by Aretha herself. Evidently she liked it enough to give it the final and most essential thumbs-up.

We didn't know about any of these interim steps until after the song had been recorded. We remained in limbo for days. Most conversations between Gerry and me went like this:

"Ya think Ahmet'll like it?"

"Why wouldn't he?"

"What about Aretha?"

"I have no idea."

"Ya think they're gonna do it?"

"God, I hope so!"

We heard nothing—not a word—until Jerry Wexler invited us to come in and listen to the finished recording.

Oh. My. God.

Hearing Aretha's performance of "Natural Woman" for the first time, I experienced a rare speechless moment. To this day I can't convey how I felt in mere words. Anyone who had written a song in 1967 hoping it would be performed by a singer who could take it to the highest level of excellence, emotional connection, and public exposure would surely have wanted that singer to be Aretha Franklin.

Few people would consider it hyperbole to call Aretha's voice one of the most expressive vocal instruments of the twentieth century. Hearing that instrument sing a song I had participated in creating touched me more than any recording of any song I had ever written. I knew that Gerry and I had delivered a song that took Jerry Wexler's title to its most romantic, emotional conclusion, and I knew that the music I had written had captured the spirit of black gospel in a way that gave Aretha something familiar she could run with—and run with it she did! But Aretha was not alone in creating that incomparable recording. She was assisted by the soaring string crescendos that wrapped themselves around her glorious vocal performance and brilliantly complemented by a solid rhythm and blues basic track and the soulful background vocals of her sisters, Erma and Carolyn Franklin.

But a recording that moves people is never just about the artist and the songwriters. It's about people like Jerry and Ahmet, who matched the songwriters with a great title and a gifted artist; Arif Mardin, whose magnificent orchestral arrangement deserves the place it will forever occupy in popular music history; Tom Dowd, whose engineering skills captured the magic of this memorable musical moment for posterity; and the musicians in the rhythm section, the orchestral players, and the vocal contributions of the background singers—among them the unforgettable "Ah-oo!" after the first line of the verse. And the promotion and marketing people helped this song reach more people than it might have without them.

But in the end it was Aretha's performance that sent our song not only to the top of the charts but all the way to heaven.

It takes a lot more people to deliver a song than most people are aware of, but you, the listener, are the most important person in the process. You complete the circle. You inspire us to write, sing, arrange, record, and promote songs that move us because we hope they will move you, too. There might still be an "us" without you, but you make us matter, and you make us better.

In 1970 I would record "Natural Woman" with a simple arrangement along the lines of the original demo. My 1970 version is slower than Aretha's and has a few chords from Arif's arrangement that weren't on my original demo.

Q: How do you follow Aretha Franklin?
A: You don't. You can only precede her.

Chapter Twenty-Eight

Sold

In 1963, with something like thirty-three top 10 hits to Aldon's credit, Donnie had begun negotiating with Screen Gems Television and Columbia Pictures to sell Aldon Music. The sale took place on April 12, 1963, with Donnie, then twenty-nine, becoming executive vice president in charge of all music publishing and recording, conducted primarily under the banners of Screen Gems–Columbia Music and Colpix Records. Al Nevins stayed on as a consultant until he passed away on January 25, 1965. He would have been fifty that year.

At first Gerry and I were unhappy about the sale, and Barry and Cynthia shared our dismay. We thought of ourselves as members of the Aldon Music family, and we were convinced that the new circumstances would herald the end of our careers. To assuage our vehement disapproval, Donnie sat down with Barry, Cynthia, Gerry, and me in the Manns' living room. He swore he'd be just as active on our behalf as head of Screen Gems–Columbia Music as he'd been at Aldon. He'd get covers just as he always had, and it would be to our advantage that he would be in charge of Colpix Records.

"Nothing's gonna change," Donnie said. "It'll only get better. I'll be able to place your songs in movies."

We were not convinced.

"You could win an Oscar!"

We thought that was too far-fetched.

Donnie gave us more examples of how he could get us theme songs for the television shows and movies he would now control. His logic was unassailable, but we were still miserable. Donnie showed singular patience in keeping the discussion going until Barry acknowledged the underlying reason we were so upset: Donnie was selling us as if we were chattel.

The problem was, we *were* chattel. For $6,000 Gerry and I had not only signed over our copyrights, we had given Aldon Music's owners, heirs, and assigns the right to sell our services. But the worst part wasn't the sale. It was the feeling that the circumstances around our professional and creative family were about to change, and the head of the family had the power to make that decision no matter how we felt about it. We were about to lose the physical location that had inspired so many songs. We would no longer be writing in the cubicles at 1650 not-really-Broadway. We would be writing at 711 Fifth Avenue in the corporate office building that housed the New York headquarters of Screen Gems–Columbia Pictures—a location in some ways as far from Tin Pan Alley, 1650 Broadway, and the Brill Building as Wall Street was from the Bronx.

Donnie's gift for persuasion won the day. Before he left he extracted a promise from the four of us to keep an open mind. Then he proceeded to come through with TV and movie themes for his writers, and he put the corporate might of Colpix Records behind artists such as James Darren, Paul Peterson, and Shelley Fabares, all of whom recorded songs by Screen Gems–Columbia Music writers. Donnie also released recordings on Colpix by writers, artists, and musicians from his stable, including Barry Mann,

Toni Wine, saxophonist Artie Kaplan, and Earl-Jean. When the Colpix release of Freddie Scott's "Hey Girl" (produced by Gerry, arranged by me, and written by both of us) made the top 10 in 1963, Gerry and I were so jubilant that we didn't object to how often Donnie said, "See? Didn't I tell you? This is great! Sheel, how great is this?" But when the successful British Invasion pushed Colpix artists off the charts in 1965, Gerry and I and the Manns started grousing again. We missed the spirit of the cubicles. We yearned for the old sense of burgeoning possibilities. And at a time when young people across America were becoming increasingly aware of corporate interests' control over their lives, we didn't like being owned by a corporation.

Hoping to diminish our discontent, Donnie called us into his office and announced that he would soon be producing a new television show featuring four young men who, he assured us, would soon become America's Beatles. Unlike most groups who came together on their own, Donnie would assemble this group through auditions.

"I mean, what better way than auditions to put a group together? They'll be great!"

"Isn't that kind of artificial?" I asked. "How can you put a group together and expect them to have chemistry when you don't even know if they're going to like each other?"

"It doesn't matter how they come together. They can't help but be successful because of all the great songs you guys are going to deliver."

Donnie went on to explain that the Monkees would need several songs for each weekly show and even more songs for their albums, which Colpix would release and cross-market through the TV show.

"The Beatles may not need your songs," he said, "but the Monkees will."

Once again, Donnie's instinct for business put him ahead of the curve. Starring Michael Nesmith, Davy Jones, Micky Dolenz, and Peter Tork, *The Monkees* TV show was a runaway hit, and so were the songs written by Donnie's writers, among them Tommy Boyce and Bobby Hart, Barry and Cynthia, and Gerry and me. Released on Colpix and widely promoted by weekly exposure on national television, our Monkees songs sold remarkably well. Our success with that group was a mixed blessing for Gerry, because the critics whose opinions he most respected considered the Monkees a manufactured group with a bubblegum flavor and no staying power. Several decades later, some of the same critics would acknowledge that the Monkees had risen to the occasion with more musical ability than the critics had originally attributed to them.

Gerry felt a little better about our association with the Monkees in 1968 after a movie called *Head* was released. Written by Jack Nicholson and Bob Rafelson, directed by Rafelson, and starring the Monkees, the film was enthusiastically embraced by the counterculture. I'd like to believe "The Porpoise Song," written by Gerry and me, was chosen for the opening of *Head* solely because it complemented the images over which it was used, but it probably didn't hurt that Donnie was in a position to advocate for its use in a Columbia picture. Notwithstanding our identification with young people rebelling against The Man, material security remained important to the Goffin family. If our lifestyle was in danger, it was not from a financial wolf at the door.

Later I would come to appreciate Donnie's timing and wisdom in selling Aldon to a multimedia corporation. If Donnie had increased his own opportunities for success, the sale had also undeniably increased the opportunities for his writers. Donnie would expand the musical knowledge of the next generation in the seventies and eighties when he presented performances on television by emerging and well-known acts, first on a late-night

ABC-TV show called *In Concert* and then as the host of a series called *Don Kirshner's Rock Concert*. Among the artists he introduced were the Rolling Stones, Curtis Mayfield, Chuck Berry, the Steve Miller Band, Blood, Sweat & Tears, Ike and Tina Turner, Alice Cooper, Led Zeppelin, Seals and Crofts, Billy Preston, the Isley Brothers, the Allman Brothers, Poco, and Kansas.

When I reconnected with Donnie and Sheila in Florida in 2010, I asked Donnie how his family was. He told me with characteristic enthusiasm how great his and Sheila's by then adult children, Ricky and Daryn, were, and how great it was to be the grandparents of five grandchildren. Of course they were great. They were Donnie's family, and they were as proud of him as he was of them. When I told him he had been right to sell Aldon Music to Screen Gems, his face lit up like a sunrise.

Donnie's heart stopped beating on January 17, 2011. When I visited with Sheila and Daryn after his memorial service, I told them something that I want to say to the world. Between his work with songwriters and his presentation of an array of groups on television that a lot of viewers might not otherwise have seen, Don Kirshner was one of the most significant influences on popular music in the twentieth century.

Donnie, babe. You were great.

Chapter Twenty-Nine

Aronowitz and the Myddle Class

The journalist Alfred Gilbert Aronowitz was born in Borden-town, New Jersey, on May 5, 1928. His articles and columns about the Beats and, later, his regular column in the *New York Post* called "Pop Scene" had a sense of immediacy and irreverence that resonated with readers who had come of age around the end of the fifties. Aronowitz first captured my husband's attention when Gerry learned that Al had known Allen Ginsberg and Jack Kerouac. Gerry's interest was further piqued by Al's relationship with the Beatles and the Rolling Stones. But perhaps Aronowitz's most compelling credential was that he was a confidant of the man who had written "The Times They Are A-Changin'."

Released by Columbia Records in January 1964, Bob Dylan's album *The Times They Are A-Changin'* was a collection of self-composed, sparsely arranged, and lyrically unsettling songs that connected with mainstream audiences. While the executives at Columbia saw huge potential income in selling the concept of rebellion to a nation of willing teenagers, other men in positions of power and influence saw Bob as a threat. That he was. Bob Dylan was empowering young people to refuse to be a cog in the military-industrial machine, and they were listening.

At twenty-two, I should have understood Bob's appeal, but I didn't appreciate until much later the social significance of his lyrics or the allure of his dry humor and unpretentious musical presentation.

Gerry got Bob immediately. He heard the call to revolution and was enthralled. The more he listened to Dylan's songs, the more frustrated he became. While Gerry had been commuting from the suburbs and achieving financial success with pop ditties about teenage love and dancing, Dylan had been honing his craft on Bleecker Street. Now Bob was exhorting young people to reject the path their parents had laid out for them and look deeper for the true meaning of life. Gerry didn't believe he could find that meaning as the person he was. He wanted to be Bob. Short of that, he wanted to know Bob.

From the day Aronowitz promised Gerry a meeting with Dylan, my husband was as inexorably drawn to Aronowitz as a boulder to the bottom of a lake. As Gerry was drawn, I was repelled. I thought that at thirty-six, with a wife and three children in Summit, New Jersey, Al was too old to hang out all night like a groupie with artists, poets, and writers at theaters and parties in hotel rooms and clubs. But such people and settings were exactly what Gerry hungered for. He found Al's invitations to be part of that scene irresistible. He didn't share my opinion that Aronowitz was trying to hold on to his youth and his currency as a member of the pop scene by associating with the likes of Brian Jones, John Lennon, Bob Dylan, and now Gerry.

It was more instinct than logic that informed my perception of Aronowitz as a threat to my family. I wanted to fight this man with his moon-shaped face, scraggly red beard, and a knowing smile that always made me feel as if he knew what I was thinking. He probably did know. It wouldn't have been difficult to discern my dislike of him or my fear that he would entice my husband away from Louise, Sherry, and me. But how could I fight someone who was not only a path to Bob Dylan but a bridge between the Beats and the new intellectuals?

Maybe the times would have tugged at Gerry even without Aronowitz. When we married in 1959 we were twenty and seventeen. Three years later we were the parents of two children. By the dawn of 1964 the responsibilities of marriage, family, and a suburban home were weighing heavily on Gerry. The dramatic societal changes that year only made him more aware of what he was missing. I thought it was my fault because I was an equal breadwinner instead of a traditional wife who stayed at home and took care of her man. But traditional wives and husbands weren't exempt from the turmoil of the period. Gerry and I were part of a larger phenomenon in which one spouse enthusiastically embraced the new mores while the other was slower to accept them or didn't accept them at all. While one member of a couple experimented with drugs, extramarital sex, or both, the other couldn't understand why his or her spouse was abandoning previously shared values.

Had I been forty-two and Gerry forty-five, I might have understood his yearning for the bohemian lifestyle he'd never had. But I was a twenty-two-year-old wife and mother losing my twenty-five-year-old husband to avant-garde ideas. I wanted my life back. Unfortunately, yesterday had a no-return policy, and today wasn't where I wanted to be. I could only hope tomorrow would be better.

I was understandably opposed when Aronowitz suggested early in 1965 that Gerry and I partner with him in forming an independent record label. When Gerry wouldn't be deterred, I applied the maxim "Keep your friends close and your enemies closer" and agreed to the plan. We called the label Tomorrow Records to memorialize our first hit and augur a successful future. Now we needed an artist. Aronowitz had a group in mind.

The King Bees were a band of five New Jersey high school seniors from Summit, Plainfield, New Providence, and Berkeley Heights who had acquired a following playing at school dances and community functions. The band consisted of lead singer and lyricist Dave Palmer; guitarist, vocalist, and composer Rick Philp; organist and vocalist Danny Mansolino; Mike Rosa on drums; and Charlie Larkey on bass. All were eighteen.

If Aronowitz thought the band would be of interest to Gerry and me, he was right. Their music had an edgy sense of urgency. Dave's lyrics and vocal presentation moved us intensely. Rick's inventive guitar parts complemented the dynamic energy of the rest of the players. The band's talent was raw but unmistakable.

Gerry couldn't wait to sign and produce the King Bees, but before we could close the deal, we ran up against a minor legal problem. A band in Martha's Vineyard had established prior use of the name "King Bees"; therefore, the New Jersey King Bees would have to change their name. Some of the Martha's Vineyard King Bees would later become part of the Flying Machine. With the changing of i's to y's and vice versa then in vogue, whether in honor or mockery of their suburban roots, they became the Myddle Class. In that spirit, though there was no conflict with any other Mike Rosa, Mike changed the spelling of his first name to Myke.

Duly renamed and respelled, the band was now free to go into the studyo.

The Myddle Class album was definitely of its time, yet the band's powerful presentation can still be appreciated today. Their well-written songs and fully committed performances embodied the tenuous freedom and impulsive energy of young men across America who knew that they could be sent overseas to die for their country at any moment. Even then, I considered Dave Palmer's lyrics on a par with those of lyricists of greater maturity. I'd like to believe that Gerry and I added value to the Myddle Class's album, but there was a reason that they already had developed a following. They were compelling. Though Aronowitz's omnipresence continued to be challenging, the one thing he brought into my life for which I will always be grateful was that band.

There would be other products of my association with the Myddle Class, but the best of them would not emerge until the early seventies.

Chapter Thirty

The Mid-Sixties

$\mathcal{E}$vents taking place in disparate areas of American life in 1965 provided a context for the coalescence of various movements for social change.

With the United States increasingly on the offensive in Vietnam, and more American troops being sent into combat, antiwar protests grew more numerous and more vociferous.

Undeterred by beatings, bullwhips, and tear gas, Dr. Martin Luther King Jr. and hundreds of demonstrators continued to march for civil rights until the Voting Rights Act was signed into law on August 6, 1965.

Alan Freed passed away with little notice.

Malcolm X was assassinated and mourned by millions.

The Beatles' albums *Help* and *Rubber Soul* soared to the top of the pop charts, with Bob Dylan, Sonny and Cher, the Byrds, and Wilson Pickett close behind.

Mainstream audiences rediscovered jazz through artists such as Bill Evans, Miles Davis, and John Coltrane, and they embraced Brazil's soft, sexy samba and bossa nova tunes recorded by Stan Getz, João Gilberto, and Antonio Carlos Jobim.

Some of the most popular films that year were A *Patch of Blue*, *Doctor Zhivago*, and *Thunderball*. Though quirky movies garnered the best reviews, the tremendous box-office response to *The Sound of Music* reinforced the contention of the conservative contingent that not everyone wanted to be a hippie.

Eddy Arnold, Sonny James, Jim Reeves, Kitty Wells, and Marty Robbins dominated the country music charts.

Ken Kesey and the Merry Pranksters took LSD.

So did Gerry.

I don't believe Gerry knew he was dropping acid the first time he ingested it. I believe someone who thought he was doing him a favor slipped it into his coffee. It wasn't a favor. After that, Gerry took LSD many more times on his own. He lost touch with reality at first for days, then for weeks at a time for many years afterward, with intermittent periods of lucidity, creativity, and wisdom. The appeal for Gerry and others who sought to "expand" their minds was the notion that lysergic acid diethylamide would make them more creative and metaphysically aware. But people on acid found it difficult to communicate and function in a world dominated by people not on acid.

When Gerry initially showed signs of paranoia, I saw nothing illogical in that. A person on acid would naturally be paranoid considering that taking LSD was illegal and officials existed whose job it was to catch and incarcerate people who'd taken it. Then he started to exhibit other symptoms of mental illness about which I should have been more concerned, but I was completely unsophisticated about such things. Apart from my brother's disability, I had never experienced mental illness in myself or anyone else. And the mental health specialists I would eventually consult knew a lot less then than is known today.

When Gerry's behavior started to become more irrational I was afraid he'd do something he'd regret later. At that point I was still thinking in terms of embarrassing rather than dangerous. I wasn't afraid he would hurt our children or me because he had never manifested violent or abusive behavior and wasn't doing so then. He just kept saying things that almost made sense but didn't, and doing things rational citizens may think about doing but don't. I didn't know whether to laugh or cry when he climbed up on a ladder and painted "Love Your Brother" on the side of our house. However, when he attempted (and thankfully failed) to seriously hurt himself, I knew it was time to call for help.

At first the doctors diagnosed Gerry as schizophrenic. Then they decided he was manic and treated him with massive doses of Thorazine to bring him down. Not unpredictably, he went into a deep depression. Though his doctors adjusted his medication this way and that and brought him in for psychiatric sessions, Gerry remained in a severely depressed state. The next treatment the doctors recommended was electric shock therapy. Because their patient was incapable of rational thought—hence the need for such a drastic remedy—the decision to give consent was legally in the hands of his young wife. To say that this was one of the most agonizing decisions I've ever had to make is to grossly understate the difficulty. I was twenty-three, Gerry was twenty-six, and our daughters were five and three. I didn't see how I could possibly decide something of this magnitude on behalf of someone else, especially when every muscle in my heart, throat, lips, and tongue wanted to shout, "NOOOOOOO!" But the doctors assured me that all the less intrusive options had been exhausted and a shock treatment would restore my husband to his normal state.

I didn't feel that I had a choice. I signed the paper, left the facility, and cried all the way home.

A decade later, Jack Nicholson would give a stunning performance as Randle Patrick McMurphy in Milos Forman's film *One Flew Over the Cuckoo's Nest*, based on Ken Kesey's novel. The film gave moviegoers, in excruciating detail, a heart-wrenching insight into the treatment I had consented to put my husband through. Nicholson gave a terrifying portrayal of what it was like to receive electric shock therapy. In Forman's fictional production, excessive wattage and frequency of shock treatments were used to manipulate the behavior of mental patients. I have no reason to believe that was the case in Gerry's circumstance, but I couldn't help but imagine him in McMurphy's situation. I didn't think I could make it through the entire film, but because I had been the one who signed the paper allowing Gerry to undergo shock treatments, I made myself watch every frame. Weeping for the young couple we'd been, I lived through Gerry's suffering and the pain of my decision all over again.

Shock therapy helped Gerry for a while in 1965, but the circumstances that had led to his ingestion of LSD in the first place had not gone away.

The summer of 1965 found Gerry in a calmer frame of mind. We were at a band rehearsal when two of the Myddle Class arrived late. Rick and Charlie talked animatedly over each other, words tumbling out of their mouths, until they calmed down enough to report the experience they'd had the night before. The act they'd gone to see at the Café Wha? in the Village was a trio featuring a young black man from Seattle who sang and played guitar in a manner unlike anything they'd ever seen or heard before.

"I couldn't believe it," Rick said. "The guy played guitar with his *teeth*!"

Charlie chimed in to describe how the guitarist had turned his amp all the way up and transformed the electronic feedback into an otherworldly musical experience. The guitarist, Jimmy James, would later become known to the world as Jimi Hendrix.

That summer, to the dismay of traditional folk fans, Bob

Dylan plugged his guitar into an amplifier and "went electric" at the Newport Folk Festival with members of the Paul Butterfield Blues Band. Later in the year he performed on electric guitar with a group known as the Hawks. I related more to Bob's electric music. Evidently, so did mainstream America, but Bob's purist fans remained adamantly vocal in expressing their displeasure. At one of Bob's electric performances in 1965 with the Hawks, when someone in the audience shouted, "Judas!" Bob told his band to play louder. No problem. The Hawks would later achieve renown as the Band.

In San Francisco, Bill Graham electrified audiences at the Fillmore Auditorium with Jefferson Airplane, the Grateful Dead, and the new visual art form of psychedelic light shows. Bill's acts and the light shows were best appreciated under the influence of the omnipresent pot smoke at the Fillmore, where a contact high was unavoidable unless you literally didn't inhale.

In Los Angeles, Brian Wilson and the Beach Boys released an album called *Summer Days (and Summer Nights!!)*. I didn't become aware of the Beach Boys' music until "California Girls" and "Help Me, Rhonda" migrated to East Coast radio. After all the hours I spent in the ensuing years enjoying the Beach Boys' *Pet Sounds* and other albums, I could see how *Summer Days (and Summer Nights!!)* foreshadowed the Beach Boys' future work, particularly "Good Vibrations"—which brings me to my encounter more than three decades later with Brian Wilson in the year 2000, when we were both fifty-eight. We were at a Songwriters Hall of Fame induction ceremony. I had come to induct James Taylor. Paul McCartney was going to induct Brian. As Brian and I waited backstage together, someone asked which of us had first used a chord that we both use frequently in our songs. Musicians know the chord as "IV over V." In the key of C, it would be F with a G bass. In the key of G, it would be C over D. I've heard people call it "the Carole King chord" or

"C over K." But Beach Boys fans might just as easily call it "the Brian Wilson chord." Whatever its nomenclature, musicians and nonmusicians alike will recognize it as the climactic chord in "Good Vibrations" when the vocals come together to create a singular, glorious, unforgettable moment:

"Ahhhhhhhhhh!"

If you're unfamiliar with "Good Vibrations," that moment alone is worth the download, which you will of course be paying for.

Brian and I agreed in 2000 to leave it to our respective fans to resolve the "first use" question. "After all," he said, "fans know a lot more about our lives than we do." We did know enough in 2000 to affirm how grateful we were to be alive and reasonably well after all our generation had been through. Just then a production assistant came to bring me onstage with James to perform "Shower the People," after which I inducted James.

Old rock and rollers never die. We just lose track of time.

In 1966 Gerry and I were twenty-seven and twenty-four. As the Vietnam War escalated, so did our involvement with the Myddle Class and their age group. Sometimes we joined our younger friends on peace marches. When we didn't have a babysitter, we brought our children with us. We continued to write enough hit songs to cover our mortgage, household expenses, and Willa Mae, whose presence in our home gave me the freedom to hang out with younger people and act like the eighteen-year-old I'd never had a chance to be. Gerry was increasingly experimenting with hallucinogenics with Aronowitz and his friends in New York, who justified such experimentation on intellectual grounds. People who expanded their consciousness were celebrated by pop culture, the intelligentsia, and the coastal news media as bold, daring, and on the cutting edge. In reality, such explorations were mostly unscientific with no built-in controls.

Such were the times in the mid-sixties, when Americans were polarized generationally, culturally, and politically. I wasn't as extreme as Gerry and Aronowitz, but I, too, was finding it difficult to reconcile my association with the corporate music industry with my self-identification with those who were contemptuous of the Establishment. People who made statements against government policies ran the risk of becoming targets of investigation by the FBI, and indeed, the antiwar activist David Harris, then married to Joan Baez, was imprisoned for draft evasion. Others expressed dissent through fashion, music, theater, or art. This made for very colorful times. The *Austin Powers* films would later put a comedic slant on the sixties, but at the time we were dead serious. The generation with which I identified was trying to stop a runaway war in a faraway land that was killing our young men as quickly as they could be impressed into service.

Ending the Vietnam War and the draft was a unifying goal for a lot of young Americans, some of whom served, though many didn't. Some men served reluctantly because they couldn't afford the college tuition that would have exempted them from the draft. But a considerable number willingly volunteered. Among those fortunate enough to return home from Vietnam were veterans who were proud of their service, who couldn't understand why they were being vilified. Extreme antiwar opponents were misdirecting their anger at the very Americans who had sacrificed the most. Gerry and I were united in our understanding of that distinction, and we were united professionally in speaking to and for our generation through our songs. But personally, we were falling apart.

Our family was under a tremendous strain. In addition to taking psychedelics with Aronowitz and hardly ever being home, Gerry was struggling with what we now call bipolar disorder. I sought relief by going to clubs, concerts, and other activities more appropriate for a younger single woman. Our daughters' yearnings were much less complicated. All they wanted was a loving, stable family with two caring parents at home. But with all the turmoil within and outside our family, the end of Gerry's and my marriage was almost inevitable.

I clung desperately to the filament of hope in the word "almost."

Chapter Thirty-One

Leaving New Jersey

*I*n 1967, when Jerry Wexler offered to sign me as a recording artist with Atlantic, my first question was, "Can Gerry produce me?"

"Sure."

"You know I'm a songwriter, not a performer. And I have kids, so I'm not willing to go out and promo—"

Wexler was chuckling.

"You think I don't know that? Talk to Gerry and let me know what you want to do."

As I drove toward the Lincoln Tunnel pondering this incentive for Gerry, I thought, What if we moved to the city? Next thing I knew I was heading down Ninth Avenue to the coolest place I knew: Greenwich Village. First I found a parking space. Then I walked among resident families with young children who appeared to be thriving. Then I began to look for a home. All I could find were cramped apartments and brownstones with concrete yards near crowded schools close to parks inhabited at night by drug dealers. Still I kept looking, hanging on to that filament, and hoping the combination of a move to the city and a producing deal could save our marriage.

It didn't.

When Gerry told me he was going to move to California without me, I didn't break down until he walked out the door. I didn't know I had that many tears. Since the disintegration of my family of origin I had dreamed of that mythical man with whom I would have four beautiful, healthy children, live in a big cheery house, and spend the rest of our lives as a happily-ever-after family. I had invested Gerry, our children, and the house on Waddington Avenue with storybook dreams and a fairy-tale ending. Waves of despair crashed around me as all those hopes and dreams were dashed on the rocks of our failed marriage. But I had no time to dwell on dashed hopes and tears. For both emotional and financial reasons, I couldn't stay in the house in West Orange. I would rent a place, if not in the Village, then somewhere in the city. I wasn't going to be any less cool than Gerry.

I found a brownstone I liked on East 10th Street near University Place at the edge of Greenwich Village and was wondering if I could afford it when we got an offer on our house. Because the buyers wanted to move in as soon as possible, I rented a garden apartment near Waddington Avenue so the girls wouldn't have to change schools. There was so much to do. I had furniture to dispose of and personal effects to pack. With the children at my mother's, somehow I got through those heartbreaking tasks.

I stood in the foyer and faced my last moments alone in what used to be our home. My sadness deepened as I walked through the empty rooms and saw the bare carpets with depressions where the furniture had been and faded rectangular areas on the walls where photographs and paintings had hung. The mural on the landing upstairs was a scene of his native Italy painted by a local artist we knew only as Mr. Cellini. The mural would remain with the house, and so would the wall of built-in closets in the master bedroom and the drawers on both sides of the bed that had contained the state-of-the-art hi-fi components on which Gerry listened at earsplitting volume to the rough mixes he brought home from the studio.

As I stood on the Yves Klein Blue carpet in the master bedroom I recalled the disbelief and grief I'd felt watching reports of President Kennedy's assassination on November 22, 1963. I remembered seeing Walter Cronkite lose control of his emotions when he delivered the news that the president had died; the shock of watching Jack Ruby shoot Kennedy's alleged killer, Lee Harvey Oswald, live on television before millions of equally stunned viewers; and the poignancy of three-year-old John Kennedy Jr. saluting his father's flag-draped coffin as it passed slowly before him. I had been informed and entertained through the black-and-white television in its carefully measured space in the wall of closets that now held nothing belonging to my family except the history we were leaving behind. That bedroom would be my answer to the question members of my generation would ask each other for years afterwards:

"Where were *you* when Kennedy was shot?"

I wouldn't miss the living room that we'd never used because the furniture was too posh to sit on, or the costly curtains and drapes that had been custom-made for the windows of that particular house. But I would miss the Thanksgiving dinners I had cooked in the kitchen and served in the dining room in an uncharacteristic annual display of culinary domesticity. I'd miss the giggles and whispers of sisterly play emanating from the girls' rooms. I'd miss the family room, the hideous red room, and the swings and the slide that had delivered Louise, Sherry, and their friends to a safe landing in the railroad-tie sandbox.

And where was my husband, my first grown-up love, my writing partner, my daughters' father? Where was my Gerry, who, when he was home, spent more time in the Eames chair in our bedroom than anywhere else in the house, sitting, thinking, absently stroking his beard?

I was about to open the front door to leave when I had the impulse to take one last look at the kitchen. All that remained of the Goffin family in that room were a few empty cartons on the floor where the Saarinen dining table had been. How anticlimactic, I thought with a catch in my throat. I walked through the foyer, opened the front door, stepped outside into the bright, sunny day, and immediately resented the weather for not mirroring my sense of loss. My sense of humor nudged me in the ribs.

You're resenting the weather? That's pathetic.

A wry smile came as I closed the door behind me. I turned and rang the doorbell. From inside the foyer came the familiar melody: do do mi mi re re re do.

Still out of rhythm.

Now I had some big decisions to make. Assuming I could afford it, the house on East 10th Street would definitely work for the girls and Willa Mae, our dog, Lika, Telemachus the cat, and me. And with Jerry Wexler's assurance that his offer didn't depend on Gerry producing me, all the elements seemed to be lining up in favor of my moving to Greenwich Village. But something kept holding me back from making an offer on that house. It might have been the pull of all the music and media celebrating California. It might have been because I didn't want to be left behind. But one thing above all compelled me to turn west. With Gerry moving to Los Angeles, there was no way I would deny my daughters proximity to their father.

In March 1968, Sherry, Louise, Lika, Telemachus, and I moved to California.

PART II

Chapter One

Wonderland

I was on the East Coast in 1967 when the Monterey Pop Festival took place in Monterey, California. By the time Woodstock happened two years later in upstate New York, I had already moved to the West Coast. In the ensuing years, every time someone asked me where I had been for both events I was obliged to confess, yet again, that I had been on the wrong coast each time.

"Holy shit! You missed Monterey Pop *and* Woodstock??"

"Yes."

Inevitably the response was, "Wow. Bummer!"

No kidding. But the real bummer was getting divorced from Gerry. When we separated he was twenty-nine and I was twenty-six. We'd been married for nine years. Though I was too upset to write with him, our conversations were civil enough that we could agree on some basic principles. We didn't want our divorce to be ugly or bitter; we would divide our financial assets equally; and the girls would live with me under joint custody.

In practice, Gerry was free to see Sherry and Louise whenever he wanted, and vice versa, so our girls didn't have to deal with the additional hardship of their parents' bickering over who got them when. But divorce at best is never without difficulty, especially for the children. On the other hand, if my daughters had been asked to compose a list entitled "What I Like About Living in California," proximity to the beach, not having to wear multiple layers of clothing, and running around barefoot in March would have competed for first position.

The day after we took up residence on Wonderland Avenue I waited at the end of our driveway with the girls for the big yellow school bus that would take them to the Wonderland Avenue Elementary School. After they scampered on board, I watched the bus make its way down the street until it passed out of view. Involuntarily, I sighed deeply, inhaling my daughters' trepidation and exhaling my own along with theirs. Then I turned, walked up the driveway, climbed into my newly leased black 1968 Mustang convertible, started the ignition, pushed the button that slowly lowered the top, and backed out of the driveway. As I drove down Wonderland, I was elated to see the tops of trees that would have been hidden by the fixed roof of a sedan. I turned right on Lookout Mountain, then waited at the light until I could fly down the canyon the way other drivers did. Released by the green, I turned right onto Laurel Canyon and reveled in the rush of wind blowing through my hair. Other drivers were cruising up and down the canyon without a specific destination, but I was going to the West Coast office of Screen Gems–Columbia Music, Inc.

Donnie had chosen Lester Sill to run Screen Gems–Columbia's West Coast office. In 1952, when Jerry Leiber and Mike Stoller were starting to attract some notice in L.A., Lester had run their publishing office. More recently he had been the "Les" of Philles Records (Spector being the "Phil") and the music supervisor of the Monkees' movie, *Head*. Screen Gems–Columbia Music was a thriving publishing operation located—where else?—in Hollywood. The building that housed it in no way resembled the corporate office building at 711 Fifth Avenue that I had come to know and loathe. The structure on the north side of Sunset Boulevard east of La Brea Avenue was three stories high with pink walls made of concrete blocks. Palm trees grew in front of a façade that resembled a car grille. After dealing for years with the expense and difficulty of parking a car in Manhattan, it was an unexpected gift to be able to drive into a free parking area where I had no trouble finding an unoccupied space. From the parking lot it was less than fifty steps to the lobby, where an elevator was waiting to transport me to the second floor.

When the elevator door opened, Lester was there to greet me. I felt comfortable with Lester partly because I had met him on previous trips and partly because he had the *haimishe* demeanor of a warm Jewish uncle. After proudly showing me around and introducing me to his staff, Lester brought me into his office and told me who was looking for material and what kind of song each artist was looking for. It was a detailed briefing by a capable, knowledgeable publisher, and it made me hopeful about my ability to continue to earn a living as a songwriter without Gerry. When it was time for me to leave, Lester walked me to the elevator and invited me to bring Louise and Sherry to his home for dinner that night.

I ran errands, gassed up the car, and got home in plenty of time to put away the groceries and unpack a few more boxes from New Jersey before I heard the school bus outside. As I ran out to greet my girls I couldn't imagine how the bus had made it up the narrow winding streets of the canyon without scraping some of the cars parked in places they ought not to have been. I should have recognized the random car-parking as an early clue to my fellow canyon dwellers' lack of respect for authority, but I was too engrossed in listening to my daughters' stories about their first day at school. Then they dropped their books in the middle of the living room floor, kicked off their shoes, and ran out the door to play Gilligan's Island in the backyard of their new friends down the street. I was so caught up in their abandon that I had forgotten for a moment that I was a parent.

"Wait!" I called. "What about homew—?"

Gone.

It's okay, I thought. Homework can wait.

Bad mom, said my conscience.

No, I thought defiantly. *Young* mom.

Amazingly, my girls did it all. They played at being Ginger, Lovey, and Mary Ann. Then they came home, washed up, changed their clothes, and finished their homework in time to leave for dinner.

The Sills lived south of Ventura Boulevard in Sherman Oaks, an attractive neighborhood in the San Fernando Valley. In contrast to the grid of streets north of Ventura, their street, Valley Vista Boulevard, wound around the base of the foothills from Coldwater Canyon to Woodcliff Road just east of the 405. Valley Vista's gentle curves gave the impression that it wasn't really *in* the Valley. Each bend in the road revealed a new image of lush greenery and brightly colored exotic plants that fairly screamed, "Look! We're even more vibrant than the plants you just saw!"

We pulled up to the Sills' house, got out of the car, and were greeted by the entire family: Lester, his wife, Harriet, their four sons (their youngest, Lonnie, was close to the age of my daughters), their female collie, and six adorable, purebred tricolor collie puppies. The puppies were so irresistible that by the end of the evening we had agreed to adopt one of them. To keep our new puppy's name consistent with the names of his litter-mates (all began with "Mac") we decided to call him Macduff.

All the Sills except Harriet would attain success in Hollywood as part of the Sill/Kaye music publishing and music supervision dynasty, now in its third generation. Harriet achieved her own success as the matriarch and fighting tigress of the Sill family. You did *not* want to mess with a Sill or with Chuck Kaye, Harriet's son from a previous marriage.

Lester's success as a music publisher was fueled by his friendships with various West Coast producers and artists. Like Lou, Lester had also earned the trust and respect of the Everly Brothers and other artists who recorded in L.A. but often flew back to Nashville to retain their original connection with their fans and their roots in country music. In addition to Lester's ability to get covers, there was also his corporate connection with movie and television productions.

I had taken a great leap of faith across a continent. But it was clear to me that there was a wealth of opportunities available to an L.A.-based Screen Gems–Columbia songwriter, and I felt that I had landed in a safe place.

Chapter Two

Where the Action Was

$\mathcal{D}$onnie had been prescient in selling Aldon in 1963 to an established company that produced both film and television projects. He had correctly intuited that the long-term prosperity of the music business lay in its connection to such projects. By 1968, though he still worked in New York City, Donnie's business and personal relationships with L.A.-based luminaries had given him a significant jump on other East Coast publishers who were just beginning to open offices in Hollywood.

Had Donnie been willing to get on an airplane he would probably have become one of the V.I.P.s who lived west of the dividing line between West Hollywood and Beverly Hills. Driving west on Sunset Boulevard, the line was unmistakable. East of the line were stores, nightclubs, office buildings, and people clad in what unsophisticated observers might have described as costumes. Sophisticated observers called such people, not unsympathetically, "freaks."

West of the line the ambiance changed abruptly. There were no stores, no office buildings, no clubs, and no freaks—only evenly spaced palm trees along Sunset Boulevard, grassy malls with carefully tended flowers, and large, gated estates with rolling lawns and rambling homes barely visible through expensively landscaped trees and shrubbery. The sidewalks were virtually empty.

Laurel Canyon was conveniently located east of the divide in the hills just above Sunset Strip. Though the neighborhood included college professors, scientists, and journalists, most residents were artists, musicians, poets, photographers, actors, directors, dancers, models, producers, and writers who had yet to achieve a West Side level of success. Canyon furniture typically consisted of a single mattress covered with an Indian-print fabric that didn't quite match the Indian-print curtains, a worn oriental rug, vinyl beanbags and cushions on the floor, and a stack of shelves made of wooden planks held up by concrete blocks or bricks on which there was a collection of books, including the *I Ching* and *The Tibetan Book of the Dead*, and a massive, eclectic assortment of well-worn twelve-inch vinyl albums. A sandblasted nautical hatch cover or a large rectangle of wood on concrete blocks functioned as a combination coffee table, dining table, and repository for the bong—a water pipe consisting of a bottle or vertical tube partially filled with liquid, and a smaller tube ending in a bowl. The bong was used to smoke what law enforcement agencies called "controlled substances." My neighbors called it hash. The décor was rounded out with guitars, incense, and candles. And no matter how impoverished the inhabitants of a crash pad were, they owned a stereo.

Shortly before the girls and I moved out west, I had flown to Los Angeles to look for a house to rent. Few things make me feel as ancient as remembering the two-year lease I signed in 1968 for a two-bedroom house in Laurel Canyon for $225 a month. The house was tucked into a hillside, with the garage at street level and the rest of the house above the garage. The stairs leading to the front door ascended between the wall of the garage and the wall holding up the front yard. Inside and out, the house had a discernible California feel to it. The exterior walls were pale peach plaster with an adobe texture. Inside, the doorways were arched, and the windows commanded enough light to make the rooms feel bigger. The floors were hardwood or ceramic tile. There were two bedrooms, two bathrooms, a living room with a fireplace, a small dining area, a place for a washer and dryer, and a kitchen with a window over the sink that would reward a person washing dishes with a view of fuchsia-colored bougainvillea draped over a grape-stake fence. There were no large trees on the property, but branches from neighbors' trees on both sides provided quite a bit of shade. Above the irises and calla lilies that grew in the lower part of the backyard was an unoccupied flat area with baked earth and prickly cactus that appeared to be a lovely desert ecosystem when I saw it in the rainy season but would prove inhospitable to humans the rest of the year.

I had chosen Laurel Canyon primarily because it was close to the Screen Gems–Columbia Music office, but with all the bands and songwriters living in the Canyon it had the added benefit of being a happening scene. It was the first time I had ever lived where the action was. Though I hadn't considered that a necessary criterion, I didn't mind. As if to validate the concept, one of my neighbors, Michael Schwartz, confided that he'd been one of the Action Kids on Dick Clark's ABC television show *Where the Action Is*. His name on the show was Mike Williams.

In addition to the actors, musicians, and songwriters on our street there were families with children the same ages as my daughters. This made the Canyon a happening place for Louise and Sherry as well. With transients tripping along the winding streets dressed in outlandish outfits, the Canyon sometimes seemed more like the back lot of a carnival than a community. Still, enough families with children lived there to give the neighborhood a semblance of normalcy. Our move had brought the Canyon yet another family with one mom, two kids, two dogs, and a cat. We weren't the only family to lack a resident dad, but another super-important person was also missing.

Prior to leaving New Jersey I had asked Willa Mae several times if she would move out west with us. Each time, she had demurred. After a week in California I called to ask again. This time she said yes. Because there wasn't room in our house for her to live with us, I helped her find an apartment in a neighborhood populated mostly with African American families. The three reasons she gave for choosing that neighborhood were social, church, and "I can drive to your house."

Drive? Yes. Emboldened by her decision to move west, Willa Mae took just enough driving lessons to learn everything she needed to know to pass the examination in California. Inexplicably, immediately after passing the test she lost confidence in her ability to make a left turn in traffic. For the rest of her life Willa Mae would make multiple right turns to get where she needed to go rather than essay a left turn.

It was my extreme good fortune that Willa Mae was willing to leave her life and her friends in New Jersey and come to California to help me raise my daughters. Her consistent presence in all our lives made so many things possible. She provided a sense of stability and continuity for my family and helped mitigate my daughters' sadness about their daddy no longer living with them. I'd like to believe Willa Mae's affection for the girls was paramount in her change of mind, though I suspect that not having to wait for buses in severe winter weather may also have been a factor. Whatever moved her to leave her friends in New Jersey, once she got to California she never looked back.

Willa Mae liked her new neighborhood very much. She wasn't so sure about mine.

If Sunset Strip was the commercial center of the pop music and club scene in 1968, Laurel Canyon was its residential center. Wanna-be rock stars and groupies waited on line at night to get into clubs on Sunset Boulevard, reveled in both the music and the scene, then crashed in the bedrooms of Laurel Canyon. You could drive along the winding roads of the Canyon any time of day or night and see people in varying degrees of substance-induced consciousness. The drugs of choice were mostly hallucinogens— marijuana, psilocybin, and LSD, or, as they were called in the parking lot of the Canyon Country Store, pot, shrooms, and acid.

As I drove up and down the Canyon in the Mustang with the top down, I could hear music from the side canyons competing with the tunes coming out of my car radio. I could never tell if the local music was live or recorded, but music was always in the air and on the air. Where there was music, there were musicians. Bands formed, broke up, and re-formed in different configurations. Rumor had it that some groups were being offered seven-figure advances. Musicians had high hopes that their band would receive one of those seven-figure checks. High hopes took on an additional meaning as the following scene repeated itself in the hillside houses during those heady times.

"Someone's gettin' those advances," a musician said as he passed what was left of a wilted joint to the next person in the circle. "Why not *us*?"

This was followed by the sound of a deep inhalation, then silence as the second musician held his breath to ensure a maximum effect from the smoke.

"Yeahhhhh...ya know?" came the slow drawl amid a haze of smoke from the mouth of the second musician. "Why *not* us, maaaan? We're the grooviest band around."

Seeing that the joint was now too small for human fingers, the next man in the circle pulled a small alligator clip out of his pocket to accommodate the roach headed his way and hoped that it would afford one last hit before it was consigned to the scarred wooden bowl that served as an ashtray.

High hopes indeed. But why *not* their band? Major record companies were ponying up millions of dollars for bands selected by their A&R man, and yes, as far as I knew, all A&R people at the time were men. Sometimes the A&R man came through big time. Paul Rothchild's decision to sign the Doors on behalf of Elektra Records paid off handsomely for Rothchild, Elektra Records, and, oh yes, also the Doors.

One of the more colorful Canyon residents was Barry Friedman. Barry lived in a house on Ridpath Drive with a pool and deck populated day and night with nude and seminude people smoking pot. I had no firsthand knowledge of this until, after seeing Louise and Sherry off to school one day, I drove to Barry's house to visit a friend, a musician from New York who was staying there. I arrived just in time to hear Barry, whom I had not previously met, announce that from that day forward he would be known as Frazier Mohawk. Just then my friend got up from his poolside chair to greet me. I observed with gratitude that he was wearing a bathing suit, and I also noted that no one among the group to whom Barry had just addressed his intention seemed to care enough to comment.

Barry's wife, Sandy Hurvitz, was a singer who had opened for the Mothers of Invention. Audience members who had come to see the Mothers left as fans of Sandy as well as the Mothers. Soon after Barry became Frazier Mohawk, Sandy began calling herself Essra Mohawk. I remember Essra mostly as a wraithlike figure wafting from room to room, but she had enough substance to write songs for other artists and record a number of albums herself.

Some Laurel Canyon residents were already famous. Others were on their way to becoming famous. Graham Nash wrote "Our

House" about the little house off Lookout Mountain in which he and Joni Mitchell lived together. Frank Zappa occupied Tom Mix's "Log Cabin" on the corner of Lookout and Laurel Canyon. Some of the Byrds lived on Horseshoe Canyon just below the Wonderland Avenue Elementary School. One Byrd provided the kids with a truly spectacular distraction from social studies. This particular Byrd liked to tear-ass around the Canyon on his motorcycle wearing a purple velvet cape. A quick-thinking teacher could have used this distraction as a *perfect* example of social studies, but that probably wouldn't have gone over well with the L.A. Unified School District.

If you haven't already guessed that it was David Crosby, I just told you.

I wouldn't meet David until seven years later, but I had already made the acquaintance of one of the Canyon's less publicly well-known residents. She was a native Californian, and she wrote lyrics.

Chapter Three

Discovering California!

$\mathcal{I}$t wasn't easy in 1968 to locate an actual native of Los Angeles in Laurel Canyon. The one I found had grown up in West Hollywood below Sunset Strip. As such, Miss Toni Stern was the perfect person to help me acclimate to my new surroundings.

Toni wrote poems with a lyrical sense that invited melodic interpretation. A friend of hers had introduced her to Lester. On one of our trips to L.A., while Gerry had been working on another project, Lester had brought Toni and me together for a songwriting session at which we began a song and a friendship. After the session, Toni took me to a popular raw-food restaurant on Sunset Boulevard called The Source where we sat outside, sipped sun tea, and ate Chinese salad with chopsticks from a wooden bowl. The scene around us was in constant motion. People streamed past in convertibles or cars with all the windows open while androgynously dressed long-haired pedestrians promenaded in white flowing robes, flowery prints, or jeans and brightly colored tie-dyed T-shirts. Toni and I talked about the people on the boulevard, their clothes, the gasoline fumes, life, love, and other things that were not only interesting topics of discussion but excellent ideas for lyrics. When we left The Source we promised to write again the next time I came to L.A.

Toni was the quintessential California girl. Before we learned how unhealthy prolonged exposure to the sun was, Toni would lie on the flat roof of her little house on Kirkwood Drive soaking up rays on an oversized beach towel. She loved the beach. Her lithe brown body was shown off to flawless advantage by a bright red bikini and a long mane of curly hair that flowed past her shoulders like a thousand sunlit rivers. Sometimes she'd impulsively take off in her Alfa Romeo convertible and drive up the coast to Big Sur, her hair blowing behind her all the way. There she enjoyed long walks in the redwood forests with her devoted German shepherd, Arf. As well as animals and nature, Toni loved books, concerts, movies, museums, plays, and other cultural diversions. Back in the city, Arf always waited patiently, without a leash, outside the restaurants Toni frequented until she came out and released him with a command.

Toni's lyrics had an unmistakable meter. She expressed thoughts and emotions in a rhythm that pulsated under accented words. The lyrics she gave me always made the corresponding music flow into my brain and out my voice and fingers. After years of interpreting Gerry's shouted suggestions and channeling his unique style of vocal expression to create the melody toward which he was leading me, I found Toni's more subtle form of guidance somewhat liberating. Her quiet way of suggesting a melodic direction encouraged me to try her ideas and explore more of my own. I still didn't know if I could write hits without Gerry, but the easy flow between Toni and me was an important step toward reinvigorating my diminished confidence. We often wrote at the piano in my house on Wonderland Avenue, where we were frequently interrupted by my daughters running in and out of their common room.

Our house in New Jersey had contained so many rooms that each of my daughters had had her own bedroom with designer furniture in a slightly different color scheme. Louise's was avocado green, white, and pink; Sherry's was avocado green, white, and yellow. Each of their rooms had been decorated with such accoutrements as colorful curtains, matching lamps, and fluffy duvets with stuffed animals lined up in a row.

Our house on Wonderland Avenue had two bedrooms—theirs and mine. I had furnished the place mostly with used furniture bought at discount on Western Avenue. At first I felt a pang of regret about the change in my daughters' lifestyle, but I was soon reminded of how adaptable children can be. The feeling faded when I saw how quickly new friends and a new environment overcame their initial disappointment at having to live in more modest circumstances. And there were new pleasures, too—not necessarily material.

Some afternoons the three of us climbed up on our roof. We marveled at the ability of the yucca plants above our house to survive with so little water. We counted the century plants near our house, so named because they were said to bloom once in a hundred years. Later we learned that the blooming cycle of a century plant is closer to twenty-five years, but that was still pretty impressive for a plant.

Sometimes I drove Louise and Sherry to Topanga Canyon, where we rented horses and rode up and down the trails as part of a group led by a seasoned trail leader whose pace was reliably followed by our horses no matter what we did with our heels or reins. And when we went to the beach in the winter, the girls especially relished the experience knowing that in New Jersey they would have been slogging through slush.

The first time my girls and I drove up the Pacific Coast Highway, each segment of the California coast seemed to have slightly different flora and fauna than other segments. I didn't know the word "ecosystem" then, but each of those segments must have been one. The entire coastline is a larger ecosystem that not only comprises the smaller ones but connects land biology with marine life. I was eager to see all of it. We loaded up the car and drove from Laurel Canyon to Malibu, then headed what started out as west and then became north on Highway 1, past Oxnard to Montecito, then Santa Barbara, Goleta, and Carpinteria. At Pismo Beach we dug in the sand with our bare heels until sunset to find grapefruit-sized clams, then we spent the night. The next day's drive included San Luis Obispo, Hearst Castle, Morro Bay, Cambria, and other stops just to take in the dramatic views along the coast. But our ultimate destination was Big Sur. Toni had recommended Pfeiffer Beach and Nepenthe as "must-see" places. We spent exquisite time in both locations and then took a walk in the forest east of the highway. Feeling very small in a grove of titanic coastal redwoods, I looked straight up and saw blue and gray sky peeking through the spaces between the clusters of small green needles. I couldn't help but wish that more people who think they're the most important thing in the world would come to that forest and walk among those redwoods. Then again, the people most in need of humility would tend to avoid places that might make them feel humble. As we walked to our car, the constantly changing interplay among the ocean, cliffs, and fog, and my happiness in being with Louise and Sherry in that place of incomparable coastal beauty made me never want to leave.

My daughters' delight in discovering California helped us get through some of the rougher patches. Gerry's and my prolonged absences from our home in New Jersey followed by our move to two separate homes was difficult for them. Knowing our actions had caused Sherry and Louise pain, I suffered for and with them. I kept remembering, missing, and, by then, idealizing our former life with Gerry. The breakup of our family was one of the most difficult things I had experienced in my relatively short time as an adult. It was all the more painful for me because it echoed my own experience as a child of divorced parents. And yet I remember those first few months in California as a simple, almost idyllic time. For one thing—a very important thing—I was in a better financial position than most divorced women. Enough money was coming in from my share of songwriting royalties that I didn't have to worry about making the rent, but not so much that I could afford to adopt the lifestyle to which so many people in the music business were praying to become accustomed.

I had experienced a taste of that lifestyle soon after I arrived in L.A. when Lou Adler invited me to a party in Bel Air at the home of John and Michelle Phillips. I wasn't keen to go, especially not alone, but curiosity trumped reluctance. Following a misunderstanding by my teenage babysitter about when she was supposed to arrive, I drove to Bel Air feeling self-conscious about arriving an hour and a half late. When I saw the line of cars parked the entire length of the street I thought I'd have trouble finding a space, but a valet waved me forward to another attendant who took my Mustang along with my keys, gave me a ticket with a number on it, and directed me to the house. Through the open front door I could see that the large entry hall was crowded with people dressed in what might have been considered rags or costumes had it not been the late sixties. Some of the clothes looked like torn pieces of cloth adorned with sequins, rhinestones, and glitter, but because the outfit in question had been purchased at great expense at one of the trendy stores on the Strip, it was not only okay to wear such an outfit, it was mandatory.

In contrast, I was wearing my standard "when in doubt" uniform: a pair of jeans, black high-heeled boots, and a long-sleeved black cotton T-shirt. It's okay, I told myself as I scanned the crowd for Lou, my unexceptional outfit will help me disappear into the background more easily. I found the bar, got a glass of carbonated water with ice, and continued looking for Lou. It was so crowded that moving from room to room was not easy. I managed to wriggle behind a couple making out and then I squeezed around a large caped person of indeterminate gender until I found a few inches of space halfway up the stairs where I could look out over the banister. There I stood, more an observer than a participant, sipping my drink and watching the parade of partygoers moving below me in a slow stream that reminded me of eastbound morning traffic on the Garden State Parkway. Above the din of recorded music, with the bass pumping at high volume and the shouted conversations among the guests struggling to be heard over the hubbub, I could almost imagine everyone thinking, I wonder how I look? Am I making a good impression?

Of course the correct answer was, "Darling, no one is looking at you. Everyone is too busy thinking, 'I wonder how I look? Am I making a good impression?'"

I didn't know what my scene was, but this wasn't it.

Chapter Four

New Friends

$\mathcal{T}$he walk to and from my neighbors' houses on Wonderland Avenue was semivertical. We learned to pronounce it "Wonderlind," as locals did, rather than "Wonderland," as Alice might have pronounced it if she had tumbled down a rabbit hole in New Jersey. Rustic houses peeped out amid luxuriant greenery and dotted the hillsides with hues not often found in nature, and there were more shades of bougainvillea than Crayola had names for.

Sherry and Louise already had friends in the Canyon. Apart from my brief forays into Bel Air, writing with Toni, and playing Discover California! with my daughters, I didn't get out much. Whenever I got the blues I found familiar comfort in attempts at solitary songwriting and playing the piano. One night, when the girls were with Gerry, I remembered that a neighbor who played guitar just for fun had invited me several times to come up and hang. On impulse, I walked up the street to his house. When I arrived, he and some of his friends were jamming. Knowing I was a musician, he invited me to sit in. At first I was reluctant, but he kept asking me to join them. When finally I did I was surprised at how much I enjoyed playing with other musicians in a casual setting. Usually when I played with other musicians it was in a studio, it was my song, and someone had just said, "Take One. Rolling!"

At first I had trouble keeping up with the spontaneous turns the music took at jam sessions. But then I began to listen to the other musicians' musical motifs and respond with respectable figures of my own. I found that the key principles were listening, knowing when to step out with confidence, and knowing when to play sparsely. Applying those principles I was able to develop a fair number of licks that I could pull out of my musical kit bag at will. This gave me the security of knowing that even if nothing fresh or inspiring came to mind when I was called to improvise, at least I could play something.

I never aspired to be in the same league as Bill Evans, Herbie Hancock, or McCoy Tyner. I couldn't imagine any great jazz pianists or other extraordinary players such as Miles Davis or John Coltrane ever having to resort to lick number 27. Few things were as exciting to me as hearing musicians of that caliber create spontaneous magic on instruments they knew inside and out. The fact that I was doing a rudimentary version of what they did gave me great pleasure.

Marijuana was present at these jams. Many players believed that pot would enhance the flow of spontaneous magic through their creative channels. Listeners thought it would help them get more deeeeeeply into the muuuuuusiiiiiiic. Marijuana may have helped both players and listeners focus more deeply on one part of the magic, but that was to the detriment of being able to appreciate the whole. If you've ever listened to music on pot—not that *I* ever have—you probably remember how hung up you got in the bass line, or the guitar solo, or the lyric the lead singer repeated over...and over...and over....

You've probably guessed by now that I inhaled during some of these jams, but I soon realized that the marijuana only made me *think* I was playing better. The fastest way to come to that realization is to listen to a recording made when you were jamming high. In the cold light of morning you hear yourself on tape playing the same mediocre riff again and again. I remember thinking, Wow. This is sooooo cool! But it wasn't cool at all. And besides, I didn't really like smoking pot. I had smoked more of it than I had wanted to when I lived on the East Coast.

The ready availability of pot and other mind-expanding substances and their use by so many of my friends and neighbors was as prevalent in Laurel Canyon as the bougainvillea, century plants, and steep winding roads. It would not be easy to maintain a healthy lifestyle. However, three things made me resolve to do that: Louise, Sherry, and my fervent desire to provide a stable home environment for them. The problem was, I wasn't sure how to define "stable."

When members of my parents' generation used the word "freedom," they had in mind the founding fathers, the flag, and representative democracy. When the following generation (mine) used the word "freedom," they meant the freedom to cast off the social values imposed upon them by their parents, and the freedom to live by their own rules, which in 1968 meant no rules. For many residents of Laurel Canyon, freedom meant the freedom to conform to the social expectations set by their neighbors, who in most cases had no expectations beyond their neighbors' willingness to smoke dope with them.

Along with newfound freedoms came newfound confusion. With no rules, no boundaries, and no blueprint, as a twenty-six-year-old divorcée and mother at a time when other women my age had not yet married, I was unsure about virtually everything. The only thing of which I was certain was that I loved Sherry and Louise more than anything in the world. Rather than feeling tied down by motherhood, I treasured having my children—not only because we loved each other so much but because I understood in a way I couldn't have articulated at the time that their presence kept me grounded in reality. Though Willa Mae was a huge help, ultimately I was responsible for the girls, the house, our dogs, and our overweight cat, whom I probably would have named Puss-in-Boots or something equally obvious. I was glad that Gerry's scholarly suggestion of Telemachus, after the son of Ulysses and Penelope, had prevailed. The photographer Jim McCrary would make our fat feline famous by including him in a photo that would become the cover of a bestselling album.* Jim's photo would also immortalize my living room on Wonderland Avenue with its hatch-cover bench and Indian-print curtains. The black Baldwin Acrosonic spinet piano on which so many hit songs had been written was behind Jim and therefore not visible in that photo.

When Toni and I wrote at that piano we hoped to have more of those hits. Sometimes we wrote with that in mind, but often we wrote simply for the joy of writing. At first our songs were recorded only as demos. Then Lou Adler recorded "Lady of the Lake" with Peggy Lipton, and Strawberry Alarm Clock released "Lady of the Lake" and "Blues for a Young Girl Gone" on their album *The World in a Sea Shell*. The Carpenters' performance of "It's Going to Take Some Time" was Toni's and my first joint appearance at the top of the charts. Later, "Where You Lead" and "It's Too Late" would find a home on the album with the corpulent kitty on the cover.

In the year 2000 Amy Sherman Palladino had the idea of

---

*Upon accepting his Grammy in 1972 for the Biggest Domestic Cat Ever to Appear on an Album Cover, Telemachus was so overcome with emotion that he could only say, "Meow." What he meant to say was, "I want to thank my tom, my tabby, and all the fat cats who oversaw the investment of my kitty. I couldn't have done it without you."

using "Where You Lead" as the theme song for *Gilmore Girls*, a TV show she had created about a young mother and the teenage daughter to whom she had given birth out of wedlock when she was sixteen. The women walk a blurry but entertaining line between being mother and daughter and each other's best friend. Before the movement known as "women's lib" had blossomed in the early seventies, Toni's original lyric had taken a "stand by your man" approach. By the time that song was released on *Tapestry* in 1971 the lyric was already outdated. When Amy said she wanted "Where You Lead" rewritten as a love song between a mother and daughter, I asked Toni if she would modify the lyric. She rose to the occasion with a version we retitled "Where You Lead I Will Follow." My by then adult daughter Louise joined me in singing the music that opened each episode of *Gilmore Girls*. This unexpected exposure carried Toni's and my song to a second and third generation. The life of a song continues to amaze me.

When Toni brought her lyrics to me they were either neatly typed on a sheet of white paper or written on lined yellow paper in her distinctive handwriting. Her lyrics were artistic visually as well as lyrically, with the verses and choruses of each song forming a unique shape on the page. As soon as I placed the lyric on the music stand of my piano I let my mind go free, not so much thinking as absorbing the meter and content. This process often brought a melody to mind even before I was conscious that one was being suggested. Sometimes I worked on the tune without Toni there, and then she'd come by the next day to help polish what I had written. Other times I wrote the music with Toni right there to change the lyric if I took the song in an unexpected direction. Though the process was different for each song, it was always fun, and it was always creative.

In 1970 I began to experiment with writing my own lyrics again, with the underlying thought that maybe *this* time I could work up the courage to play them for someone. It was difficult to shake the memory of earlier times when, during some of the more discouraging periods of my marriage, I had tried to prepare for the possibility of having to earn a living by writing my own lyrics. I had been so intimidated by Gerry's gift, his intellectual capacity, his skill, and his success that I could never bring myself to show my lyrics to anyone. Often I didn't even finish them. After having worked with Gerry for so long and knowing the level of excellence of which he was capable, I would stop myself in mid-lyric, thinking, Why bother?

It was Toni's generous approach to songwriting that first inspired me to think that maybe I could write lyrics on my own. A second wave of inspiration would come in 1970 from someone I had met a few years earlier.

Chapter Five

The Night Owl

$\mathcal{I}$ was twenty-five and still living in New Jersey in 1967 when I ran into two of the Myddle Class in a music store on West 48th Street. Rick and Charlie were there to look at guitars, and then they were going to a club in the Village to catch a band they knew.

"You gotta come see these guys," Rick said. "They're unbelievable!"

The Flying Machine was playing four sets a night. With Gerry in the studio and the girls in New Jersey with Willa Mae, I could catch an early set and be home by eleven.

The Night Owl Café was bustling when we entered. Charlie and Rick immediately recognized three of the Flying Machine among the people milling around the bar. As my eyes adjusted to the darkness the musicians greeted each other with what appeared to be some kind of secret handshake. Then Rick introduced me to drummer Joel "Bishop" O'Brien, and Danny Kortchmar, who sang, wrote, and played guitar. Charlie added that Joel and Danny had been two of the Martha's Vineyard King Bees. Then Danny introduced me to Zach Wiesner, the Flying Machine's bass player.

Following Zach's glance, I noticed an extraordinarily tall man with long hair standing off to one side of the bar.

Following my look, Danny brought me over to the tall man and said, "James! Say hello to Carole King." James Taylor mumbled something like, "Hrrph, harya," then turned and covered the distance to the dressing room in several strides. Danny looked at his watch. It was time for their set. Danny, Bishop, and Zach quickly followed James.

Years later, James would tell me that he had so much respect for my songs that when Danny introduced us he didn't know what to say, but at the time I felt like an unwelcome intruder.

"I should go," I told Charlie.

"You're already here," he said. "Just stay for one set."

"Trust me," said Rick. "You'll be blown away!"

With that, Rick took my arm and guided me toward the center of the club where some people were already seated in church pews. We were seated at a table barely big enough to hold a candle, drinks, and an ashtray. A waitress materialized to take our order, which arrived just as the Flying Machine began to file onto the stage. James pulled a mic toward his acoustic guitar, Zach and Danny plugged in their instruments, Bishop picked up his sticks, and the stage lights went up.

From the moment I heard the first notes out of James's guitar, I was mesmerized. When the band came in on the downbeat of the first verse and James began to sing, I felt as if I were witnessing a long-lost friend who also happened to be an angel. Rick was right. I was blown away. As much as James tried to blend in with the band, his stage presence was unmistakable. His songs and the quality of his voice evoked an astonishing range of emotions. His modest demeanor was authentic and endearing. He told stories and jokes between songs with a dry, self-deprecating sense of humor, and his banter with Kootch, Zach, and Bishop was witty and familiar. His joy at being onstage was apparent and infectious, and when he threw his head back to hit the high notes, there was no doubt about it: James Taylor loved to sing.

After the set James was swarmed by audience members eager to tell him how good he was. Though I shared their opinion, I didn't relish being part of an after-show crush, and I was a little gun-shy following our earlier encounter. I was also experiencing that sense of borrowed time that mothers of young children often feel when they're out having a good time. I decided to head back to New Jersey without saying goodbye to James or the band. Charlie and Rick walked me to my car, and I drove home to suburbia.

Like so many other bands who had come to New York, the Flying Machine believed that a record deal was all that stood between them and their ascent to the top of the charts. After all, their main songwriter was James, whose gift for singing and songwriting was manifest. Danny, in addition to being an accomplished guitar player, was also an excellent songwriter. And Zach was James's cowriter on "Rainy Day Man." But the potential of the Flying Machine would not be realized in that incarnation. As the seasons of New York changed around the smoky clubs in which hopeful bands played, the atmosphere inside remained the same, as did the availability of hard drugs in Greenwich Village. In addition to being one of a number of bands competing for the attention of A&R men, the Flying Machine was struggling with James's addiction to heroin. In the fall of 1967 the hopes of the band were dashed to "pieces on the ground."* In desperate need of help, James called his father, Dr. Isaac Taylor, a professor at the University of North Carolina. Ike drove to New York and brought his son home to Chapel Hill.

---

*James wrote, "Sweet dreams and flying machines in pieces on the ground" two years later in his song "Fire and Rain."

After several months, James felt that he had recovered sufficiently to look for another career opportunity. His decision to fly to London turned out to be fortunate. Peter Asher was already known to the world as half of Peter and Gordon when the Beatles put him in charge of A&R for Apple Records, a division of the Beatles' Apple Corps, Ltd.* It was Kootch who suggested to Peter that he give James a listen, and Peter had the wisdom to sign James immediately. The result was James's eponymous first album.

The first time I listened to the songs on *James Taylor* I thought, I could hear these songs a thousand times and never grow tired of them.

That theory would be tested and affirmed.

---

*The name "Apple Corps" was created by the Beatles, thereby proving that I'm not the only songwriter unable to resist the appeal of a truly bad pun.

Chapter Six

Kootch

Accounts differ about when the Fugs were formed—1964 or 1965—but all agree that Ed Sanders and Tuli Kupferberg were the founders. Tuli was a Beat hero who published magazines called *Birth* and *Yeah* and sold them on the street in the East and West Village. Sanders's operation, Fuck You Press, published *Fuck You: A Magazine of the Arts*, which he sold at his Peace Eye Bookstore on Avenue A in the East Village. The name Fugs was reportedly derived from Norman Mailer's use, in his novel *The Naked and the Dead*, of "fug" as a substitute for the word everyone knew it replaced.

After the Flying Machine broke up, the Fugs hired Kootch. He brought with him a killer driving rhythm guitar and a seemingly unlimited supply of outrageous licks. But his real love was black music in any form. Danny was a good-looking kid from Larchmont, New York, an affluent town in lily-white Westchester County. Coming of age under the heavy influence of R&B, soul, blues, gospel, and jazz, he had listened and practiced until he had mastered some of the sounds of the guitar players he admired in the genres he favored, and then he had listened and practiced some more.

Danny's gig with the Fugs didn't afford him much of an opportunity to develop his skills in his preferred genres, but it did come with a couple of distinct advantages for a young man: it was a steady job, and the Fugs attracted plenty of women willing to provide companionship. Often, after the show, Danny would emerge from the stage door wondering if he would wind up going home with one of the young women waiting to hook up with someone in the band. It never occurred to Danny—handsome, smart, funny, and reasonably well brought up—to be anything other than nice and polite to the girls waiting outside. This of course made the girls want to have nothing whatsoever to do with him. They had come to hang out with the bad boys and by all that was unholy that's what they were going to do. Thus it was Tuli and Ed coming out the door—snarling, cursing, and projecting all the dark glory of their outrageous personae—who got all the chicks.

Danny was just beginning to think about leaving the Fugs when an L.A. band called Clear Light offered him a job if he was willing to move to California. Kootch left the Fugs, flew to the West Coast, and moved in with a group of hippies and musicians living at the home of Frazier Mohawk. The hazy discussions around Frazier's coffee table often included the observation that living in Laurel Canyon was a much more desirable option than, say, getting killed in the jungles of Vietnam. Southern California was the center of everything fresh, young, and current. The beautiful people, the gorgeous weather, the burgeoning music scene, and the free and easy lifestyle were a siren call to young men around the country, and they were responding in droves. One was a musician I'd known on the East Coast who would add a lot more than music to my life.

Chapter Seven

The City

*A*fter the dissolution of the Myddle Class, the Fugs hired Charlie Larkey to play bass. At the end of 1967 the band comprised Kenny Pine, Ken Weaver, Kootch, Charlie, Tuli, and Ed. Charlie was playing with the Fugs in New York when he learned that they had been booked in L.A. for three days in April 1968. By then it was common knowledge that Gerry and I were separated. When Charlie called to invite me to one of the Fugs' concerts, I said yes. After the concert, he came home with me and stayed for the next three nights. When the Fugs' engagement was over and Charlie had to go back to New York, we kept in touch by telephone. After two months, our conversations across the miles led to a big decision for both of us. Two months later Charlie gave notice, flew west, moved into the house on Wonderland Avenue, and began looking for a gig in L.A. He picked up a few studio sessions and sat in at clubs, but he wasn't getting the regular paycheck he'd had with the Fugs.

When Clear Light broke up, Danny, too, was without a gig. Since Danny and Charlie both thrived on playing live with other musicians, Danny started coming over to jam with Charlie.

"We gotta keep our chops up," Danny said as he lugged his guitar and a Fender amp up the stairs.

Taking the amplifier from Danny, Charlie agreed.

"If we don't have calluses, we're not practicing enough."

Charlie plugged Danny's amp into an outlet in the living room, then picked up his Fender bass, which was already plugged into his Ampeg B-12 bass amp. I said, "Right on," flashed the two-finger peace sign, then went into the kitchen to prepare the only vegetarian entrée I knew how to make: nut loaf.

At first I tried to stay out of the way when the guys jammed, but inevitably I wanted to hear a bass and guitar on one of Toni's and my new songs. And just as inevitably, after the three of us had played the song a couple of times, it took only the utterance of names such as Otis Redding or Miles Davis to get me to play soul and jazz tunes with them. But I was less reluctant than I had been at my neighbor's house. Playing with Charlie and Danny was not only fun, it greatly enhanced my jamming skills. As the number of licks in my kit bag went up, so did my confidence and understanding of jazz. And Kootch had a gift for exhorting other musicians to play, write, and sing beyond what they believed was the edge of their ability. During our jams Danny challenged Charlie and me to be badder (in the sense of better) by planting himself in front of us in classic Kootch stance, with a facial expression that seemed to say, "I'm the baddest mutha-fuckah around. Whatta *you* got?"

Years later, Danny told me he hadn't been thinking that at all. It was an expression of concentration. He was simply doing what he always did when he played with other musicians: listening, learning, and figuring out what he could play that would help establish a groove, augment the tune, and not get in the way of the other players.

Seeing how much I enjoyed playing with them, Charlie and

Danny became more assertive in trying to convince me to perform. They wanted me to record an album of my songs with them as my band and then we'd take the band on the road. But I would commit no further than agreeing to go into the studio with them.

One day we were discussing possible producers when Charlie said, "You know Lou Adler. Why don't you call him?"

I did know Lou Adler. After leaving Donnie's employ, Lou had become one of the most successful producers, managers, and publishers in Southern California. He had founded two labels, first Dunhill, then Ode. Among the artists and titles with which Lou was associated in 1968 were "California Dreamin'" by the Mamas and the Papas, "San Francisco" by Scott McKenzie, "Eve of Destruction" by Barry McGuire, and other recordings by artists including Johnny Rivers, Shelley Fabares, and Spirit. Remembering how enthusiastic Lou had always been about Gerry's and my demos, I got his number from Lester and reached him at his office. I told him I was in a band and invited him over to hear Charlie, Danny, and me. He said he'd be over later that afternoon.

After hearing the three of us in my small living room, Lou didn't seem all that excited. But I took hope from his encouraging words when he left. We didn't have long to wait. As soon as Lou got home he called to offer me a recording contract.

"Not the band," he said. "Just you."

This was not an unfamiliar scenario, but this time I stood up for my bandmates. I told Lou he needed to sign the entire band, and I made it clear that I was no more willing to go on the road than I had been when he was with Aldon.

"Just albums," I said. "No promotional tours, and no club gigs."

"No problem," Lou said.

Lou signed the three of us to his label, Ode Records, at that time distributed by Columbia Records. With encouragement from Lou, Lester, Toni, Charlie, and Danny, I began to feel comfortable as part of a recording band. Everyone took me at my word that I didn't want to perform live and turned their focus wholly toward the studio. But even a recording band needed a name.

"Hmm," mused Danny. "We're all from New York....Why don't we call ourselves...." He paused, then exclaimed with as much enthusiasm as if he had just discovered penicillin, "the City!"

That's how quickly it happened. One minute we had no name. The next, we were in the studio recording as the City. We wanted to keep the band to just the three of us, so we took Lou's suggestion and hired Jim Gordon to play drums on the album.

The title of the City's first and only album, *Now That Everything's Been Said*, was the name of a song I had written with Toni. We recorded that song, a song by Margaret Allison called "My Sweet Home," and ten others that I had cowritten with either Toni, Gerry, or Dave Palmer, the lead singer and principal songwriter for the now defunct Myddle Class. Gerry and I were still in transition. We were speaking but not collaborating on songs. Though Gerry wasn't directly involved in the recording of *Now That Everything's Been Said*, we had already cowritten six of the songs on that album: "Snow Queen," "Wasn't Born to Follow," "A Man Without a Dream," "Lady," "All My Time," and "Hi-de-Ho (That Old Sweet Roll)." In 1970, Blood, Sweat & Tears would release a version of "Hi-de-Ho" from their album *Blood, Sweat & Tears 3*. The BS&T version, featuring the vocal of David Clayton-Thomas and the band's distinctive horn section, would rise to #14 in *Billboard*.

Danny wrote these liner notes thirty years later for a rerelease of the album in 1999:

> *It seems like a million years ago when Carole, Charlie, and I sat in the living room of Carole's Laurel Canyon house and worked these tunes up. Even though we had a group name, this*

was Carole's record all the way. She would sing or play parts to Charlie and me, and once we got it right, we could hear how great this record was going to be.

By the time we went into Sound Recorders in Hollywood, I was pumped. This was the first album I had ever played on and I was thrilled to be working with the people at the top of their game. With Lou Adler producing and Jim Gordon on drums we went into Armin Steiner's studio [Sound Recorders]. I soaked it up like a sponge and for me it was a learning experience of a lifetime.

The City album remains a great example of Carole's brilliant writing skills, Lou Adler's legendary production sensibilities, and Jim Gordon's amazing musicality.

The seeds of the enduring classic album Tapestry were planted here, and I consider myself extremely lucky and proud to have been a part of it all.

We all considered ourselves extremely lucky. In fact, when the album was finished, we thought it was brilliant. Even without touring, we had no doubt that Now That Everything's Been Said was destined for huge success. The next step was for Charlie, Kootch, and me to pose for album cover photos in hippie garb (i.e., our everyday attire). Columbia's art department hired Jim Marshall to take photos in various locations around Los Angeles consistent with the theme of a city. Executives at Columbia were so enthusiastic that they flew Charlie and Jim to New York so Jim could photograph Charlie eating a hot dog next to a street vendor, and other New York–specific activities. In the late sixties, record companies were not afraid to spend whatever it took to create an artistic cover or produce a creative album. To my knowledge, none of Jim Marshall's photos of Charlie in New York ever made it onto the album.

I was twenty-six when Now That Everything's Been Said was

released in 1968. Charlie, Danny, and I expected it to zoom to the top of the charts within, at most, a few weeks. Individually and together we optimistically imagined the album's success as if it had already happened. Danny and Charlie kept telling each other, "It's a great album. The City is gonna be number 1 with a bullet!" The album didn't get above 500 with an anchor. It never even charted.

Did the material fall short? Was something lacking in the presentation? Was it because I was unwilling to go on the road to promote the album? Whatever the reason, our disappointment at the failure of the album to chart would pass, but our joy at having written and recorded the City's first and only album would endure. As would the music.

Chapter Eight

Truth Is One, Paths Are Many

After the demise of *Now That Everything's Been Said*, Charlie told me he wanted to get a place of his own. He told me this gently as he held me and reminded me that he had gone from living with his parents to rooming with friends in New York to living with me. At twenty-two, Charlie had never lived alone.

At twenty-seven, I couldn't argue with his logic, but it was little Carol who heard the news, and she wasn't taking it well. All she—I—could do was hold on to him tightly, as if that would keep him with me. At last, after promising that he would always love me (a promise kept), Charlie stepped back and began to gather his things. As I watched him drive away I blamed myself, yet again, for my inability to keep two people together who loved each other.

At first we remained close. Charlie couldn't wait to show me the room he had rented over a garage on Stanley Hills Drive. Outwardly I mirrored his enthusiasm, but I couldn't believe that he had left the house on Wonderland Avenue (read: *me*) for such a minuscule space. I couldn't imagine a family of mice living inside it, let alone a six-foot-tall man with an upright bass, a Fender bass, several amplifiers, and a black-and-tan German shepherd named

Schwartz. After a while I came to view the little studio as Charlie's Declaration of Independence and stayed away.

A natural consequence of our separation was that first Charlie, then I, began to date other people. It was 1969. It was okay to love lots of people. Indeed, it was mandatory. But human nature hadn't changed as much as the sixties had led us to believe. It was painful to think of Charlie seeing other women, and I cried every time I came home from one of my own infrequent dates. I didn't want to date. I wanted Charlie. Letting go was proving incredibly difficult, and yet I knew it was a necessary step toward empowering little Carol to become the woman she had the potential to be. However, reaching that objective would require me to overturn my generational indoctrination that I needed a man to complete me, and achieving *that* objective would require me to find my center.

I did find my center, and a man was involved, but not in the way you might expect.

I began taking hatha yoga classes at the Integral Yoga Institute on Benda Place near the convergence of Barham Boulevard, Cahuenga Pass, and the Hollywood Freeway. In addition to hatha poses, called asanas, the classes incorporated meditation, chanting, relaxation, and breathing techniques. I found these practices so healing emotionally and physically that I signed up to teach them to others. I attended discussion groups and volunteered in the kitchen, where my knowledge of vegetarian recipes expanded from nut loaf to include two entrées, three salads, and four desserts. Only a block away from the sea of traffic on the 101, the Institute was a harbor of peace, joy, love, and learning. I looked forward to meeting its founder.

C. K. Ramaswamy Gounder was born in South India on December 22, 1914. He grew up to become a successful businessman with a wife and two sons. After his wife passed away, Ramaswamy left his sons with their grandmother and went on a spiritual quest. He walked through jungles, forests, and caves and climbed mountains until he arrived in Rishikesh, where he found his spiritual master, Swami Sivananda. In 1949, Sivananda ordained Ramaswamy as Swami Satchidananda. The name was a compound of three Sanskrit words (*sat*, *chid*, and *ananda*) loosely meaning "truth," "knowledge," and "bliss."

Satchidananda came to New York in 1966 at the invitation of the artist Peter Max and established the original Integral Yoga Institute in an Upper West Side apartment. Disciples received and disseminated Satchidananda's wisdom with single-minded devotion. Following customs in his home country, they showed their reverence by calling their religious teacher "Gurudev," kissing his feet, and surrounding him with flowers. Though he accepted such tributes with grace, he often reminded them that he was simply a teacher. He made no financial requests. There were no requirements for service at the Institute and no compulsory level of practice. He asked only that his students learn whatever they were ready to learn.

Gurudev's flowing orange robes, hair, mustache, and beard were consistent with what most Americans thought a swami should look like, but the consistency stopped there. He drove a car, wore a wristwatch, and could repair anything from a camera to a carburetor. I was drawn to him because he didn't ask me to retreat from worldly life but showed, by example, how I could bring the principles of yoga into my daily life. Gurudev asked us to look for service in everything we did, be it folding laundry, smiling at the irritating woman at the DMV, or not getting angry at the driver of the motorcycle who had just aggressively cut us off.

"Karma yoga is action," he said. "And every action is karma yoga."

Most people thought karma referred to good deeds that could later be withdrawn from the bank of good fortune. Gurudev

taught that every selfless action was its own reward. He also promoted interfaith pluralism. The message that every religion could
lead a sincere seeker to the same goal would become the focus of
Gurudev's lectures and actions in his later years. His motto, "Truth
is one, paths are many," struck me as a beautiful way of expressing
my wish for everyone to live in harmony.

With the lilt characteristic of his South Indian accent,
Gurudev would speak softly at discussions.

"We are all wanting to get to the same place. If you are going
one way and I am going another, let us agree that neither way is
better. Let us embrace all ways together. Always together."

And then he would chuckle because he had just made a pun.

Gurudev had a gift for using simple analogies to help people
incorporate complex theological concepts into their daily lives.
In the summer of 1969 he gave the opening invocation at Woodstock. Whether speaking to twenty people or an audience of
thousands, Gurudev exuded a calm, easy confidence. He never
proselytized, only spoke of what was possible. He believed that
his purpose was to guide people to their spiritual connection with
each other and with whatever form of higher power they were
ready to embrace—or not.

I was already in tune with most of what he was saying, but I
found a deeper connection through his analogy of a candle in a
windstorm being blown in all directions, its flame flickering. The
owner of the candle is fearful that the flame will be extinguished
by the wind. A neighbor gives the fellow a glass chimney to put
around the candle. Now the owner can see that the flame will
burn steadily and brightly no matter what's going on around it.
Now he knows he has nothing to fear.

"The peace within us is the flame," said Gurudev, "and the
chimney is our awareness of our relationship to each other and
to God."

When Gurudev said "God," I took it to mean God by whatever name. Twelve-step programs use the phrase "God as I understand God" to cover all the names and concepts people use to describe the life force that animates and inspires them. Gurudev's analogy of the candle was a reminder that if we have faith in our relationship with everyone and everything in the universe, the flame of our inner peace will remain constant through life and death. My understanding of this concept made me stronger.

Sometimes Gurudev gave me personal advice, but he never took it personally when my inner rebel chose not to follow it. He knew I needed to learn in my own way and in my own time. Gurudev attained Samadhi on August 19, 2002. He was eighty-eight when he left his body. I was one of his many friends, disciples, devotees, and students around the world who mourned his passing and celebrated his life.

By combining Gurudev's wisdom with principles from my Jewish heritage, reaffirming my dedication to excellence, responsibility, fairness, and compassion, and incorporating all those things into what I hoped was a commonsense approach to theology, I found my center—or so I thought.

I would come to learn that a center isn't a destination. It's a journey.

Chapter Nine

Three Really Excellent Things

*T*he first really excellent thing happened when I resumed writing with Gerry in 1969. As much as I enjoyed writing with Toni, it felt good to write with Gerry again. I continued to write with Toni and also, separately, David Palmer.

Lou had moved Ode's distribution and offices to A&M Records, of which the "A" was Herb Alpert and the "M" was Jerry Moss. Raise your hand if you can think of a trumpet player before or since Herb Alpert who was able to parlay a series of easy pop hits into an empire as hugely successful as A&M.

Herb and Jerry had purchased Charlie Chaplin's former studio, at the corner of Sunset Boulevard and La Brea Avenue, and converted it into a compound of A&M offices. Conveniently located fifteen minutes from Laurel Canyon and ten minutes from Wallich's Music City on Sunset and Vine, the former movie lot provided a casual, independent environment for Alpert, Moss, Adler, and the day-to-day employees who facilitated A&M's creative and business endeavors. With a dress code ranging from casual to outrageous, an easygoing executive management style, comfortable recording studios with state-of-the-art equipment, and an assortment of low-lying buildings with glass-paned doors, large windows, and balconies with lots of plants, A&M offered my generation of fugitives from the East Coast gray-flannel fifties a congenial atmosphere conducive to creative thinking. While the executives, business people, album cover artists, recording engineers, and assistants prospered in the informal ambiance of A&M's offices, the writers and artists whose music underwrote the operation were lionized.

With the City album in the cellar, Lou had invited me to his new office to propose that I record another album for Ode, this time as a solo artist.

"Look," he said. "If an artist doesn't record a song of yours that you really like, you can record it and release it on a Carole King album. That'll get your song out there. Isn't that what you want?"

Yes. It was.

Between Lou's logic and the attraction of working at A&M, I agreed to strive for success as a solo recording artist. But then I developed a new boundary. I didn't want to be a star.

Everyone around me thought I was out of my mind. I was being offered an opportunity for which so many people had been praying their whole life and all I could say was, "Please believe me. I don't want to be a star." My rationale was that I viewed success and stardom as two different things. Successful recording artists were played on the radio, were respected by the public, and had longevity. The songs they sang moved and inspired people. Stars were hounded and mobbed, their privacy was nonexistent, and they were under constant pressure to reach #1 and stay there.

Kootch and I had a recurring conversation about this. One day, while he was sitting on my living room couch holding a cup of strong black coffee, he expressed once again his strongly held opinion that I had what it took to be a star, and I should settle for nothing less.

"And you shouldn't aspire to be just any star," he said. "You should be the biggest star there is. You got what it takes to be number *one!*"

"But Danny, stars fall."

"Yeah," he said, setting his cup down on the hatch-cover coffee table. "But it's pretty fuckin' great to be at the top. The top is where you want to be!"

"I don't want to be number one," I said. "There's no place to go but down. I'd rather be number five, or even number ten, and stick around longer."

I didn't realize I was expressing a guiding principle of my career. I was hoping for career longevity, and to my utter amazement and eternal gratitude I achieved it. And if that weren't enough, one of my albums would actually reach #1 and stay there for a very long time. But Danny and I engaged in such conversations before *Tapestry* was released, when I had no way of knowing what my future held. I just wrote songs, worked hard, created each day's blueprint from scratch, and hoped to high heaven that I was doing all the right things to give my daughters and myself a good life.

High heaven must have thought I was doing the right things, because in spite of intermittent relationship confusion, 1970 was humming along pretty smoothly. Louise and Sherry seemed to be flourishing, I was cowriting songs prolifically, and our household seemed almost normal considering the rapidly changing times. I was practicing yoga. And I was dating occasionally, though not with much enthusiasm.

Then the second really excellent thing happened. Charlie came over, told me he wanted to build a life with me, and asked me to marry him. Oh, joy!!! We began planning a wedding and reception to be held on September 6, 1970, in the front yard of what would once again be *our* house on Wonderland Avenue. Charlie, too, was Jewish, which made it easy for our respective families and us to agree that a rabbi would perform the ceremony. Though I was rebellious in other ways, major family occasions always seemed to bring me back to my roots. My attachment to Judaism was more about tradition than religion. I liked the chain of familiar rituals that had sustained generations before me, and I didn't want to break it.

I was twenty-eight and Charlie was twenty-three the day we were married. My friend Stephanie made a simple white A-line wedding dress for me. It was ankle-length, with a scoop neck, long sleeves, and no lace. A garland of white flowers, woven by Joel O'Brien's then wife, Connie, cascaded through my hair. We honored the custom of men covering their heads at Jewish services by providing yarmulkes. Though our friends were dressed in varying degrees of unconventional attire, the ceremony was traditional. Charlie wore tails and a top hat that added eight inches to his already six-foot-one height. I was five foot two in my bare feet.

Charlie was waiting with the rabbi in front of the chupah when I made my entrance. At eight and ten, Sherry and Louise were achingly beautiful as they accompanied me. They wore long-sleeved sky blue and mint green dresses that I had made to match their eyes. My making their dresses was a tribute to my Grandma Sarah and her sister, Lillie, who as new immigrants had contributed to the support of their families by working as seamstresses in their homes.

Louise and Sherry stood just behind me during the entire ceremony. Though I clearly heard the rabbi say, "I now pronounce you man and wife," little Carol heard, "I now pronounce you a family." Charlie broke the glass with a firm stomp of his heel, and then amid the chorus of friends saying "Mazeltov!" we sealed our vows with a kiss, for which Charlie had to bend way down while I stood on tiptoe. Then we stepped away from the chupah. Friends and family members crowded in with congratulatory hugs, kisses, and handshakes. Watching Louise and Sherry alternately running around happily with their friends and interacting comfortably with Charlie's and my friends, it struck me that some of Charlie's friends weren't much older than my children.

How happy I was! And oh, how blissfully unaware I was that I would now have to balance the needs of a younger husband with those of two children who weren't his biological offspring, and somehow fit my own needs into the picture.

The third really excellent thing that happened in 1970 was that I was reintroduced to James Taylor, and this time he was fully present.

Chapter Ten

Sweet Baby James

I recorded and released three albums for Ode between 1968 and 1971, beginning with the City album. Lou produced *Now That Everything's Been Said* and *Tapestry*; Gerry Goffin and John Fischbach produced *Writer*. Though I didn't realize it then, I view those three albums as a trilogy, with a progression from *Now That Everything's Been Said*, through the slightly more confident *Writer*, and culminating with the elements that contributed to the success of *Tapestry*. But there was an additional element in *Tapestry*. If Danny's observation is true that the seeds of *Tapestry* were planted in the two prior albums, then the influence of James Taylor brought water and sunlight.

In 1969 "sunlight" might not have been a word that sprang to the mind of Peter Asher in connection with James. After producing James's first album in London, Peter accompanied him back to America, dropped him off at a rehab center on the East Coast, then went on to Los Angeles. Peter's mission was to put together a band and produce an album on which James's voice and guitar would be the focal points. Among the musicians Peter assembled were Danny Kortchmar on guitar, Russ Kunkel on drums, Chris

Darrow on fiddle, Red Rhodes on steel guitar, and alternately on bass* Bobby West, John London, and Randy Meisner.† When Danny suggested to Peter that I play piano, Peter asked Danny to bring me over for a rehearsal that would be scheduled as soon as James arrived in L.A.

The day after James landed, I went with Danny to Peter's house. I was already a fan of James's songs. I was also a fan of Peter and Gordon. In addition to their string of hits including "A World Without Love," "Nobody I Know," and "I Go to Pieces," the duo had recorded "Crying in the Rain."

Peter's house on Longwood Avenue in the Wilshire district was an elegant old home. Describing a house in Los Angeles as "old" wasn't a negative. It simply meant that the house had been built as long ago as thirty years. With his trademark red hair and eyeglasses, the man who answered the door could only have been Peter. His British accent, upper-class background, and natural generosity made him a casting director's dream for the role of sociable host. He embraced Danny, then welcomed me with a warm handshake. As we walked through the foyer I could see other rooms. In contrast to the elegance of the exterior style and location, inside, the décor resembled that of a rehearsal studio. The living room was devoid of furniture in any conventional sense. There were acoustic and electric guitars set in stands, a set of drums in front of large arched windows, several microphones, two guitar amps, one bass amp, a couple of mismatched straight-backed chairs in front of a large fireplace (the latter showing no evidence of use), a few odd tables on which to put drinks, charts, pens, and ashtrays,

---

*Lee Sklar did not play on *Sweet Baby James*.

†Randy Meisner was a founding member of Eagles. N.B.: Many people say "the Eagles," but their friend Steve Martin reports that Glenn Frey has always insisted that the band's name is Eagles without "the." Official Eagles material released by the band supports Martin's story.

several stools for the bass and guitar players, stereo components and speakers on the floor, and wires everywhere. There was also a grand piano. And there was James, sitting on a tall wooden stool tucked into the curve of the piano.

It was the first time I'd seen James since the Night Owl. He was now twenty-one. He didn't notice us at first because he was playing the guitar softly, his head bent with close attention. Once again I had the impression of how tall and angular he was, and even with his head down, his presence was compelling. When he looked up and saw Danny and me, he looked blank for a second. Then, realizing that it was Danny, James smiled broadly, set his guitar into a stand, unfolded his body, and stood up to embrace his friend.

Danny said, "James. You remember Carole."

James turned to me and said, "Sure!"

As we shook hands and smiled with mutual pleasure, our eyes met. That was the first moment of our decades-long friendship.

Peter had booked the rest of the band to arrive later so that James and I could play, just the two of us, before they showed up. I sat down at the piano and played a few chords. Nice piano, I thought as James picked up his guitar. Soon James and I were playing and singing songs we both knew—some by him, some by me, and some by other artists.

Magical...? Transformative...? Timeless...? Adjectives fall short. It was as if I were playing with an extension of myself. Every time I thought of a chord or note that I wanted James to play or sing at that moment, he was already there. Our musical vocabulary was the same, and we found that we had an impeccable vocal blend. Piano, guitar, chords, notes, and vocal harmonies rolled around each other like puppies playing in a pile of newly cut grass.

After a while, James asked Danny to join us. Danny leaped forward, plugged in his guitar, executed a few licks, and then the three of us were jamming. As a trio we had a similar familiarity, but with Danny added there was an exponential increase in volume and energy. We might have continued for hours, but Peter was listening for the doorbell. As soon as the rest of the band arrived, we stopped playing, exchanged greetings, and then we began to rehearse the new material.

With Peter producing, James recorded *Sweet Baby James* at Sunset Sound in 1969.

That year, in addition to being a mom to my seven- and nine-year-old daughters, I played and sang on James's album, recorded my own *Writer* album, and wrote songs and made demos for other artists. After Warner Bros. released *Sweet Baby James* in February 1970, James started appearing in small venues around the United States to promote the new album. As his manager, who was also a friend, Peter traveled with James and did his utmost to keep him clean and sober. He wasn't always successful in keeping the darkness of James's addiction at bay. Even so, James's talent and charisma shone through brightly enough to build a following.

The next time I saw James was in the summer of 1970. As before, he was staying with the Ashers, and Danny had invited me to join him in catching up with his old friends. Peter's house had changed quite a bit since I had last been there. Now the interior had an elegance to match the outside. Peter's spacious living room still had the fireplace and grand piano, but without the drums to block the view I could see the greenery framed by the large arched windows. There were new stereo components and speakers in a proper cabinet, two sofas, several comfortable armchairs, small side tables with coasters on which one could set a drink, and a coffee table on its own legs.

Danny had already told me that James was preparing to go on a college tour to further promote *Sweet Baby James*. The band would include Kootch on lead guitar, Lee Sklar on bass, and Russ Kunkel on drums. On this visit, after about twenty minutes of casual conversation, James migrated over to his guitar and picked it up. Danny plugged his guitar into an amp artfully tucked among the décor. I sat down at the piano. With Peter encouraging us, clapping, singing along, and sometimes joining in on acoustic guitar, we played whatever came to mind. We laughed, sang, and let the music pour out of us. We were four individual musicians riding a collective wave of easy enjoyment.

When at last we stopped for a break, Peter seized the moment and invited me to join James's band on tour. I was no more inclined to go on the road than I'd been previously, but Peter had anticipated my concerns about leaving Charlie and the girls. He explained that going on the road with James wouldn't take me away from my family for long periods of time. The tour would involve six to eight college shows on weekends during the fall of 1970, with trips home in between.

The opportunity to play music with James again was difficult to resist. After consulting with Charlie, the girls, and Willa Mae, I said yes.

It was during one of those weekends that I wrote "So Far Away" completely on my own. I had Charlie in mind personally and James in mind musically. James's songs can be deceptive in their apparent simplicity. They're actually quite complex and not always predictable. James creates subtle distinctions that make every verse and chorus not quite like any other, yet each new section feels completely familiar and natural. I was so inspired by James's writing style that I began to incorporate it into my own songs. I had developed the skill of writing for other artists in the Aldon years. Though I wasn't writing *for* James, it was his voice I heard in my head while I was writing "So Far Away."

It was on a night during another one of those weekends— more than a year after Neil Armstrong and Buzz Aldrin took "one small step for [a] man, one giant leap for mankind" on the actual *moon!*—that James figuratively dragged me kicking and screaming to the front of the stage. Later, I learned that he had been looking for an opportunity to help me make the transition from sideman to performer. Once he'd made the decision that the transition would happen that night, he was more assertive about it than I'd ever seen him be about anything.

With all due respect to the astronauts, from where I sat, the moon was a lot closer than the front of the stage.

Chapter Eleven

Pre-Loved

$\mathcal{I}$'ve always enjoyed being a sideman. For the record, it is "side-man" regardless of gender. It was especially fun to be a sideman with Danny, Russ, Lee, and James, who went out of their way to make me feel welcome. As the focus of attention, James had the responsibility of directing the flow of the show and making sure the audience was having a good time. Part of his audiences' enjoyment came from James's generosity in showing off the musicianship of members of his band, to whom he always gave plenty of latitude to stretch out within the framework of a song. Sometimes I was so entertained by the musical interplay among my bandmates that I forgot what I was supposed to be playing. Along with the audience, I was in awe of Danny's guitar work. I couldn't fathom how he managed to come up with so many different inventive solos night after night. As the tour progressed, I became quite comfortable as James's sideman.

As I write this, I remember my grandmother saying, "Kehdeleh dollink, dunt get too comf'tah-bull."

What happened next was the opposite of comfortable, and I never saw it coming.

Most of the songs James performed were self-penned, but sometimes he sang other people's compositions. Originally released by the Drifters in 1963, Gerry's and my song "Up on the Roof" was one of James's favorites. It was on the set list the night we were to perform at Queens College.

Usually James performed the first part of his set alone, accompanying himself on acoustic guitar. James and I were waiting with the rest of the band in the backstage area when the house lights flickered, signaling that the show was about to begin.

James leaned down and said, "I'd like you to sing lead on 'Up on the Roof' tonight."

It was a long moment before I fully absorbed what he had just said.

"Oh, no...n-no...please...James...I couldn't...I mean... *you* sing it so beautifully..."

I stopped, took a breath, and exhaled as I spoke.

"James," I said. "Don't make me sing lead in front of all those people!"

James wasn't having it. "Don't worry," he said. "They'll love you."

"James, I can't do this. It's my alma mater!"

"You'll be fine," he said. "We'll do it in your key."

Oy, I thought. He knows my key.

"Tell the band," he said, unnecessarily, since they were right there. And with that he hoisted his guitar and strode onstage. A few audience members caught sight of him and began clapping; it became a wave of excitement and then an ocean of applause from the entire audience.

I stood immobile. They were welcoming James. They didn't know me. I was James's piano player. And I was terrified.

That night James played and sang, as he always did, with confidence and authority. There was no sign of shyness when he sang. And when he spoke to the audience between songs, his down-to-earth demeanor gave the impression that he was speaking completely off the cuff about whatever had just come into his mind. Normally his performances and patter had a calming effect on me, but not that night. He was so good. I couldn't imagine following him.

Soon it was time for me to go on as James's sideman. Thankfully, my fingers played the piano part on "Fire and Rain" and "Country Road" without my having to consciously direct them, leaving my mind free to careen around the white-knuckle edges of panic.

Some friend! I thought over the quarter-note chords in the first verse of "Fire and Rain." Why is he putting me on the spot? Is he *really* going to make me do this?

Not only was he going to make me do it, he was going to make me do it without a rehearsal! With terror running through my head like a team of track racers sprinting for the finish line, we ended the song that preceded "Up on the Roof." Prolonging my agony, James chose that moment to introduce the band, player by player, as he does at some point during every show. That night, he saved me for last. Before saying my name, he mentioned some of the songs that I had cowritten that the audience was likely to know. Then he announced that I had gone to Queens College. When the audience applauded I wasn't sure whether they were applauding for me, the songs, or their school.

Then James pronounced my name.

"Ladies and gentlemen: Carole King!"

I could either freeze in place and pray that the stage would open up and drop me into the basement, or I could go ahead and sing the song. I took a breath and brought my hands to the piano.

As I played the opening chord, the lights around me dimmed, leaving me alone in the spotlight. My voice came out sounding timid.

When this old world starts getting me down
And people are just too much for me to face . . .

I continued through the second verse and began the first bridge.

On the roof it's peaceful as can be . . .

I was wondering how I would make it through the rest of the song when suddenly I felt the audience make that infinitesimal yet impossibly vast transition from tentative to attentive. I may have been unfamiliar to them, but the song wasn't.

And there the world below can't bother me . . .

They were with me.

By the time I got to the second bridge, to my surprise, I was there, too. I looked over at my bandmates, and every man had a big smile on his face. The biggest smile was on the face of my sideman, James Taylor, who was playing and singing, in my key, parts that fit perfectly with what I was doing.

Together we sang:

On the roof's the only place I know
Where you just have to wish to make it so
Let's go up on the roof . . .

The audience's warmth filled me with confidence. I played the lead piano instrumental with gusto, and then some of the audience joined us in singing the last bridge. My mind was still running along parallel tracks. On one track I was performing; on the other I was tremendously touched to see all those people holding hands, swaying, and singing along with James and me.

Right smack dab in the middle of town
I found a paradise that's trouble-proof . . .

On one track I was aware of leading the audience; on the other I was thinking, Leave it to Gerry Goffin to find such an evocative description of an earthly paradise—"trouble-proof"—and have it rhyme with "roof."

When the song ended, the audience clapped and cheered and wouldn't stop. They loved the song and, as James had predicted, they loved me because I'd written it. I basked in the applause, and when they still wouldn't stop, James waved me up and I took a bow. Then James stepped up to the microphone and everyone, including me, remembered whose show it was. I sat down, flushed with exhilaration, while the audience became quiet, ready for the next James Taylor song. As before, I had no idea what my fingers were playing, but thankfully they still knew what to do.

Later that night, in one of those insightful moments that come just before we fall asleep, I understood that rather than putting me on the spot, James had given me a priceless gift. He had set me up for a favorable reception from the audience. James's introduction and choice of song had virtually guaranteed that I would be pre-loved. My inaugural experience as a lead performer was successful because of a thoughtful send-off from a generous, caring friend. I will always be grateful to James for putting me on the path to become a confident performing artist, and also for being an excellent example of how to perform unselfconsciously with joy and integrity.

Chapter Twelve

Musical Studios

*P*eople often ask if I knew, when I was recording *Tapestry*, that it would become one of the biggest-selling albums in popular music, or that it would touch so many people.

How could I know that? I was simply doing what I'd always done—recording songs that I had written or cowritten. I was the musical half of the writing team through whom the songs had emerged. I wasn't in the same league vocally as Aretha Franklin, Joni Mitchell, or Barbra Streisand (whom I considered *"real* singers"), but I knew how to convey the mood and emotion of a song with an honest, straight-from-the-heart interpretation. If quality of songs and integrity of presentation were factors in *Tapestry*'s success, so were the timing of its release, an extraordinary confluence of good luck, and the determination of Lou Adler to ensure that the album would be heard by as many people as possible.

Except for my publishing rights, which were owned by Screen Gems, Lou was directly involved with everything I did as a performing artist. He was my manager, record company, and producer. It was Lou who helped select the songs to record, Lou who chose Hank Cicalo to be our recording engineer, and Lou who made sure we got studio time at A&M. With the Carpenters recording in Studio A and Joni Mitchell recording *Blue* down the hall in Studio C with Henry Lewy engineering, Lou and I would be recording with Hank Cicalo in Studio B.

Seven blocks east, Peter and James were recording *Mud Slide Slim and the Blue Horizon* at Sunset Sound with Richard Orshoff at the control board. A constant stream of singers, musicians, friends, and family flowed in and out of the recording studios along Sunset Boulevard. At A&M we commuted down the hall. Sometimes we commuted between A&M and Sunset Sound. In New York I would have walked the seven blocks. Now that I was living in Los Angeles, where people thought nothing of driving half a block to buy a newspaper, I adopted a "when in Rome" policy. When I wasn't working on my own album I drove to Sunset Sound to play as a sideman and sing background on James's songs. Sometimes I rode over with Kootch, who was playing on both albums. Periodically James came over to A&M to play acoustic guitar and sing background on my record. Physical proximity to me and romantic proximity to James brought Joni's beautiful voice to both James's and my albums. Sometimes it seemed as if James and I were recording one massive album in two different studios.

Studio C had a reddish wood Steinway piano that everyone said was really special. One morning I was able to slip in and try that piano out. I couldn't help but agree; there really was something extraordinary about it. It felt good to play, and its exceptional sound resonated with Lou and Hank as well. Unfortunately, the red Steinway also resonated with Joni and Henry Lewy, which led to Joni and me vying for time in Studio C to record basic tracks. Unknown to me at the time, Hank made several attempts to move the red Steinway into B, but Joni and Henry wouldn't allow it.

When we learned that Studio C was available one night, we grabbed it. First Charlie and I arrived, then the rest of the rhythm section, then Lou. The band that night consisted of Charlie on electric bass, Joel O'Brien on drums, Danny on guitar, and me at the piano. All of us including Lou milled casually around the coffee machine discussing the relative merits of various Thai restaurants, the new speakers at the Whisky, and which jazz saxophonist currently reigned supreme. We felt no particular sense of urgency until the studio manager came in to inform Lou that we had Studio C for only three hours and then Joni was coming in.

We scrambled to our places in the studio and rehearsed "I Feel the Earth Move." Hank made a few microphone adjustments and then we began recording. I usually sang during rehearsals but didn't sing while we were recording a basic track so I could focus on the interplay between my piano and the other instruments. It took no more than three takes for us to get the rhythm track for "I Feel the Earth Move" that is still heard today on the *Tapestry* album. To suggest an earthquake, I concluded with a continuous cluster of notes on the piano cascading rapidly downward in pitch until the band and I ended the run together on a final C bass note. Later, while mixing, Lou made the executive decision to leave out my earthquake ending. He thought the last thing the public should hear was my voice singing the words "tumblin' down." Lou was right to leave the earthquake ending off the album, but in concert I still perform it as originally recorded.

After "I Feel the Earth Move," Charlie switched to acoustic bass for "You've Got a Friend" and "(You Make Me Feel Like A) Natural Woman." By keeping technical adjustments to a minimum on both tracks, Lou and Hank were able to capture on tape the close musical and personal connection between Charlie and me. We managed to complete three basic tracks before Joni arrived. Rather than putting us under pressure, the knowledge that we had limited time in Studio C had energized us, made us more efficient, and set a towering standard for the rest of the album.

After a few more sessions in B with the rhythm section we completed all the basic tracks and went on to overdubbing vocals, additional keyboards, and a string quartet. Now that we no longer needed Studio C, we were ready to take advantage of what Hank had said all along were the attributes of B. In 2010, Hank shared with me on the phone his recollections of the *Tapestry* sessions and A&M's studios:

"We never worked on *Tapestry* in Studio A. The Carpenters had it locked up. I didn't like A for you anyway. It was too big. We could never get that intimate feel. And C was too small. B was just the right size. All the great studios in town were the size of B.

"I liked that I could set a mood in B with the lights. And I always put the players where everyone could see each other. Your piano was in the middle of the room, with the drums where you could see them and the drummer could see you. I put everyone around you in a semicircle so everyone could see you because you conducted with your head. I always changed the control room lighting for the mood of the song, and I did the same with the lighting in the studio."

I never knew any of that.

Chapter Thirteen

Technology

$\mathcal{I}$ was lucky to have Lou Adler as a producer and Hank Cicalo as a recording engineer. Some producers claimed to be able to "fix it in the mix," but that phrase was never in Hank's or Lou's vocabulary. They knew that a mix could turn out well only if they had captured a great performance, and they created an environment in the studio and control room that would be most favorable to that outcome. They also knew that a bad mix could ruin a great performance and they worked diligently to make sure that never happened on their watch. I believe that along with the talent of all the writers and musicians, it was Hank's skills in the mixing room combined with Lou's instinct and A&M's state-of-the-art equipment that put *Tapestry* across the finish line.

In the early seventies, state-of-the-art equipment included a console that I found beyond my ability to comprehend until an assistant engineer explained that it consisted of multiple identical modules. Sound was recorded through magnetic reel-to-reel tape and analog recording machines with calibrated motors that moved the spools of tape at a predetermined speed. If we wanted to lower the key so I could reach a high note, Hank slowed the machine down and then brought it back up to speed after I had sung the note. Did I sound like a chipmunk? No one would notice. An editing or splicing block with slots for a straight or angled cut allowed an engineer to cut and reconnect audiotape with precision. Did we want to take out everything between the end of the first verse and the beginning of the third chorus? A skilled engineer with a sharp razor blade and an even sharper sense of where the downbeats matched could do that.

During the overdub phase of *Tapestry*, Lou suggested that I layer background vocals in my own voice on some of the tracks. In the early sixties Gerry and I had accomplished layering by recording back and forth between two machines, but after a few overdubs the tape became too noisy. That didn't stop Donnie from releasing Little Eva's "The Loco-Motion." Most people would say that the first sound on that recording was the locomotive snare drum. Not so. The first sound on that track was tape hiss from all the overdubs back and forth. But a clean recording of layered overdubs was possible in the early seventies because of Sel-Sync,* an innovation that allowed me to hear previously recorded material through a "play" head at the same time as I played or sang new material onto a blank track through a "record" head. Somehow the technology compensated for the physical gap between the play head and the record head and synchronized the timing of the old material with the new. For an artist who thrived on improvising new layers over previous ones, Sel-Sync was a godsend.

After mixing came mastering. A master was a disc cut on a lathe with a stylus that converted the recorded signal into grooves

---

*Sel-Sync (Selective Synchronous) recording was developed at Ampex in the mid-fifties primarily by Ross Snyder, Mort Fujii, and Les Paul. Les Paul brought the concept of multilayered sound-on-sound performances to public popularity in 1951 with the voice of his wife, Mary Ford, on "How High the Moon" and "The World Is Waiting for the Sunrise."

on the disc. The master was used to stamp out the mothers from which vinyl records were pressed. Like photo negatives, mothers were the reverse of the final product. Where masters had grooves, mothers had ridges that would recreate the grooves in the vinyl. I understood master-mother-vinyl, but I would never understand how sound became grooves. The good news was, I didn't need to. My job was to create a song and perform it, then watch in awe as highly skilled people used technology to convey music from microphones to tape, then to a master, a mother, and ultimately a vinyl disc with a label and a hole in the middle.

In the fifties and early sixties singles were predominant. Singles were seven-inch black vinyl discs that played at 45 revolutions per minute, with a one-and-a-half-inch hole in the middle of each disc. On a multispeed phonograph, playing 45s required individual plastic adapters or a drop changer that fit over the spindle. A drop changer held up to ten 45s stacked several inches above the turntable. When the phonograph was turned on, the first 45 would drop and the sound would be transmitted through the stylus to an amplifier and speakers. After the first disc finished and the needle reached a predetermined spot near the center post, the machine swung the arm out of the way. The second disc would drop down, and so on, one at a time, until all ten discs were stacked on the turntable. Sometimes the needle got stuck and played a scratchy sound until the arm was lifted manually. It was beyond our imagination that producers of something called "hip-hop" would deliberately put the sound of scratching from a stuck needle on a track and call it music.

In the early seventies long-playing albums (LPs) were favored by most music fans. LPs were twelve-inch vinyl discs meant to be played at 33⅓ revolutions per minute. Singles were still being pressed but were used mostly for promotion. Artists were shunning the industry's prior custom of releasing albums with one hit and eleven tracks of filler. Instead they strove to include as many high-quality tracks as a disc could accommodate. Other advantages of an LP were that a listener didn't have to get up as often to change the record, and the twelve-inch-square covers could be adorned with the psychedelic art, photos, lyrics, and liner notes that listeners prized almost as much as the music.

Continuous-loop eight-track players were popular in rural communities because they traveled well in cars and trucks. Cassette tapes took over in the eighties until compact discs replaced them in the nineties. By the dawn of the twenty-first century most people's CD collections had disappeared into their computers, where they reappeared on the screen as MP3s and other dots, letters, and numbers that enabled consumers to download for free what they used to have to pay for. Distraught record companies aimed lawsuits at consumers like buckshot until Apple hit the bull's-eye with iTunes.

The equipment we used in 1970 was a link in a chain of audio technology that some say began with the sixteen-inch transcription discs, or V-discs, on which Billie Holiday's performances were recorded. Today we can see audio on a computer screen. We can record, change, manipulate, and even create notes, sounds, tempos, loops, and other elements of rhythm, melody, and words. If I sing "tonigh" and I want to hear that final "t," I can copy and paste an audio image of the "t" from the end of the word "beat" elsewhere in the song, so then we hear "tonight" as I intended to sing it. Using software such as Pro Tools and Auto-Tune, an artist can record a sophisticated, multilayered track on a laptop at a desk in a hotel room for (depending on which hotel) less than it cost back in the day to rent, let alone purchase, a studio-quality multi-track machine. The technology is changing so rapidly that some recording applications in use today could be obsolete by the time you read this.

Technology is not necessarily helpful in my hands. Trying to record and manipulate audio takes me away from the emotional trajectory of a song. In the hands of engineers such as Hank Cicalo and, in my later studio work, Rudy Guess, technology can be another instrument. Some might argue that it's the most important instrument because it records and enhances all the others. Others believe technology is making music less musical. Which brings me to a question I'm asked consistently in interviews and discussions:

"Has today's technology lowered the quality of music from that of previous generations?"

I believe that as long as people have hearts and minds and the capacity to laugh, cry, dance, feel, and fall in and out of love, a good song will always find an audience because it connects us to our humanity. If technology can help people make that connection, I'm a fan.

Chapter Fourteen

Tapestry Snapshots

I was so deeply involved in the making of *Tapestry* that it's difficult for me to describe those happy, productive weeks in a logical or linear fashion. But these random scenes remain vibrantly alive for me in memory snapshots:

- James and Joni sitting on adjoining stools, their heads almost touching as they whisper to each other and share a private moment before Hank is ready for them to sing background harmonies on "Will You Love Me Tomorrow."

Though James and Joni are singing on separate mics, their closeness is an almost physical presence. I can't tell you what specific frequency it occupies, but the intimacy between them can still be heard and felt on this recording.

- Me at the microphone recording a scratch vocal with utter abandon, knowing I don't have to strive for perfection.

After a basic track has been recorded, I quickly record a scratch or guide vocal so other musicians and vocalists can hear the song while overdubbing additional parts. Because I love singing over a great basic track my musicians have just delivered, the scratch vocal is often my most heartfelt performance, and just as often we can't use it because I'm too hoarse from having sung the song multiple times while the musicians were learning it.

- The sight of my face in the glass between studio and booth reflecting my joy as I improvise layered vocals and keyboards over the basic track and lead vocal.

I have no idea what I'll do on the next overdub until I sing along with what's already there. Layer by layer, I weave an aural tapestry out of sound waves. Some of my favorite moments in recording are when I hear a perfect vocal or piano part come out of me with no plan or forethought. Even better: it was captured on tape!

- Having just finished a take, I'm in the dimly lit studio waiting for Lou to tell me what he thought of my performance.

I see Lou talking to Hank, but I can't hear them through the triple glass window. The talkback button, controlled by Lou, is my lifeline.

- Me sitting on a high wooden bench in Studio B surrounded by a Hammond organ, a couple of electric keyboards, assorted microphones and cables, and the omnipresent candles and incense.

The dim light makes it difficult for me to see the keyboard controls as I search for the right sound to create a dark, spacious mood for the recording of "Tapestry."

- Me fussing with my headphones to get them in the correct position so I can hear what Lou is hearing in the control room and also hear live in the room the string quartet playing the arrangement I wrote the night before.

As I prepare to conduct the quartet I worry that I won't do it right, but the musicians encourage me to conduct with whatever movement comes naturally. "Don't worry," they say. "We'll do the rest." And they do.

- Lou, Hank, assistant engineer Norm Kinney, the musicians, and me crowded in the control room listening to the take that Hank has just recorded with such efficiency that not one creative moment was lost. I have no idea that Hank is building a sound that will endure through many decades.

Playback for a band can sometimes be fraught with "more me" syndrome, with each player wanting to hear more of his or her part. Lou wisely keeps my vocal down for the band playback so they can enjoy hearing themselves way up in the mix, but everyone knows that the final mix will have a more realistic balance, i.e., more *me*.

- Charlie in the studio punching in a bass note.

The technology to move a note up or down on a computer screen has yet to be invented, but with Sel-Sync it takes less than a minute to punch in the right note. A wry-smile truth among bass players is that the best take is invariably the one with the bass mistake. If the band achieves a good performance without a bass mistake, we know we haven't peaked yet.

- Lou quietly making suggestions, keeping the process going, never allowing anything to compromise the integrity of a song or the relatively simple presentation that will become a hallmark of my work.

- My daughters and their friends flowing in and out of our sessions in jeans or long dresses with their hair pulled up in flowered headbands.

The only time Louise and Sherry weren't allowed in the studio was when the RECORD light was on. Otherwise they and their friends wandered in and out at will. Sometimes, when I had to work at night, Sherry or Louise, at home with Willa Mae, would call to ask if they could pleeeeeease do their homework in the morning.

"No," I'd say. "You need to do it tonight!"

Other times—inconsistent mom that I was—I'd say, "All right. Just don't forget to set your alarm!"

Sometimes the girls needed me to settle a dispute about who left whose sweater crumpled in a ball at the bottom of their closet.

"No, Mom, it can't wait. We need you to deal with this now!"

"I don't care whose sweater it is," I said, channeling King Solomon. "You pick it up, your sister can hang it up, and then both of you go finish your homework!"

I may have been a professional songwriter and recording artist in the hallowed halls of A&M Studios, but to my daughters I was the homework police.

Chapter Fifteen

In Retrospect

One of my greatest joys as a songwriter has always been hearing different interpretations of a song. I've mentioned Gerry's and my original demo of "Natural Woman" starting out one way, the version Aretha released being considerably different, and my version on *Tapestry* representing a third way. My live performance of "Natural Woman" with a full band is unlike either of my earlier versions. Since Aretha recorded what I consider the definitive version, "Natural Woman" has been recorded by many great artists, among them Céline Dion, Mary J. Blige, and (with a small but important lyric adjustment) James Ingram, Rod Stewart, and Bobby Womack.

To develop such interpretations, an artist typically works with a producer. Some producers are more effective than others. Lou Adler was one of the most effective in the business. Among his many attributes, for me the most valuable was his ability to give his artists a safe space in which to be creative. Lou had ideas of his own, but he saw himself mostly as a facilitator. Like all the great sidemen, he knew when not to play. In addition to offering his own ideas when they were needed, Lou listened carefully to my suggestions, and if they couldn't be implemented at the time, he would remember and find a way to incorporate them. It's difficult for me to give an example because our respective ideas are so thoroughly integrated into the whole album. And even as he was minutely attentive to every detail, he never lost sight of the big picture. For Lou that meant preserving the soul and integrity of the music while coordinating the work of the artist, band, engineers, graphic artists, photographers, and business people to create a package that would be commercially successful. In 1970, when many producers and recording artists purported to disdain commercial success, the kid from Boyle Heights never lost sight of it.

Our strengths were complementary. Where I lacked patience, Lou persevered through extreme tedium and repetition. He could listen to the same thing over and over with intense concentration on infinitesimal but important details. Often Lou and Hank handled the preliminary stages of mixing and then had me come in with fresh ears. After they had spent hours experimenting with where to put the cymbals and percussion in the stereo pan in relation to Danny's rhythm guitar and my piano, I'd come in and say, "Try bringing the reverb down on my lead vocal at the beginning of the first verse," and then other things would fall into place. It was a team effort in which each of us contributed valuable ideas.

It was during the mixing of *Tapestry* that I discovered a listening perspective that I called the "other room listen." I asked Hank to play an almost final mix a few times with the door open while I went out to the lounge, got a cup of tea, skimmed through a magazine, and exchanged pleasantries with one of the studio employees on her way to the ladies' room. Hearing the mix with only partial concentration allowed my subconscious mind to lead me directly to any necessary corrections. It might be a too-soft piano fill, a too-loud snare drum, or the lead vocal out of balance with the background vocals. But when a mix was right, the "other room listen" confirmed it.

Another system of checks and balances involved listening on a variety of speakers. Mostly we listened through the massive Altecs that dominated the corners of the control room with a bass level that foreshadowed the woofers on wheels that would emerge later in the twentieth century. As well as listening through the Altecs, Lou often listened through headphones so he could hear the discrete left, right, and center separation more clearly. Years later, when I asked Lou why he used the headphones so much, he said, "I always liked hearing your voice and piano in the middle of the top of my head." As we got closer to a final mix we switched alternately to smaller speakers such as the Auratones* perched on the bridge of the console or the tinny, monaural car radio speaker directly in front of us that replicated the conditions under which most people would be listening. If a mix sounded good through all four systems, we took it to the next level: the "overnight listen" in which we brought acetates home, played them on our respective stereos, and got further input from friends and family members.

Lou came up with the sequence of the tracks on *Tapestry*. On analog vinyl albums and cassette tapes there was an interval approximately midway through, during which the listener had to turn the product over. Until CDs made that interval obsolete, an album sequence had to take that pause into account. Knowing that pacing could make or break an album, I suggested several different orders for Lou to try, but we always kept coming back to his sequence. Now I can't imagine it any other way.

There was an actual tapestry. Inside the original double album cover is an image of the needlepoint I worked on when I wasn't

---

*Auratone speakers were used in the seventies by many studios for what is now called "nearfield monitoring." In the eighties, Yamaha NS10s replaced Auratones as the industry standard for nearfield monitoring. Yamaha has since discontinued the NS10s, reportedly because they can't get that kind of wood any more.

playing or singing. You can see where I stitched the words "thank you" before I gave it to Lou.

People often preface their *Tapestry* story with, "You've probably heard this story a million times." But each individual account of how *Tapestry* affected someone's life is important to me because it's important to that person. While we were recording the album I wasn't thinking about all the people who might be affected by it, nor was I thinking about the level of success it might attain. I just wanted to get the songs on tape, enjoy the process with friends and fellow musicians, and maybe get some radio play. Hearing years later from people who grew up in countries around the world about how much the album had meant to them was something I couldn't have imagined. Whatever the reason, I'm thankful that I was given this uncommon opportunity to create something that touched so many people in a positive way.

Tapestry's success was undoubtedly facilitated by its release at a time in twentieth-century cultural history when people were beginning to turn inward to explore the emotions about which other songwriters and I were writing. The contemporaneous success of *Tapestry*, *Sweet Baby James*, Joni Mitchell's *Blue*, and other great albums by singer-songwriters who performed their own songs seems to bear that out. Reviewers dubbed us "singer-songwriters." In an earlier century we would have been called troubadours.

Chapter Sixteen

The Troubadour

*I*n the early 1970s, a booking at Doug Weston's Troubadour in West Hollywood could put an artist on a fast track to fame. That was the case with many singer-songwriters, including Jackson Browne, Joni Mitchell, and Elton John. Doug's club had a reputation for being an encouraging place both to be and see a new artist. Audience members who had enjoyed a performer's early appearances there took even greater pleasure in going back to see that performer at the Troubadour, knowing that she or he was drawing huge crowds in much larger venues. I didn't know until later that Doug's contracts required performers to come back and play the club periodically for very little money no matter how successful they became. My first appearance at the Troubadour was as an audience member.

When I learned that James Taylor was scheduled to headline at the club for a week starting November 24, 1970, I was just thinking about how much fun it would be to see my friend play there when Peter Asher rang to ask if I was available to play those dates as a member of James's band.

I was.

Peter then called Lou to enlist his help in persuading me to open for James as an artist in my own right. With *Tapestry* about to be released, Lou was happy to make that call. He was less happy, though not surprised, when I told him I wasn't ready to do an entire set on my own, and I definitely wasn't ready to do it at the hottest club in town.

"You're already going to be playing with James," Lou said. "All you have to do is sing your own songs just as if you were playing for friends in your living room."

"It's not the same."

"Remember when you told me how much you enjoyed performing 'Up on the Roof' in James's set?"

"Ye-es," I said, wishing I hadn't told him that. "But that was just one song in someone else's show. It's not the same as performing a whole set."

"Would you feel more comfortable if Charlie played string bass with you on some of the songs?"

"Maybe."

"What if we brought in the rest of the string quartet?"

He was referring to violinist Barry Socher, violist David Campbell,* and cellist Terry King.

It *would* be a beautiful presentation.

"Okay. I'll do it."

Charlie and I rehearsed, the quartet and I rehearsed, and I rehearsed alone until I felt as prepared as I would ever be. I made a long burgundy-colored velvet dress for opening night. My hair would be done by—no one. It was my hair. I wouldn't require much makeup either. I was a natural woman in life, and that's who I'd be at the Troubadour.

---

*David Campbell and Bibbe Hansen are the parents of the composer, recording artist, and performer Beck.

On opening night there was a line around the block. This was not unexpected. James's show was reportedly one of the best around. More than two-thirds of the crowd were record industry people and friends of James. The rest were fans. There was overlap in that many industry people were James's friends, fans, or both. When the show finally started, it was well beyond fashionably late. Every table was filled to capacity, with barely enough room for the waitresses in their skimpy outfits to sidle past each other with their trays held high above their heads to deliver the overpriced drinks that were the lifeblood of Doug Weston's income stream.

As the opening act, I wouldn't have a chance to ease into any kind of comfort zone. There would be no pre-loved introduction. The lights would go down and then I would be *out there*, just me and a piano and three hundred people expecting me to be really good. Charlie and the quartet would join me later in the set.

Looking down from the dressing room upstairs, I could see the stage. It was little more than a platform, roughly twelve by six feet, which stood two and a half feet above the audience. I checked my hair in the mirror. It was still my hair. I double-checked my makeup, now even more natural because my blush and lipstick had faded. I began whispering to myself: "...friends in my living room...friends in my living room..."

Then it was time. The lights dimmed to half and I walked down the stairs. From the sound and light booth, a disembodied voice intoned, "Ladies and gentlemen...Carole King!" and the house went to black except for the bar and the stage. I walked onstage and bowed to acknowledge the audience, then I walked over to the piano, sat on the bench, and looked down to make sure that a glass of water had been placed next to the upstage leg of my piano. (It had.)

My first song was "I Feel the Earth Move." I played the pounding bass notes of the piano intro and then launched into the first verse. I was too nervous to remember to sing as if I were singing for friends in my living room, but, as usual, the song carried me through. I completed the earthquake ending and then waited five agonizing years during the infinitesimal pause between the ending and the audience's realization that the song was over. Their response was encouraging. I bowed my head and said quickly, "Thank you very much," and bent down to take a sip of water. Sitting up again, I ventured a shy smile over my right shoulder to acknowledge the audience members who would mostly see my back because I was facing the other way. Then I started the boogie blues shuffle that kicked off "Smackwater Jack." Thank God the song was up-tempo. It was fun to sing. After the last chord rang out, the audience was genuinely warm, which made me less nervous about my singing, but I still had no idea what to do or say between songs other than "Thank you very much." My sense of theater was telling me that I needed to say something more, and I needed to say it right then, before the third song. My mind was racing.

Should I welcome them? Good evening, ladies and gentlemen. No. Too formal.

I could ask if everyone could hear me...or how they liked my dress...or I could bellow, "Are ya ready to rock and roooooooollll?"

No, no, and *no*.

As the applause began to die down I saw six people at a table in the back talking animatedly to each other about something I was certain had nothing to do with my performance. The rest of the audience was looking at me expectantly. Panic began to set in. What should I say?

All of a sudden, the same voice that had introduced me came over the loudspeaker.

"Uh, Carole...we're gonna have to ask everyone to leave the club in an orderly fashion. Don't worry, it's just a rumor, but the L.A.P.D. heard that there might be a bomb in here."

I didn't think. I just spoke.

"As long as it's not me."

The audience's laughter broke the tension, and everyone filed out as directed. People were in a surprisingly good frame of mind considering what had just been announced. Twenty minutes later we were escorted back into the club with the assurance of the L.A.P.D. that there was in fact no bomb. With everyone reseated, I came back to finish my set, and what do you know? I was happy to be there! Not only was I excited about the songs I was playing, but the interruption had just forced me through a barrier that had been there only because I had created it. Once surmounted, it disappeared and the audience responded with unbounded enthusiasm. Performing wasn't something to fear; it was merely a larger circle of collaboration. The more I communicated my joy to the audience, the more joy they communicated back to me. All I needed to do was sing with conviction, speak my truth from the heart, honestly and straightforwardly, and offer my words, ideas, and music to the audience as if it were one collective friend that I'd known for a very long time.

I had found the key to success in performing. It was to be authentically myself.

Chapter Seventeen

J Is for Jump

In 1970 Danny and Charlie formed a new band with Ralph Schuckett on keyboards, Michael Ney on drums, and Gale Haness singing lead. Their name, Jo Mama, was a play on the "yo'mama"* verbal sparring they'd heard among jazz musicians.

At first Jo Mama rehearsed in the living room of the house where Gale and Michael were living as a couple. Then three transformative events occurred. First Gale changed her name to Abigale. Then she changed boyfriends from Michael to Danny. Rehearsals were predictably awkward until the third event, in which the band decided by one vote short of unanimous to replace Michael with Joel O'Brien.

Abigale was a powerful performer with an impressive vocal range. She was equally at home singing pop, hard rock, soft rock, gospel, soul, jazz, and R&B.† She was also, as Danny put it, "easy

---

*The "yo'mama" ritual originated with black male slaves. Because they weren't allowed to engage in physical violence, they traded verbal insults: "Yo'mama so ugly she..." "Yeah? Well, yo'mama so dumb she..." And so on.
†A starring role in 1974–75 at the Roxy Theatre in West Hollywood as Janet in *The Rocky Horror Show* would add show tunes to Abigale's list of genres.

on the eyes." With Abigale singing lead, Jo Mama accumulated a repertoire that few white bands could pull off with credibility. They released two albums on Atlantic: *Jo Mama* in 1970, and *J Is for Jump* in 1971.

Following the warm reception in 1970 of James and me at the Troubadour, Peter asked me to open for James and then play as a band member in James's upcoming nationwide tour. We would be away for three weeks, home for a two-week break, then out again for another three weeks. The offer grew sweeter when Peter proposed to have Jo Mama open the show before my set. The James Taylor–Carole King–Jo Mama show would be a three-act extravaganza in which we would all play in each other's sets, culminating in a grand finale in which everyone, including both drummers and both bass players, would join James onstage to bring the show to a rousing conclusion.

Charlie's vote in favor was already cast. He was excited about the opportunity to play, first with Jo Mama, then in my set, and then again in the finale. It took me a little longer to get there. Peter's offer had tremendous appeal, but three weeks was longer than I'd ever left my girls. However, I did have someone reliable to stay with them, and I'd be with them for two weeks in the middle of the tour. After I said yes, I, too, was excited. Being on the road would be an adventure, it would be musical, and it would be fun.

Considering the variety of personalities, romantic attachments, and number of shows on the schedule, a collection of stories from the 1971 tour alone could surely fill a book. What I remember most is the feeling of being part of a big family. This is a common phenomenon on endeavors such as tours, films, shows, circuses, carnivals, and archaeological expeditions, and probably even more intensely so in military service. Thrown together by a common mission, far from home for an extended period of time, people inevitably develop a strong bond. A social hierarchy evolves based on the group's perception of how essential a person is to the overall effort. On tour everyone has an important role, but the buck stops with the headliner, which thankfully on that tour I was not. On a concert tour the headliner is at the top of the pile (a) because it's his or her name on the marquee, and (b) because s/he is paying everyone. The corollary is that the headliner is responsible for making sure the show goes smoothly. It doesn't matter how bad s/he might feel. A headliner has to show up and be a shining star onstage every night.

James was that shining star, and yet he was egalitarian. Every night he began the show by walking onto the stage in street clothes, which looked exactly like his stage clothes. Because headliners usually weren't seen onstage until later in the evening, James's early appearance caused a buzz that gradually built until the entire audience realized: Oh my God, it's James Taylor! They cheered and applauded wildly until James calmed them down with a raised hand, gave Jo Mama a warm introduction, then left the stage.

At first Jo Mama played to half-empty houses while people were still coming in, but once word spread about the unique format of our show and the excellence of Jo Mama, the house was close to full from the jump (for which J was).

And that was only the beginning.

Chapter Eighteen

Herding Cats

*T*he word "cat" as a synonym for musician originated in the world of jazz. My personal definition of a cat is a skilled musician who cares about excellence, values the integrity of the music, and plays his or her instrument with a commitment to enhance the piece. A true cat plays for the sheer joy of playing. Under my definition, orchestral players and background singers also qualify, though orchestral players might not use the word "cat" to describe themselves.

Ever since there have been traveling bands and orchestras, someone in the position of tour manager has had to deal with the inherent difficulties of trying to move a group of cats from point A to point B. Before civil rights became law in the sixties, tour managers with big bands had to contend not only with the natural propensity of cats to scatter but also with the logistics of "white" and "colored" lodging, dining, and bathroom facilities. Add female singers of whatever color into the mix and you have a logistical nightmare far beyond the challenges that faced our tour manager, Jock McLean, in 1971—not that Jock's job was easy.

One morning we had to wake up to catch an impossibly early flight to the next city. Upon leaving our room, Charlie and I saw a couple of musicians (who shall remain nameless) whose rooms were on the same floor. Having gone to sleep barely an hour earlier after a night of drinking and heaven knows what else, they had managed to put their bags out for pickup by the bell staff and were waiting for the elevator. When it arrived, the two cats stumbled into it and we entered behind them. Both were wearing sunglasses. Each peered at the other as if he were unsure whether he was looking at the face of the other guy or his own face in the mirror. Each was probably thinking how messed up the other guy looked and hoping he didn't look that bad. No one spoke. A full three minutes elapsed before any of us thought to look up at the lighted floor numbers. With a sudden rush of clarity, I realized that the numbers weren't changing.

"Oh! Right!" I said, and pushed "L" for lobby.

As soon as the elevator stopped and the door opened, Charlie and I stepped into the lobby. The two cats remained in the elevator, drifting in and out of their early-morning fog. Jock was paying the group's bill at the cashier's desk when he noticed a familiar pair of boots inside the elevator. As the door began to close, Jock ran over and pushed the "up" button just in time. When the door reopened Jock escorted the musicians onto the bus, where they slept soundly in their seats until we arrived at the airport. After Jock had checked the rest of us in, he went back for the two cats and escorted them to the boarding gate, where they slept until it was time to get on the plane. They slept all the way to the next city, and if we hadn't had a gig that night, they'd probably have slept until a reasonable hour for a rock musician to wake up, typically defined as midnight.

James and I both relied heavily on our cats. Even though we

didn't use all the same players, we made no distinction between his cats and mine in terms of affection and respect.*

The first show of the tour began with James's introduction of Jo Mama. With half the audience still drifting in, the members of Jo Mama were uncertain how their set would be received, but they played with a nervous energy that the audience members who were paying attention perceived as excitement. By the end of their set, they looked and sounded confident enough to elicit a fair amount of applause. The band took an exultant bow and left the stage. The lights went up for the first intermission, and the crew began to reset the scene.

Fifteen minutes later I was waiting in the wings. I wouldn't say I was afraid, but the butterflies in my stomach were keenly aware of the importance of my first solo appearance ever on tour. When they called "house to black," most people were back in their seats. The spotlight found James as he walked onstage to introduce me. I entered from stage right, walked to center stage, and reached up to hug him. He reached down to return the hug, waved to the audience, then exited stage left. I walked over to the piano and sat down. It was a very big stage, and I was alone on it. As I prepared to play for thousands of people, I took a breath. Then I dove in and performed the first few songs of my set solo.

Considering how shy I had been about performing, I was surprised at how comfortable I was. During the solo part of my set I really did feel as if I were playing in a living room (albeit a large one) for a receptive audience. And rather than detracting from the

---

*Abigale sang and Charlie, Joel, and Ralph played in my set and Jo Mama's. I played in James's and my sets. Lee and Russ played in James's set. Danny played in all three. After the 1971 tour, Craig Doerge would replace me in playing keyboards for James. Danny, Lee, Russ, and Craig would become known as the Section—so named because everyone wanted to use them as their rhythm section.

intimacy, Charlie's entrance drew them in. Later, when we played the Los Angeles Forum before an audience of twenty thousand people, I didn't believe we could achieve a comparable level of intimacy. Just before my set that night I had peeked out from the wings and watched the streams of people walking back and forth across the various levels, buying souvenirs, getting refreshments, and going to and from the restrooms. With so many diversions for the audience, I didn't know if I could connect with them. But as soon as I hit the first notes on the piano, I forgot how many people I was playing for. As at the Troubadour, I had the sense of playing for a familiar, collective friend.

Often I began my set with "Song of Long Ago" and played "I Feel the Earth Move" second, but sometimes I opened with "Earth Move" to get the crowd (and probably myself) going. On future tours with drums and an electric band I would perform it much later in my set. A full band would allow me to indulge in another of my favorite ways of connecting with an audience—a full-on rock performance with me up front and a cat playing my piano part. I love leading my band and the audience in a rock concert experience in which every musician is giving his or her all with peak energy and volume, yet with professional awareness and control. I love to watch an audience become caught up in the sizzle of the groove and the heat of the beat, clapping and dancing, up on their feet.

Gloria Steinem once called me the first woman to give a downbeat. Though I've given many downbeats, I'm not sure I was the first, but my experience has always been that gender doesn't matter to cats as long as they respect the bandleader as a fellow cat. Being a sideman taught me that nothing makes a cat happier than having a good song to play and a leader who recognizes a cat's ability to play it.

Such was the case for every cat on tour in 1971. The fact that I was one of a close-knit group of musicians having a fantastic time performing onstage sustained me for a while. But the grind of touring affected each of us. It hit me one morning toward the end of our second week, when I woke up depressed. I was tired of being on the road. I didn't know that few touring bands enjoyed the amenities we did, or that many bands slept on a bus and rarely made use of hotels, airports, or comfortable hygienic facilities. I should have been thankful that our travel included a nightly hotel room with a clean, comfortable bed and a hot shower. But I was weary of going from airport to hotel, with little time to do more than fumble around in my suitcase for toiletries and something to wear the next day. Every night I grabbed a shower and a few hours' sleep, then rose to the jarring ring of a wake-up call the next morning, followed by "bags out" and a quick breakfast before boarding the bus to the airport. We flew, landed, got on a bus to the venue, where we did a soundcheck, played the gig, then got back on the bus and went to the hotel, and so on. Most of the time we were booked to play three nights in a row followed by a night off. Every night off was a welcome respite. It was also a night of vocal rest as long as I didn't go out with the band to a restaurant or a smoky club in which I had to shout to be heard by someone sitting across the table. The monotony of the routine, the constant travel, and living out of a suitcase were wearing me down. I missed being home, I missed my daughters, and hearing on the phone how much they missed me only made me feel worse. But I wasn't the only musician to succumb.

After performing in Philadelphia, we had a night off before hitting the road again. When Charlie offered to take me out to dinner, just the two of us, the prospect alone lifted my spirits. I spent the afternoon walking, shopping on Philly's cobbled streets, and looking forward to a lovely evening with my husband. We were just leaving the hotel when one of the band members came in. We exchanged waves and went on our way, unaware that our friend was nursing a bad case of the blues. It was his birthday, his loved ones were far away, and he was lonely. No one on the tour knew it was his birthday, so no one thought to look in on him. Returning to the hotel a few hours later, we learned that our friend had caused quite a commotion. The cat with whom he roomed had brought home a couple of bottles of liquor from Hospitality. After waving to us, our guy had gone up to his room, drunk as much as his body could absorb, and proceeded to destroy the television and toss several lamps, chairs, and other pieces of furniture out the window.

Wow! I thought. This is the kind of thing people do in movies about rock bands. At first my inner adolescent thought, Groovy! But then my outer rational adult understood that our friend had acted out what I'd been feeling earlier. It was the blues run amok, and it wasn't groovy at all. There was some good news: no one had been hurt by the projectile furniture, and our friend hadn't thrown himself out the window.

The next morning our bandmate was appropriately contrite. Not surprisingly, he was also extremely hungover. While the rest of us checked out, Jock, on behalf of James and Peter, apologized to the hotel manager and paid for the damage. Then everyone got on the bus. From that point on, we did whatever Jock told us to do. Unload. Stand here and wait as a group while I check you in. Okay, here are your boarding passes. Go directly to Gate 39 and wait until I join you. We'll board the plane as a group. Do not leave the boarding area for any reason whatsoever.

And so it went: airport, hotel, soundcheck, gig, hotel. No wonder our companion melted down. Soon the first segment of the tour would be over and we'd all get to go home for the break. All we had to do was get through the next few days. Our friend probably would have had to work for free for the rest of the tour to pay off his debt, except that James and Peter never asked him to pay it back. Not one penny.

Chapter Nineteen

Showtime 1971

$\mathcal{B}$eing home for two weeks was a welcome relief from the road. I spent a few days reacquainting myself with such basic tasks as making a bed, washing dishes, and going to the bank in lieu of receiving a cash per diem. Just when living at home was beginning to feel normal, just as I began to settle in to the rhythm of getting the girls ready for school, feeding the dogs, buying groceries, and picking up our clothes from the dry cleaners, it was time to leave for our second stint. Though I didn't act out my blues as dramatically as my bandmate had done, I understood his impulse. Even with friends on tour, even with my husband there, I often felt lonely and isolated. Normal life seemed a distant dream.

Later I would learn that there's a predictable probability of depression midway through a tour. Mine was exacerbated by our two-week break at home, which had lasted just long enough to foster the illusion that the tour was over. But in 1971 I knew none of that. As time away from home grew longer, tempers grew shorter—until showtime. No matter how badly any of us might have been feeling before a show, from the moment James walked out to introduce Jo Mama, all negative feelings were forgotten.

David Crosby used to say that the two hours onstage were heaven and the rest of his life was hell. I sincerely hope that David is enjoying more offstage hours of heaven now. Though I've always valued my life offstage, I've come to share his view of the hours onstage. When a performer is connecting with an audience, all's right with the world. People who saw the James Taylor–Carole King–Jo Mama shows tell me that what they remember most about the show was all the really good songs well performed by musicians who so obviously enjoyed playing with each other that the feeling was infectious. From the first chord of Jo Mama's set to the last chord of James's second encore, the intensity of emotion built to a climax that promised to be nothing less than kick-ass. When everyone came back onstage for the grand finale, there was no doubt. We were having a party.

Usually James took his first encore with his band, then we took a "James and his band" bow and exited the stage. Invariably he was called back for a second encore, which he performed solo with his acoustic guitar. Often, though not always, it was "Sweet Baby James."

I remember what happened at every performance after James's second encore as vividly as if I were there right now.

James is standing in the wings wiping perspiration off his hands, face, and neck with a towel. He chugs water from a mug and waits for the applause to become insistent enough to compel him out for a third encore.

As the applause builds, Jock holds a blue jacket that James had bought at Nudie's* as a tribute to the country music part of his

---

*Nudie Cohn's clothing store in North Hollywood was *the* place to go if you were a country singer, a cowboy, or a rock star wanting country credibility with pizzazz. Customers clothed by the "Rodeo Tailor" included Roy Rogers, Porter Wagoner, Gene Autry, and Elvis Presley. When I lived in California I often saw Nudie driving around in one of his "Nudie-mobiles"—big convertibles customized with western paraphernalia such as silver coins, horseshoes, pistols (presumably unloaded), and longhorns from an actual steer. Nudie died in 1984.

roots. The jacket is festooned with rhinestones, sequins, and other glittery objects. James puts on the jacket, and Abigale joins me in the wings. The exact right moment depends not only on the level of applause but also on how quickly the crew can roll the platform with the second set of drums onstage. As soon as we get a signal from the crew that both sets of drums are in place, Abigale and I enter from stage right. At the same time, all the cats except the drummers enter from stage left. All but Ralph are holding their instruments. The drummers step through the middle of the upstage curtain and climb up to their kits. Danny, Lee, and Charlie plug in. Ralph sits at the Hammond organ, and the crowd claps harder, establishing a rhythm of their own as they chant, "More! More! More! More!" They now know that James really *is* coming back. (Did they ever doubt it?)

Abigale and I are wearing jeans, Frye boots, and identical tight-fitting red short-sleeved T-shirts. Abigale's mane of curly red hair catches the light and flickers with shades of crimson and gold as we position ourselves in front of the single microphone on a stand downstage right. We raise our hands high in the air and bring them together repeatedly over our heads in the universal sign for "Clap with us!" while Russ and Joel rhythmically pound the bejeezus out of their respective drum kits. Clapping their own hands overhead, Danny and Ralph join us in encouraging the audience to clap with us—not that the audience needs any encouragement. They're already at a pitch of excitement bordering on frenzy. Now Charlie and Lee begin to improvise rhythmic syncopations to complement what the drummers are playing.

At last James steps out from the wings. The noise of the crowd becomes deafening as his adoring audience welcomes him back. The jacket alone raises the level another decibel. Holding his guitar mid-neck, James walks toward center stage and waves to the crowd with his free hand. Just before he gets there he stops, inclines his head slightly to acknowledge first the band, then the audience, and then he takes the final step that places him directly in front of the center-stage microphone. He positions his guitar and begins to sing: "Come on, brother, get on up, and help me find this groove," to which Abigale and I respond in harmony, "Groo-oove"—and we're off!

We finish with a classic Big Rock Ending, and the audience explodes with approval, clapping and cheering through our final group bow and departure from the stage, with all but James exiting stage anywhere. The final solo bow belongs to the headliner, and James takes it with gratitude. He exits, the house lights come up, and the show is over.

Everywhere we played, everyone left the show on a high note. We couldn't account for how anyone might feel an hour later, the next morning, or the following afternoon, but during every show we belonged to the people in the audience, and they belonged to us. The 1971 tour set a standard that would become a blueprint for the rest of my performing life.

If only there had been such a blueprint for my nonperforming life.

Chapter Twenty

Addition, Family Style

As the tour drew to a close I was a mass of conflicting emotions. I was excited about going home to my girls, but I had enjoyed performing with James and Jo Mama so much that I was sad to think that we wouldn't be doing those shows anymore. Others must have been thinking along similar lines, because the energy level at the last show was even higher than usual. If the decibel level and range of emotions had been elevated before, they were off the meter that night.

And then the tour was over.

As soon as I walked in the door of the house on Wonderland Avenue, my sadness disappeared. The enthusiastic greeting I received from Louise and Sherry mirrored my own delight at seeing them. Our dogs' wagging tails and "Pet me! Pet me!" noses under our elbows only added to the joyous confusion of our arrival. My first thought on awakening the next morning was heartfelt gratitude that I was free of the airport–soundcheck–gig–hotel routine. I eased back into domesticity as seamlessly as if I'd never been gone.

Before *Tapestry* was released in March 1971, I had told Lou that I would do the tour, but I wanted no part of the public relations machine in which recording artists were expected to help the record company generate sales. Lou respected my wishes. He fielded all requests and kept me from having to do interviews. Just when I was thinking how happy I was to be enjoying a comparatively simple life, my twenty-nine-year-old body announced a major new development. I was expecting my third child.

My twenty-four-year-old husband was over the moon. This would be his first child. With two children already in our household, adding a baby wouldn't cause as big a change as it might have for a couple with no children, though we definitely would need to move into a bigger house. The word "simple" no longer described our life. Before I could fully absorb the implications of this new development, Peter called to say that he was thinking of bringing the James Taylor–Carole King–Jo Mama show to his country of origin. Would Charlie and I be available that summer to travel around the United Kingdom?

We would.

Though we had to find a new house and prepare for a baby, Charlie and I were young enough to think we could do it all. During my previous pregnancies I had worked in the studio literally up until the day of delivery. As long as I didn't leap around onstage, the baby and I would be fine. And because the UK bookings coincided with the girls' summer vacation, Sherry and Louise, now nine and eleven, could come along.

James also brought someone important to him. In one of my memory snapshots of the UK tour, Joni Mitchell is sitting on a long wooden bench in the hospitality area backstage with one leg drawn up under her as she sketches line drawings of Louise and Sherry. On another bench Louise is playing an acoustic guitar almost as big as she is, while Sherry is drawing on a sketchpad, her long hair partially covering one side of her face. Joni is motionless except for her drawing hand. Her pencil moves rapidly and purposefully as it transmits the essence of what she sees to the expressive images emerging on each page. As Joni continues to sketch, her long blonde hair glows with the late afternoon light streaming in behind her through the french windows that frame the verdant summer forest of the Ullswater Lake Country. In Joni's sketches, which she generously gave to Louise and Sherry, her visual artistry captured something fundamental about the spirit of each of my daughters that can still be seen in the woman each has become.

The UK tour ended, and then it was fall. The girls went back to school, and Charlie and I began settling into our new home. The house on Appian Way sat on a steep hillside atop Laurel Canyon. Though most of its outdoor space was unusable, it had plenty of room inside. The living room was two stories high, with a tall fireplace, a cathedral ceiling, and a balcony with a wall of bookshelves. To the *I Ching*, the *Tibetan Book of the Dead*, and other books and albums from the Wonderland Avenue house we added books about stages of a healthy pregnancy, what to name a baby, and how to prepare for home birth.

A couple we knew who'd had a healthy baby at home the prior year recommended Dr. Nial Ettinghausen as a midwife. Dr. E. was a D.P.M., a Drugless Practitioner of Medicine who combined watching and waiting with calm, knowledgeable guidance and prudent intervention. He had successfully delivered hundreds of babies at home with an extremely low rate of unusual incident or the need for transport to a hospital. We had some trepidation about home birth, but the support of our family physician as well as his offer to be on call calmed our concerns.

As winter approached, my baby and I grew bigger. We wouldn't know its gender until it was born. When an X-ray taken by Dr. E. in the ninth month showed the fetus sitting straight up, I thought, Aww. Doesn't it look cute sitting up like that! I didn't realize that it should have been upside down for a headfirst presentation. When Dr. E. pointed out that it was in breech position with its derrière likely to emerge first, Charlie became anxious, and so did I. But our family doctor reassured us. Dr. E.'s years of home birth experience had included many safe deliveries of healthy babies in breech presentation. Since I had already delivered two healthy children, I was a good candidate for a successful breech delivery. And he, an M.D., would be less than twenty minutes away if, God forbid, anything went wrong.

Molly Norah Larkey was born in robust good health on December 31, 1971—not on our kitchen table, but in our kitchen. Dr. Ettinghausen had brought a nurse, a delivery table, and all the necessary equipment. Our childbirth classes had covered everything from how labor would progress to how to breathe and how to push. Naturally, when the time came to propel the baby out I forgot all the instructions. I tried pushing a few times with no apparent effect, then I gave one final, massive, superhuman push that felt as if I were expelling a Volkswagen. Dr. E. caught the baby and quickly flipped it over to reveal a vigorous little girl with a perfectly shaped head.

For the next ten days, Charlie spent every waking moment gazing at the miracle of Molly until he had to go back to work. To help me care for Molly I had the indefatigable Willa Mae, Molly's sisters, and her two grandmothers, who had flown out to the West Coast to meet their new granddaughter as soon as they heard the news. In between cooing over the baby, our mothers told us how relieved they were that the birth had gone well. When they had given birth to us in the 1940s, women routinely went to hospitals. At the end of a weeklong stay, the new mother was sent home with bottles and instructions on how to make formula for her tightly wrapped little bundle of joy. Our mothers had considered themselves "modern" women because they'd had access to good medical care in a germ-free environment. Our choosing to give birth in the manner of their mothers' generation had caused them some consternation. However, it didn't bother my grandmother. When my mother told her that I was planning to deliver her great-grandchild at home and breastfeed her, my grandmother's response was, "So vot's so un-yuzhull?"

In the early seventies, few hospitals offered a birthing environment that combined medical resources with the social benefits of home birth. Today many hospitals offer birthing rooms with a homelike environment and enough room for doctors, nurses, equipment, a father or other birth partner, and older siblings. Ironically, more women are having babies at home in the twenty-first century because they can't afford to go to a hospital.

I became pregnant again in the summer of 1973 and continued being a homebody, alternately working as a singer and songwriter. That pregnancy was less challenging physically than my pregnancy with Molly, but it seemed to last a lot longer—especially toward the end. During those months I wrote the songs for my album *Wrap Around Joy* with David Palmer, then Lou Adler produced the album and assembled some of the finest musicians in L.A. to record the tracks. "Jazzman," featuring Tom Scott on saxophone, would emerge as the most popular song from that album, reaching #1 on November 9, 1974.

Charlie was twenty-seven and I thirty-two when our son, Levi Benjamin Larkey, arrived on April 23, 1974, in the customary headfirst presentation. After that our kitchen reverted permanently to its conventional use, and so did my body. Levi would be my last child.

Chapter Twenty-One

Mommy and Grammy

$\mathcal{T}$he year 1972 started off on a high note after Molly's arrival. Then, on March 14, I attained the highest pinnacle of success to which a recording artist and songwriter could aspire: I was awarded four Grammys for my work on *Tapestry*. I didn't accept the awards in person because the ceremony was in New York and I wanted to stay in California with my new baby. Along with his own Grammys, Lou accepted mine. With *Tapestry* now a multiplatinum-selling album that had wildly exceeded my teenage dreams, I didn't know what to do with my success. I didn't want the problems that came with being famous, and I didn't want my private life to be public. I just wanted to do what I'd been doing as a wife and mother before the success of *Tapestry*. I made clothes for everyone in the family, tended our small garden, and occasionally went out for sushi lunch in Little Tokyo with my friend Stephanie. I taught at the Integral Yoga Institute and attended cooking classes at The Source. I continued to embarrass my Goffin daughters by bringing their vitamins to school. And I continued to bring home health food instead of the Cokes, Pepsis, and potato chips that Sherry wanted. When I said for the umpteenth time that health food was better for her, Sherry retaliated by saying, in a perfect imitation of my voice, "It's nutritious!"

Charlie was home a lot that year. When he wasn't playing with Jo Mama or helping care for Molly, he was in his studio practicing. He was determined not to miss the important moments of Molly's first year. When we were invited to dinner, a party, or some other social event to which neither of us was interested in going, Charlie was usually the one who said no on behalf of both of us. I didn't mind. Charlie was better than I at saying no.

I also continued to write and record songs. Because I was breastfeeding, I brought Molly with me to the studio. I had a bassinet that looked like a rectangular wicker basket, which I kept near the piano when I was recording. When I was working in the booth the bassinet was on a bench near the console. Molly didn't seem to mind the noise and the activity. When she was ready to sleep, she slept. When she was awake she looked at the lights and the people and kicked her feet in the air with what looked like pure pleasure. When Charlie was in the studio he held her whenever he wasn't recording. She cooed at him and made adorable baby faces at whoever else picked her up until she was ready for what only her mama could then provide. These lines from my song "Goodbye Don't Mean I'm Gone" described my life in 1972.

> But it's all I can do to be a mother
> (My baby's in one hand, I've a pen in the other)

In a song called "Weekdays" I articulated the struggle by many women of my generation to balance feminist goals with traditional wife- and motherhood. The woman in that song was a character I created along with others in the *Fantasy* album.

Weekday mornings
Coffee smell in the air
After you've gone and the children have left for school
I'm alone and I think about all the plans we made
I think about all the dreams I had
And I wonder if I'm a fool

Weekday midday
I've got the marketing done
Plenty to do but nothing to tax my mind
That's all right—it's a habit
Heaven knows I can always watch the daytime shows
And I wonder which story's mine

She loved a man she knew little about
After so many years of trying
So many years of doing without
Oh, but what's the use of crying

Weekday evenings
We sit and I realize
You've dreamed, too, and I kind of understand
I've been with you and you need me to take care of you
But we'll work it out so I'm a person, too
And we'll help each other out the best that we can
'Cause I'm your woman and you're my man

After *Tapestry* I would write and record six more albums for Ode: *Music, Rhymes and Reasons, Fantasy, Wrap Around Joy, Thoroughbred,* and *Really Rosie.*

Each of the six albums after *Tapestry* went either gold or platinum. *Music* sold over two million. All were extraordinarily successful by any standard short of the one established by *Tapestry*. People often ask me if I was disappointed when subsequent albums didn't do as well. Some are skeptical when I say no. But I never expected *Tapestry* to achieve the success it did, and I saw no reason to expect that level of success to continue. I was just glad I could keep writing, recording, and making a good living while enjoying a normal life. The meaning of "normal" was open to interpretation, but in 1972, the year I turned thirty, my life felt pretty normal to me.

Chapter Twenty-Two

Divergence

*M*y definition of a normal life continued in 1973 with my caring for Molly, being supportive of Charlie, chauffeuring two increasingly busy schoolchildren around, and writing and recording new songs. Charlie's definition of a normal life included playing in three bands, none of which was Jo Mama. That band had broken up. One of Charlie's bands featured David Foster on piano and William Smith—"Smitty"—on organ. Another featured Dave Palmer, with Danny Douma on guitar, John Ware on drums, and, at one point, Michael McDonald on vocals and keyboards (yes, *that* Michael McDonald). But the band that would become Charlie's main gig was the David T. Walker band, featuring David T. on guitar, Clarence McDonald on keyboards, Harvey Mason on drums, Charlie on bass, and Ms. Bobbye Hall, a petite woman who made big sounds with percussion instruments.

As a fellow musician I understood why Charlie enjoyed playing with David T.'s band. They were such superb players that I hired them to play on my *Fantasy* album. Rather than being a collection of songs in random order, that album had a connecting story and a predetermined sequence, and I had written every song with the specific intention of singing it myself. Just before *Fantasy* was released in 1973, Charlie and Lou suggested I promote it by going on tour with the David T. Walker band as my rhythm section.

Promoting an album had never been sufficient inducement to get me to go on tour, but what interested me was the chance to share with an audience how much fun I'd had writing and recording it.

Lou sealed the deal when he said, "Not only will you be playing with David T.'s band, you'll be playing with everyone's dream horn section."

He was referring to George Bohanon on trombone and euphonium, Dick Hyde, also called "Slyde," on trombone, Oscar Brashear on trumpet, Gene Goe on trumpet and flugelhorn, and Tom Scott and Mike Altschul on saxophone.

Though the *Fantasy* tour didn't last as long as the 1971 tour, it, too, was successful. More than one hundred thousand people attended our free concert in Central Park.

And though record sales never approached the level of *Tapestry*, the *Fantasy* album was critically well received. I enjoyed that tour very much, but as soon as we got home I readily slipped into my comfort zone of domesticity. Charlie took a different direction. I had always respected his dedication to music, but he was now taking it to another level. He played so many late-night club gigs that I rarely saw him.

It was probably just as well that I had come up through the ranks of the music business without having to play late-night club gigs, because I'm not a late-night person. I'm an inveterate diurnal. I'm one of those really inconsiderate early-morning people that nocturnal people hate. Never giving a thought to whether someone might be sleeping in the next room, I rattle the cereal box, clink the spoon while stirring my tea, and yell at the top of my lungs to a dawdling child, "Hurry up or you'll miss your bus!"

Nocturnals enjoy watching the sun come up only when they're making their way home after having been out all night. I prefer to watch the sun rise after I've slept for eight hours.

And that was the problem. Charlie and I still cared for each other, but we were spending almost no time together. Our disparate schedules continued through 1974 and part of 1975. Some couples are able to preserve their emotional connection from different cities or on different shifts, but our overlapping hours were simply not enough. We tried marriage counseling, discussions, therapy, and other options without success until we felt that we had exhausted all possibilities available at the time.

Sadly, "at the time" was all we had. With tremendous sorrow on both our parts, we separated, then divorced. But we remained united in our resolve to be the best possible parenting team for our children. Charlie was a devoted father and a considerate coparent. Indeed, he would provide stability for our kids when my life choices were less than stable. Our shared commitment to our children's well-being and mutual respect for each other's rules even when we disagreed gave our kids a solid foundation. Had they tried to play us against each other, they wouldn't have been successful. Grounded in their well-being, Charlie and I navigated cooperatively what is often treacherous territory for divorced parents and their children.

Even after our lives diverged to include other partners, Charlie and I remained friends. Periodically we wondered if we might have tried harder to work through our problems and, in so doing, perhaps could have stayed together. We'll never know, but we're grateful for our shared history of love, respect, children, grandchildren, friendship, and music. We had the chance to make music together again in 2001 when Charlie played on "An Uncommon Love" and "Oh No Not My Baby" for my *Love Makes the World* album. Written with Gerry and recorded with Charlie, "Oh No Not My Baby" could have been subtitled "Husband Reunion."

I could not have predicted in 1975 that Charlie's and my relationship would turn out to be an unconventional success story. All I could
see then was another failure. After Charlie and I divorced I lost my
center. Sometimes I felt as if I were floating away like the red balloon
in the movie *Le Ballon rouge*. After Charlie moved out I found it too
heartbreaking to stay in the house on Appian Way with the memories it held of our life together. Thankfully I could afford to move. My
Goffin daughters didn't want to leave the Canyon, but when I found
a house on Encinal Beach in Trancas they were okay with that. Plus
we had cool neighbors. Cheech Marin lived next door. His partner
in comedy, Tommy Chong, lived just across the Pacific Coast Highway. Louise and Sherry knew two of Tommy's daughters, Rae Dawn
and Robbi, from school in Laurel Canyon. Neil Young lived in a cot-
tage nearby on Broad Beach. Lou Adler and some of his friends lived
on Carbon Beach. And J. D. Souther and Don Henley with Eagles
shared a house just up the hill from mine.

Because so many of my neighbors were celebrities, the invitations I accepted brought me to high-profile events and parties. I
found myself spending social time with people actively seeking the
very visibility that I had tried to avoid. Some celebrities were more
intellectually curious than others. In addition to being a stellar ath-
lete, Kareem Abdul-Jabbar had a vast knowledge of jazz and its place
in history. But more often I found myself in the company of people
who enjoyed gossiping about who was wearing what, who was dating whom, who'd had plastic surgery, and what the best places were
to see and be seen. Even now I can't explain why I continued to
socialize with such people. Perhaps I was still trying to make up for
my high school years, when I was rarely invited anywhere. But without Charlie to say no for me, I found it difficult to say no for myself.

Though I was grateful that my family and I were free of serious
problems such as illness or poverty, I was challenged by the much
less serious problem of living a lifestyle I loathed, and I was upset

with myself for continuing to pursue it. I was becoming a parody of a pop star. I began to dream of buying some land in the mountains with a small house and a much larger organic garden than the plot I had tried to cultivate on Appian Way. I had the means and freedom of workplace to make such a move, but I couldn't find a way out. When I complained about my life to less affluent friends, they were predictably unsympathetic.

"Poor Carole," I imagined them saying as soon as the door closed behind me. "Her BMW is more than a year old and her champagne's gone flat."

My escape from the fast lane was set in motion the night Don Henley hosted a thirtieth birthday party for J.D. John David Souther had been born in Detroit on November 2, 1945, and raised in Amarillo, Texas. Known variously in 1975 as a country rock singer, songwriter, actor, friend of Eagles, and companion of Linda Ronstadt, John David had written one of my favorite songs. Linda's performance of "Faithless Love" on her 1974 album *Heart Like a Wheel*, with a gorgeous harmony by J.D., twanged every string of this city girl's heart.

It was a good two hours past my bedtime that November 2 in 1975 when Henley sent someone down the hill to invite me up. I could hear the sounds of music and celebration from my room, and it sounded like fun. With the kids asleep, a nanny in the house, less than two hundred feet between the children and me if they needed me, and my ability to say no completely inoperative, I saw no harm in joining the party.

With each step up the hill I came one step closer to meeting a man who would bring momentous changes to the lives of my family and me. He would lead me to some of my highest highs, my lowest lows, and, ultimately, to a place I would call home for a very long time.

PART III

Chapter One

Shepherd

At the top of the hill I saw a cluster of people standing outside Don Henley's house. Though I didn't know them, they waved to me, and I waved back. Inside, I recognized Glenn Frey at the buffet table. We hadn't met, but what the heck.

"Hi, Glenn," I said. "How're ya doin'?"

He looked up, answered, "Great, how're you?" and then went back to filling his plate with ribs, chicken, gravy, and mashed potatoes.

I walked toward the open glass doors leading to a deck on the ocean side of the house. The late fall breeze carried a touch of chill along with the sharp fragrance of the Pacific Ocean. Just inside the doors I saw Henley talking to a tall blond man.

"Hi, Don," I said.

He said, "Hey," gave me a hug, and introduced the blond man as Rick Evers. Don preempted the party question I wasn't going to ask ("What do you do?") by telling me about the sheepskin coats Rick was making for him, J.D., and Eagles manager Irving Azoff. The question "Why would someone living in Southern California need a sheepskin coat?" crossed my mind, but all I said was, "Hi, Rick. Nice to meet you."

"Nice to meet you, too," he said in a husky voice.

Don said, "Show her your coat."

Rick went outside and came back in holding a light tan sheepskin coat. He put it on. Immediately I became more interested in both the coat and its maker. The coat was stitched with hand-cut leather thongs and decorated with beads, antler buttons, and other rustic artifacts. On Rick's slightly undernourished six-foot-one frame, the coat looked bold, striking, and artistic. His long, shaggy blond hair seemed to flow seamlessly into the ragged edges of the wide collar. If a person were looking for attention, wearing such a coat would definitely attract it.

Don stayed with us a few more minutes, then left to mingle with other guests. Rick took off the coat and escorted me over to a couple of comfortable chairs in a corner. He helped me into one of them, draped the coat on the back of the other, and excused himself. A minute later he was back with a couple of glasses of water. He handed one to me and set his glass down on a side table, then we began a discussion of topics ranging from sheepskin coats to American Indian culture, music, politics, and things we didn't like about L.A.

With blue eyes, a square jaw, and a wheat-colored mustache, Rick was ruggedly handsome. He was exciting, passionate, and not a celebrity. He didn't care who was dating whom, or wearing what, or whether the Lakers had won or lost. I had assumed that he was staying at Don and J.D.'s house, but as the conversation progressed I learned that he was living in a red Chevy van with Rusty, his large yellow mixed-breed Labrador retriever. This revelation should have been a warning signal, but I chose to perceive the living arrangement as bold and adventurous.

When I told Rick about my dream of living closer to nature,

he offered to drive my children and me around the mountains of Colorado, Utah, and Idaho.

"I've lived in all three states," he said. "I know a lot of things you might find useful."

I listened avidly to his stories about living in the mountains and asked him a lot of questions. He answered all of them with a calm confidence I found reassuring. And there was no mistaking the sparkle in his eyes. He was attracted to me, and I was attracted to him. We were sitting near an open window. I didn't notice the chill that had begun to creep into my bones until I looked around and saw that we were among the last remaining guests. When Rick saw me shiver, he stood up, picked up the sheepskin coat, and wrapped it around me. That's when I allowed pheromones to elbow common sense aside and invited him to spend the night at my house.

"What about Rusty?" he asked.

"Of course. Bring Rusty, too."

Rick and Rusty would stay a lot longer than overnight.

In hindsight, I probably should have asked Rick these two questions: "Why are you living in a van?" and "Are you by any chance psychotic?" But he was so handsome and interesting, and he was going to lead me to people and places I would have never encountered without him. One such person was Roy Reynolds, an artist who lived in eastern Idaho with his wife, Mon'nette (Mo-NEET). Roy had previously been a cowboy and an alcoholic, but by the time I met him he had quit drinking and had bought an Appaloosa colt to celebrate his sobriety. He named the colt Whiskey and channeled his tendency toward addiction into training the colt and making art. Roy painted the canvases that would become the album art for *Simple Things*. In 1977, in an act of characteristic generosity, Roy gave Whiskey to me. Standing a little over sixteen hands, that horse had more charisma than most movie stars.

A few years later, as I traveled around the West, poems, songs, and stories written by cowboys about their horses would inspire me to write a song about my equine buddy.* Whiskey's lifetime was just right for a horse, but too short for a friend. In a perfect heaven Whiskey is romping with Seabiscuit.

Early days with Rick were a natural high. He was so excited about our future that every day felt like an adventure. But adventure didn't come cheap. It required gear. The first thing Rick and I bought together was an old Dodge Power Wagon, though technically it wasn't "we" who bought it. Rick found the Power Wagon through an ad in the paper. Though its body was rusty in places, it could haul a large family and lots of camping gear. With four-wheel drive it could, in theory, go anywhere. We had it painted metallic brown to camouflage the rust.

In the seventies—oh dear, this is *so* embarrassing—hippies named their cars. The first car I owned (as opposed to leased) in California was a white Volkswagen station wagon. I thought of it as female and named her Carma. With its beefy body and muscular engine, we deemed the Power Wagon to be a male, named him Shepherd, and registered the vehicle in Idaho with personalized plates reading SHPRD. Between 1975 and 1977, Rick and I covered thousands of miles in Shepherd traveling back and forth between California, Utah, and Colorado with Levi and Molly in search of what Rick had now begun to refer to as "our" dream. On one trip to Colorado we visited Dan Fogelberg, who lived in Boulder. On Rick's advice, and with Dan's blessing, I began working with members of a band called Navarro that Dan sometimes played with. Their musicianship was inspired and full of energy, and I enjoyed their company. Navarro, Rick, and I traveled between Boulder and

---

*"Whiskey" was released in 1979 as the B side of the single "Move Lightly" from my album *Touch The Sky*. "Whiskey" did not appear on that album.

L.A. to write and play music together. Soon Navarro and their families and friends became my primary social circle.

Shepherd carried us to a number of magnificent places in Colorado, to any one of which I might have happily moved, but I wanted to explore other areas before making a final decision. In Utah, Rick, my Larkey children, and I clambered up and down glorious red desert rocks and, along with copious amounts of water, drank in spectacular views of changing colors as the sun moved across the sky. And when I saw a stream flowing uphill in the Wasatch Mountains, I would have been receptive to anything a Utahn told me. But from the moment we crossed the state line, Idaho's landscape had me in its grip. I was enthralled by the wide-open spaces of the high volcanic desert in which cows and horses grazed peacefully in large pastures on spacious farms against a vast panoramic backdrop of majestic snowcapped mountain ranges. I was humbled by a sense of infinite space and natural beauty unlike anything I'd ever experienced before. My field of vision widened to capacity as I tried to take in a full view of all that land on which there appeared to be absolutely nothing.

Of course there wasn't "nothing." Tens of thousands of organisms thrived there, from wild plants and herbs and creatures large and small to birds and insects that coexisted in symbiotic harmony. But what I perceived then as "nothing" was the absence of any sign of human habitation for miles. After spending so much of my life walking on the streets of New York, driving on the parkways of New Jersey, or sitting in traffic on the freeways of Southern California, always within sight and earshot of teeming humanity and the rumbling vehicles that conveyed people from place to place, I was awestruck by the very idea of all that land with no visible indication of human beings on it.

When I did encounter human beings, I found Idahoans' directness, simplicity of lifestyle, and readiness to help others refreshing.

It wasn't that New Yorkers and Angelenos weren't kind or helpful, but in Idaho helping strangers seemed to be a way of life. Folks never hesitated to stop whatever they were doing to pull someone's car out of a ditch or help a neighbor with a chore. I had the impression that people in Idaho had more spare time than city people. Of course, had I said that to a farmer or rancher, she or he probably would have said, "Yeah? And just how much spare time do ya think I have?" even as the man or woman was climbing off a tractor and spending whatever time it took to pull my car out of the ditch.

If L.A. was the fast lane in 1975, Idaho was the extremely slow lane. Idahoans took pride in saying, "Idaho is what America was." One night Rick and I went to dinner with a couple who spent quite a bit of time trying to determine whether "Boy-see" or "Boy-zee" was the correct way to pronounce the name of Idaho's City of Trees. The husband, originally from California, favored "Boy-zee." The wife, as did most Idahoans, said "Boy-see." I say "Boy-see" because that's how Rick pronounced it. I couldn't believe how much time was spent on a question that is always resolved in the same way: both are correct.

At another evening meal, this time at the home of a much larger family, all the adults sat around the supper table and debated for an hour whether a neighbor's truck had thrown a piston or a rod. And on a third occasion the topic was whether Barb's Toll House cookies tasted better with half a cup or a whole cup of chocolate chips. Was that even in question?

What wasn't in question was that during the nine years I had lived in Southern California I had never stopped thinking of New York as my home, but after less than a week, Idaho was already vying for that position.

Chapter Two

Mores Creek

In 1975, with only six gates, Boise Airport met the definition of a sleepy little airport. I first saw it from Shepherd on a road trip to visit Rick's adoptive mother. Luey Noble lived in a small house on five irrigated acres less than a mile from the airport. Rick's sister and brother-in-law, Mollie and Don Culley, lived on the property with Dennis, their eight-year-old son. They kept horses, dogs, cats, birds, chickens, and a cow on the small farm. They cared for the animals in the morning before they left for their jobs in town, then they came home and tended them again at night. The Culleys weren't the only family to work multiple jobs while struggling to hold on to their property and way of life against encroaching development. For the Culleys and others it would be a losing battle. Open spaces and five-acre farms near Boise Airport have since given way to subdivisions, industrial parks, and massive structures with enough parking spaces to accommodate all the passengers who now use that airport, which, as I write this, has at least thirty-two gates and can no longer be considered "sleepy."

At first, when Don and Mollie said they were going to do

chores, I assumed they meant washing dishes, making the bed, and sweeping the kitchen. Wanting to be a considerate guest, I offered to help. That's when I learned that on a farm "chores" meant getting up at 4 o'clock on a winter morning and slogging to the barn through slush, mud, and manure to feed the animals, milk the cow, and gather eggs. As a guest, my participation in chores was voluntary. For my hosts it was mandatory. A few years later, when I was responsible for the twice-daily care and feeding of farm animals, I would learn the meaning of "mandatory." I would find it extremely challenging to leave my warm, cozy bed to go up to the barn in temperatures as low as 45 below zero, but I would also find caring for those animals grounding and rewarding.

Living in Idaho and visiting Los Angeles seemed a much better idea than the reverse. I could continue my professional career no matter where I lived. Even so, though I wrote and released a number of albums after I moved to Idaho, the perception in the industry was that I had dropped out. I suppose that if you measure a person's standing in the music business by her position on the charts or her presence at star-studded parties, I did drop out. But I felt as if I were dropping *in* to real life—or as real as life can be when you have financial security beyond the reach of most of your neighbors.

Rick and I began the search for our dream place by driving northeast along the Boise River on Highway 21 toward Idaho City. The first property we looked at was about a half hour out of Boise in the highlands above Mores Creek, a tributary of the Boise River. The two brothers who owned the property could have been anywhere from forty to seventy-five. Each wore denim overalls that might have been blue at one time but had evolved to a nondescript slate color. They lived together in a one-room cabin roughly twice the size of a hot-dog stand. A table covered with bills, envelopes, and other papers stood beneath a wall covered with girlie calendars from the 1940s. Unwashed dishes filled the sink, and there were black grease stains everywhere. The cabin reminded me of the back office of a filling station I'd walked through in rural Connecticut when I was a teenager.

To make conversation, I asked if either of them were married.

"Oh, no, ma'am," one of the brothers drawled. "We find it's cheaper to rent 'em."

When Rick asked if we could view the property, the brother who had answered the "married" question led us out the back door to an old crew-cab pickup that would hold all four of us. Rick sat in the passenger seat. The other brother climbed in back with me. As we bumped along the two ruts that served as a road, Rick asked about water.

"Are there any hot or cold springs?"

The brother who had answered the "married" question replied, "Yep." Evidently he was the more gregarious of the two.

We waited for him to continue. When he didn't, Rick and I exchanged a look in the mirror as if to say, What do we have to do to get information out of these guys?

The gregarious brother stopped the pickup, pointed to a stand of red willows, and said, "Ya got a cold spring right there."

"How can you tell?" I asked.

"Ma'am? D'ya see them willas?"

"Yes."

"Wa-al," he said, "where ya got willas, ya got water."

"Sure," I said, trying to sound as if I had already known that.

"Ya see," he said. And he stopped as if that were his complete thought. Then, with the extra patience shown to a city slicker by a man raised in the country, he added, "That's how it works."

He shifted into first and started driving again. The taciturn brother decided it was time to end the discussion.

"No water, no willas."

I had just received my first lesson in the lore of the land from a couple of locals. Other valuable lessons would come later, including that sewage flows downhill, payday's on Friday, and the weather in Idaho changes every five minutes. In fact, right after "Idaho is what America was," the phrase I would hear most often in my adopted state was, "If you don't like the weather, wait a few minutes."

The brothers' land wasn't suitable for our purposes, and neither were several other properties we viewed along Mores Creek. We wouldn't find our dream place for nearly two years, but in the intervening months we had an unexpected encounter that led to an extraordinary evening in New York with a man who had changed the world.

Chapter Three

Taxi Driver

While living in Laurel Canyon I had traveled back and forth to New York frequently to visit friends, family, and other songwriters and musicians with whom I enjoyed working. After I met Rick I continued to travel to and from New York, but never without him. From the moment I saw Rick in his remarkable coat, he and I were virtually inseparable. More accurately, Rick was inseparable from me. That he insisted on going everywhere with me didn't make me as uncomfortable in the beginning as it made my friends and family. Though they were glad I was happy, they thought Rick too possessive. That opinion was initially brought up by Rick, who had a keen sensitivity to anyone's slightest possible dislike of him. He dismissed their judgment and said they were jealous of the love he and I shared. Caught in the middle (a place with which I was not unfamiliar), I tried to accommodate everyone. I allowed Rick to come everywhere with me, and I tried to assuage the fears of my friends and family by telling them it was my choice to have him with me. They didn't believe me. Because they didn't know what else to do, the people who loved me let me know that they were there if I needed them, and then they gave me the space that Rick was building so industriously around the two of us. I could have set the concept to music had someone not already written it as a nursery rhyme: "Everywhere that Carole went, Rick Evers was sure to go."

Early in our relationship Rick told me that he was a big fan of the Moody Blues.

"Anyone can be a fan of the Beatles," he said, "but it takes a really tuned-in person to appreciate the Moody Blues."

When he said he would die to meet John Lodge, Justin Hayward, or Graeme Edge, I assumed he meant it figuratively. Rick never met the Moody Blues, but he did meet a Beatle, and he didn't have to die to do it. All he had to do was go to a movie with me on a winter night in New York in 1976 after a business meeting, at which he was of course present. We went to a cinema on the Upper East Side to see *Taxi Driver*, in which Robert De Niro delivered one of the best-known lines in twentieth-century movie history when he looked in the mirror (as Travis Bickle) and said to his reflection, "Are you talkin' to *me?*"

Just about everyone who has seen the film remembers that moment. I remember it, too, but the rest of the movie was eclipsed by other events that night.

Soon after that scene I became aware of an insistent call of nature. I eased out of my seat, sidled past the people in my row, and found the ladies' room. As I emerged from the stall, the face I saw reflected in a mirror was instantly recognizable as that of Yoko Ono. Yoko was at the sink washing her hands when she looked up, saw me in the mirror, and recognized me. I suppose one good thing about having a famous face is that you don't have to introduce yourself.

Drying her hands, Yoko asked, "Do you live in New York?"

I pressed down on the soap dispenser and said, "No. I came for business meetings and to visit my family."

While we completed our ablutions, Yoko confided that she and John were enjoying their night out at the movies very much. "This is the first time we've gone out together since the birth of our son." From news reports that had provided a waiting world with the announcement of Sean Ono Lennon's arrival on October 9, 1975, I knew that their son had been born several months earlier.

"Oh, you must be so happy. Congratulations!"

Yoko moved toward the exit ahead of me. Just before she pushed the door open, she turned and volunteered that they would be leaving the theater soon. "Would you like to visit us at our apartment?"

"Sure," I said. "Er...I'm here with my boyfriend. Is that okay?"

"Of course. You must bring him, too."

As we entered the darkened theater together Yoko pointed to where John was sitting and whispered that they would be leaving before the movie was over. When I saw them get up, my boyfriend and I were to do the same and meet them at the back of the theater.

Incredulous, I whispered, "You're not going to stay for the end of the movie?"

"No. We never do."

As I made my way back to my seat I pondered the concept of never seeing the end of a movie. Rick glanced up when I arrived, then immediately turned his attention back to the screen. I tugged his sleeve to get his attention and whispered that I was going to get up again before the end of the movie, and when I did, he should follow me. It must have sounded very mysterious to him, but he nodded and returned to the movie.

I could no longer concentrate on Travis Bickle. I couldn't stop thinking about Yoko's invitation, and I was intrigued by her exit plan. Not wanting to miss Yoko's cue, I kept looking in their direction. When at last Yoko and John stood up, so did two men behind them. I, too, stood up. Rick followed, keeping an eye on the screen all the way out. We trailed Yoko and John to the back of the theater and slipped out the door after them into the brightly lit, nearly empty lobby. One of the two men with them escorted us to the exit doors, where an old-fashioned woody station wagon was waiting.

To my surprise, neither the vehicle nor the Ono-Lennons seemed to attract anyone's notice. The whole operation took less than a minute. One man helped Yoko into the back seat and instructed Rick and me to scoot in on either side of her. The second man quickly helped John into the back of the station wagon, where John immediately assumed a prone position. The man who had helped Yoko climbed into the front passenger seat while the second man closed the tailgate and raised his hand to hail a taxi.

As the woody sped away I asked the driver, "Do you do this all the time?"

"Yes," he said. "We have to."

Of course, I thought. Security would be a major concern for anyone charged with protecting a Beatle. And if you happened to be responsible for the Beatle who lived with Yoko Ono, the need for security would be even higher because, among millions of fans who mourned the Beatles' breakup, many blamed Yoko.

Thinking about security, I remembered a frightening experience of my own. After my free concert in Central Park in 1973, a crowd of overenthusiastic fans had broken through the fence and surrounded a limo with Charlie and me inside. As I tried to get the terrified driver to inch forward slowly, the fans, who had worked themselves into a frenzy, began to rock the limo. These were ostensibly people who *liked* me. Fortunately, three of New York's Finest showed up before anyone was hurt and persuaded the crowd to disperse.

Now, as we sped across Central Park toward John and Yoko's home in the apartment building known as the Dakota, I realized that my scary fan experience was insignificant compared to what the Beatles had to deal with *all the time*. When it came to the Beatles, the fanaticism of some people knew no bounds. Hey, I knew what it meant to be a Beatles fan. I had been one when I first met them in 1965.

I'd been on my way to retrieve my car after a meeting with an A&R man when Al Aronowitz hailed me outside the Warwick Hotel. Seeing the crowd gathering behind stanchions off to one side of the entrance, I remembered having heard on the radio that the Beatles were in residence.

"Wanna meet the Beatles?" Al said, in the manner of a street guy offering to sell me a watch.

Unaware of the circumstances, I said, "Sure!"

Al said he was on his way up to see the Beatles. What he didn't tell me was that he was trying to earn insider points by smuggling four young women up to their suite. It was a completely unsolicited enterprise by Aronowitz. After all, it wasn't as if the Beatles needed his help in finding female companionship.

Whatever Al said (and, I'm guessing, gave) to the leader of the phalanx of security officers through whom all potential visitors needed to pass, it worked. The next thing I knew, I was in the service elevator with Aronowitz and four young women. When we arrived at the Beatles' suite, whatever Al said (and, I'm guessing, gave) to the gatekeeper got us in the door.

Inside the Beatles' suite, a huge party was going on with a lavish amount of food, drink, smoke, and a high probability of substances I wouldn't have wanted to know about. I immediately separated myself from Al and the four women and set out to achieve my personal goal of meeting all four Beatles. I had arrived with an advantage. Early in their career Paul and John reportedly had said that they hoped to become the Goffin and King of the United Kingdom. I had taken this to mean not that they hoped to marry each other and live in New Jersey but that they aspired to be successful songwriters. I was grateful for the compliment and hoped that my uninvited presence in their suite would do nothing to diminish their respect.

Making my way through the gaggle of groupies and hangers-on, I saw my first Beatle: Ringo Starr. I introduced myself and he responded with a look of recognition. This was good. I welcomed Ringo to America, and he thanked me in his distinctive Liverpudlian accent. Then someone waved him over and off he went.

I didn't have to go very far to find George Harrison. He spoke kindly, quietly, and briefly. George was not the most extroverted Beatle, but my next Beatle, Paul McCartney, was outgoing and congenial. He welcomed me as if we were at a social gathering rather than a scene. He went on for several minutes about how much he and John had always enjoyed and respected Gerry's and my songs, even going so far as to cite specific songs and artists. Then, in what seemed to be emerging as a pattern, someone actively engaged Paul's attention and he turned to that person, though not before gripping both my hands and thanking me for coming.

My last Beatle sighting was John Lennon. Surrounded by several women, none of whom appeared to be his wife, he looked... how shall I put this?

High.

I barely had time to say, "Hi, John. I'm Carole King..." when he interrupted with a remark so disrespectful that I cannot remember what he said, but I do remember how I felt. I had proffered a face of friendship and he had responded with a figurative slap. Had I been mature enough to realize that pushing the edge of decorum was a reflex for John at that stage of his life, I might not have taken it so personally. But I was very young, and I took it very personally.

There was no reason to stay after that. I left through the front door of the suite with no idea that I would have an opportunity to learn directly from John eleven years later why he had been so rude.

Chapter Four

John and Yoko

$\mathscr{T}$he woody's sudden stop for a red light at Central Park West and 72nd Street returned me abruptly to 1976. When the light turned green the driver crossed Central Park West and pulled into the Dakota's motor court, where the man who had taken a cab from the cinema was already waiting for us. (Where's *that* taxi driver when you're late for a meeting?) In a smooth series of motions, he opened the tailgate and helped John out while the fellow in the front seat opened the front passenger door and the rear door on my side, helped me out, and retrieved Yoko. By the time Rick stepped out the first man had already escorted the couple into the lobby. The second man told us to follow John and Yoko, but once Rick and I got inside there was no sign of them. We waited in the lobby while the second man told the driver of the woody where to park. Then he escorted us up to John and Yoko's apartment. Make that John and Yoko's *apartments*, plural. The Lennons had been systematically buying up apartments in the Dakota and as of that evening owned several floors. They didn't own the entire building. Roberta Flack resided in the Dakota, and so did Lauren Bacall.

After exiting the elevator we passed through several rooms on our way to the area in which we would spend the evening. The décor was minimalist. Every room was white, and the few pieces of furniture in each room were also white. I have no recollection of seeing baby Sean, who we were told was with a nanny. I do recall someone bringing us green tea and an assortment of Japanese-style appetizers in white dishes, but what I remember most is that John was radiant with happiness. Against the cool white background of his apartment, at ease with his wife, John was sociable, outgoing, and contented. The angry writer of "Run for Your Life" and "Gimme Some Truth" was nowhere to be seen.

"Y'know, I quite like being a house-hoosband," John said, the traces of having grown up in Liverpool still evident in his speech. A Liverpudlian may move to New York but he'll never stop referring to the season after spring as "soom-eh." This does not apply to Paul, whose ability to mimic anything he's ever seen or heard allows him to lose his Scouse accent at will.

John continued, "Everyone's got soomthin' to say about how Yoko's takin' me away from makin' music, and how she's deprivin' the world of me talent, but bein' a house-hoosband is me talent right now, and I'm pleased to be doin' it. A man's got a right to do what he wants, now, doosn't he."

It wasn't a question.

Though I could somewhat relate, Rick was relating with every bone in his body. With everyone around us complaining that he was taking me away from my music and my friends and family in California, Rick bonded instantly with Yoko. He told her he thought it was completely unreasonable and unfair that she was being so vilified by Beatles fans for taking "their" John away from them.

There was one small elephant in the room, visible only to me: the memory of John being rude to me at the Warwick. I took a deep breath, then went for it.

"John, do you remember meeting me a long time ago?"

"Remind me."

I wasn't sure if that meant "Yes" or "I've met millions of people and I haven't the slightest idea what you're talkin' about," but I plowed forward.

"We met at the Warwick Hotel in 1965," I said, not elaborating on the exact nature of how I got up there. "When I introduced myself to you, you were very rude. Why?"

He paused before saying, "D'you really want to know?"

He did remember.

"It's because I was intimidated."

I stared, uncomprehending.

"You and Gerry were sooch great songwriters. I couldn't think of anything to say that didn't sound stupid, so I did what was coomf'table and made the smart remark."

Now I was embarrassed.

"John, I'm sorry. I didn't mean to remind you of that night. It's just that I've so often wondered what was in your mind and wished I could ask you about it. Really, it was such a long time ago."

"Well, that's all right, then," he said, taking another sip of tea. "No hard feelings, right?"

Relief washed over me as I replied, "Right."

"Well, now," he said, setting down his cup of tea and turning to Rick. "Let's hear what yer man's thinkin' about."

Rick was more than happy to take over the conversation. He had a lot to say. In his account to John about what we were planning to do with our lives he revealed quite a few things he hadn't told me. Apparently Rick identified more strongly than I'd realized with the precept of the counterculture that involved preparing for Armageddon. He told John and Yoko that he considered himself a survivalist. He wanted us (me) to buy a place deep in the woods that he could outfit with everything we'd need to survive after society collapsed, as Rick believed it must inevitably do. He said the place we were looking for would allow us to be self-sufficient. We would live near water, grow our own food, and stock up on whatever we couldn't grow such as fuel, medicine, and other necessities. When the time came, we'd build a new society from there.

As Rick provided more details to John and Yoko about his plan, I felt a shiver of apprehension. I had heard him allude to such ideas before, but I'd had no idea that he'd already formulated a detailed plan to prepare for the end of the current social order. I was dependent on that social order for my income. Living as survivalists didn't seem reasonable or realistic for me or my family.

Without knowing that Rick, too, had been adopted, John had intuited that Rick was in some ways a kindred spirit, and he listened respectfully. When Rick finished laying out his vision for our future, John's response revealed the innate compassion of this man who had already influenced the lives of so many people.

"Well, now," John said. "I couldn't do that. I'd have me bag of rice, but what about everyone else?"

John's remark not only mitigated my apprehension but touched me so deeply that for a few moments I stopped thinking on a conscious level. I know he said other things along those lines, but I don't remember any of the details. I remember only the purity of his compassion and how I felt it envelop me like a warm blanket. Sitting in the glow of his happiness and inner peace I realized that if John Lennon could ignore what others were saying and live his life exactly as he wanted to with love and compassion, then so could I.

Dear God, I thought, please take care of this good man.

That good man would enjoy nearly five more years of happiness before being murdered outside the Dakota on December 8, 1980, by a man whose name will not appear in this book. The man with whom I spent an evening in 1976, so famous and sought-after, had been surprisingly down-to-earth. I wish I had told him how inspiring his song "Imagine" was for me. It's still the simplest, most powerful, and most hopeful answer to questions such as these that keep driving me to be a better person.

Why do people do cruel things to each other? Why can't we live in a world without greed? Why can't people take care of each other and resolve their differences cooperatively?

Imagine.

Sherry and Louise in Laurel Canyon, California, 1969 *From the Carole King Family Archives*

With Lou Adler and Hank Cicalo at A&M Studios, 1970 *From the Collection of Lou Adler. Photo by Jim McCrary*

Recording *Tapestry* with Danny Kortchmar, Russ Kunkel, Charles Larkey, and Ralph Schuckett *Jim McCrary/Redferns/Getty Images*

Working on "the" tapestry, 1971 *From the Collection of Lou Adler. Photo by Jim McCrary*

With James Taylor and Joni Mitchell recording "Will You Love Me Tomorrow" at A&M Studios, 1971 *From the Collection of Lou Adler. Photo by Jim McCrary*

Grammys, 1972 *From the Collection of Lou Adler. Photo by Jim McCrary*

Recording *Fantasy* album with David Campbell and baby Molly, 1973 *From the Collection of Lou Adler. Photo by Jim McCrary*

Rick Evers, 1977 *From the Carole King Family Archives*

With Rick Evers at Kirkham Hot Springs, Idaho, 1977 *From the Collection of Roy and Mon'nette Reynolds*

Molly and Levi at Welcome Home, 1977 *From the Carole King Family Archives*

Milking a goat,
1978 *From the Carole
King Family Archives*

Spring skiing, Burgdorf,
Idaho, 1978 *From the Carole
King Family Archives*

Homeschooling Levi,
1978 *From the Carole
King Family Archives*

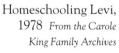

With dad visiting
Idaho, 1978 *From the
Carole King Family Archives*

Skiing with Molly
and Levi in Burgdorf,
1980 *From the Carole
King Family Archives*

Splitting wood, 1981 *From the Carole King Family Archives*

Idaho garden harvest, 1981 *From the Carole King Family Archives*

Rick Sorensen, 1981 *From the Carole King Family Archives*

Wedding, 1982 *From the Carole King Family Archives*

Testifying in DC for Northern Rockies Ecosystem Protection Act (NREPA)
MCT/McClatchy-Tribune/Getty Images

The Living Room Tour, 2004 *Photo by Elissa Kline*

Chapter Five

A Different Kind of Hit

*R*ick Evers had told me early on that he expected to leave this mortal plane at thirty-three because that was the age Jesus had been when he died. Rick also believed that before he left this mortal plane he was destined to have a profound influence on the world through his music. Despite objective opinions to the contrary, Rick considered his songs melodic and had no doubt that his lyrics contained messages that the world wanted to hear. He was convinced that he was a good enough singer to achieve renown equal or superior to that of the Moody Blues. My professional opinion was that he had a long way to go to match the success or the talent of the Moody Blues, but I was smitten enough to believe that anything was possible with this man.

After our visit with Yoko and John, Rick's determination to become a star kicked into overdrive. He didn't see his lack of musical training as a drawback. He thought of it as an asset that made him more original than songwriters and performers with an actual knowledge of music. He compared his rudimentary guitar playing in unconventional tunings to Joni Mitchell's inventive tunings, and he viewed her success as a logical consequence for himself.

Rick's way of applying himself to the pursuit of stardom was to insinuate himself more deeply into my songwriting and recording. He became my songwriting partner by verbalizing ideas that he expected me to turn into songs—which I did. As Rick pushed himself more persistently into all aspects of my life, it was clear to everyone but me that he thought our association would accelerate his rise to fame. The indications were there, but I was a woman in love. I didn't become aware of the net of Rick's behavior tightening around me until I was too enmeshed to get out.

It's really difficult for me to write this.

Rick Evers physically abused me—not just once, but many times.

This is even more difficult to write.

I stayed.

As powerful as my initial attraction was, it had become even more so with my view of Rick as the sole person who could help me move out of L.A. It was a view he did everything to encourage. The more dependent on Rick I became, the more the net tightened. The more it tightened, the more dependent on him I became. The more I lost myself, the more disposed I was to believe Rick when he characterized himself as the only way I could find myself. It was a self-destructive cycle in which I willingly participated.

The first sign of Rick's abusive nature had occurred early in 1976, just three months after we'd met. I was in the bedroom putting away some folded laundry when Rick entered the room and asked about a phone call I had received earlier. He wanted to know who it was. I answered truthfully that it was someone in my business manager's office. Without warning, he struck me with his right fist. He hit me hard, as if he were in a boxing ring, except he wasn't wearing gloves, and he wasn't in a boxing ring.

What...? I thought as I crumpled to the floor holding the left side of my face. Did Rick just *hit* me??

I never saw it coming. I had been putting Rick's jeans in a drawer. Now I was on the floor, sobbing, with tears of pain and outrage soaking my cheeks. I couldn't tell which hurt more, my face or my heart. Meanwhile, Rick, seeing me on the carpet holding my face and weeping, broke down completely. Seemingly aghast at what he had just done, he picked me up off the floor, sat down on the bed, and cradled me in his arms. Now he was sobbing inconsolably and swearing that it would never happen again.

"Oh my God, Carole, I'm sorry, I'm so sorry. Oh, baby, I can't believe I hurt you. I love you so much. I didn't mean to hurt you. You're my lady. I would never do anything to hurt you."

The man who had just hit me was crying harder than I was. He began chanting, "I'm sorry, baby, I'm sorry, so sorry. I'll never do it again, never, *never* again. I love you so much. I'll do anything to make it up to you. I promise, I'll never, ever hurt you again."

Foolishly, I believed him.

Rick was on his best behavior for the next couple of months. He was sweet, kind, loving, and generous—until the next time. It happened the same way, without warning. As before, we were in the bedroom. I had just said something perfectly innocuous when, Bam!!! Again I crumpled to the floor, but this time I was less shocked and more outraged.

"Why did you *do* that??"

Rick broke down. He dropped to the floor and held me while he sobbed and repeated, "Carole, oh baby, I'm sorry. I'm so, so sorry. I promise, I'll never do it again."

After a while he pulled back and regarded the left side of my face. Seeing that it was beginning to swell, he lifted me up, laid me tenderly on the bed, and went to the kitchen to get some ice. He came back into the bedroom with the ice wrapped in a towel and applied it gently to my face. Feeling the cold seeping through the towel, I thought, Look how lovingly he's taking care of me. It was so thoughtful of him to get the ice. He's so remorseful. And he did say he'd never do it again.

The memory of how far I was willing to go to rationalize Rick's behavior is beyond even my own comprehension as I write this, yet it was I who did the rationalizing.

Wasn't it?

Well, yes, it was me. But it wasn't me.

Okay, then, who was it?

It was a woman who let herself be manipulated into a dangerously abusive relationship by a man with so much emotional hunger and misguided sensitivity that he could intuit her every insecurity and play her like the musician he wanted to be. It was a woman who didn't want to let go of her belief that the relationship was fundamentally as good as she had always wanted a relationship to be. This woman—it's so difficult to say "I"—*I* thought of his tender moments as his normal state of being and viewed the moments of abuse as anomalies.

I developed a litany of excuses: He's helping me find my home in the mountains. He's under so much pressure because he's getting all this negative energy from my friends. Everyone resents him for taking me away from them. It's hard on a man when a woman makes all the money. He never hits me in front of the children.

The list could have gone on endlessly. And not one of the excuses justified my staying.

During 1976, Rick would allow just enough time to go by for me to believe that our relationship consisted of nothing but peace, love, joy, and happiness—and then, Bang!!! I never knew what would set it off. Maybe Rick thought his journey to stardom wasn't happening fast enough. Maybe I was getting too much attention. Perhaps I had been on the phone with a female friend a little longer than he thought I should be. (By then I knew better than to be on the phone with a male friend.) Each time something set Rick off, his insane jealousy and explosive temper would take over and he'd throw a jab at my face with his fist. His fist!! After a few such times you'd think I would have figured out that this was a pattern and removed myself from harm's way, but I was beyond rational thinking. I was completely lost. The relatively confident woman I had been had all but disappeared. Externally I appeared to be going about my work and my life as usual, but inside I had become a small distant creature wrapped in fear, shame, and guilt.

Every so often, a vestige of the woman I used to be would ask in a tiny voice from a far corner of my mind: Why are you staying with this man? But rather than look for an answer, the manipulated woman to whom the question had been directed—there I go again; I—ignored the question and continued to let my abuser off the hook.

One of the most appealing things about Rick was that he knew how to come up with activities that were fun. My younger children in particular seemed to enjoy those activities. I often described Rick as "good to my children." My Larkey children never reported otherwise, nor did I ever see him being anything but kind to them. Had I ever seen or heard about him lifting a hand to Molly or Levi, I would have protected them. I would have taken my children and left without a backward glance. But because I didn't value myself in the same way, I didn't protect myself. With his twisted sensitivity, Rick knew exactly how far he could go and still retain his emotional hold on me. He knew that he would lose me instantly if he said a cross word to the children, so of course he never did. The truth is, Rick never felt the need. He felt safe in the company of children, animals, and the elderly. It was prime-of-life adult humans—specifically women, and at the time, most specifically I—who threatened him the most.

It took me a long time to realize that Rick had a very serious problem. It took me even longer to admit that I, too, had a problem. By staying, I was complicit in creating a space in which the abuse could recur. The same gift for denial that had led me to commit so readily to Rick in the first place allowed me to characterize his irrational anger as an aberration. I set it aside, as if it weren't part of our "real" relationship. My reluctance to leave was exacerbated by the psychological bond that formed between us every time he became abjectly apologetic. When he cried and said he was sorry, swore he didn't mean it, and promised he'd do anything to make it up to me, *I* felt sorry for *him*. And then when he avowed his undying love and devotion, I was so grateful to be kissing and making up that I was willing to believe whatever he said.

It was a perilous yet irresistible dynamic. One moment I felt completely powerless. The next moment, all the power shifted to me. Rick was so full of remorse that I could say anything at that moment with impunity. I could speak my truth and tell him with righteous passion all the things I expected from him. With conflicting emotions obliterating any possibility of levelheadedness, I was drawn in again and again by Rick's repentance. I so desperately wanted to believe him.

Before Rick I couldn't imagine myself in such a relationship. I thought abuse happened only to women who were uneducated or unsophisticated, women with no money or confidence whose fathers or other male family members had been alcoholics or addicts or bullies asserting control through physical and sexual abuse. My father had done none of those things, nor had any other man in my life. I had my own income and a prior history of worldly success. I had plenty of friends and family members to whom I could have turned for help. I could have left Rick with complete safety. I had always been judgmental about women who stayed in abusive relationships. I'd always thought, If I ever found myself with a man like that, the first time he struck me I'd be out of there in a New York minute. I would *never* stay with an abuser. Until I did.

And through it all, my career went on.

Chapter Six

Definition of a Friend

*T*hroughout 1976 Rick and I continued to be joined at the hip. At the studio, while I was recording he sat in the lounge, smoked, and made phone calls. He walked up and down the aisles with me at the grocery store. He sat in the salon and read while I had my hair cut, and when I went out to promote *Thoroughbred* he came on tour with me. My band members were Russ Kunkel on drums, Lee Sklar on bass, Clarence McDonald on keyboards, Ms. Bobbye Hall on percussion, and Doyle Hoff, Waddy Wachtel, and Danny Kortchmar on guitar. Often Lou Adler traveled with us. Everyone on that tour had a good rapport with Lou, with me, and with each other. That year the definition of "with me" included Rick, with whom no one had a good rapport. My band would have enjoyed that tour a lot more had it not been for the constant presence of my boyfriend. Rick's moods and behavior were the hub around which the emotional wheel of my 1976 tour revolved.

One event stands out in my memory because it revealed the strong character of one of my bandmates in particular. It was less than ten minutes before a concert in the Midwest when Rick exploded at me in the dressing room. This time the manifestation of his fury was verbal, leaving me physically undamaged but deeply upset. When my production manager knocked and announced, "Showtime!" I honored the long-established tradition of "the show must go on" and followed him to the wings. Heartened by the roar of the crowd when the house went to black, I walked onstage, bowed and waved to the audience, sat at the piano, and was sufficiently in the moment to deliver a plausible performance and respond warmly to the audience. But a part of my mind was preoccupied with what kind of mood I'd find Rick in when I came offstage.

On that tour, audiences typically invited me back for multiple encores. Usually I performed the first encore solo, then I brought the band back onstage for the second encore. During that first encore I couldn't stop thinking about Rick. I finished the song, took a bow, and came offstage looking for my boyfriend. He was nowhere to be seen. Probably he was in the dressing room. I drank some water and waited to see if the applause would die down. It didn't.

During the second encore we rocked hard, loud, and evidently capably enough that the audience kept up a continuous level of clapping and cheering throughout the song. When we came off-stage, again I looked for Rick, but I still didn't see him. With more than five thousand fans now stomping, applauding, and calling for a third encore, I caught my breath, wiped my face and neck with a towel, and gulped more water. Just as I was about to walk back onstage I heard a commotion from the direction of the dressing rooms on the other side. Every neuron in my brain was telling me that Rick was involved. I wanted so badly to find out what was happening, but the applause was becoming more insistent. Hundreds of lighters and matches illuminated the venue. More than ten thousand feet stomped in rhythm as people chanted, "More! More! More! More!"

It's difficult to explain how a performer senses the exact right moment to come back out. The timing is crucial. Too soon and there's not enough excitement to warrant your reemergence. Too late and the audience's enthusiasm begins to wane. Early in my career as a performer I tried to preempt the myth of the unplanned encore by staying onstage and confessing that I had already planned to do another song, but the audience didn't want to hear that. On another occasion I skipped the encore altogether, leaving a very unhappy audience making sounds that rhymed with "shoe." I wish I could have a do-over on that one.

What I learned after trial and error was that audiences enjoy the encore ritual. There's a predictable rhythm to the custom of an audience applauding a performer back onstage. A request for an encore is a gift given by an audience to let the artist know that she has given a worthy performance. And they respond with even more enthusiasm when the artist is modest enough to convey with sincerity that she had no idea that she was going to be applauded back onstage. The truth is, we never do know. We may hope and prepare for an encore, but if we're lucky enough to retain some humility, we do not take it for granted.

The night of that concert in the Midwest, the third encore was of course unplanned. (Excuse me; I have to go feed a hungry myth.) On the off chance that a third encore might be requested, I had prepared "You've Got a Friend," a song I often perform solo. On that tour I performed it with the band.

Years later, when I was called upon as an actress to feel conflicted, I didn't need to look any further than that moment when I was desperate to find out what was going on with Rick at the same time that my fans were calling for me to do one last song. With my sense of theater telling me that the demand was at peak intensity, professionalism prevailed. I went onstage, bowed my thanks, sat down at the piano, and took a moment to collect myself while giving the band enough time to assemble before joining me onstage. Looking toward the stage left wings I saw...no band.

Okay. I would start the intro myself and carry on until they showed up. I played the introduction, then started the verse, expecting Danny to come in.

When you're down and troubled, and you need some loving care...

No Danny.

Close your eyes and think of me...

No Waddy, and no Lee. No Clarence, Doyle, or Bobbye.

I kept all my attention and energy focused on the audience and played the rest of the first verse alone. I no longer expected the band. As I began the first chorus with "You just call..." I heard Russ's brushes softly accenting the backbeat on his snare drum. I looked up. There was Russ sitting at his kit with that calm, reassuring smile that adds light to any stage on which he's playing. No one else joined us. For the rest of the song, all I could think about was how Russ typified everything about which I was singing. We finished the song, took the final "band bow" as a duo, then left the stage as the audience, now with happy tearstained faces, continued to applaud until the house lights went up. I don't know why that song always does that to people. All I have to do is sing it. Even a cappella, everyone sings along and all fights are forgotten for five minutes and twelve seconds.

But not all fights had been forgotten that night. As soon as we came offstage Russ headed straight for the band dressing room. I asked a crew member if he knew where Rick was.

"I saw him leave the building a few minutes ago."

I watched the guy as he headed toward the stage for the load-out, then I walked past the monitor mixing board and saw Danny, Waddy, and Lee outside their dressing room. They were berating someone I couldn't see. "Someone" turned out to be Lou. The musicians had had it up to *here* with Rick's moods and disruptive behavior and wanted to leave the tour. With Danny, Waddy, and Lee equally indignant in communicating their outrage and Russ standing nearby in support, Lou was trying to soothe the troubled waters and apparently having no luck.

"Fuck this shit," Danny exploded to Lou. "You get me on a god-damn plane tomorrow. I'm fuckin' outta here!" Waddy and Lee echoed their agreement.

The house lights and backstage lights were up, but I was completely in the dark.

"What happened?" I wailed. "Would someone *please* fill me in?"

They did.

From what I could ascertain from their overlapping narrative, Danny had come off the stage after the second encore with his fist in the air saying, "That was FUCKIN' GREAT!!" For no apparent reason and with no warning, Rick had knocked Danny cold. That was the commotion I'd heard earlier. Lee had stayed with Danny while Waddy and Russ wrestled Rick into the bathroom. As Danny described it later, "Russ wanted to take Rick's head off, but then Rick started saying, 'I'm sorry, I'm sorry, I don't know what came over me.'" Waddy and Russ had stayed with Rick while Lee went back to the dressing room with Danny. When Russ heard his cue he left Waddy with a now contrite Rick and joined me onstage. Apparently Clarence and Bobbye had absented themselves as soon as they saw there was a scuffle, as had Doyle, who had previously known Rick in Utah.

Realizing that Rick had driven my band beyond the limits of their endurance, I apologized profusely and said, "Please don't leave." But then the pressure of not knowing where Rick was became too much for me and I said, "I have to go." If anyone could calm the band down and persuade them to stay, I knew Lou could. I needed to find my boyfriend.

I went to my dressing room, changed to street clothes, and prepared to leave the venue. As anxious as I was to see Rick, I spent the entire car ride back to the hotel in dread of seeing him, a feeling that turned out to be justified. The moment I entered our hotel room he began to make a huge scene, going over in excruciating detail everything that had happened with the band from his point of view (i.e., it was everyone else's fault) and citing all the wrongs that had been done to him from day one by everyone from Clarence McDonald to a catering assistant two cities ago. I was afraid he would take his frustration out on me physically, so I just listened, nodded compassionately, and made occasional exclamations of compassion such as "Ohh." The good news was that, other than having to listen to his tirade, I endured no physical abuse that night. When at last his anger was spent, he became affectionate and then we went to bed. The next morning, Rick was more subdued. He didn't exactly apologize, but he nodded to Lou and the band and kept a respectful distance.

I will never forget Russ's calm professionalism in setting aside his personal feelings and coming onstage to finish the show with me. I'm still deeply touched by the willingness of my bandmates to endure being with Rick before and after the altercation. And then there was Lou.

"None of us want to be around him," Lou had said, "but Carole needs you to stay more than you need to go."

Twenty words.

Years later, when I discussed that night with Danny, he assured me in no uncertain terms—and let me say that with Danny, there are never uncertain terms—that the band had stayed because of the music, and because they cared about me.

"Money had nothing to do with it," Danny said. "No amount of money could have made us stay if we didn't want to."

I knew that.

To my great relief, Rick, Lou, the band, and I got through the rest of the tour without further incident. The same could not be said about Rick and me after the tour.

Chapter Seven

Tributaries

One of the most incomprehensible things about women who stay in abusive relationships is not just that they don't leave, but that they don't want to leave. For more than a year I had suffered physically and emotionally from Rick's violent outbursts. By 1977, after all those weeks and months, I had to know he wouldn't change. I should have left. I could have left.

So why did I stay?

It's well known that women have the ability to forget pain. If we didn't, no woman would ever have a second child. That ability helped me forget the bad times and allowed me to think of Rick as the man I wanted him to be. After he hit me, the power shift gave me the illusion of control for a while. And I still believed I needed Rick to help me find the place of my dreams.

I kept hoping that once we left L.A., Rick's anger would disappear. His disposition did lighten considerably when we found the perfect place on Robie Creek, a tributary of Mores Creek off Highway 21 between Boise and Idaho City. The day I signed the check, I, too, was happy. I had just become an Idaho landowner.

In the mid-seventies, most of the land along Robie Creek was relatively undeveloped. After leaving the paved highway we had to negotiate two miles of rocks and potholes on a winding dirt road to get to the property. I was okay with that. I found it infinitely preferable to sitting in stop-and-go traffic on the Santa Monica Freeway. The property had a flat area near the creek with enough room for a large garden, a small pasture, and the double-wide trailer that would accommodate our family until we could build a more permanent log home. We had already chosen a site higher on the property along Ashton Creek, a small, year-round tributary of Robie Creek. The place felt entirely rural, yet we were only a half hour out of Boise. It was the best of both worlds.

Back in L.A., school had just let out for summer in 1977. I arranged for someone to stay in the house on Appian Way, packed our belongings, and prepared to move my family to Idaho. With Charlie's cautious consent, Levi, Molly, Sherry, Rick, and I began the thousand-mile drive to Robie Creek without Louise.

At seventeen, Louise had just finished her junior year in high school. When I told her we were going to move, she unambiguously let me know that she did not wish to relocate to "an isolated place in the middle of nowhere." I was so set on going that I convinced myself it was okay to allow her to stay in L.A. She was determined to finish high school, she was competent and responsible, she had just been signed to a record deal with an advance, seventeen was almost eighteen, and she would be living near her father.

It was a seriously misguided decision on my part. As much as Gerry loved his children, his illness made him incapable of being a responsible parent. If anything, Louise was Gerry's responsible parent. That she graduated from high school and made a good life for herself is a tribute to her. She never lost sight of who she was, and she persevered in the face of adversity. She turned my leaving her to fend for herself into an opportunity to develop her own strengths. She learned how to play multiple instruments and wrote and recorded her own songs. In 1984, she moved to London and became part of the UK community of songwriters and musicians. After she returned to L.A. in 1994, she went out on tour in 1996 with Tears for Fears, playing lead and rhythm guitar and singing backup. Louise has been a productive member of the music community ever since, pausing only to have two sons and be the attentive parent to them that she would have liked her parents to be to her.

As the parent of a minor child, I could have insisted that she move with the rest of us. Or I could have given up my dream in support of her well-being, as many parents do for their children. Or I could have waited a year to move. But even if waiting had been in my nature, it wasn't in Rick's. Louise was already on a path to becoming the woman she wanted to be. She would have been miserable in Idaho. It's likely that I didn't force her to go because of my core characteristic: I just wanted everyone to be happy.

Do I regret leaving her? First, I have to reject the word "regret." I find regret, shame, and guilt unhelpful. Instead of carrying those feelings around with me, I figure out how to apply them to my future behavior. At that point they stop being regret, shame, or guilt and become a lesson learned. I don't feel great about my decision. But then I ask myself what I might have done differently. My dream was to leave California and live in a place very different from L.A. If I hadn't met Rick, I would have found some other way, some other place, and, most likely, some other man.

Speaking years later about this, Louise said, "Eventually I came to understand that you found peace and sanity in Idaho. But I wouldn't have made the choices you did. I must have had angels watching over me."

Sherry was fifteen that June. With even less interest than Louise in a rural lifestyle, she protested loudly and frequently. Notwithstanding her piteous pleas that she didn't want to leave her friends, I gave her no choice. She would come with me to Idaho and attend Boise High in the fall. The sole attraction for Sherry was that she loved horses and had been riding and caring for a palomino mare named Sweetheart. When I offered to trailer Sweetheart to Idaho, Sherry continued to protest, but at a lower volume.

As it turned out, there was another attraction. In California she would have had to wait until she was sixteen to get a driver's license. In Idaho teenagers could then legally drive at fourteen. In theory fourteen was a tender age, but in practice many kids in Idaho had learned to drive tractors while sitting on the lap of a parent. It wasn't much of a leap for them to drive cars and trucks as soon as they could see through the steering wheel. Idaho law would allow Sherry to legally drive herself to and from Boise every day. Her route would include the unpaved stretch of road along Robie Creek during a particularly icy winter. Her vehicle was a CJ5 Jeep, about the size of an army Jeep, with sturdy snow tires, four-wheel drive, and a roll bar. I was immeasurably thankful for such precautions when Sherry had several minor vehicular mishaps and suffered no injuries. Evidently she, too, had angels watching over her.

Although it was I who precipitated the move, I had my own moments of doubt. Having spent most of my life around people and buildings, the first time I went for a walk alone in the woods I felt uneasy as soon as I lost sight of people and buildings. After a couple of months of such walks I felt more comfortable among rocks and trees. I cherished walking in the rain and watching little streams merge into bigger ones. I loved the cool quiet of the glade along Ashton Creek. My new surroundings taught me to appreciate solitude and nature. Though I continued to be surrounded by nature, solitude would become a rare commodity.

Rick had named the place "Welcome Home." The name was prophetic. We had a profusion of visitors, virtually all friends of Rick. Soon a pattern developed. First they came to visit. Then they came to stay. Before long Welcome Home became a sort of commune, with Rick as its social center and me as its financial center. It might have been a typical seventies commune except that only one of its residents had a steady income. It was a good thing my songs were generating enough money to ensure that my family would have enough to live on if I were reasonably prudent. As long as I defined "reasonably prudent" as making more than I spent, I was meeting that definition. The definition of "my family" was another matter entirely. At Welcome Home the concept of family was elastic. Still, I was living my dream. Our garden was producing abundantly, and our little community was enjoying the fruits (and vegetables) of everyone's labor. With Rick's dark side seemingly left behind, I was optimistic enough to commit to a third partner. On August 24, 1977, the day Rick and I were married, I was thirty-five and Rick was thirty. Louise, in L.A., was seventeen. Sherry was fifteen, Molly five and a half, and Levi three. I didn't know Rusty's age, but he, too, was in attendance.

I spent many enjoyable evenings listening to music sung and played by my new friends and neighbors not just from Welcome Home but from up and down Mores Creek. From Idaho City to Boise, whatever the genre—usually country, bluegrass, folk, or pop—and whatever a person's economic status or educational background, everyone participated, even if only by clapping along. Maybe a gal couldn't pay her phone bill that month, or maybe a fella couldn't afford a TV, but somehow these long-haired denizens of southern Idaho managed to come up with enough money to buy a guitar, a banjo, a fiddle, a string bass, a tambourine, or a preowned set of drums.

Another essential item was a device for listening to music. Most often it was an eight-track, though for some it was a cassette player or a car radio. There was no question about my new friends' priorities: music was at the top of everyone's list. At first I was skeptical, but after I heard the enthusiasm and, in some cases, skill with which these untutored players executed complicated maneuvers on their instruments, I could see that they had their priorities in order. For most of my life my connection with music had happened in solitude. It was highly educational for me to play with and listen to this group of mostly unschooled musicians who, rather than aiming for commercial success, seemed to be playing music purely for the love of it.

As it turned out, that wasn't exactly the case. They might not have been *aiming* for commercial success, but more than a few of my new friends harbored a fantasy of becoming the very thing that I was assiduously trying not to be—a star. This was true for no one more than Rick. The extremes of our relationship had manifested themselves the previous year in songs to which Rick had contributed, and songs I wrote on my own. My internal conflict could be heard in "To Know That I Love You," cowritten with Rick, and "God Only Knows," which I wrote alone. These and eight other songs became the ten tracks on *Simple Things*, my first album for Capitol Records.

Not all the songs on *Simple Things* reflected conflict. "One" was a pure expression, unfiltered through Rick, of my long-held belief that each of us has the power to change the world. I wrote "In the Name of Love" to assuage my grief and comfort others after Willa Mae passed away. And I was inspired to write "Hard Rock Café" after I drove past a bar with that name in downtown L.A. and then, on another occasion, dined in a Main Street eatery with that name in a small Idaho town. I was not yet aware of the Hard Rock Café with 1950s décor in London that would become the flagship of a world-renowned chain of restaurants.[*]

In previous discussions with friends in coastal cities about whether anxiety or serenity inspired better art, I had always held that good art could be made just as easily from a place of contentment. However, in practice, without the tumult, stress, and competition typically found in cities I found that I had no interest in writing three-minute pop tunes. My children, my garden, and the additional horses we acquired (one being Whiskey) occupied most of my time. While I was living what I thought of as a normal life, I was neglecting my music. The impetus to write that year came mostly from Rick's need for recognition, which he believed was imminent, and my contractual commitment to deliver another album to Capitol.

---

[*]Founders Peter Morton and Isaac Tigrett reportedly named the Hard Rock Café in London after that same bar in downtown Los Angeles. That bar also appears in a Henry Diltz photo on the Doors' 1970 album, *Morrison Hotel*.

Chapter Eight

Inundated

*I*n January 1978 my commitment to Capitol brought my three youngest children, Rick, and me back to the house on Appian Way. The title of the album I had come to record was *Welcome Home*—an irony not lost on me as I looked out the window and watched the rain pouring down on the eucalyptus trees and ravines of the Hollywood Hills.

That January, Los Angeles was inundated with rainstorms— not just average, ordinary, run-of-the-mill precipitation, but massive, torrential, dripping, splashing, umbrella-crushing, gully-washing vertical streams of water. Cars parked below Mulholland Drive on the city side of Laurel Canyon were swept down to the intersection of Hollywood Boulevard, where their owners found them the next morning, bunched up side-to-bumper in ponds of murky water that had formed overnight at the bottom of the Canyon. It was mudslide season. Rocks and trees responded to the call of gravity and blocked streets and roads faster than CalTrans could remove them. Unaccustomed to that kind of weather, a lot of native Southern Californians called in sick rather than drive to work in a downpour. Among those who ventured out, many plowed into each other's cars, which forced tow-truck drivers and insurance adjusters out of the comfort of their homes. Now they, too, could plow into other people's cars. On the other hand, not even the deluge après Louis XV could have kept transplanted New Yorkers home. Reports that the floor of Art's Deli was under six inches of water did not deter regular customers from showing up in East Coast foul-weather gear to get a corned beef on rye with a half sour pickle and a Dr Pepper.

My emotional life matched the weather. Outwardly I did my best to function normally, but inwardly I was in turmoil. As happy as Rick had been in Idaho, for him the idea of the children and me going to L.A. without him had been unthinkable. When we arrived at the house on Appian Way it was as if he had parked his evil twin in a closet and traded places with it. His dark disposition reemerged, and once again he accompanied me everywhere, which of course included the studio. It was only during rare moments when he left the room that I experienced the enjoyment I usually felt in that setting.

One morning Rick said, "Go ahead. I'll come later."

I was puzzled, but I said, "Okay," and drove to the studio. Though I was concerned about where he was and when he'd arrive, I found his absence liberating, almost exhilarating. That feeling continued uninterrupted. Rick never showed up. When I came home he offered no explanation of where he'd been, and I didn't ask. A few days later he again told me to go on without him, but he did come to the studio a few hours later. His periodic absences continued through the rest of January. It was unnerving. I couldn't fully relax because I never knew when he might turn up.

Nearly a week after my thirty-sixth birthday in February, Rick picked me up at the end of a session. My question "How was your day?" made him angry. I was afraid he'd lash out at me, but he didn't. When we got home he stayed in the car and smoked a cigarette while I made sure my kids were where they were supposed to be. They were. I kissed the children, paid the babysitter, and sent her home. Exhausted, I went to my room, took off my shoes, climbed into bed, and fell into a restless sleep.

At 2:02 a.m. I awoke and saw Rick sleeping next to me. I turned my head and registered the time on the clock. Then I turned my face up toward the ceiling and lay on my back, motionless. I knew who Rick was, but I couldn't remember who I was. At that moment, if someone had asked me my name I would have drawn a blank. Suddenly I heard someone ask a question. It might have been I, but I hadn't spoken. It was as if I were outside myself hearing the question being asked in my mind.

"Who am I?"

I sat up slowly, attentively, the way people do at night when they think they've just heard something but aren't sure. Rick hadn't moved. I waited, but heard nothing more. I stepped quietly down from the bed, and started to go . . . where? Where was I going? I couldn't remember why I had gotten up. Suddenly my perception shifted and I was regarding myself as if through someone else's eyes. I watched myself walk over to the window and look out. Then I saw myself turn from the window and, with a movement like that of a silk scarf slipping off a mannequin, the woman I was watching slid down and collapsed on the rug at the foot of the bed. At that moment she—I—curled into a fetal position and disappeared. I had no thoughts. I had nothing, and I was no one.

Then I heard another question in my mind as clearly as if I had spoken it aloud.

"Where's me?"

An answer grew out of the nothingness and shaped itself around the person I was experiencing as not-me. It wasn't sudden, like a thunderbolt. It was an unguent, a healing sense of possibility that slowly permeated my consciousness, a balm that soothed my soul, reanimated my body, and infused my mind with a renewed sense of identity and purpose. I had no idea where it came from. If I'd been looking for something resembling what people define as God by whatever name, I didn't find it. It found me.

I began to recollect what I knew about myself. My success as a songwriter, my musical gift, my joy and responsibilities as a mother, and the financial independence that had defined me in the past were all still part of my present. If I didn't have the will to leave Rick, maybe I could learn to live with him in a more healthy way. Meanwhile, I would continue to be the best mother I could be, finish my album, and, since professional counseling was readily available in the land of la-la, I would seek such help. With clarity and resolve, I stood up, walked to the bed, climbed in, and immediately fell asleep.

A few hours later, I woke up before Rick did. I went downstairs, called a friend in a later time zone, got a name, and somehow managed to book my first therapy session without Rick finding out. For each of the next few therapy sessions I came up with what I hoped was a credible story. Each time, when Rick didn't object, I thought it was because my explanation was plausible and nonthreatening. I didn't know that he had rekindled his interest in something he didn't want me to know about. I was so grateful to be able to discuss my deepest feelings with someone other than my husband that I didn't question why he was slackening his constant oversight of me.

It took only a few sessions for me to learn that I had power within the relationship that I hadn't been using. Perhaps the simplest, most tangible result of my therapy was my discovery that "No" was a complete sentence. I didn't need to explain or apologize. However, discovering wasn't the same as doing. I would have to actually say no and mean it, or nothing would change.

The first time I hazarded saying no to Rick he was sitting on one of two sofas in the living room. I was sitting on the sofa opposite him. He had just announced that he wanted "us" to buy a sailboat as soon as I finished the album.

A sailboat??? I thought. No way! But Rick had already launched into his presentation. His eyes twinkled with anticipated pleasure as he said, "Baby, it'll be great! Think of how much fun the kids will have!"

I pictured Levi, Molly, and Sherry on a sailboat.

"Carole. You work so hard. You deserve a real vacation. Don't worry about Welcome Home. Our friends'll take care of it."

The idea of a sailing trip did sound very appealing.

"Trust me. Wasn't I right about Welcome Home?"

His case had just slipped away. He had lost it when he said, "Trust me." But he didn't know that. He came over to where I was sitting, put his arms around me, and made his closing argument.

"Baby, you'll see. Sailing on our own boat will be a great thing for you and the kids."

No, I thought. It won't.

Was this the right time to say no?

With Rick's arms still around me, I marshaled my courage, lifted my head, looked him in the eye, and said, "No."

He let go of me, pushed himself back, narrowed his eyes, and held my gaze for a long moment. I met his gaze and waited for the blow. It never came. He averted his gaze, then looked back at me with bewilderment. Then he stood up and walked out of the room. I stayed on the sofa and pondered what had just happened. He was gone for the length of time it would take to smoke a cigarette. When he returned he acted as if nothing had happened. The smell of fresh cigarette smoke on his clothes triggered a recurring childhood memory of my father coming out of the bathroom. The association might have weakened my resolve, but I was not going to allow that to happen. Rick never brought the subject up again.

On two subsequent occasions when Rick wanted something equally out of the question, each time my answer was, "No." Each time I braced for him to be angry or violent, but he took each no passively, then acted as if he'd never mentioned the wanted thing in the first place.

Obviously everyone's experience is different. Simply saying no may not be the best solution for everyone. But if you're a victim of abuse, you may find it helpful to know that you're not the only one who's endured what you're going through, and that no matter what your abuser tells you, what's happening is not your fault. There are good, kind, caring people and organizations that exist to help you.

If you're suffering from physical or sexual abuse, go to a safe place as soon as you can and call the National Domestic Violence Hotline at 1-800-799-SAFE (7233) or 1-800-787-3224 (TTY). Or, from a safe computer (to which your abuser does not have access), go to http://www.thehotline.org.

PLEASE GET HELP! You deserve to be safe.

In my situation, against all logic, it seemed that the more I had tried to please Rick to avoid his wrath, the more abusive he became. As soon as I stood up for myself with confidence and clarity, his violent behavior stopped.

At the time I thought my newly acquired ability to say no was the reason Rick never hit me again. I didn't realize that he was preoccupied with something he wanted even more than control of me.

Chapter Nine

The Final No

While I'd been mixing *Welcome Home*, unbeknownst to me, Rick was becoming increasingly addicted to cocaine. He wasn't snorting it recreationally; he was shooting it. Between work and my responsibilities as a mother, using any drug in any way was the farthest thing from my mind. I was hooked on the high of living close to nature—a high I had been reluctant to interrupt, but I had to earn a living. Working in the studio without Rick had restored my confidence. I stopped resenting L.A. and treasured whatever time I could spend with my four children. Every day was a gift, a joyous celebration of rediscovery.

I had asked, Who am I?

I was *this* woman. And this woman was slow to catch on. Before 1978 I had seen no evidence of Rick using drugs. As far as I knew, my husband had two addictions—cigarettes and coffee. Later I would learn that he'd had a history of shooting speed, and that prior to meeting me he'd been living in the red van with a woman from Utah and her young son. The day before the party at which I'd met Rick she had taken her son and gone back to Utah to get away from his drug abuse and the physical violence he sometimes visited upon her. True to form, Rick had never hit the boy—as if that made it okay.

Rick was smart enough to shoot up far from where I conducted my daily activities so I wouldn't find out about his forays into that shadowy world. It worked. At first I was so grateful that he wasn't hitting me and that I could see friends without him that I didn't fully grasp the implications of the changes in his behavior. It wasn't just the cessation of his jealousy and violence. Usually, when I came home after a mixing session, the first thing I did was check on the children. After determining that everything was as it should be, I would look around the rest of the house to see if Rick was around. He wasn't often home, but when he was I usually found him in our bedroom pacing and muttering to himself. Sometimes I heard him preaching in a hoarse voice to a nonexistent listener about arcane spiritual and religious concepts. Other times I found him writing furiously, filling notebooks with colored-pencil drawings of spaceships, flames, and elements of American Indian design. He wrote copiously, covering pages with what he believed was visionary poetry and art.

As Rick's bizarre behavior intensified it reminded me of my previous experience with the mental illness of a loved one. I had just made the decision to consult a medical professional and was going to do so the following day. I never got to make that call. The night I completed the final mix of *Welcome Home* I parked the car and came into the house in a celebratory mood. Rick wasn't there, but the babysitter was with the children, and thankfully all was well. The next morning I woke up very early. Rick wasn't in bed. I checked all the rooms upstairs, but he wasn't in any of them. With all three of my kids still asleep, I went downstairs, put water on to boil for a cup of tea, and looked in every room downstairs. No Rick. I went back to the kitchen, put a teabag in the cup, and poured hot water over it. While it was steeping I entered the bathroom next to the kitchen and saw several drops of dark red blood on the white tile floor. With the flash that comes when something has been right in front of your eyes the whole time but you've never really seen it, I understood that not only had Rick been injecting cocaine, but he had come in during the night and had shot up in the house where my children lay sleeping.

At that moment I made the decision I should have made the first time he hit me.

Not knowing how soon Rick would return, I woke all three children. Levi and Molly, still sleepy, dressed themselves while Sherry and I hastily packed a few bags, and we all left the house. We drove to Louise's to let her know why we were leaving and make the necessary arrangements from her phone. Though Louise was living on her own and didn't interact much with Rick, I made sure she knew that she was not to go to our house under any circumstances until further notice.

My impulse was to get as far away from Los Angeles as possible, but I didn't think it was a good idea to go to Welcome Home. I saw my options as either New York or Maui. I have no idea why Maui came to mind, though warm weather and sandy beaches may have been factors. Probably I thought that a faraway island would be the safest place to go to figure out what to do next. A few hours later, Sherry, Molly, Levi, and I were on a plane to Hawaii. I didn't have more than a few days of figuring before a definitive decision was made for me. Using the phone in our rented condo, Sherry called a friend of hers who also knew Rick. After listening in silence for what seemed like an unusually long time, she handed the phone to me with a horror-struck expression on her face and uttered one word.

"Mom?"

Rick had been found dead of an overdose of cocaine in a location believed to have been the shooting gallery where he'd been buying and injecting the drug. That's what my husband had been doing while I was recording *Welcome Home*.

Richard Edward Evers had been born on January 6, 1947. He died on March 21, 1978, nearly three months after his thirty-first birthday. He was less than two years shy of the age of demise he'd predicted for himself.

I could no more describe my jumbled emotions that night than I could describe the colors in the exquisite Maui sunset. That particular sunset was so spectacular that I wondered if Rick had sent it from wherever he was. I was filled with a deep sense of loss, not for the man Rick was when he died, but for the man with whom I had fallen in love. Before I had seen his dark side, I would have described Rick Evers as full of joy. How could that man have a dark side? How could he take himself out of this world? Had my saying no driven him to drug abuse? Was it because my work had taken us away from his beloved Idaho? Of course I wasn't to blame for Rick's death, but when we lose someone unexpectedly, we often ask what we had done that might have contributed to the death of our loved one, or what we didn't do that might have saved him or her. Usually the answer is, "Nothing." But still we ask.

The next day I flew back to Los Angeles with my kids. One question had already been answered: Idaho was our home, and Idaho was where I wanted to be. However, Idaho was not where Sherry wanted to be. When she asked if she could stay in L.A., I assented. It took several weeks to deal with the aftermath of Rick's death and find someone to stay in the house on Appian Way. After that, Molly, Levi, and I flew back to Boise. As the plane took off and I watched L.A. recede from view, suddenly, silently, I began to cry. I had just lost someone close to me, and all the complicated parts of the story fell away. At thirty-six, I was a widow.

At Welcome Home, with spring unfolding and its abundance of life renewing, I was comforted and inspired by nature's optimistic outlook. While Molly attended school in Idaho City, Levi played with friends at home. I did my utmost to keep happier times with Rick foremost in my memory and those of the children. Rick's friends helped me take care of Welcome Home, and I continued to support them financially. I worked in my garden, rode and cared for the horses, hiked up and down Ashton Creek, and did mundane, necessary tasks such as washing dishes, doing laundry, and taking out the garbage. After everything my kids had been through, they seemed to be flourishing, as were the horses and garden. Rusty was the lone exception. You could see the question in his eyes and in everything he did: Where is he? At first Rusty stayed with us, then he moved in with another Welcome Home family, then another. He belonged to all of us, and yet to none of us.

Throughout the spring and summer I allowed myself to feel grief and, yes, anger. But I also worked diligently to replace such feelings with positive memories. It had been Rick who had provided me with the extra motivation I needed to get out of L.A. He had introduced me to the mountains, the beauty of the land, and the simple decency of so many people in my adopted state. And though I would rather not have lived with an abusive person, doing so had given me compassion for people in similar situations and helped me reaffirm that if I exercised the will and determination with which I believe every one of us is born, nothing would keep me down.

It was a crisp morning toward the end of August when I walked up the hill with Molly and Levi to meet Molly's school bus. The blue jacket on one of her classmates reminded me of the clear blue sky reflected in Rick's eyes our first morning at Welcome Home. I remember him sitting on the front porch steps with a steaming cup of coffee cradled in his hands, watching the sunlight creeping down his beloved Idaho mountains.

That vivid image set off a series of recollections. As I made my way back down the hill with Levi, memory snapshots were flipping through my mind.

- Me standing on a big rock on the bank of a creek in the summer of 1977. I'm wearing a tank top and cutoffs and feeling the shock of icy-cold creek water splashing over me while Rick, his golden hair backlit by the sun, plunges his naked body into a swimming hole. Emerging dripping wet, Rick raises his arms to the heavens in a triumphant V.
- Rick carrying a chain saw down Ashton Creek after cutting wood with his friends who live above us on the property. First smelling, then seeing his favorite person in the world, Rusty begins to bark ecstatically.
- My young son and daughter being scooped up by Rick. He swings them around, then embraces them both in a bear hug. As he laughs with delight at their obvious enjoyment of his impromptu display of affection, he looks over at me to see if I'm watching. (I was.)
- Rick strumming the guitar in one of his unorthodox tunings, seemingly oblivious to everything except the pure pleasure of making music.

We were approaching the double-wide. Tucking away my memory snapshots, I opened the door, took off my jacket, and got Levi settled with a bowl of cereal. As I sat in the kitchen with my son, my youngest child, the Benjamin of the family, I experienced one of those rare moments of peace during which I wasn't thinking or doing anything. I was just being. It didn't last long. Gently returning to the world, I recalled the tenderness that Rick had always shown to the elderly, animals, and very young children. Then I thought about the peace that he had experienced so rarely in life, and I hoped with all my heart that he had finally found it.

Chapter Ten

Not Bergdorf Goodman

With Rick gone, the financial arrangement at Welcome Home caused some of the more responsible members of the community to announce their plans to move elsewhere. I, too, thought about moving elsewhere, but I didn't know where. All I knew was that I wanted to stay in Idaho and I didn't want to live in a city. I considered the idea of a place even farther from civilization that would be small enough for me to handle on my own, but inertia kept me from taking action.

During my time in Idaho I'd come to believe that it was mandatory for everyone to drive an old pickup and own a Labrador retriever. Toward the end of August, when a friend of one of the women living at Welcome Home drove down for a visit, her arrival in a pickup with a black Lab in the passenger seat did nothing to disprove that theory. On her way out, the visitor, whose name was Joyce, stopped by the double-wide and invited me to come up and visit her the following weekend.

Seeing Levi and Molly, she said, "Bring the kids. They'll love it."

"Where do you live?" I asked.

"Burgdorf," she replied. "About thirty miles northeast of McCall."

"Bergdorf?" I repeated, mentally visualizing the name the way a woman from New York would spell it. "There's a Bergdorf Goodman near McCall, Idaho?"

Joyce burst out laughing.

"No, Carole. It's not a store. It's a little town with cabins around a hot spring. Come on up. You'll see."

Joyce was still chuckling as she climbed into her truck and drove up the hill.

Burgdorf was an unincorporated little town where a community had been established in the latter half of the nineteenth century around a natural hot spring in a magnificent mountain meadow. In 1978 the town comprised roughly twelve cabins of varying sizes and shapes. The cabins had seen better days, and the largest building, once a hotel, had fallen into disrepair. The town was owned by a brother and sister who lived, respectively, in McCall and Boise. Scott and Gretchen Harris allowed members of the public to stay in the cabins for a minimal charge. They didn't need to advertise. Word of mouth brought campers, hikers, and families in the summer, hunters in the fall, and cross-country skiers and snowmobilers in the winter. Virtually no one came in the spring because Warren Wagon Road was too bare in some places to snowmobile or ski, and too deeply covered with snowdrifts in other places to drive.

Over the years the Harrises had hired serial caretakers to live on the premises year-round and collect rent for the cabins on behalf of the owners. The price of an overnight stay that year ranged from five to ten dollars, depending on a cabin's size and condition. There was no maid service, room service, electricity, telephone, or plumbing in any of the cabins. If you wanted drinking water you could either bring your own or haul it from a seasonal spigot in a nearby Forest Service campground. An unheated outhouse up the hill from each cabin served as a toilet. Heat was provided by a cast iron heat stove and a cookstove in each cabin fueled by wood from a well-stocked woodshed. There was no bedding. You slept in your own sleeping bag either on a pad on the floor or on top of a bare mattress covered with mouse droppings that you'd have to brush off before you put your pad on the bed. Some of the cabins had a loft accessible by a removable ladder.

Molly, Levi, and I drove up the Friday of Labor Day weekend. Joyce, who was that year's caretaker, showed us to our cabin. Molly and Levi would sleep in the loft. I would spend the night on a bed that I zealously cleared of mouse droppings before I unrolled my pad and put my sleeping bag on it. It surely was not Bergdorf Goodman.

Hot water was abundant on the property. Natural hot springs underground fed two small pools under a roof supported by four poles and three walls. At approximately 130°F, the water in the covered pools was too hot for human beings, but the effluent from those pools fed a much larger pool under the open sky. At 115 degrees, that pool was the main attraction for visitors. At first contact the large pool felt too hot. Everyone made the same series of sounds upon entering. First they said, "Ooh! Oh! Ow!" Then came the inevitable "Ahhh-hhhh" as the person relaxed into the heat of the water. Everything that had seemed so important a few seconds earlier had just moved to a back burner. Such was the magic of Burgdorf.

It wasn't like Baden-Baden, a spa town where rich Europeans went to "take the waters" in Germany's Black Forest and enjoy fine wine, excellent cuisine, and luxury hotels. Burgdorf was rustic, simple, and wonderful. For a mere five dollars, which I gave to Joyce over her protests, my kids and I got to spend the night in a warm cabin and enjoy a soak in a large natural hot springs pool under the stars, which, as I recall, were spectacularly clear and brilliant in a moonless sky that weekend.

Chapter Eleven

Teepee Rick

*W*hen I look back at my relationships with men, I see a pattern. As a child my strong will was juxtaposed with wanting to please my father. As a teenager I knew I wanted to write songs and earn the respect of people I hoped would someday be my peers, and though I took some important steps on my own along that path, my ambitions were powered in part by the pride I knew my dad would take in my accomplishments. Though my mother, too, took tremendous pride in my achievements, I took her approval for granted. By the time I was a grown woman, seeking the approval of a man had become a firmly established element of my psychological framework. And because my father had been so effective in solving problems and making things happen, I grew to believe that it was easier to take strong, steady action toward a goal with a man to help me get there.

Gerry Goffin's determination to succeed in the early sixties had driven me harder than I might have driven myself. Not only did we write more songs in service of the pressure he felt to provide for his family, but we wrote better songs because of his insistence on excellence. In the late sixties I had become a recording artist with the consistent encouragement of Charlie Larkey, Danny Kortchmar, and Lou Adler. And in 1970 I became a performing artist after James Taylor pushed me forward. Though I was never romantically involved with Danny, Lou, or James, all were mightily influential in my development.

Given this pattern, it's not difficult to see why I believed I needed Rick Evers to help me move my family to a slower-paced, natural environment.

That September weekend in 1978, I wasn't looking for anyone to teach my children and me how to live more fully and richly on the land in the wild and woolly western state I now called home. But if I had been looking for such a person, could anyone have been more suitable than someone called Teepee Rick?

Saturday morning dawned brisk and sunny. Molly, Levi, and I enjoyed a delightful 115-degree soak in the pool. We walked to the campground to refill our water jugs, then set out to explore the little town. We were curious to see what was inside the structures that hadn't been rented out. It was the second of September. The fall colors were already beginning to promise October splendor. Patches of leaves among the groves of aspens were quaking orange and gold against the evergreen forest of mostly lodgepole pines. Burgdorf Meadow held a variety of glorious tall grasses and the last wildflowers of the summer season. The leaves on the low-lying bushes on the hillsides above the meadow had already turned red. White clouds punctuated the crystal blue sky with Rorschach-like images ranging from double exclamation points to white bunnies in love.

Molly, almost seven, had been a voracious reader since she was four. As if by magnetic attraction, it was she who first poked her head into what Joyce had called "the library cabin." All three of us were immediately drawn in by the accumulation of books left by visitors over the years. The library cabin policy was simple: anyone was free to take a book or leave one. Burgdorf's readers had left so many books that we found selecting a single book as difficult as eating just one potato chip. When we emerged from the library cabin an hour later with our selections, we saw Joyce waving to us from the porch of her cabin just above us.

"Come on up and have a cup of tea with us," she called.

Us? I thought as we scrambled up the hill.

The children had no interest in entering a dark cabin on such a beautiful day. Molly wanted to stay on the porch and read, while Levi was more interested in the paints that Joyce had set on a table outside. After getting the kids settled on the porch I followed Joyce in. At first I couldn't see anything. Then my eyes adjusted to the darkness and I saw two men in the cabin. One was sitting on the edge of Joyce's bed, which doubled as a couch. Joyce introduced him as "Che" (as in Guevara). The other man was sitting on a worn brown vinyl beanbag chair with his long legs crossed in front of him. He was industriously tamping a pipe.

"Carole," Joyce said. The long-legged man looked up. "This is Teepee Rick."

Rick Sorensen was relaxed and comfortable as he smoked his pipe. He was an entertaining storyteller whose dry humor added to listeners' interest in what was already a good story. From the banter between him and Che I gleaned that Rick had a girlfriend with whom he lived in a teepee that he moved seasonally. In the late spring and summer they lived in McCall, where Rick worked as a carpenter and his girlfriend as a nurse. During the summer they boarded their horses in McCall or Cascade. Together they earned enough to pay for their own food, the horses' board, and winter supplies for them, their dog, and the horses. In the late fall, just before the first big snow closed backcountry roads for the winter, Rick trailered the horses and hauled the teepee to his mining claim on the South Fork of the Salmon River. Hence the nickname Teepee

Rick. He performed the required mining activities to keep his claim active, but the Mining Law of 1872 didn't allow permanent structures on such claims. Hence the teepee.

Rick and Che had come to Burgdorf to hunt. Many Idahoans depended on the skill of their family's hunters to bring home an elk or a couple of deer during the legal season, the dates of which varied from year to year but usually began after the males had rutted and the females were carrying next season's young. Idaho Fish and Game monitored the populations of various species of wildlife and adjusted the regulations each year. Normally only male elk and deer were taken unless Fish and Game determined that there was an excess of females that year. Prior to living in Idaho I had not been a fan of guns or hunting, but I was beginning to learn that there was a natural order between animal herds and my Idaho neighbors. Responsible humans were part of the ecosystem. Hunting was a way of keeping populations of wild animals in balance while providing human families with a source of protein. I didn't hunt, but I did eat. I was mostly vegetarian and ate almost no meat, but I didn't condemn those who did eat meat. I could only hope that those who hunted would do it in a respectful manner.

As the conversation went on I learned that Rick was thirty and that his girlfriend was less than enthusiastic about going back to the South Fork that winter. I listened to Rick and Che tell stories in Joyce's cabin until my kids came in to tell me that they were bored and hungry. The guys were planning to go out early the next morning. Soon they would tub, then they would sleep in the hayloft in the Harrises' old barn to save the cost of a cabin rental. I said good night, brought the kids back to our own cabin, and gave them dinner.

Later, after the children had gone to sleep, I asked Joyce if she would come over and stay with them while I went to take a tub under the stars. I figured the guys would have already come and gone and I'd have the pool all to myself. I walked to the upper end of the big pool, got undressed, and left my clothes on the bench. In that decade, many among my generation didn't wear bathing suits even in daylight. I wasn't wearing one that night, but I wasn't concerned. I was alone, and even if someone else had been there, it was too dark to see anything. I paused to look up and marvel at the clarity of the stars against the dark sky. Then I sat down at the edge of the pool and slid into the water.

Ooh! Oh! Ow!...Ahhhhhhh...

Splash!

Someone was at the lower end of the pool. I called out.

"Hello?"

Two male voices called back.

"Hello!"

They belonged to Rick and Che, who swam up to my end of the pool. There we expanded our earlier conversation until Che announced that he was overheated and ready to call it a night. Rick and I stayed and talked about people we knew, places we'd been, and opinions we shared. We created a waterfall of words that tumbled over, but couldn't hide, our mutual attraction.

The next time I looked up, the stars were in a completely different configuration than when I had first arrived. My fingers were wrinkled, I was much too warm, and Joyce was undoubtedly keen to get back to her cabin.

I was just beginning to climb out when Rick pulled me back in.

Chapter Twelve

Reading, 'Riting and 'Rithmetic

Rick and Che left early the next morning. I didn't stay long enough to find out whether they bagged whatever it was they were hunting. On Monday afternoon I said goodbye to Joyce, loaded the kids and our gear into our sturdy Jeep Wagoneer, and drove back to Robie Creek. With Molly now in second grade and Levi in kindergarten, every weekday morning I walked the children up the hill to catch the yellow school bus to Idaho City, and every afternoon I waited at the top of the hill for their safe return. Back in the double-wide I admired the kids' crayon drawings and Molly's workbook pages with motherly love and supportive compliments. I attached their drawings to the refrigerator with magnets with a folksy kitchen theme that I'd found at a grocery store in Boise.

Toward the end of September, Rick Sorensen called to say that he was on his way to Boise. I invited him to visit me at Welcome Home. He arrived with John, a medium-sized tricolor canine of unknown origin. On a walk up Ashton Creek the next day Rick told me that he and his girlfriend were breaking up. He had worked out a deal with Scott Harris to fix up one of the old cabins at Burgdorf in exchange for being allowed to live rent-free in that cabin over the winter. Then he asked if I would consider bringing Levi and Molly and spending the winter with him. It didn't take me long to decide. I had already been thinking about a change of location, I liked Rick, and it would be an extraordinary adventure. The fact that we would be snowed in from November to April was less a deterrent than an incentive.

The next three years turned out to be an unparalleled learning experience for all four of us, though it's fair to say that the memories my Larkey children have of that period are somewhat less pleasant than mine. They were young, and they missed their father. My forcing yet another Rick on them as the predominant male figure in their daily lives wasn't easy for them. While I recall those three years as alternately peaceful, adventurous, frustrating, educational, challenging, and fun, my children would probably add "disempowering" to the list.

One thing it was not was boring.

With our ability to live at Burgdorf dependent on the whim of the owners, I became keenly aware of every moment as something to be fully experienced and treasured. Our stay could come to an end at any time, and when it did, it could never be replicated. That fall we continued to get our drinking water from the campground spigot. We filled several large containers and hauled them up the road to our cabin in a rusty red wagon with wobbly wheels. When there was too much snow on the ground for the wagon, we hauled the containers on a plastic sled using a rope of braided orange baling twine. Molly and Levi took turns pulling and riding on the plastic sled and another sled roughly the same vintage as Rosebud that we'd found in the old hotel. After the Forest Service drained the campground pipes for the winter, we chopped through the ice on the little creek that flowed through the campground and filled our containers directly from the creek with a large ladle. No one ever camped upstream in the winter, so we figured the water was potable.

We washed our bodies, clothes, and dishes at the pool, though not all in the same water. We used biodegradable soap to wash ourselves at the lower end of the big pool. Then we rinsed off with a bucket below the pool. Our washing machine/automatic dishwasher was a huge round washtub that previous residents had placed beneath a vigorous stream of water that flowed continuously out of a large pipe at the lower end of the main pool.

We stacked our dirty dishes in a white five-gallon bucket that stood in the corner of our cabin. When the bucket was full, the next time we headed for the pool we brought the dirty dishes with us on a wagon or a sled, according to season. We put the dishes in the washtub below the pool, added biodegradable soap, scrubbed the dishes with a brush, then dumped the dirty water and put the dishes under a smaller pipe that bypassed the pool with clean water originating in one of the upper pools too hot for people to bathe in. By the time we'd finished washing ourselves, our geothermally heated gravity-powered automatic dishwasher had finished washing the dishes. We used a similar technique for laundry and squeezed excess water from the clothes using an ancient hand-cranked wringer in a shed next to the washtub. Then we hauled the wrung-out clothes back up to our cabin and hung them on a line above the stove to dry. It was astonishingly efficient considering that we had no electricity. We didn't know the term then, but we were leaving a minimal carbon footprint.

Our cabin was heated with wood. At night we lit candles and kerosene lamps with glass chimneys and read by the light of a Coleman lantern. Levi and Molly slept in the loft in sleeping bags. Rick and I slept in a bed in the main part of the cabin under flannel sheets, several layers of wool blankets, and a buffalo robe that Rick had used in his teepee. We acquired a cat to keep the mice (and by extension, their droppings) under control. We also acquired another dog, a Lab-shepherd mix. In a tip of the hat to Rick's Norwegian ancestry we named him Thor and pronounced it "Tor." John and Thor kept the cat under control and the cat kept the mice under control. We didn't have to worry about cars, so our pets were free to chase each other in a safe, open environment. The remaining residents at Welcome Home took care of my horses. Rick's horses wintered in a town called Cascade at a lower elevation than mile-high Burgdorf with its short grazing season. We kept a couple of goats in the barn for milk. Milking goats twice a day is considered a chore, but I found it satisfying to perform this service both to the goats and to the half of my family that drank the milk. While Rick and I liked goat milk, my children emphatically did not.

We had no phone, no two-way radio, and, in 1978, no email. We communicated with the rest of the world by ski-mail. Visitors on cross-country skis brought our mail, and we sent messages and mail out with them or other skiers. Sometimes a neighbor would snowmobile in and pick up or deliver supplies. We kept up with current events through a radio powered by two alternate twelve-volt car batteries that our neighbor periodically charged for us. In some ways our life at Burgdorf was complicated, but in other ways it was simple. Living this way brought everything down to basics.

Let me see. Was there anything I could add that might make it even better?

What about another job?

Our isolation left me no choice but to homeschool the children. At first I had tried to work with the Idaho City public school and send assignments back and forth, but mail delivery was too erratic. Then I inquired at the McCall elementary school, where one of the teachers suggested I sign up for homeschooling. The Calvert School offered an accredited program used by American diplomats abroad and other families who either needed or chose to teach their children at home. Developed and refined by respected educators, Calvert's curriculum had been proven worthy over time and was flexible enough to allow for sporadic mail.

It was mostly I who taught Levi and Molly during the three school years we lived at Burgdorf. The curriculum included the three R's, which I had always thought of as a child's first lesson in misspelling: reading, 'riting and 'rithmetic. It also included music, mythology, and mycology as well as astronomy, biology, geography, history, French, and Spanish. The books they sent captured not only my children's interest but also my own. After we had covered the required course materials on a given day I allowed the kids' questions to expand the discussion. Often Rick chimed in with his own knowledge and opinions.

I loved teaching. My original career plan had been to teach, but until I homeschooled my own children I'd had no idea how enriching it could be. We were all thirsty for information, and together we drank it in. I believed then, and still believe, that the most important thing a teacher can convey to his or her students is a love of learning. Though difficult to test, a pupil's love of learning is the key to mastery of any subject. I saw and encouraged that in my own two pupils, and I was confident that they were receiving a high-quality, if somewhat unconventional education.

Calvert's curriculum was designed to be taught for three hours every weekday morning for 180 days. This would leave afternoons free for activities such as helping out on the family farm or doing other chores. In our family, afternoon activities included skiing or swimming, which we put under the heading of physical education. When I saw that Molly and Levi were learning so much so quickly that they were reluctant to end the school day, we began doubling up on lessons. Sometimes we covered two sessions in a day by including a break for lunch and then another hour or two of study before P.E. On this schedule we were able to complete the work of an entire school year by March. And though we were physically isolated, we learned a lot from the people from various parts of the world who came to Burgdorf and shared stories with us around a stove in someone's cabin or at the pool. This gave the children a much broader perspective than they might have received from a more traditional school experience.

Although I took some liberties with the recommended schedule, I was scrupulous about the rules when it came to learning and testing. I made sure that I taught every last detail of the required material. More to the point, I made sure that my pupils *learned* every last detail of the required material. I conducted the tests according to Calvert's rules as strictly as if my children's lives depended on it, which, in many important ways, they did. Perhaps the best evidence that homeschooling wasn't deleterious to my children is that Molly graduated cum laude from Columbia University, and several years later Levi earned a Ph.D. from the University of Texas. My older female relatives would have enjoyed hearing me introduce my son as "*Doctor* Larkey."

I may or may not have been a good teacher, but my pupils were fantastic learners.

Chapter Thirteen

All-Weather Friends

With no television, we tuned in to the weather. Not the weather *report*; I mean the actual weather. I needed to know what to wear to the barn to milk the goats in the morning, or which boots the children should put on to sled down the driveway behind our cabin, though the latter probably didn't matter since the boots inevitably came off.

Cross-country skiwear decisions were less difficult. We'd simply put on lots of layers and remove or add them according to need. However, with wax-based cross-country skis, determining which wax to use was particularly challenging. We had a shoebox with tins of wax ranging from white through shades of blue and green to yellow and red. There was also something called klister, literally meaning "paste" in Norwegian. Its use often resulted in snow sticking to our skis in huge clumps. I *prayed* that conditions wouldn't require the use of klister. In order to select the right wax, not only did we need to know the weather, but we needed to know the difference between fresh, old, warm, or cold snow and snow with high or low water content. And we needed to know how quickly the conditions for which we had just waxed would be obsolete as soon as we skied out of the shade into the sun.

A NATURAL WOMAN

Above our kitchen table was a horizontal picture window approximately five feet by three that offered a view of Burgdorf Meadow, the
mountains around it, and the sky. Having already spent some years in
the backcountry, Rick was astonishingly accurate in predicting the
weather, which included, in the winter of 1978–79, sunny and cold,
sunny and colder, thick soft flakes of snow, sleet, and, during one
particularly windy blizzard, snowing sideways. Usually when it was
cloudy or snowing the temperature rose to just below freezing, around
31°F. Rick explained that this was because the cloud cover kept the
warmth of the earth from rising above the clouds. On clear nights the
temperature plummeted to somewhere between –10° and –25°F, but
after the sun came up it rose to double digits above zero. The lowest
temperature during my three winters at Burgdorf was –45°F, a temperature that is exactly the same number in both Fahrenheit and Celsius.
Temperatures between –20° and –45°F were a frequent occurrence in
late December and January. But not every day in January was cold.
Every year we enjoyed a few days of Chinooks—warm winds that, in
contrast with 45 below, made me feel as if I were in Hawaii.

With our road vehicles parked at a friend's house in McCall,
we kept a couple of snowmobiles at Burgdorf in case of emergency.
Sometimes I rode into town for supplies and to call friends and
family. I always felt more secure scheduling such trips to coincide
with those of our neighbor who lived six miles away and could fix
anything mechanical with little more than duct tape and a wire
hanger. Toward the end of one such trip, while I was waiting in
town for my neighbor to finish the last of his errands, I decided to
call a friend in L.A. who had expressed concern about my decision
to move to the backcountry. After all I had been through with
Rick Evers, she was afraid that I had jumped into a different kind
of insanity. As I stood in a phone booth and dialed the number,
I watched the lights coming on around Payette Lake as the short
winter day began to give way to the long night.

I was as glad to hear my friend's voice as she was to hear mine. After responding to my question about what was going on in her life, she asked how I was doing. Shifting from one foot to the other in the increasingly cold phone booth, I enumerated all the things I was doing and how much I was enjoying them until I ran out of steam. My friend paused and then spoke.

"You hike up to an outhouse first thing in the morning, then you haul your family's drinking water from the creek. No matter how cold it is, you go to the barn every morning to milk the goats, and do it again at night. You chop wood, tan hides, mend clothes, grind wheat by hand, bake your own bread, teach your children, and last week you, Rick, and the kids skied twelve miles round trip to visit Rick's brother."

"I love doing all those things," I said. "They make so much more sense than driving up and down the Canyon to bring one kid to this friend's house and another kid to that after-school activity, or shopping for clothes and furniture, or for that matter buying overpriced groceries wrapped in plastic."

"I just don't get it. You could be dining at the finest restaurants, drinking champagne, eating caviar, taking limos, and going to movie premieres. Instead you're performing tasks that any woman in her right mind who could afford it would be asking her 'people' to do. Why would you want to give that up?"

I'd heard variations on that question from other friends and read similar questions in letters from fans who missed seeing me on tour. The way most of them put it was, "Why have you dropped out?" I might have answered, "I thought I dropped in," but that wasn't the answer they were looking for.

Why had I "dropped out"?

Because when I said I wanted to get back to the land, I meant it. Notwithstanding a local saying that there were only two seasons in Idaho—winter and the Fourth of July—there were in fact four seasons, each of which brought me great pleasure. I loved liv-ing within earshot of a creek in a forest with a view of mountains and meadows. And I was grateful to wake up every morning hun-dreds of miles away from the fast lane.

Obviously, it was easier for me economically than for many natives of my adopted state. I had a dependable source of income, and though I had chosen to be where I was, I could leave at any time. Indeed, I did leave frequently for work and to spend time with my Goffin daughters. And though I was perfectly comfort-able living without electricity and other modern paraphernalia, I was glad to have the occasional use of telephones, tape recorders, electricity, penicillin, and modern medical and industrial conve-niences that had been unavailable before the twentieth century. But Burgdorf was affording my children and me a rare opportu-nity to live as close as we could get in modern times to a basic, down-to-earth way of life.

I wanted to say all that and more, but it was getting really cold in the phone booth.

Instead I said, "I'm okay. Really, I am."

Just then I heard my neighbor approaching on his snow machine. He was hauling a cargo sled with our groceries and other items under a tarp.

"That's my ride. I have to go."

"Okay," she said. "I just want to say two more things: I love you, and I can't believe you're not writing songs or playing music at all."

Tears came to my eyes as we said goodbye. I hung up the phone, stepped out of the booth, put on my helmet, and climbed onto the back of my neighbor's snow machine. Then, with a cloud of smoke and the distinctive sound of an accelerating two-stroke engine, we were off.

Chapter Fourteen

Gretchen's Piano

*I*t wasn't as if I'd made a conscious decision at Burgdorf not to write songs or play music. It just seemed to work out that way. Knowing that there wouldn't be room in our cabin for a piano, I'd brought a guitar, but I hadn't taken it out of the case since we moved in. I listened mostly to the tapes Rick played on our battery-powered cassette player. In a one-room cabin, when one of us listened to music, everyone listened.

Among Rick's favorites were the Grateful Dead, Bob Dylan, Willie Nelson, Merle Haggard, Patsy Cline, and Waylon Jennings. I not only listened but sang along to "Fire on the Mountain," "Don't Think Twice, It's All Right," "Mama Don't Let Your Babies Grow Up to Be Cowboys," "Mama Tried," "Crazy," and "Put Another Log on the Fire." Though I was not unfamiliar with country music, listening to it every day reminded me that the best country songs had a great story, a well-crafted lyric, and a performance that made you laugh, cry, or both.

One night, after hearing Jerry Jeff Walker sing about an Austin bootmaker named Charlie Dunn, Rick said, "You should go to Austin and record an album with Jerry Jeff's band."

"Interesting," I said, and immediately put it out of my mind.

Several nights later we were entertaining a couple of Rick's friends who had skied in when one of them asked if I'd ever played the piano in Gretchen's cabin.

I had not.

I knew that Gretchen occupied her cabin rarely in summer and never in winter, but it was her cabin and I respected her privacy. Even if I'd been inclined to check out her piano, which I did know about, the cabin was unheated, which wasn't conducive to keeping a piano in tune. But I was intrigued enough to ask the skier to call Gretchen when he got to McCall and see if she'd give me permission to enter her cabin and play her piano. Two days later word came in with another skier that Gretchen had said yes.

The following morning I hiked up the steep hill to Gretchen's cabin in knee-deep snow. Idahoans call it "post-holing," because each step leaves a hole deep enough to support a fencepost. I had no objective beyond seeing just how badly out of tune the piano was, or if it was even playable.

How badly out of tune was it? The piano was playable; it just wasn't listenable. But in this situation my lack of perfect pitch was a blessing. Removing my gloves, I sat on the bench and played a chord. Ouch! It was way out of tune. But I heard it in my mind as it was supposed to sound. I played another chord, and then another. I stopped counting after the fourth chord. I just kept playing while my brain, in neural self-defense, replaced the out-of-tune notes with the correct ones. But then I encountered another obstacle. The outside temperature in the sun was –5°F. Gretchen's cabin was in the shade and therefore at least ten degrees colder. After a while my fingers became too frozen to continue playing, and I went back home to warm up. As soon as I could feel my fingers again I resolved to learn how to play and write music on guitar.

The linear layout of chords on a piano was second nature to

me. In contrast, the square configuration of chords on frets was as foreign to me as the Cyrillic alphabet. At first I found it difficult to adapt, but the thought of putting on layers of clothing, post-holing up to Gretchen's cabin, and playing an out-of-tune piano until my fingers froze motivated me to persevere. That February I wrote most of the songs for my next album on guitar. I also turned thirty-seven.

When Rick again suggested that I record with Jerry Jeff's band, the next time I went to McCall I reached out to some of the players. In March 1979, I left Molly and Levi in Rick's care, flew to Austin, and recorded *Touch the Sky*. The Austin cats not only added a country music sensibility to every song but were even more talented than Rick had predicted they'd be. To this day I'm convinced that keyboard player Reese Wynans had fourteen fingers, but I couldn't prove it because the extra four automatically retracted when anyone was looking.

I spent the rest of 1979 alternately living at Burgdorf and visiting my Goffin daughters. While I was there I collaborated with other songwriters, including Gerry. In January 1980, I returned to Austin to record a fourth album for Capitol. This time Rick and the children came with me. Sherry flew down from L.A. and took the cover photo for *Pearls: Songs of Goffin and King*. That album comprised new versions, with me singing, of nine vintage hits that Gerry and I had written in the sixties and a more recent composition by the two of us called "Dancin' with Tears in My Eyes." *Pearls* brought together a mélange of the men in my life that included my current boyfriend and two ex-husbands. I had written the new song with Gerry, who wasn't in Austin, but Charlie was there to play bass on the entire album. In addition to his being an outstanding bass player, a friend, and a cooperative coparent, I knew Levi and Molly would enjoy having both parents with them in

the same city. The situation was fraught with potential for dishar-
mony, but Rick seemed to take it in stride.

I didn't think about it at the time, but it's possible that I
was attempting to answer the questions that John Lennon had
answered for me in "Imagine." A similar question would become
a permanent part of twentieth-century American pop culture a
decade later when Rodney King, stammering with emotion, would
ask, "Can we...can we all get along? Can we...can we get along?"
In the twenty-first century Mr. King's plaintive appeal would probably have been Auto-Tuned, set to a beat, uploaded, and viewed
as entertainment by millions within an hour of the initial news
coverage.

For so many years, I, too, had wondered why people couldn't
get along. In 1980, while I was recording *Pearls*, it almost seemed
as if we could.

Chapter Fifteen

The Eighties

The morning of December 9, 1980, as usual, I was the first one up. The fire in the heat stove had died down to embers. I had gone from being cozy in flannel sheets to shivering in a frosty cabin where my every exhalation was visible. I opened the damper and the draft, fed the stove, and turned our battery-powered radio on at a barely audible level. In preparation for walking up to the outhouse, I put on my robe, hat, boots, and my right glove. As I was pulling on my left glove, I thought I heard the announcer say something about Lenin. I thought, Why is he talking about a deceased Bolshevik leader? I turned the radio up slightly and realized that the newscaster wasn't talking about Vladimir Lenin. He was talking about John Lennon, and I thought I had just heard him say Lennon was...dead??

Horrified, I woke Rick up and we listened to the report together. I thought back to the evening I had spent with John and Yoko and how sad it was that Sean would grow up without a father. I thought about how unfair it was that just when John was hitting his stride as a happy, healthy man living with his family in productivity and peace, his life had been cut short by an appalling act of violence. I thought about the psycho who had singled John out for whatever reason and taken him away before his time.

For my generation, the murder of John Lennon was more than the loss of an icon. It was a loss of hope. We who had lived through the previous three decades had been catapulted into the eighties, which seemed a lot like the fifties except without the innocence. Politically, the rise of conservatism was a déjà vu some people didn't want to see again. Musically, things were pretty cool. Rockabilly was back in style, and the girl groups of the fifties inspired the more independent women who came to prominence later in the eighties. The Bangles, the Go-Gos, the Wilson sisters (collectively known as Heart), and the Motels' Martha Davis not only wrote their own songs and played their own instruments but in some cases also produced their own albums.

In the eighties we had Live Aid, Farm Aid, Band Aid, and "We Are the World." A list of Quincy Jones's accomplishments would have to include his shepherding all the "We Are the World" stars into one room and getting them to perform as an ensemble at full diva power while behaving reasonably well to one another. I would have wanted so much to be at that session, but I was too out of touch to hear about it until after the fact. I participated in more events later in the eighties, but most of my experience of the first couple of years of the decade was filtered through my self-imposed isolation in the backcountry. We did listen to the news enough that I was aware of people whose names became so ingrained in twentieth-century cultural history that the name alone evokes the memory of that person's story. To wit: Tawana Brawley; Mikhail Gorbachev; Bernhard Goetz, known as the Subway Vigilante; Ferdinand Marcos, the corrupt president of the Philippines, and his wife, Imelda, whose name would become a metaphor for a woman who owns too many pairs of shoes. I heard pronouncements from James Watt, President Reagan's secretary of the interior, who set out so blatantly to reverse all efforts to preserve the environment that conservationists didn't think there could ever be a worse secretary of the interior. And reading about Ayatollah Khomeini and Lech Walesa in newspapers brought in via ski-mail made me thankful that I had the radio as an alternate news source or I would never have known how to pronounce their names.

In 1982 Jane Fonda's Workout brought fitness into the lives of women across America who wanted to look and feel more healthy. Aerobics classes and athletic clubs sprang up like daisies in a field. Women who had never stretched a leg wore dancewear to the grocery store and tried to look as if they had been practicing ballet for several hours when they suddenly remembered they needed a head of lettuce.

As women tried to break through the glass ceiling, massive shoulder pads came back in style along with rolled-up sleeves and oversized suit jackets. Perhaps we thought we might have more credibility if we were built like football players.

In the spring of 1981, my wardrobe consisted mostly of T-shirts, flannel, and denim flecked with hay.

Chapter Sixteen

Moving Day

One of Burgdorf's main drawbacks was that the owners could ask us to leave at any time. Another was the public road over which (depending on the season) cars, campers, snowmobiles, or commercial logging trucks roared past our cabin and the pool. During the winter of 1980–81, we let it be known through our ski-mail system that we were interested in purchasing a place in the backcountry with more privacy. Though not necessary, a natural hot spring on the property would be desirable.

In the spring of 1981 we heard about a ranch for sale in central Idaho. First we arranged for someone to stay with the children; then, with the direct route still closed, we drove the long way round. Turning off the paved highway, we went down a hill, crossed the river on an old-fashioned steel bridge, and continued along the dirt road to the west gate of the property. Above the open gate we saw a sign on a wooden crossbeam with the name of the ranch and smaller posted signs saying "Private Property" and "No Trespassing."

Good, I thought.

We pulled up to the main building. One of the owners came out to show us around. A visitor from the city might have described the buildings as old and run-down, the kind that realtors euphemistically call "fixer-uppers." I saw them as rustic and historic.

With water of prime importance in the arid West, this property was unusual in having more than enough to supply the dwellings and irrigate the fields. The Salmon River, though not adjacent, was close by. A sizable creek that ran past the buildings was warmed by hot springs that originated on federal land upstream along a geological fault line. A hot spring on the property flowed from a hillside into an upper pool that emptied into a lower pool. The effluent from the lower pool coursed into the creek, which met the Salmon River with a stunning display of cascading waterfalls at the confluence.

When we had completed our tour of the property I told the seller that private ownership of the road was very important to me. She said the road outside the ranch was public, and because she and her husband had run a business that served the public, they had left the ranch gates open most of the time. However, she assured me that the road within the ranch was private and open to the public by permission only. She and her husband had affirmatively asserted their private ownership by locking the gates at least once a year.

The place seemed perfect for our needs. Due diligence was the next step. After my Boise attorney confirmed that all water and mineral rights were in order and the road within the property was private, I made an offer, the sellers accepted, and I became the owner of a ranch in central Idaho.

We moved out of Burgdorf on Friday, June 26, 1981. I had always known our stay was finite, but as I watched the last dilapidated gray wooden building recede in the rearview mirror, I could almost feel the rush of air as Father Time slammed the door behind me. If only it had been a literal rush of air. Our progress on the winding dirt roads was too slow to generate even a small breeze. Our caravan consisted of Rick's 1955 Dodge pickup, my Jeep Cherokee, the CJ5 that Sherry had driven on Robie Creek, a one-ton silver truck, and a two-horse trailer. Rick's brother drove Silver, and a friend of his drove the CJ. Though a crow could have covered the distance in a couple of hours, it took us the better part of a day to arrive at our destination. By the time all the vehicles, people, dogs, cats, goats, horses, and mules had passed through the log portal leading to the residential compound, everyone was hot, dusty, and thirsty.

The compound consisted of the main building, three medium-sized buildings, and eight small cabins. All were constructed of logs and had red shingle roofs. The seller had told us that in addition to serving as her family's home, the main building had functioned variously as a stagecoach stop, a restaurant, an inn, and a lodge. We parked along the road that curved alongside the main building and turned off our vehicles. As the dust drifted away, I found the complete absence of motor noise a welcome contrast to the relentless racket of the previous ten and a half hours. But the quiet didn't last long. Rick got out of his truck and began to unload the horses and the goats while the rest of us opened various vehicle doors. Dogs, cats, and children leapt out of confinement and scattered in all directions in search of water. The dogs and cats headed straight for the creek. Rick tied the goats and equines to a conveniently located hitching post, then he, his brother, his friend, the children, and I drank from a garden hose attached to a tall outdoor standpipe with a pump handle that, when lifted, released a flow of water. After we had slaked our thirst Rick led the horses, mules, and goats into a nearby pasture to graze while I filled a metal tub with water for them. After releasing the animals, Rick brought the horses' lead ropes back to the trailer, pointed to the main building, and directed Levi and Molly to start carrying their things inside.

"There?" I asked, daunted by the building's immensity.

"That's where we're going to live," he said, and went off to unload the saddles and other tack.

The lodge was approximately seventy-five hundred square feet, with six bedrooms upstairs and as many rooms downstairs. I knew that the previous owners had run a restaurant, so I shouldn't have been surprised when my first view of the huge commercial kitchen revealed oversized pots and pans, a professional mixer on a stand, a walk-in refrigerator, an ancient wood cookstove with two ovens, an eight-burner gas stove with two more ovens, a large upright freezer, and a pizza oven, all of which the owners were leaving behind. After having lived for three years in a very small cabin, I was intimidated by the magnitude of the kitchen, let alone the entire house.

During our prepurchase visit I had envisioned us living in the two-story cabin 150 feet up the creek from the lodge. It had two good-sized bedrooms upstairs and an open area downstairs that could work as a kitchen, dining area, and living room. A covered porch off the living room overlooked the creek. Large windows in every room would bring every season of the great outdoors inside. While Levi and Molly were exploring the lodge, I asked Rick to walk over to the creek cabin with me. We stood on the porch while I tried to explain why I thought we should live there. My impassioned advocacy for the creek cabin may have been driven in part by my realization that someone would have to clean all twelve rooms in the lodge, and I knew exactly to whom that job would default.

I said, "If we lived here we'd have this wonderful view of the creek."

But Rick had already made up his mind.

"You'll want all that room when the rest of your family comes to visit."

I was not unfamiliar with "good for the children" as an argument in favor of something my husband or boyfriend wanted, but Rick's point was valid. I watched him stride back to the lodge and lingered for one last look at the creek.

Then I turned, walked quickly through the cabin, and headed toward the Cherokee to unload boxes of food into my humongous new kitchen.

Chapter Seventeen

Bars and Benches

The first mining operation in the Boulder–White Cloud Mountains reportedly began when a miner named Robinson filed a placer claim on a tributary of the Salmon River in the seventh decade of the nineteenth century. The claim became known as Robinson's Bar (the name was later changed to Robinson Bar). With hand tools and shovels wielded mostly by Chinese immigrants, Mr. Robinson installed an extensive network of ditches and sluice boxes to divert water from the creek for the purpose of extracting gold. Remnants of those ditches still exist at that ranch.

A placer is a natural concentration of heavy minerals (such as gold) deposited by gravity and water. Placer mining involves the use of water to separate the heavier minerals from lighter materials such as sediment or sand. Panning, sluicing, and dredging are all methods of placer mining.

"Placer" was one of many words I learned in my adopted state, where folks speak the same language as the rest of America—and yet not. Some words have different meanings in the Wild West than, say, on the South Side of Chicago, where "draw" could be a tie game between the Cubs and the Phillies, or it could be something an artist does. In Idaho a draw is the place between two hills down which water flows.

In common usage, reference to a draw is made in the late fall when a man holding a rifle says, "Y'see that big bull elk up that draw?"

"What drawer?" I asked the first time I heard a hunter use the word. I was imagining the place in my bureau where I kept my socks.

"See'm up there?" he said, using the barrel of his rifle to indicate a standing dead tree toward the top of the hill. "He's right behind that snag."

After puzzling for a moment over how a pulled thread on a sweater could obscure a bull elk, I queried, "Snag? Where?"

The hunter pointed again to the standing dead tree, behind which were some branches. Suddenly some of the branches moved. They were the rack of the aforementioned bull elk, which had no sooner moved than the hunter raised his rifle, aimed, and Kaboom!! Suddenly the elk was no longer behind the snag up the draw. It was good luck for the elk (though not for the hunter) that the hunter had missed. When last seen (at least by me) the elk was bounding up the hill with his rack and the rest of him intact.

In New York I had always understood a bar to be a place where you ordered whiskey, and a bench to be where you sat while you drank it. In Idaho, a bar is a flat piece of land along a creek or a river, and a bench is a larger flat piece of land higher up, not necessarily near water. In the context of mountains, "flat" can mean anything between horizontal and steeper than the face of a cow.

Not to put too fine a point on it, in Idaho a bar can also be a place where you order whiskey and a bench something you sit on while you drink it. The town in which I vote has several of both kinds of bars and benches within the space of a quarter mile.

To keep things fair and balanced, a future lesson could cover subway etiquette and priority positioning for hailing a taxi on Broadway in inclement weather. Hint: the optimum position is in front of a person who is already trying to hail a taxi, unless he or she is wielding a large umbrella, in which case you'd be better off looking for a bench in a bar.

Then there's the meaning of bar as in lawyer, and bench as in judge.

Chapter Eighteen

New Neighbors

Among the first things Rick and some of his friends did after we moved in was to repair pasture fences and secure the coop, which we promptly filled with chickens. The coop had a small enclosure so the birds could range safely outdoors during the day. We were the delighted beneficiaries of the hens' efficiency (with essential help from the rooster) in converting leftover food waste into eggs that tasted bright yellow compared to the bland off-white flavor of eggs from corporate poultry. The horses, mules, and goats must have thought they'd died and gone to heaven with all that space and grass. Our domestic cats stalked and pounced on rodents while our dogs chased the cats, the rodents, each other, and the feral barn cats we had inherited.

My children's and my activities that summer included unpacking boxes, cooking for ourselves and Rick and all the men helping him, eating, washing dishes, housecleaning, laundry, riding horses, milking goats, gathering eggs, hiking, gardening, baking, canning, swimming in the creek, and swimming in the pool. Rick's activities included swimming as well as equine care, building, repairing various structures, and oversight of other people's activities. It was a lot of work, but the results were commensurate with the amount of effort expended, as opposed to the naked, heartfelt labor an artist can put into a project for months or years only to watch it go unappreciated by an indifferent public.

Charlie had just moved to a Los Angeles suburb with good public schools. Toward the end of the summer we agreed that it was time for Molly, now nine, to return to the public school system. Levi would stay in Idaho with me. Rick's friend Che, now called Richard, would live in the caretaker cabin with his son, who was the same age as Levi. I would homeschool both boys.

During the summer we had spread out and occupied most of the rooms in the lodge, but when I returned from delivering Molly to Charlie in late August (a delivery only slightly less painful than her birth) the cooler morning temperatures made it clear that we were going to have to contain ourselves in a smaller space within the lodge. The roof was poorly insulated, and there were too many cracks between the logs to chink them all before winter. Rick hung blankets over doorways to close off most of the rooms in the house. Our family would occupy two bedrooms above the kitchen, laundry room, and dining room. As with the multipurpose room in our cabin at Burgdorf, we would eat, read, sew, do crafts, and conduct lessons in the dining room. There was an indoor bathroom off the laundry room—two amenities for which I was very grateful. Though I already missed Molly, I knew she would thrive in California with her father. I had adapted to the size of the lodge and felt completely at home there. I was so glad to find peace and contentment in my new environment that I was unaware of a developing situation that would make it increasingly difficult to retain that perspective.

The seller had told us that a couple in their sixties, Thurlo and Dorothy French, were the social center of a small group of summer homeowners four miles downriver. A couple of days after we moved to the ranch we had driven down to meet the Frenches and let them know that although I was planning to lock my gates, they and their immediate neighbors were welcome to drive through, and so were their guests. As Rick handed the paper with the combination to Thurlo, Dorothy surprised me by saying, "I've been listening to your *Tapestry* album for years. I just *love* your song 'Beautiful'!"

"Well, aren't you nice to say that!" Then, quickly, to take the focus off me, I said, "Your home is so lovely. Did you build it or was it already here?"

Dorothy was more than happy to talk about herself and her home. Our conversation continued along typical lines of new neighbors getting to know each other. The Frenches were so pleasant and hospitable that on the drive back upriver I remarked, "Aren't we lucky to have such agreeable neighbors!"

Our home lay along the Salmon River between Stanley (pop. 100) and Clayton (pop. 26). Farther downriver was the county seat, Challis (pop. 2,500).* In order to acquaint ourselves with our new community we had subscribed to the local weekly, the *Challis Messenger*. One popular column reported that this family had motored to Idaho Falls to welcome a new granddaughter and that family had driven to Salmon to visit an aging parent. Another column gave gardening tips while waxing poetic about seasonal changes in Round Valley and the surrounding mountains. There were obituaries, church news, 4-H Club news, and school news. I was inspired to characterize the writer of each letter to the editor with a simplistic, wholly subjective formula: if a writer expressed an opposing view she was opinionated; if he agreed with my view he was impassioned.

The sheriff's report detailed a bleaker side of the community.

---

*Population numbers are approximate for 1981.

One of the most common incidents, particularly in winter, involved someone driving off the road into the river. Local residents had a saying: "There's two kinds of people 'round here: them that's driven into the river, and them that's gonna drive into the river." I had no wish to be included in either classification. More often than not, an excessive intake of alcohol by someone was involved. With three bars in Clayton and a handgun in just about every household, violence sometimes erupted in the form of a shooting. Sometimes the consequences were deadly. A few months after we moved in, a woman living a few miles upriver was arrested and later convicted of killing her husband with a shotgun.

There were also public notices in the weekly paper. By law, it was required that the minutes of the monthly meetings of the county commissioners be published in the *Messenger*. I found the minutes of little interest until one day in the summer of 1981 when Rick called me over to show me what he had just read. The minutes reported that Thurlo French had come to the meeting to ask the commissioners to declare the road that ran through Robinson Bar public. Thurlo went on to say that he hoped that a declaration of public road by the commissioners would force Carole King to open her gates so the public could continue to drive through her property.

Excuse me??

Chapter Nineteen

Trials and Tribulations

The next morning, Rick and I drove downriver along the steeply winding road to the Frenches' place. When we arrived, the Frenches behaved as if nothing were amiss and warmly invited us in.

Doing his utmost to contain his consternation, Rick stood his ground, looked down at Thurlo, and got straight to the point.

"I was just wondering why you found it necessary to go to the commissioners to get something you already have."

Thurlo mumbled an answer that was difficult for me to hear, but it sounded as if he was saying he appreciated that I was letting them drive through my property. Then he said, more audibly, that although he had other ways of accessing his property, he liked driving through the ranch.

"Only reason I spoke up at the meeting," he declared, "is 'cause I wanted to make sure other folks could still come through. Hope there's no hard feelings."

No hard feelings? Was he serious??

He hadn't denied that he said and did what the minutes reported. He and Dorothy continued to offer explanations and excuses that didn't make any sense, nor did they answer Rick's question. Finally, frustrated and bewildered, we left.

Erring on the side of generosity, I continued to allow the Frenches to drive through the ranch. Even after we read that they and their neighbors were persistent in asserting that I had no right to lock my gates, I allowed all of them to drive past our home until the predictable annual occurrence of snow closed the road for the winter. At that point I sent a letter to the Frenches giving them one last opportunity to confirm that I had a legal right to lock the gates to my property. When they declined to do so, I thought, Okay. That's it.

First I notified the Frenches and their neighbors that they no longer had permission to drive through my property. Then Rick changed the combination. The next time we saw the Frenches was in federal court in Boise the following year.

I'm not sure how much time or thought Custer County's attorney put into the document she wrote on behalf of the county unilaterally declaring my road public. I had never seen or heard about the declaration of public road until I read about it in the *Messenger*. No one from the county had ever notified Rick or me. They simply declared my private property public and considered it a done deal. It was on the basis of no notice and no hearing that my Boise attorney advised me to file suit in federal court charging Custer County and the Frenches with violating my constitutional rights.

At the trial the Frenches and other witnesses for the defense swore to tell the truth, the whole truth, and nothing but the truth, and then they proceeded to say things that left me incredulous. As I watched people take the stand, one after another, and make allegations about the history of the ranch that impugned my name and reputation, I thought, How can they say these things with a straight face? Rick and I had given them the combination in good faith, and the Frenches initially had responded with appreciation. How did we become their enemy? Why were they doing this??

I had suspicions that there were industrial interests not among the named parties. We were given to understand that the Frenches' attorney was working for them pro bono. He also happened to represent a large mining company with an interest in access to the mountains above my ranch. And although I don't recall this being disclosed to me before I bought the property, a Forest Service official had reportedly urged the commissioners to declare the road within the ranch public during my predecessors' ownership.

Few people in rural Idaho had the financial resources to fight the government. I suspected that those seeking to take my property were counting on my not having the will to fight back, but I had both the will and the resources. Even so, I started out slipping backwards. In the federal case, the county was on trial to defend its purported violations of my constitutional rights, but the opposing lawyer and his witnesses treated me as if I were the one on trial. When the Frenches' lawyer puffed himself up and said, "We don't cotton to outsiders coming in from New York and blocking public access to a public road!" I didn't cotton to being characterized as the outsider in question.

Pausing to gather indignation until it reached the bursting point, he expounded further, "Why, that road's been public ever since the ohhhhhld stagecoach came through back in eighteen sixty-two!"

With the location and history of the ranch and the roads and trails around it a matter of public record, I believe that the Frenches' lawyer either knew or should have known that the road within the ranch had not been public since 1939, and that I wasn't blocking access to so much as one inch of public land. But his claims were duly reported and widely disseminated. Few people outside the courthouse heard the truth. I had already fired my original Boise lawyer. Now I watched helplessly as a second Boise lawyer let far too many opportunities go by without making what even I as a layman thought were obvious objections to the defense counsel's tactics.

At last the defense rested. The judge ruled that he couldn't deliver a decision until I could prove that I had been damaged, and I couldn't prove that I had been damaged until I had proven that the road was mine to lose in the first place. The federal case was put on hold until such determinations could be made in the proper venue, which was state court. The "action to quiet title" that I would have to file would be decided in Challis, the very town from which the declaration of public road had emanated.

The misinformation repeated most often by the Frenches and others was that the gates had never been locked in all the years prior to my ownership of the ranch. No one disputed that the entire length of Robinson Bar Road used to be the only road, that it used to be public, or that Robinson's Bar had been a stagecoach stop in the nineteenth century. And everyone agreed that after the highway had been constructed on the north side of the river in 1939, Custer County had legally abandoned the old road on the south side, which by law gave ownership of the road to the adjacent landowners. Outside the ranch, ownership transferred to the United States Forest Service; within the ranch, to the ranch owner. That happened in 1939. With public trails available outside both gates, my assertion of ownership of the private road within the ranch would not deny any member of the public access to the public land around the ranch.

The declaration purported to reclaim the road through a state law that held that a road, having been open to the public for five years and maintained at public expense for five years, could be declared public. My claim was that there was a constitutional defect in that law (and consequently in the declaration) because the law failed to provide for notice or a hearing.

Before the dispute, local lore was consistent with what the seller had told me, that previous owners had locked the gates at least once a year to affirm their private ownership. But we couldn't prove it because no one would come forward to testify to that on the witness stand. With the federal trial on hold pending a state court ruling, it seemed like a good time to look for another lawyer. It was a good thing Steve Millemann agreed to represent us when he did. Custer County was about to escalate the dispute.

Chapter Twenty

Criminal and Quiet Title

*I*t was a beautiful Indian summer day in October 1981 when three deputies drove up the river and parked outside the locked gate on the west side of my ranch. In full uniform, with hats, badges, and sidearms, they entered my property on foot. They continued on to the residential area and headed for the lodge. Having already seen them approaching, Rick and I stepped out to greet them before they could knock.

"Hi there!" I said brightly. "Pretty day, isn't it?"

"Yep," one of them said, looking around as if to verify that this was indeed true. "Sure is."

"Been a dry summer," Rick said.

"Yep. Sure has."

"Creek's gonna get lower before the snow flies."

"Prob-lee."

There were several more exchanges between the men about natural phenomena, during which I silently noted the incredible beauty of the blue sky and the sun shining through the golden aspen leaves quivering among the lodgepole pines. At last one of the deputies—I'll call him Larry—broached the subject they had come to discuss. Almost apologetically, he volunteered that they had been dispatched by the sheriff and instructed by the county attorney to order me to unlock my gates and to arrest me if I didn't comply.

"Arrest me? On what grounds?"

"On the grounds that you're blocking a public road."

"On what does the county base its claim that the road is public?"

The two deputies who weren't doing the talking shifted uncomfortably from one foot to the other. None of the three men seemed to know exactly how to answer that question. However, they had been sent on a mission, and they didn't want to go back to Challis with the gates still locked and me not in custody. They looked at each other.

"Uh . . . I don't know," one of the other deputies hazarded. "You, Larry?"

Larry didn't. Nor did the third deputy.

When they left, the gates were still locked, and I wasn't in custody.

The next day Larry came back alone. He was still in uniform but minus his hat, sidearm, and sidekicks. He had returned with the county attorney's answer to my question about grounds for my arrest. It was the declaration of public road, which he handed to me along with a summons requesting my appearance in the criminal case of *Custer County v. Carole King Evers*.

With the federal judge waiting for a legal determination of whose road it was, and now with a criminal case against me, I had no choice but to file an action to quiet title in Challis, where a state judge would preside. It was my call whether to have the matter decided by a judge or a jury. There was some risk in leaving the decision in the hands of a single judge who might or might not be sympathetic, but I believed that was less risky than leaving it up to twelve people in a community whipped to a frenzy over my supposedly having denied them the right to drive on a road that had been used by the public ever since the ohhhhhld stagecoach stopped there.

This now made three cases in which I was involved.

Prior to being litigants, neither Rick nor I had felt the need to change our common-law cohabitation status, but now we felt the time had come. We became husband and wife on May 3, 1982.

I probably could have earned a degree as a paralegal with all the hours I spent working with Rick and Steve to understand the ramifications of every "whereas" and "herewith" in the documents pertaining to our case. In addition, I was still homeschooling the boys, milking goats, and doing all the other activities that made up the fabric of my daily life. I was also working on several music projects and visiting my other three children in New York and Los Angeles. Something had to give. It was with a heavy heart that I brought my son to live with his father and sister and attend public school in California.

Rick took on the job of detective, a role he clearly relished. Though he hadn't been formally educated beyond high school, he had a high native intelligence. He enjoyed strategizing, and he was good at it. One day he sent Richard to Challis to make copies of the cassette tapes of the commissioner meetings at which my road had been discussed. Those tapes were supposed to be available to the public. I didn't actually expect the commissioners to allow Richard access, but he came back with twenty-two tapes on which he had copied all the original tapes. On one we heard the commissioners debating whether they should ask their attorney to write up a declaration of public road. On another we heard one of the commissioners asking, with an unmistakable contextual reference to me, "What if she sues us?" That question and the discussion around it clearly established the commissioners' awareness that they might have been doing something actionable.

Having obtained a smoking tape, we now turned our attention to getting information from the Forest Service. It took some doing, but their files supported my position that the road within the ranch was private, that I had every right to lock my gates, and that I wasn't blocking public access to any public land.

I had purchased a 1982 Franklin computer with primitive software that allowed me to catalog each document, type in fields of information, and search for that information later. Each search took several minutes for the computer to cycle through the data, but I didn't mind. It was a lot more efficient than searching through physical notes, documents, and our collective memory. After analyzing the documents in this way for a couple of weeks, we were able to pinpoint information about the Forest Service's deficiency of maintenance and other things that were useful to Steve. We now had more than enough documentation to get the criminal case dismissed. But first we had to prevail in the quiet title action.

During that trial in 1985 the claim that the gates had never been locked prior to my ownership was repeated over and over by the Frenches and others. An elderly lady who had lived on the ranch for many years during the first half of the twentieth century made a compelling witness when she said in her slightly cracked elderly-lady voice, "I lived at the Robinson Bar Ranch for over thirty years, and we never, *ever* locked those gates!"

Watching that elderly lady and then sexagenarian Dottie French deliver with impunity what I believed to be inaccurate information, my education in Trial Law 101 began with Lesson 1: it is virtually impossible to impeach the testimony of an elderly lady. Lesson 2 was that *two* elderly ladies delivering the same misinformation are even more difficult to impeach. Disproving such testimony rarely sits well with a judge or a jury. Fortunately, Trial Law 101 included a third lesson. The most effective way to impeach the testimony of however many old ladies is to come up with your own old lady who not only testifies truthfully but brings pictures and a diary.

Working with a private investigator, we found an elderly lady who had visited the area in the 1940s and was willing to fly up from California to tell the truth. From her wheelchair she testified that the gates had been locked when she and her husband had driven up to the ranch many years ago. She brought photographs, a diary, and her own very convincing testimony. The opposing lawyers, of which there were now seven, ignored Lesson 1 and tried to impeach our elderly lady, but her testimony held up through cross-examination. After the trial—four years after Thurlo French had initially sought relief from the county commissioners for a problem he didn't have—Judge Arnold Beebe reviewed our elderly lady's evidence along with the documents Rick and I had obtained from the Forest Service and ruled that the road within my ranch was private. With the judge's decision in my favor, all criminal charges were dismissed and the commissioners settled the federal case out of court.

Not surprisingly, opposing counsel appealed Judge Beebe's decision. Their appeal had the effect of extending the illusion of credence to their claim for another three years. The status of the road within the ranch continued to be perceived by the public as unresolved until the Idaho State Supreme Court upheld the trial judge's ruling in 1988 and the news media duly reported that information. Even so, confirmation of my victory didn't stop some of the mud from sticking. To some of the local old guard, I would always be the wealthy outsider who had locked them out of their God-given right to drive any-damn-where they pleased. Some folks in the American West never would give up on the idea that blocking motorized access to any land whatsoever is a crime just short of Murder Two—unless the land in question happens to belong to one of the local old guard.

Yee-ha.

Chapter Twenty-One

One to One

*I*t seemed that no matter what else was going on in my life, I was inevitably drawn back to music. Concurrent with the road fight were periods during which I was motivated to write and record songs. In 1982, the professional work that was both my joy and my livelihood brought me to Austin to record my first album for Atlantic Records. A generous reviewer might have called *One to One* an eclectic mixture. A more blunt assessment would have been that the songs had no unifying thread.

Though Rick Sorensen never collaborated on a song with me, I internalized and communicated some of what I believed to be his views in "It's a War," "Lookin' Out for Number One," and "Little Prince"—all written in Gretchen's cabin. But there were also songs with upbeat lyrics. I was the sole writer of "Golden Man" and "(Love Is Like a) Boomerang." I'd written "Golden Man" about Rick Evers early in our relationship, and the opening and closing choruses of "Boomerang" expressed my long-held belief that love is worth the risk.

Then there was "Life Without Love," penned by Gerry Goffin and our daughter Louise. That was the first song I ever recorded that I had not written.

But the best song was arguably the title song. With its exquisitely crafted lyrics by Cynthia Weil, I wasn't surprised when Atlantic released "One to One" as the first single, but I was truly surprised when it hit the top 40. It probably didn't hurt that I did some live performances that year, or that the message in "One to One" was consistent with what people wanted to hear from me. Such was not the case with "Goat Annie." Few of my fans could relate to that song, and more than a few wrote to ask why I had included it on the album. The answer is, I wrote it to celebrate the independent spirit of the woman who had inspired the fictional Goat Annie. How could I not include it? I shared the opinion Jerry Jeff Walker was said to have expressed about records:

"A record is exactly that—a record of what you're doin' and thinkin' at a certain time."

One to One had been exactly that. And so it was with my second Atlantic album. Released in 1983, *Speeding Time* combined my exposure to some of the people I'd met in rural Idaho with a desire to incorporate some of the sounds of the eighties. *Speeding Time* was—how shall I put this?—not warmly received. I knew that people wanted more songs from me along the lines of those in *Tapestry*, but I was older now, and my life was different. I had written some of the songs for *Speeding Time* with Gerry, and I wrote others on my own in a small studio Rick helped me set up in a little-used room in the part of the lodge that had been the stage stop. As I wrote, I ran an eight-track reel-to-reel tape to record what I called a docu-demo. Unlike a demo to present a song to an artist, the purpose of a docu-demo was to document a song as it was emerging so I could refer back to a moment of creative magic that I might otherwise have lost. I employed a Linn drum machine that gave me the ability to approximate, with the touch of a finger, the sounds a human drummer makes. I also had a Roland Jupiter-8 synthesizer with presets that attempted to replicate the sound of a string orchestra, a horn section, or any other instrumentation I wanted. What I did not have at Robinson Bar was immediate access to a recording engineer or a community of cats.

Studio musicians were having problems of their own. Synthesizers were beginning to replace them in the studio. Producers were thinking, Let me see. $1,000 for a machine, one time only? Or $10,000 per track for an orchestra? And the machine doesn't require a ten-minute union break every hour.

But I didn't take my friends' jobs away. I used my synthesizer as a writing tool and then went to L.A. to record with actual musicians. However, after I recorded the live tracks, since the sound of the eighties was all about synths, I felt compelled, however misguidedly, to add electronic sounds to what the live musicians had played. It was not my finest hour as an arranger.

I invited Lou Adler out of semiretirement to produce *Speeding Time*. I'm still not sure why he agreed to do it. That album included some of the worst songs I've ever written. I believe I may have hit a career low with "Chalice Borealis," though of course I didn't feel that way at the time. Still, some songs from *Speeding Time* have held up. Lou and I closed a circle when we recorded a version of "Crying in the Rain," on which I sang both Everly Brothers' parts and added—finally!—my own third harmony. And I still smile when I hear "One Small Voice," which I composed after rereading Hans Christian Andersen's *The Emperor's New Clothes*. I'd like to believe that my performing "One Small Voice" in three different American presidential campaigns had nothing to do with my first two candidates losing.

After spending time back in 1977 with David Crosby and his pale young girlfriend, Nancy Brown, my perception of their relationship had inspired me to write the music and lyrics for "Alabaster Lady." That song was really more of an epic, but it, too, appeared on the *Speeding Time* album. I thought it was incredibly generous of Crosby to remain my good friend even after he heard that lyric in which I was highly judgmental of him.

Sometimes songs reveal layers that not even the writer fully understands at first. When I wrote "Alabaster Lady" I thought I was speaking to Nancy Brown. Later I realized that I was also speaking to myself. "Alabaster Lady" is one of those songs that came *through* me, rather than *from* me. As soon as I recognize that a song is coming through me, I try to get out of the way and let the process be guided by whatever is driving me beyond what I think of as craft. People have different names for whatever inspires them, but anyone who's ever created anything from that place knows exactly what I'm talking about.

Craft is when you sit in front of a blank page, a musical instrument, or a computer screen, and wonder how you're going to come up with a second verse, the next chapter, an irrefutable argument in a legal brief, or that certain-to-get-you-admitted paragraph in a college essay. Artists, actors, and choreographers undoubtedly experience a similar agony contemplating their chosen medium. When I experience such agony I'm usually contemplating a hastily scribbled verse and maybe a chorus that I'm trying to shape into something resembling a good song.

When I hit a wall I usually stop and do something else. This effectively turns the problem over to my subconscious mind, which keeps working on it under the radar. When I return to the task, my subconscious has often solved the problem before my ego has time to assert control. When the ego is in charge, that's when the work is coming *from* you. You may still be doing good work but the ego allows doubt to creep in.

First you agonize. How will I ever finish this?

Then you ponder. How did I ever come up with this?

Then you wonder. Is it good enough?

I offer this as the opinion of one woman: when the thing you're creating comes *through* you, you know it, and it's much better than good enough.

After *Speeding Time*, I didn't release another album or tour again for five years—unless you count performing for political purposes.

Chapter Twenty-Two

Ronald Reagan's Opponent

$\mathcal{D}$isclaimer: if you disagree with my political views, feel free either to skip this chapter or substitute the name of your preferred candidate.

The first time I dipped my toe into the waters of a presidential campaign professionally had been in 1972 when Lou asked me to perform in a concert he and Warren Beatty were putting on for Senator George McGovern. Lou had called the concert "Four 4 McGovern." With not a single conservative among us, the "Four" were Barbra Streisand, James Taylor, Quincy Jones, and me.

In the fall of 1983 I reached out to everyone in the Idaho congressional delegation for help with my road fight. A staffer in every office sent me back a standard form letter over the senator's or representative's mechanically reproduced signature thanking me for writing and saying he sincerely appreciated hearing from me, but the courts were the appropriate jurisdiction.

Thank you, I thought. I'm already in court.

I tried writing to senators from other states, but the universal response was that they couldn't help me; I needed to write to my own senators. I remained in a bureaucratic circle until one of my letters reached Oliver Henkel, who was then managing Senator Gary Hart's campaign for president of the United States. Oliver, whom everyone called "Pudge," wrote back immediately to say that although Senator Hart couldn't help with my road fight because it wasn't in his state, would I consider supporting the senator's bid for the 1984 Democratic presidential nomination?

When Pudge asked me to support Senator Hart's campaign in 1983 I knew three things about the candidate: he was the junior senator from Colorado, he was running for president, and he had hired a campaign manager with chutzpah. When I told Pudge I needed to know more about Senator Hart, he sent me some position papers, speeches, and Senator Hart's recently published book, *A New Democracy*, in which he presented his plan for governing the United States. I was sufficiently impressed to ask Pudge what he wanted me to do. He was prepared with an answer.

In December of 1983 Senator Hart's campaign was in desperate straits. Volunteers were stuffing envelopes by candlelight with freezing fingers in an unheated office in Washington, D.C. The phone and power companies hadn't been paid for several months. The power was already cut off, and the phones—the lifeline of a campaign—would be next. Pudge said that if I did a concert for Senator Hart in Denver it would raise enough money to keep the campaign going until the New Hampshire primary in February. When I agreed to do it, Pudge put me in touch with a volunteer in Manchester, New Hampshire, who would put the concert together.

In addition to being a deeply committed supporter of Senator Hart, Will Kanteres was a realtor in a family-owned business. He had no experience in promoting concerts, but he was willing to learn. I hooked him up with Barry Fey, a professional concert promoter in Denver. Together Barry, Will, and others from the campaign managed to pull together a concert that raised enough money for the campaign to pay its past-due bills and cover other basic necessities until February. When I asked some of my musician friends to participate, all were generous enough to donate their time.

When I met Senator Hart after the concert, he was appropriately appreciative. After that, whenever our paths crossed on the campaign trail I was impressed every time by how intelligent and visionary he was. He would continue to be both as we moved into the next century. After taking himself permanently out of contention for the presidency, Senator Hart would continue working to educate elected officials about how they could improve our government. Notably, Senator Hart and Senator Warren Rudman, a former Republican senator from New Hampshire, would submit a bipartisan comprehensive report several years before September 11, 2001, with detailed suggestions for how the United States could prepare more thoroughly and effectively to avert a terrorist attack.

After the concert in Denver I was so inspired by Senator Hart's ideas that I agreed to do several more concerts in Iowa and New Hampshire early in 1984. My commitment to the campaign attracted others, including a man whose name at birth had been Wolodia Grajonca. Born to a Jewish family in Berlin in 1931, nicknamed Wolfgang in his early childhood, the boy was lucky enough to get out of Germany before the rise of the Nazis. Eventually he arrived in the United States, where he would become known as Bill Graham. Among Bill's accomplishments were that he had founded both Fillmores (East and West) in the sixties, and he also managed the Grateful Dead. In 1984 he was a legendary promoter in San Francisco. If an artist wanted to play in any venue in the Bay Area, Bill was the guy to call.

A couple of weeks before the New Hampshire primary, Will and I met with Bill about booking the Warfield Theater in March for another concert for Senator Hart. Though Bill knew nothing about the candidate, he looked me in the eye and asked, "Do you know him?"

"Yes."

"Do you like him?"

"Yes."

"Do you really think he'd make a good president?"

"Yes."

"Okay. On your say-so, I'll hold the Warfield Theater."

This was not a corporate decision made by a committee. This was a personal commitment involving some risk. But Bill Graham wasn't afraid of risk.

On February 28, 1984, less than a month before the concert at the Warfield was scheduled, Senator Hart roared past the pack of eight Democratic candidates to win the primary in New Hampshire. The next day, Bill Graham called me.

"I don't know how you knew," he said, "but I'm glad I trusted my instinct. We're gonna put on a terrific concert in March, and our guy's gonna win!"

He was right about the first part. It was a terrific concert. By June my band and I had done a total of twelve concerts that raised more than a million dollars for the Hart campaign. This startling number impelled the journalist Bryant Gumbel to inform me, during a morning interview on national television, that I qualified as a special interest. I told Bryant that I was simply bringing people in to learn more about my candidate.

"Once they hear from Senator Hart," I said, "the voters will be his to keep or lose."

Knowing that the Democratic National Convention would be held in San Francisco that year, Bill decided to book another concert for Senator Hart at the Warfield. This show would take place during the week of the convention and would feature multiple artists.

The frustration of the road fight had been temporarily eclipsed by my enthusiasm for the campaign. With both these projects in my life, any hope I had for peace and tranquility in the near future was virtually gone. If I had any brain cells left, the gathering of energy and ambition at the Democratic National Convention that week overpowered them all. Delegates from every state, having vied aggressively at home for the opportunity to attend, showed up with costumes, bells, whistles, flags, hats, balloons, signs, and enough vigor to party for five days and five nights while working every room they were in to collect hearts, minds, names, and ideas.

As I walked from one state delegation to the next on the convention floor to make my case for Senator Hart, I had the opportunity to observe how complicated a convention can be, and that was in the 1980s. It seemed as if every fourth person was a voting delegate, with at least two members of the press for each delegate. The rest were people working the floor on behalf of the competing campaigns, as I was doing. The maneuvering of the minions was as unceasing as the flow of the Sacramento River toward San Francisco Bay. Simply moving through the crowd required the skills of a New Yorker with experience navigating Macy's the morning of a white sale. Luckily, I still possessed those long-neglected skills.

That week I also got to see for myself how little control we voters have concerning information we receive from the news media. Early in the morning on the first day of the convention, I had just turned the news on at low volume in my hotel room when I saw a video clip that appeared to show demonstrators outside the Moscone Center being beaten with clubs by a team of S.W.A.T. policemen. By the time I got to the TV and turned the volume up, the anchor was introducing the next story.

Oh no, I thought. I hope this doesn't turn into another 1968.

It wasn't another 1968, but not for the reason you might think. In 1968 most news programs reported news wherever they found it. By 1984 the news media had become more savvy about selecting what they would and would not report. Editors and producers had learned that showing demonstrations, especially those involving violence, had the potential to encourage others to demonstrate and possibly, God forbid, start a movement. To my knowledge, not one subsequent news program on that or any other station reported the Moscone Center story or showed that clip again. It was as if the demonstration and the beatings had never happened.

A little after noon I was being interviewed about my support for Senator Hart by an anchor at the station on which I'd seen the clip. I said as much about my candidate as I could squeeze into the short time allotted between commercials, then, during a break, I asked the anchor why her station had suppressed the news of the beating of demonstrators by the police. She was obviously aware of it, because she looked extremely uncomfortable. Finally she said, "The producers believe they're being more responsible by not showing it."

I said, "It's news. You need to show it." She disagreed. When we came back from the commercial, she marshaled all her skills as an interviewer to make sure that she retained control of the conversation until my segment was over. But her vigilance was unnecessary. I wasn't there to embarrass the news media. I was there to tell people why I thought Senator Hart would be a great president. I had felt compelled to mention the news suppression off air only because I was hoping to appeal to her conscience and possibly get her to air the clip. Ha! Color me naïve.

Senator Hart lost his bid for the 1984 Democratic nomination to Walter Mondale. The former vice president had had years to solidify his intraparty following, which, along with his "Where's the beef?" commercial, made Mondale's nomination inevitable. In hindsight, I doubt that it would have mattered who won the Democratic nomination in 1984. Saint Peter probably couldn't have defeated the popular Republican incumbent, President Ronald Reagan.

Of course I had known there was a chance Hart might not win, but I had never allowed myself to think about that as a possibility. Gary Hart was going to be inaugurated in 1985. Period. When that hope vanished, I went back to Idaho and vowed to stay out of politics—a vow I didn't keep. I would be drawn into politics again and again by my joy in finding common purpose with other Americans who loved their country as much as I did, who had come to politics not out of fear, hatred, or greed but because they wanted to make the world better. I did take one thing away from the Hart campaign that no defeat will ever diminish: the friendship of more than a few exceptional people. The time I spent on the campaign trail in 1984 had made me stronger for the battles that lay ahead in Idaho.

Chapter Twenty-Three

Prosecutorial Discretion

*I*n spite of the road fight I was thankful to be living at Robinson Bar. In the spring I loved watching the "reveal" as melting snow uncovered new life pushing from every inch of ground and from every branch and bush. In the fall I reveled in the golden glory of the aspens and the orange shimmer of kokanee salmon in the rivers and creeks. I took pleasure in seeing the stars reflected in the pool as twinkles of light that scattered in patterns with every ripple. I was reassured by the rhythm of the seasons that I experienced with all my senses. I felt renewed by all the living things that grew, grazed, flew, swam, and hibernated at different times of the year. When the negativity of the road fight threatened to engulf me, I could always find comfort in some small gift proffered by nature, almost as if in consolation.

After the quiet title decision in our favor, I was eager to get back to a more positive frame of mind. Before the trials I had always believed that people were inherently good. Now that the battle was over, I longed to rediscover my faith in human nature. But Rick seemed unable to let go of his belief that justice had not been sufficiently served. He turned his attention to the Forest Service official who had encouraged the commissioners to declare our road public. I agreed with his assessment of the man's wrongdoing, but I was weary of living in an adversarial atmosphere. Wasn't it enough that we had won? Apparently it wasn't. Rick obtained a transcript of the official's testimony and pored over it. Then he called me over, held up the papers triumphantly, and pointed out at least eight instances of what he viewed as perjury. I could see that he was excited about the possibility of retribution, but I didn't relish the prospect of yet another battle. I was excited about life after litigation. When Rick asked me to go to Challis with him to file charges and request that the new county attorney prosecute the official for perjury, I balked.

"You don't have to be a party to the case," Rick said. "The People will be the plaintiff. All you have to do is be a witness."

He kept after me until I agreed.

"All right," I said, climbing into his truck. "But this is absolutely the last time I'll testify in this matter."

As it turned out, neither of us would testify in this matter. I was about to learn Lesson 4 in my hopefully soon-to-be-ended legal education: prosecutorial discretion can trump justice. You and three witnesses can apprehend a killer standing over a bleeding dead body with a smoking gun in his hand and the bullet holes in the body a perfect ballistic match to the aforementioned gun. If the prosecuting attorney chooses not to prosecute, the killer walks.

The Custer County magistrate went as far as issuing a subpoena for the official to respond to the allegations, but the county prosecutor declared a conflict, and the Idaho attorney general ultimately declined to prosecute.

Hearing that the official had been transferred to another state was good enough for me, but it wasn't good enough for Rick. He spent a substantial part of each day in his rocking chair staring out the window, tamping and refilling his pipe, and complaining about the unfairness of prosecutorial discretion. I understood his frustration with the capricious nature of the judicial system, but we had prevailed in that very judicial system. Why couldn't he be happy with our victory and move on?

I didn't know enough at the time to diagnose it, but it's possible that Rick was suffering from depression, and that my attempts to be cheerful and encourage him to move on at my pace made him feel even more frustrated. What I did know was that Rick's state of mind was casting a pall over everything I had loved and appreciated about him. I began to turn in the direction of seeing my children more often, songwriting, recording, and other activities that I hoped would restore peace and joy to the forefront of my life.

PART IV

Chapter One

All Over the Map

$\mathcal{I}$n the early eighties, alternately isolated from the world and in the thick of it, I bridged the gap by listening to news reports. As the eighties rolled out, I found myself more in the thick of it than not. To recap:

On January 21, 1981, while Ronald Reagan was rolling up his newly inaugurated presidential sleeves to deal with a variety of responsibilities affecting humankind around the world, I was deciding such things as when to haul water from the creek and what wax to put on the children's skis.

President Reagan's responsibilities would include freeing hostages in Iran; ending a strike by air traffic controllers; invading a tiny Caribbean island called Grenada; bonding with the United Kingdom's prime minister, Margaret Thatcher; recovering from an attempt on his life; deregulating the financial market; promoting trickle-down economics; and reducing government spending except for "Star Wars," the Strategic Defense Initiative that he told us would prevent nuclear obliteration of the United States by the Soviet Union.

I turned forty on February 9, 1982. That same year I recorded my

One to One album, performed in concert, and filmed a performance and interviews in Austin for a video I released that year, also titled *One to One*. I traversed the continent between California and New York to spend time with my children, act on the stage, and appear on TV. I traveled to Boise to meet Rick for court appearances and lawyer meetings. Back at home I strategized with my husband, composed letters seeking congressional help, and wrote songs.

The quiet title trial alone might have filled 1985, but when producers Laura Ziskin and Sally Field asked me to score and write songs for *Murphy's Romance*, and the director, Martin Ritt, offered me a small role in the film, how could I say no? The score featured my piano, a string quartet, and the saxophone of David Sanborn. David Campbell did the orchestration. Lou Adler produced the soundtrack album for *Murphy's Romance*, which as of this writing has yet to be released. The score and songs took quite a bit of time to create; the acting role, considerably less. Don't blink or you'll miss my moment as Tillie. Later that year director Rick Rosenthal cast me in *Russkies* as the mother of a twelve-year-old boy played by Joaquin Phoenix, then called Leaf Phoenix. My mother played my character's mother. The film was scheduled to be shot in Key West, Florida. When I went on location the children stayed in L.A. with Charlie. Rick remained in Idaho.

In 1986 Charlie became involved in a project that required him to be in Florida for an extended period of time. To keep the children from having to change schools, he asked if I'd take over as the resident parent in L.A. during the 1986–87 school year. Rick had never made any secret of his loathing for L.A. and declined to join me, but he did agree to the arrangement and promised to travel back and forth for what he referred to as conjugal visits.

The intricate travel dance in which my husband, my ex-husband, and I were engaged did nothing to ameliorate the problems developing between Rick and me. The range of the dance increased in 1986 when Sherry asked me to come to New York as much as possible during the last months of a difficult pregnancy in which she was confined to bed. Traveling back and forth between New York, L.A., Idaho, and London—where Louise was living—I racked up thousands of frequent flyer miles. I was forty-four when I became a grandmother on October 24, 1986.

When I held my grandson for the first time I nuzzled his little face, counted his fingers and toes—ten, twenty, yes, all there!—and pronounced him, with no bias whatsoever, the handsomest baby in the world. I held him long enough to mutually imprint that we were family, then I reluctantly gave him back to his mother. Sherry settled the baby in a comfortable position for both and then posed a question with so much tact that I would have recommended her for a position in the State Department had she not just taken on an eighteen-year commitment.

"Um...Mom? What do you want Dillon to call you?"

I looked at her as if she were from another planet.

"Grandma. What else would he call me?"

Nomenclature would not be one of the ways I would try to postpone getting older.

At forty-four, not only was I a grandmother but I was the mother of two adult women and two active teenagers, one of whom was a twelve-year-old Jewish boy. With his own son unable to participate in the Jewish traditions of his ancestors, my father turned his attention toward the next male in line. In the fall of 1986, when I told my dad I was going to be based in L.A. until the following June, he said, with the air of a casual suggestion, "You know, Levi's going to be thirteen next April. You might want to think about his bar mitzvah."

It was unusual for my dad to express a heartfelt wish with such delicacy. I could tell how important it was to him when he continued in the same understated manner.

"You shouldn't have any trouble finding a good rabbi in L.A."

My dad needn't have worried. I was of similar mind. And he was right; I had no trouble finding Stan Levy, a rabbi whose day job as a practicing lawyer kept him independent of having his sole income subject to the whim of a congregation. This left him free to perform his rabbinical duties answering only to God and Mrs. Levy.

Since I had to drive Levi to and from Stan's study classes, rather than drop my son off and wait in a nearby café, I asked Stan if I might sit in.

"Of course."

His consent was a threefold gift to me: a joyous reunion with learning, a reconnection with the history of my forebears, and an opportunity to witness how much Levi and the other boys, including Stan's son Joshua, were absorbing from the discussions.

As 1986 rolled into 1987, my roots were spread among far too many places for any to take hold. As much as I had tried to make a home for my family in Idaho, life kept taking me elsewhere. Chief among the advantages of being in L.A. was getting to spend more time with my Larkey children. Other benefits were the availability of new and interesting professional experiences, the joy of having neighbors who didn't hate me, and proximity to the popular culture that many Angelenos believed would help them stay young. Of course I didn't need to be in L.A. for any of the latter three things. New and interesting experiences seemed to find me no matter where I was. Joy was in my heart, even in difficult times; the key was remembering that. As for staying young, if someone had then told me, "Good luck with that!" I wouldn't have listened. As far as I knew, I *was* young.

An unanticipated stroke of good fortune came to me in 1987 when I met Rudy and Lorna Guess. With so many activities to keep track of, I needed a personal assistant. When Lorna applied for the position she mentioned that her husband was a guitar player but didn't elaborate further. Lorna proved so capable, intelligent, and industrious as my assistant that inevitably she became my professional manager. In addition to appreciating the benefits of her advocacy, I found it very satisfying to watch her win respect in an industry that is not always welcoming to strong, smart women in management. After I hired Lorna, the first time I needed to record a demo it seemed quite natural for me to do it in Rudy's studio and have him play guitar. I quickly discovered that Rudy was an extraordinary guitar player with a musical sensibility similar in many ways to mine. Where it was different, his knowledge expanded my own repertoire and skills. He was also an excellent recording engineer. Increasingly I came to rely on Rudy as a cowriter, coproducer, engineer, bandmate, and musical director.

In Lorna Guess I found a wise, bright businesswoman, a gracious teammate, a sympathetic sounding board, a bold innovator, and a creative partner who saw where I wanted to go and helped get me there.

In Rudy Guess I found a comrade with a calm approach to solving problems. His strength of character, understated generosity, clarity of purpose, sense of wonder, and sunny smile made everyone's life better.

In both I found two of the greatest friends a person could ever hope to have.

My son's bar mitzvah took place on a perfect spring day in April 1987, with the Pacific Ocean as a backdrop. As Rudy and Lorna came to be known, the Guessae (pronounced Guess-eye) attended along with other friends and family members. Rick came to L.A. for the occasion and was in a rare and delightful humor the whole time. It was the last time I would see him that way.

Chapter Two

City Streets

In November 1987 I was cast in a play written by Hindi Brooks called *A Minor Incident*. It ran for a month at the West Bank Café Theater in New York. Paul Hipp played the young man injured in the accident that Hindi had written about to begin the play. In addition to being an actor, Paul was a singer, songwriter, and guitar player whom I had met before. It was by sheer coincidence that he was cast in *A Minor Incident*. I had met Paul when he was putting all his talents to use in an off-off-Broadway show called *Rockabilly Road* that featured, among others, Paul and my daughter Sherry. With dark good looks and a robust baritone voice, Paul had been so strongly influenced by rockabilly that he sometimes appeared to be channeling Elvis Presley. A year later he would achieve acclaim, first on London's West End, then on Broadway, playing the title role in the musical show *Buddy: The Buddy Holly Story*.

During our run at the West Bank, Paul and I began writing and performing together. He and his band had a regular gig playing the 1 a.m. to 4 a.m. shift at the Red Lion Café on Bleecker Street. When he invited me to a rehearsal on one of our days off, I zipped my black Telecaster guitar into a padded gig bag, hoisted the bag on my back, took the subway, and walked up Bleecker Street affecting casual familiarity with the Village until I remembered that I had earned that familiarity as an audience member. On my way to the Red Lion I passed several locations of clubs at which I had witnessed some of the great jazz players and emerging rock bands more than two decades earlier. With the exception of the Village Vanguard, most of the clubs were gone or had new names.

Jamming on guitar with Paul and his band was so much fun that when Paul invited me to sit in with them it was an easy yes. With Paul and Mark Bosch covering all the guitar parts, as long as they kept my guitar level down no one would notice if I made mistakes. The truth is, no one noticed much of anything. By the time 1 a.m. rolled around, most of the people in the club were several sheets to the wind. Even so, the waitresses kept bringing drinks to the tiny tables. The more drinks they imbibed, the louder the patrons talked, which made other patrons talk even louder. After fifteen minutes of performing mostly for ourselves, Paul turned the mic over to me. With Paul handling harmonies, I sang "Will You Love Me Tomorrow." Most of the patrons conversed right through my performance, which significantly increased my appreciation for musicians who regularly play the 1 a.m. shift in a bar.

One or two people looked up with a vague sense of recognition. I could almost see them thinking, Is that...? No. Can't be.... But I could tell who knew for sure by their attention and the knowing smiles and nudges they gave their tablemates.

My connection with Paul was fun and musical, but not physical. Wanting to share my life in New York with Rick, I had invited him to come see me in the play, an invitation on which he had not yet taken me up. A couple of days after I told him that Paul and I were playing on Bleecker Street, Rick came to New York unannounced. When he showed up at the apartment where I was staying, I was surprised but glad to see him. I wasn't sure how he felt but I assumed he was tired after hours of travel. That night he attended the play. Then he came to the Red Lion to watch Paul and me perform. The next day he flew back home and moved into the cabin on the creek—the very cabin in which I had wanted us to live.

To be fair, the woman Rick had met in Burgdorf had told him that she wanted a simple life. Inexplicably to him, I was being drawn back into a scene for which he had little regard, and that scene included a young man with whom I was spending more time than with him. Rick had made a big change from his chosen lifestyle—at the time, that of a mountain man—to live in the more modern-day world to which my children and I were inextricably connected. Where was his wife?

From my point of view, the man I had met in Burgdorf was then doing everything necessary to support his chosen lifestyle, and he had made me laugh with his dry sense of humor. Where was that man?

It was possible that our economic inequality, the complicated nature of my work and family, and the stress of years of litigation had contributed to the decline of our relationship. Whatever the reasons, although our divorce wouldn't be final until the following year, our marriage was effectively over.

In May 1988 I attended one of Bruce Springsteen's Tunnel of Love concerts at Madison Square Garden. The phrase "blew my mind" unquestionably applied to that concert. In addition to the band's scorching musicianship, Bruce and Patti Scialfa were newly in love. Not only did Patti's three-octave vocal work complement Bruce's raw, gritty singing style, and not only was her attire exactly right for the theme of a carnival, but the chemistry between Bruce and Patti was electrifying. Old songs, new songs, it didn't matter to Bruce's fans. We loved every minute of every song. We loved the carnival atmosphere. We loved the expanded horn section.

And we loved watching the Boss and the Big Man (saxophonist Clarence Clemons) lean up against each other with the affection of longtime friends delighted to share their musical history with fifteen thousand other friends. Two and a half hours after the first welcoming roar from the audience, I was elated to have attended that energetic and emotionally charged rock concert and at the same time disheartened because I didn't think I could ever make an audience that happy. But soon my dejection gave way to action. I had already written a few new songs. I added a few more, re-signed with Capitol Records, and recorded the *City Streets* album at Skyline Studios in New York with Rudy Guess playing guitar and coproducing. Among the many first-rate musicians who responded to my invitation to join me in the studio were drummers Steve Ferrone, Omar Hakim, and Max Weinberg; saxophonists Branford Marsalis and Michael Brecker; and Eric Clapton.

I was recording that album when Rick called me at the studio to tell me that the Idaho Supreme Court had upheld Judge Beebe's ruling and the ranch road was now legally confirmed as private. His delivery of the news was followed by a pause during which I could almost imagine his unspoken thought: *And aren't you ashamed of yourself for not being home with your husband to acknowledge how much a part of the victory he was?*

My husband was very much a part of the road victory, and yes, I did feel his pain about my not being there with him. But then I remembered his gloomy outlook when I was there, which made me not want to go home, which added fuel to his frustration, which kept me away. And there was the inescapable reality that I had work that brought in necessary income that I couldn't do at home. My work took me to places of which Rick was openly contemptuous, places where I interacted with people about whom he complained on a daily basis. My children lived in some of those places, and they and their fathers were some of those people.

Hearing what I interpreted as a reproachful silence at the other end of the line, I sensed a hunger in Rick for someone I no longer believed I could be. My own hunger for artistic creativity and optimism was too strong. As I tried and failed to find words to express my appreciation, the silence grew painfully uncomfortable.

What I thought he was hoping to hear was, "I want to be with you so much that I'm putting my album on hold and coming home tomorrow. I promise I'll stop running around and stay home with you."

What I said was, "Thank you."

I replaced the handset. The ranch, the road fight, and the man who was still legally my husband began to recede. However, like objects in a rearview mirror, they were closer than they appeared and would remain so for a long time.

I was exceptionally happy with the *City Streets* album and was actually looking forward to going on tour to promote it. (Yes, I did just say that!) I incorporated some of the elements from Bruce's show that had inspired me. Obviously I wouldn't have Bruce, Patti, Clarence Clemons, or someone with whom I was newly in love, but I would have a well-designed set, gorgeous lighting, a collection of both new and familiar songs, and a stellar nine-piece band led by Rudy and me. Though not everyone in the tour band had played on the album, all were ready, willing, and able to rock the outdoor venues known as "sheds."

The City Streets Tour lasted for two and a half months during the summer of 1989. It was the longest I had ever been away from my Larkey children, though I did build in some days off that allowed me to visit them. When I first learned that we would be traveling by bus I envisioned something like the Trailways bus that had brought my mother and me to Florida in 1951. But touring on a bus designed for the specific needs of a touring band turned out to be so much better than flying from city to city that a bus became my tour transportation of choice from then on. Note to reader: this was true only if none of the choices was a private jet.

Because few women who have been pregnant would ever describe being with child as "easy," let me just say that my daughter Sherry's pregnancy with her second child in 1989 was uncomplicated enough for her to sing backup and play percussion alongside Linda Lawley on the City Streets Tour. Linda's husband, Danny Pelfrey, played saxophone, guitar, and other instruments. Sherry's husband, Robbie Kondor, played keyboards. Lorna's husband, Rudy Guess, played guitar and sang backup. We were one rockin' family. Several months after the tour ended, my biological family increased by one with the birth of Sophie Leann Kondor on October 17, 1989. I have no doubt that my granddaughter's experience of a tour in utero contributed to her decision early in life not to become a professional musician.

Knowing that my fans wanted to hear songs from *Tapestry*, I gladly delivered them. They were probably a little surprised when I liberated my inner Chrissie Hynde by strapping on a low-slung guitar and slamming out a hard-driving rhythm with my band, but I appreciated that my audiences were kind enough to indulge me. Our last song before intermission was "Jazzman." After the apex of Danny Pelfrey's last saxophone solo, I climbed up on the piano to propel the band as they increased the intensity of the Big Rock Ending, then I gave them a cutoff by jumping off the piano. That was so much fun it should have been illegal.

Chapter Three

McCartneys in Tokyo

$\mathcal{I}$n 1990 I took the City Streets Tour to Japan. One afternoon, with no show that night, I went off on my own to sightsee in Tokyo. I meandered up one street and down the other with no destination in mind. I crossed lanes, avenues, and alleys to explore little shops with lacquered dishes, silk kimonos, or luggage. Every fourth storefront was a sushi bar, each of which would have been impossible to walk past had they not all been closed between lunch and dinner. After another leisurely hour of strolling, I walked into a giant electronics store where hundreds of sounds were competing for my attention at peak volume. Equally loud visually were the displays in Japanese of vividly colored neon logos flashing so brightly that I wondered when the heavy metal rock band would appear. I didn't stay to find out. Emerging onto a noisy street that seemed silent by comparison, I looked around to get my bearings and saw that all the street signs were in Japanese. There were no signs in English, and I didn't see any landmarks that I recognized. I had no idea where I was. I could speak enough Japanese to order sushi, but that wouldn't get me back to my hotel.

None of the people I stopped on the street spoke or understood English. There were phone booths, but they required Japanese coins and an ability to read instructions in that language. With cell phones not yet in common use, I had no way to call anyone. I began to feel a sense of panic. The interplay of people and vehicles in motion under signs I couldn't read was making me dizzy. I had just sat down on a bench when I remembered that the desk clerk had given each of us a card at check-in with the name and address of our hotel in English and Japanese. Oh, God. Did I bring it? I rummaged frantically around in my purse until... Yes! I stood up, hailed a taxi, and showed the driver the card. He nodded with understanding, beckoned me in, and delivered me to my hotel.

The revolving door spun me into the lobby, where I saw some of my companions having a drink. They waved me over and excitedly informed me that Paul McCartney and his band were playing at the Tokyo Dome that night.[*] Did I want to go?

Yes! Definitely!

It didn't take long for my tour manager, Joe Cardosi, to confirm that Paul's people would set aside twelve tickets. Looking at his watch, Joe told us we had barely enough time to go upstairs to freshen up and meet our transportation outside the hotel.

"Ten or tails," Joe warned on his way to the elevator. "Ten" was the number of minutes before departure, and "tails" were the taillights a latecomer would see pulling away.

No one was late. At the venue we descended en masse from the vans and headed to the box office expecting to find twelve tickets in my name. But our tickets could not be found.

"Anata no onamae wa?"

---

[*]Paul's band in Tokyo comprised Hamish Stuart on guitar and vocals, Robbie McIntosh on guitar, Chris Whitten on drums, percussion, and vocals, Paul Wickens on keyboards, and Linda McCartney on keyboards and vocals.

"Carole King."

"A-noh, group-u . . . ?"

I gave the Japanese pronunciation of my name. "Karoru Kingu."

"So sorry, other namu?"

Joe said, "Try Cardosi."

No tickets.

My band and crew were disconsolate as we stepped away from the window. I thought, I am not going to give up. There *has* to be a way.

Before I could finish saying, "Let's go to the stage do—" Joe was already headed that way.

The stage door had several levels of security. Joe's use of my name got us through the first and second levels, but we could not get past the third. With only a few minutes left until showtime, we were stuck in an anteroom adjacent to the backstage area. Suddenly a door at the far end of the anteroom opened. Through the opening we saw several men walking past holding instruments. We assumed they were Paul's bandmates making their way to the stage. Maybe I could get one of them to vouch for us. I was just about to call out when a man holding a bass guitar came into view. Was it . . . ? It was!

"Paul!" I called. Paul McCartney stopped, peered into the room, and stared intently at me.

"Is that Carole?"

"Yes, it's me! How's it going?"

"Well, just great," he said, stepping into the anteroom, revealing Linda standing in the doorway behind him. Paul handed his bass off to a member of his crew, took Linda's hand, brought her over, and said, "You remember Linda."

Of course I remembered Linda. Who didn't remember Linda? In my case, in addition to what I knew *of* her, I had actually met her at several public occasions, but we had never conversed. There had been so many people, greetings, photographs, and questions from the media around her and Paul that there hadn't been a chance to say anything more meaningful than "Hello"—if that.

"We're about to go on," Paul said. "D'ya need a seat?"

"Well, I thought we had seats, but apparently we don't."

"No problem," he said. "How many d'ya need?"

"Twelve," I said, mentally cringing. I didn't want to be pushy, but I couldn't bear to send any of my friends away. I needn't have worried. When you're Paul McCartney, finding twelve seats at literally the last minute is not a problem. Paul directed an assistant to look after us and then said, "We always leave right after the show. Why don't you join us at our hotel afterward?"

"All of us?" I asked. "Aren't we too many?"

"Not at all." He took Linda's hand with one hand and retrieved his bass with the other. "Right, then. See you anon!"

Then he and Linda turned and walked through the doorway leading to the stage.

Twenty seconds later we heard a roar from the audience indicating that the house lights had just gone down. Our ticket broker (whose former band had made musical history) would make his entrance in less than two minutes.

I was convinced then, and still am convinced, that Paul emerged from his mother's womb performing. In addition to being musical *and* outgoing, he's a consummate professional. He knows what his audiences have come for, and he gives it to them. That night not only did he give his Japanese fans Paul McCartney, he gave them as close to the Beatles as Paul McCartney could get without George, Ringo, or John. Among the songs Paul performed that night were "Can't Buy Me Love," "The Long and Winding Road," "The Fool on the Hill," "Good Day Sunshine," and "Eleanor Rigby." He also performed some of his post-Beatles hits, including "Band on the Run," "Jet," and "Live and Let Die."

Paul ended his show with a long, energetic version of "Hey Jude," by the end of which everyone was chanting the "Nah nah" part. Following each chant, Paul executed yet another seemingly impossible set of vocal gymnastics around the words "yeah" and "Judeh." When at last "Hey Jude" ended, Paul and the band took a bow, then everyone left the stage. I joined the audience in applauding loudly, but I was disappointed that Paul hadn't performed "Yesterday." Oh well. I knew how it was. A performing artist with so many well-known songs to his credit couldn't possibly perform everything everyone wanted to hear in one show.

Silly me. I had been so caught up in how terrific the show was that I forgot the rhythm of a concert. Of course Paul came out for several encores, the first of which was an acoustic version of "Yesterday." The other two were "Get Back" and the three-part epic "Golden Slumbers/Carry That Weight/The End."

Now the show was over, and wasn't that a dandy way to spend a night off.

The Japanese had the unique ability to rock, roll, roar, get rowdy, and then file out of their seats in an orderly fashion, row by row. As we waited for our turn to exit, Joe, Lorna, Rudy, and I reminisced about the early days when Paul and Linda were first falling in love. We all knew that Linda, née Eastman, had been born into a wealthy family and had achieved success in the sixties as a photographer of sought-after rock performers. Linda had incurred the wrath of millions of the mostly female fans of the Beatles when she married one of the most sought-after rock performers. After the Beatles broke up, when Paul formed his band Wings and included Linda in his shows, she was widely panned by critics and excoriated for daring to play and sing with Paul and his other more experienced musicians. But that night at the Tokyo Dome, I couldn't help but be impressed by the improvement in Linda's musical skills. My respect for her had grown in other ways as well. I admired her for persevering in the face of relentless criticism, for her activism on behalf of animals, and most of all, for being a source of happiness for Paul. I hoped that I would have the opportunity to tell her that.

After the show my group and I made our way to the hotel where the McCartneys were staying. One of their assistants met Joe in the lobby and escorted all twelve of us up to the area where a lot of other people were waiting to see Paul and Linda. The McCartneys' entourage on the road included some of their children, teachers, the band, band family, the crew, some crew family, and a multiplicity of personnel essential to run the intricate machinery of a behemoth concert tour. I would have bet money that the traveling population on that tour exceeded that of many American towns.

The McCartneys' very specific culinary requirements had increased the size of their entourage by the number of people it took to shop for food and cook for the entire assemblage. I've never encountered a more impressive buffet on tour. Notwithstanding Linda's criteria that no food could be served that had ever had a face, the vegetarian menu was varied, organic, and delicious. I'm probably not the best judge of how it was for nonvegetarians because my own taste in food mostly coincided with Linda's, except that I sometimes ate fish. My band and crew were usually seen at mealtimes tearing into mounds of bacon and eggs or double helpings of fried chicken and mashed potatoes, but even they raved about the excellence of the vegetarian cuisine.

Considering the show he'd just put on, I couldn't believe how much energy Paul still had. Watching him and Linda move through the room I was struck by the way they seemed to move as one, much as they seemed to move through life. It was impossible to imagine Paul without Linda or Linda without Paul. Linda might not have been movie-star beautiful, but she had a natural beauty that emanated from her blue eyes and radiant smile. I could see how she might have impressed the rock stars who had allowed her to take their pictures.

When Paul and Linda reached my group they spent more than a polite amount of time with us. Up close, I could see that Linda had removed her show makeup. Her freckles and natural blush on a face framed by her straight blonde hair gave her an earthy, girl-next-door appearance. When Paul spoke, of course everyone's eyes were on him. When his attention was momentarily diverted, Linda kept the conversation going. When at last Paul was pulled away to greet other visitors, my group dispersed and I found myself standing with Linda, face to face, just the two of us. She began to talk about the challenges and joys of motherhood. I listened and commiserated. Then I told her how grateful I was to have spent so much time living in relative privacy with my Larkey children in a simple, natural environment. Linda said that she probably would enjoy something like that, but Paul's fans would never allow him to get that far away. Just then Paul called her name. She squeezed my hand and then went to join him, leaving me with a more personal appreciation of her devotion to Paul and their children. I thought, If Linda can inspire this kind of feeling in people, no wonder Paul is happy.

My friends and I were gathering to leave as a group when Paul and Linda walked over to where we were. That's when Paul showed yet another side of his talent for entertaining. He described a recent appearance on *Late Night with David Letterman* with a gift for mimicry that was startling in its accuracy. Playing the respective roles of David Letterman and Paul Shaffer, McCartney completely captured the essence of both men. When Paul McCartney quoted Paul Shaffer, he *became* Paul Shaffer. Replying as Letterman, his facial expressions and voice morphed into those of Letterman, right down to Dave's Hoosier accent.

Finally it was time to say goodbye. I hugged Paul, then, taking Linda's hands in both of mine, I told her how much I had enjoyed visiting with her, and how very much I had enjoyed her performance that night. When I specifically complimented her solid rhythm on the keyboard and her tight vocal blend with Paul and the others, Linda's eyes became moist. She thanked me and embraced me. Then she stepped back.

Eight years later, on April 17, 1998, Linda McCartney succumbed to breast cancer. She left a legacy of love, family, respect for all living things, and her remarkable photographs. She was fifty-six.

Chapter Four

A Quiet Place to Live

I was able to tour and travel in 1989 and 1990 in part because Charlie willingly absorbed the day-to-day responsibilities for our two teenagers, and in part because two young friends from New York and L.A. moved to Idaho to help take care of my ranch. Elissa Kline and Erik Gillberg signed on for a year and stayed for seventeen, leaving only when the son they had raised at the ranch through early childhood began asking if he could live closer than four miles away from his nearest friends. While they were still at the ranch, when I was on tour, I was comforted to hear about Erik's and Elissa's discovery of their individual creativity as they and Ian explored the inner worlds that so often make themselves known when one lives at nature's pace. They *get* it, I thought with mixed emotions, wishing I, too, could be there. I might have composed a song about how much I longed to be in a quiet place had I not already written one in 1973.

All I want is a quiet place to live
Where I can enjoy the fruits of my labor
Read the paper
And not have to cry out loud

In the years after I wrote "A Quiet Place to Live" I experienced times of peace and times of turmoil—which could describe anyone's life. But in 1990, the year I turned forty-eight, my life was anything but quiet.

After Rick's and my divorce became final in June 1990, I was eager to return home and again experience my ranch as a place of tranquility. But fate had something else in mind. First Disney asked me to film a video, paradoxically called *Carole King: Going Home*, that would include interviews and concert footage from the City Streets Tour.* Then in December I was cast as a teacher in an *ABC After-School Special* called "It's Only Rock and Roll," shot in Pine Bush, New York. There I became friends with John Gibbons, an actor who played one of my students. The math of me at forty-eight and him at twenty-seven added up to, at most, a brief encounter. That encounter lasted for six years during which we accumulated a wide range of adjectives that described our time together. "Quiet" was not one of them. Between John's exponentially increasing collection of cassettes and, later, CDs, his sporting equipment spilling out of every closet, and the multitude of his frequent and lively visitors, the continual wind from the opening and closing of doors made me feel as if I were rooming with a tornado.

John and I made frequent trips to L.A. On one such trip in the fall of 1991, I went to write with Brian Wilson at his studio. Brian had two pianos. I sat at one and he at the other. Listening to him noodle around with familiar chord clusters, I was reminded not only of how much Brian had contributed to popular music but also of how much I had personally enjoyed his work. Even when Brian had had problems functioning in what most of us think of as "the

---

Carole King: Going Home was subsequently released as a DVD.

real world," he had always been a pure, perfect channel for the music of the gods.

That Saturday we worked for a little over an hour on a riff in E-flat that Brian had come up with. We experimented with chords and harmonies around the recurring phrase, "Rock, rock, rockin' and a-rollin'," until our collective span of attention ran out. As I began to gather my things I had an impulse to tell Brian that I thought the tune we had started sounded like a quintessential Brian Wilson song. But before I could say a word, he remarked that he thought our little ditty sounded exactly like a Carole King song.

We agreed to meet the following afternoon to finish the song, but I never made it.

The next morning I went for a hike alone. I didn't realize that a trail leading down a steep cliff was a false trail until I lost my footing. I bumped and slid all the way down a sixty-foot cliff. The muscles of my left buttock took every bump with what felt like the force of a sledgehammer. After the first few bumps I lost count. Finally I landed on the beach below the cliff. My left foot hit first and took all the shock. My body crumpled onto the sand. Then I rolled onto my back. I had been fully conscious the whole way down, and as I lay there, panting, I was aware of my surroundings. I wiggled my toes, legs, arms, and fingers. Then I rolled my head from side to side. Every stimulus was followed by the response I was hoping for. Then, lying on my back with my left knee pointing skyward to form a triangle, I was just thinking how miraculous it was that I had survived the fall and avoided injuring my spine when a bolt of pain struck with what I imagined was the force of a meteor. It was the most excruciating pain I had ever known. On a scale of one to ten, I would have rated it at seventeen had I been able to speak. All I could do was moan. My awareness was reduced to a core of agonizing pain, at the periphery of which I sensed rather than saw people coming to help. A helicopter arrived to provide me with speedy transport to a hospital. It also brought EMTs who did their utmost to ease my pain and prevent further injury until they could get me to an emergency room. The medication they gave me brought the level of pain down to about fourteen, which allowed me to convey John's phone number to one of the bystanders before I was evacuated.

In the emergency room, a doctor examined me, gave me a prescription for stronger pain medication, and released me into the care of John, who had come to take me home. Though he drove as slowly and carefully as he could, I felt every seam in the road. Every time we drove over anything rougher than polished asphalt I emitted a gut-wrenching cry. On the way home he stopped to fill the prescription and gave me a pill that we both hoped would take effect before he carried me up the stairs to where we were staying. Once he got me upstairs he laid me gently on the couch and helped me with basic needs through the night, but the muscles in my buttock had been so badly bruised that I couldn't stop moaning. The next day John took me to a different hospital. At the first hospital's emergency room I had been in so much pain from my banged-up buttock that no one, including me, noticed any other injury. When an orthopedist at the second hospital heard that I had landed on my left foot, he immediately ordered an X-ray. My foot had been broken in three places. I remained in the hospital for eleven days. It took six months after that for my bruised buttock and broken bones to heal enough for me to walk without assistance, and another six months of intense physical therapy to achieve normal functionality.

During the third night of my hospital stay, as I lay in bed waiting impatiently for the next painkiller, tears of self-pity began streaming down my cheeks. Why *me*? I asked. The answer came, not in words, but in the realization that I had been given an opportunity to expand my compassion and knowledge of human nature.

I had experienced firsthand what it was like to live with mind-numbing physical pain so intense and so inescapable that drugs could relieve it only briefly, if at all. And in addition to the care and attention I received from John, I got to witness and simultaneously benefit from the competence and generosity of all the medical professionals I encountered, including physical therapists and practitioners of alternative medicine. The entire experience from injury to recovery convinced me that medical caregivers deserve a special wing in the Hotel Afterlife with extra helpings of caviar, champagne, and chocolate.

Five days into my stay I remembered my missed appointment with Brian Wilson. I felt terrible about having stood him up and called him as soon as I could. Brian was sympathetic and relieved.

"I was worried about you," he said. "I'm sorry you got hurt."

"Yeah," I said. "Me, too. I can't wait to finish what we were working on."

Brian said, "You work on getting better, and we'll write again soon."

"Soon" turned out to be fifteen years.*

---

*I recorded two songs with Brian Wilson in 2006: Gerry's and my song "I'm Into Something Good" and a composition of Brian's called "Good Kind of Love."

Chapter Five

The Troubles

$\mathcal{M}$y pain was nearly gone and my injuries mostly healed in the summer of 1992 when John came home even more excited than usual. He'd just been invited to go to Ireland to spend a week with four of his friends sightseeing and visiting some of their relatives. When he asked, "Would you like to come along?" I had my bags packed before he got to the question mark. In keeping with the budget of most of the group, we stayed either in bed-and-breakfasts or, strictly separated by gender, in the narrow twin beds of the boys' and girls' bedrooms of the modest homes of the relatives. There would be not the slightest opportunity for sexual congress between unmarried guests in our hosts' Irish Catholic households.

We spent a staggering amount of time in pubs.* The people we met were unfailingly friendly, humorous, and helpful. In Ireland, when you ask people for directions, they don't simply tell you how to get there. A man will get in his car and lead you there—never

---

*Some people drink. I make bad puns and leave them in warm paragraphs to ferment.

mind that it's thirty kilometers each way. If you ask a woman for directions, she'll be equally helpful. She'll send her brother, husband, or son.

One night John and I met a young woman from Belfast—I'll call her Dierdre—who was putting herself through law school by working as a waitress at a pub. When she invited us to join her for a visit to her family's home we were eager to go in spite of the danger, or, for some in our group, because of it.

The conflict known as "the Troubles" between Irish Catholics and Protestants in the six counties of Ulster had been going on since the seventeenth century. This made visiting Belfast a good deal more of an adventure for us than, say, a visit to Ennis in County Clare. The warring factions' respective names for the six counties sounded almost the same. Catholics considered the six counties in "the north of Ireland" part of the Irish Republic, while Protestants considered the counties a separate entity called "Northern Ireland." You did not want to use the wrong name with the wrong people.

As we drove north toward the disputed territory we had to pass through several checkpoints. At each checkpoint our rental car was thoroughly searched for bombs and other weapons. There were no exceptions; every vehicle was searched. After being cleared to enter Belfast, we found our way to Dierdre's house. There we were greeted warmly by a gathering of relatives that included our friend, her mother, her aunt, and, soon after we got there, her father and uncle arriving home from work. We were sitting in the parlor chatting with the family when Dierdre's twelve-year-old brother came in. Dierdre whispered to us that the lad was several hours late arriving home from school. During our conversation about matters ranging from the price of cotton fabric in America to the optimum amount of dill to put in a salad, you'd never have known how worried his mother had been. Now that he was home, she didn't berate him or ask questions. She simply told him to wash his hands, then she went into the kitchen with her sister to start serving dinner while Dierdre organized seating around the table.

Almost impossibly, there was enough room and food for all of us. Dierdre's father led us in saying grace. Then massive plates of stew, mashed potatoes, soda bread, and salad were passed around along with pitchers of lemonade and iced tea. It was only when everyone had a full plate and had begun to eat that the boy told us the reason for his delayed arrival. One of his mates had been killed in a fracas between Catholics and Protestants. When our lad had arrived at school, the authorities had asked him to accompany the adults delivering the news to his friend's family. Dierdre's brother gave us the details as matter-of-factly as an American twelve-year-old might have come home and reported to his family at dinner that one of his teammates had broken his ankle during football practice.

I found the boy's unemotional delivery more frightening than anything I'd seen in the newspaper or on TV. I found it difficult to wrap my mind around the fact that children were speaking about the killing of friends and relatives as if such killing were a matter of course. Even more horrifying, it *was* a matter of course.

At the end of our week in Ireland we flew home to America, leaving the children of Belfast in Belfast. But I couldn't leave behind the memory of mothers waking up every morning to see their husbands off to work and their children off to school knowing that there were more than even odds that someone known to each mother, maybe one of her own family, maybe even—Jesus, Mary, and Joseph forbid!—her own child, would be killed that day. How could they ever begin to fix such a problem?

Put the mothers in charge.

Chapter Six

Colour of Your Dreams

I was powerless to fix the Troubles, so I redirected my frustration into creating songs that I hoped would lift, educate, or entertain a listener. If I got it right, a song might do all three.

I wrote the songs for *Colour of Your Dreams* variously in California, Idaho, and New York and recorded them piecemeal in 1992 and 1993 with Rudy Guess at his studio in California. I released the album in 1993 in partnership with Hilton Rosenthal on a small independent label called Rhythm Safari. The 1994 Colour of Your Dreams Tour was memorialized in a video titled *Carole King—In Concert.** In addition to the members of my band, *In Concert* featured Slash of Guns N' Roses as my guest. My decision to pair musically with Slash was perplexing to many of my fans, but I was being true to my custom of expanding my repertoire to include musical styles with which I was relatively unfamiliar. I had been inspired to write "Hold Out for Love" by Slash's guitar work on "Sweet Child O' Mine." When Slash came to Rudy's studio to play on my song, the parts I had been imagining in my head came alive with his

---

Carole King—In Concert was subsequently released as a DVD.

passion, energy, and the skill of a good musician who knew exactly what I wanted. When Slash performed live with me on "Hold Out for Love" on the Colour of Your Dreams Tour, I got a tremendous kick out of watching audiences' skepticism turn to appreciation.

Why "Colour" with a "u?" For the same reason I still call a cell phone a "mobile" (rhymes with "no guile"). I had been in Ireland. When I travel I tend to pick up accents, customs, and spellings. The Irish spellings and names for certain things stayed with me long after I had returned to the United States. Another thing that stayed with me was the result of time I had spent with Irish film-makers, notably Neil Jordan and Jim Sheridan. After my return to America, I was moved by a number of films to write songs for *Colour of Your Dreams*. A decision by the leading male character at the end of *After Dark, My Sweet* prompted me to write "Lay Down My Life." The impassioned monologue delivered by Sean Penn as Terry Noonan in *State of Grace* led to "Just One Thing." And I wrote "Wishful Thinking" after watching *Let's Get Lost*, Bruce Weber's documentary about jazz trumpeter Chet Baker. Filmed in 16-millimeter black-and-white, Weber's stark documentary pulled no punches in showing Baker's tragic deterioration from a char-ismatic, talented young man in the 1950s to a wasted junkie in the 1980s. As painful as I found the film, it put me in the right mood to write a song about the desire for something unattainable. In addition to being a song about romantic yearning, "Wishful Thinking" embodied my wish that Chet Baker's personal history had not turned out as badly as it did.

I wrote and recorded "Now and Forever" at the request of Penny Marshall, who was directing a film called *A League of Their Own* about female baseball players in the 1940s. I had expected the biggest hurdle to be delivering something Penny liked. When I heard that she was going to use my song over the end-title credits, I was elated. And then I got the Call.

I picked up the phone with a cheery "Hello?" and heard a voice say, "Caaarole?"

I didn't need caller ID (not yet in common use) to tell me who it was. If I'd had any doubt, I would have known for sure when I heard Penny say, "We have a prahhhblem."

With Madonna starring in the movie, the problem was that Madonna's contract required Penny to use one of her songs over the end-title credits. With Solomon-like wisdom, Penny put Madonna's song over the end titles and shot a new sequence for the beginning of the film over which she used "Now and Forever."

I took so much pleasure from learning to play, on guitar, a song from R.E.M.'s *Out of Time* album called "Losing My Religion" that I was moved to write, on guitar, the song "Colour of Your Dreams." As at Burgdorf, composing on guitar helped me write more simply because I was limited to the chords I could play on that instrument. I was thrilled to have Rudy's expertise to put across ideas I had imagined but couldn't play. Knowing his abilities, I often wrote with what Rudy might play in mind. One of my favorite things to do when we were recording was to "play Rudy." With the tape rolling, I communicated through body language where I wanted Rudy's solo to go next. He never failed to understand and deliver the music I was hoping to hear, which he took to the next level by adding improvisations of his own.

And in "Friday's Tie-Die Nightmare," with phrasing reminiscent of that of Bob Dylan, I described a dream I'd had about the New York City subway.

It was not my first song about the subway.

Chapter Seven

Lessons from Underground

*M*y relationship with the subway began before I was born. My pregnant mother rode it frequently because she had already learned Subway Lesson 1: when the subway runs smoothly, as it does most of the time, it's the most efficient and affordable method of getting around New York City.

A destination on the same side of Manhattan is a straight shot on a local, with the possibility of catching an express along the way. One of my earliest experiences of Murphy's Law occurred at a station where I had to decide whether to wait for an express or take the local that had just pulled in. A local makes more than twice as many stops as an express. If I got on a local, inevitably the express roared by while the local was slowing down for one of the stops the express didn't have to make. If I got off the local at the next stop and waited for an express, three locals would come and go before the next express showed up. By guessing wrong and arriving late time and time again I learned Subway Lesson 2: the only way to catch an express is to leave early enough to make the entire trip on a local.

After I achieved public recognition, friends and family members counseled me to stop taking the subway. But I didn't take their advice because I, too, had mastered Subway Lesson 1. Anyway, people on the subway rarely recognize me, and when they do, they either know I don't want to be bothered, or they think, That's not her. She wouldn't be takin' the subway. With few exceptions, New Yorkers tend to be matter-of-fact about celebrities. One day I was part of a crowd rushing from the 1 train at Times Square to catch a crosstown shuttle when a well-dressed man in his forties strode up alongside me. Without missing a step, he said, "Carole King! What are *you* doin' takin' the subway?"

Keeping up my own stride, I answered, "Same thing you are. Tryin' to get from point A to point B!"

I was one of the last to squeeze into the shuttle before the doors closed. The well-dressed man didn't make it, but as the train pulled out, its metal wheels screeching around that first long curve, I saw him smiling. I'd like to think it was because he appreciated my answer, but it was probably because he had just seen another shuttle pulling in.

The subway is most useful during rush hour, when it's especially difficult to get a taxi. Change of shift for most taxi drivers is at 4 p.m. I know this because of all the years I spent trying without success to get a taxi to pick me up between 4:00 and 5:00 in the afternoon. On the rare occasion when a driver stops and admits you—which he will do at that hour only if your destination is directly on the way to his company's garage—it's a mixed blessing. It's rush hour. Delay is inevitable. Surface streets are filling up with commuters' cars headed toward bridges and tunnels. You have eight minutes to get to your daughter's dance recital downtown, and where are you? Sitting in traffic at a dead stop, watching the meter tick up waiting time while trains are racing unobstructed below you. Five minutes later, seeing that traffic hasn't moved, you think, This is ridiculous! I'll get there faster if I walk. You pay the driver and exit the taxi only to find that it's starting to rain.

When the weather is bad, it's remarkable how similar taxis are to birds in a flock who change direction all at once. When the "Off Duty" light of every taxi in Manhattan goes on simultaneously with the first drop of precipitation, you'd best have either an umbrella or a MetroCard.

The subway is a fascinating place to people-watch. I spent many hours in the fifties and sixties on what was then called the BMT.* During the forty-five-minute ride between Sheepshead Bay and Times Square I often passed the time making up stories about the people around me. In the late fifties most of my narratives went as far as my imagination would allow. This woman with the red-rimmed eyes has just come from losing an argument with her husband. That man with the tortoiseshell glasses hates his job. The gaunt woman in the brown coat is on her way to yet another doctor to see if this one can cure what all the other doctors have told her is an incurable illness. The man grading papers is a teacher. (Duh!) The man sitting in front of me is an inconsiderate boor. Why? (And here's where imagination stops and reality kicks in.) Because I'm on my way to the city, I'm visibly pregnant, and I'm hanging precariously on to the strap above him while he, an apparently healthy adult male, is studiously reading the same page of the *New York Times* over and over. I can almost hear him thinking, If I make eye contact with her, I'll have to give her my seat, so I'm not gonna look at her.

And he didn't look at me. Not once.

There must have been a coffee factory under the Manhattan Bridge. I never found out where it was or if it even existed, but I will forever associate the aroma of roasting coffee with the V and

---

*There were three subway lines when I was growing up: BMT, for Brooklyn-Manhattan Transit; IRT, for Interborough Rapid Transit; and IND, short for the Independent Subway.

M shapes of the painted brown steel braces framed against the sky as they did the important work of holding the Manhattan Bridge together. The journey across the bridge gave Manhattan-bound commuters ten minutes of daylight before the train descended into a tunnel beneath the cobblestone streets of the city.

Observing my fellow riders, I began to see a pattern. Some days everyone looked good to me. The fellow with the early-morning grumpy face whose ratty trench coat needed cleaning might have been handsome under other circumstances. I saw beauty in the countenance of a college student who was frantically trying to clamp a bunch of papers back into her aptly named loose-leaf notebook before we arrived at her stop. And in the full-moon face of a heavyset woman with several chins whose burgundy-colored pumps appeared too small to contain her feet, let alone her entire weight, I caught a glimpse of the slim, attractive girl she had once been.

Other days everyone looked ugly. I viewed the group of teenage kids playfully shoving each other as a bunch of juvenile delinquents planning to rob the woman standing next to me, or worse, *me.* I was annoyed by the tall woman with flaming red hair and mismatched rouge who was stinking up the entire car with a corned beef sandwich that she was eating on the fly. At the time I didn't think about the possibility that she might have had to skip breakfast so she could get to the electric company in time to pay the bill. And the word "ugly" categorically defined the slightly balding middle-aged man pressed up too close against me with his coincidentally roving hands. ("I was just trying to keep her from falling," he might have said, had he been asked.) At first I felt violated. Then I became defiant. I was *not* going to be a victim. I jammed one of my spike heels hard into his ankle. The man gave a muffled yelp and quickly took his hands off me.

I'm not sure exactly when I figured out that the way I perceived others on a given day was a reflection of how I was feeling. I do know that rather than revealing itself in something like an Aha! moment, the realization was subtle. It came to me gradually, like... Ohhhh...right.

That realization was Subway Lesson 3, which turned out to be the basis for my first subway song, "Beautiful." And rather than it being a conscious thought about which I intentionally sat down to write, it emerged on its own. And because "Beautiful" is one of those songs that came through me, I was unaware of a professional detail about the song until a fellow songwriter pointed it out: there are no rhymes in the chorus—unless you count stretching "will" into "weel" as a false rhyme for "feel."

> *You've got to get up every morning with a smile on your face*
> *And show the world all the love in your heart*
> *Then people gonna treat you better*
> *You're gonna find, yes, you will*
> *That you're beautiful as you feel*

As a songwriter, of course I would have put rhymes in the chorus. As an instrument, I never noticed.

It's been years since I rode a BMT train, and subway tokens have gone the way of the passenger pigeon, but I still believe Subway Lesson 3 to be as true as it was the day I learned it. I still believe that everyone is beautiful in some way, and by seeing the beauty in others we make ourselves more beautiful.

Chapter Eight

Blood Brothers

I had the chance to reacquaint myself with the subway in 1994 from April through December when I starred in a Broadway musical written by Willy Russell. *Blood Brothers* had been playing to standing-room-only crowds both on London's West End and New York's Broadway. Producer Bill Kenwright was preparing to put an additional production on the road starring the leading lady then on Broadway, Petula Clark. He had already established a model of success with interchangeable female pop stars with an alto vocal range in the lead role. Knowing that I possessed an alto range and acting experience, he wanted me to replace Petula on Broadway. No audition would be necessary. All I had to do was agree to a six-month commitment to perform eight shows a week and the role was mine.

I was fifty-two when I began my run as Mrs. Johnstone (pronounced Johnston). Being onstage for most of the show eight times a week left me with no time or energy for my own music. After every evening performance I collapsed into the back seat of a town car and was thankful to have such a luxury. I found moments of normalcy in folding laundry, going to my favorite restaurant for lunch, taking the subway around town, and, weather permitting, walking, unrecognized, around my city of birth. It was on one of those walks that I came upon the familiar faded reddish brown stone building in which I had studied drama, dance, and music at the High School of Performing Arts. I couldn't go in because it was after hours, but from visible signs and posters I inferred that it was still a school, only now it had a business curriculum. When I peered in through the barred windows the old staircase looked exactly the same. I could almost hear and see my fourteen-year-old classmates hurrying to the next period propelled by a dream that drove them to the exclusion of almost everything else. I touched the cornerstone and silently conveyed the news that, after thirty-eight years, I was starring in a Broadway show.

Offstage, when I wasn't walking or taking the subway, I spent most of my time eating, sleeping, or exercising. I needed to keep up my strength for what I considered a demanding role on a grueling schedule until I saw Glenn Close in *Sunset Boulevard*. Once I got to know my fellow cast members I realized that for them an eight-show-a-week schedule with the concentrated energy required for every show was not only normal but desirable. Playing Mrs. Johnstone was a lot more challenging emotionally than physically. In my own life I try to keep pain at bay, often to the point of denying its existence. Yet in order to be credible as a woman who suffered as Mrs. Johnstone did, I needed to draw on my own suffering. Every performance ended with my character in despair because her adult twin sons had just been shot to death. Mrs. Johnstone blames herself. When the boys were infants and she was a single mother of seven living in extreme poverty, a childless woman of means persuaded her to give her one of the babies by preying on her superstitious nature and fear that if she didn't give the baby up she would lose all seven of her children. As the run progressed I found it increasingly difficult to step away from my character's anguish. There couldn't have been a worse time for me to be going through menopause. On the drive uptown one night, after a particularly harrowing immersion in Mrs. Johnstone's misery, I watched the quarter moon set over New Jersey and wondered why I had allowed myself to be drawn back into acting when I'd already had a perfectly good career in music. But I had taken on the role, and I would not only see it through but extend my commitment through December 31, 1994.

In the rare quiet moments during my final performance that New Year's Eve, I could hear the roar growing louder outside the theater as people converged on Times Square for the traditional dropping of the ball. The emotions of my character merged with my own. I was simultaneously elated to be playing Mrs. Johnstone for the last time and sad that she and I and the cast and crew were parting company. It was 11:45 when I took my final solo curtain call with the tears of both my character and me streaming down my face.

Fifteen minutes later I was drinking champagne in a cast member's apartment near the theater with John, the cast of *Blood Brothers*, and their significant others. I heard the crowd counting down, loud and live, on the street below while I watched the ball drop on television. And then it was 1995.

Chapter Nine

Ireland, Again

$\mathscr{I}$ spent most of January 1995 on an island in the Caribbean with John. I was thankful that my list of activities—sunning, snorkeling, swimming, sailing, and sleeping—did not include suffering. Renewed and refreshed, I went back to the mainland with absolutely nothing on my schedule. When John asked if I wanted to go back to Ireland for a few months while he explored prospects for work in the Irish film industry, I was all for it, and not only for his benefit. Ireland had some terrific songwriters, and I was more than ready to go back to music.

We flew to Dublin, rented a house on Heytesbury Lane, and drove north to visit Dierdre and her family in Belfast. We were delighted to find them in much happier circumstances. The IRA and Ulster Protestants had laid down their arms the previous year. There was no longer a need for barricades, vehicle inspections, or armed soldiers patrolling the streets. I dressed warmly against the February chill and strolled openly with John and Dierdre among the residents and tourists in the shops on Donegall Place and Royal Avenue. If I found the effects of the truce uplifting, it must have been a remarkably liberating experience for the residents of Belfast to walk around their city without fear.

The truce and the economic expansion of the mid-nineties had brought positive changes to Dublin as well. In 1992, while walking at night in Temple Bar (a neighborhood along the River Liffey), I had seen a disproportionate number of men and women in various stages of intoxication sprawled on the streets outside the Temple Bar (a pub named after the neighborhood—or was it the other way around?). My inference was based on the nearby array of empty discarded plastic cups, each of which had likely contained a pint of draft Guinness, Harp, or Smithwick's (pronounced Smiddicks).

In 1995, the neighborhood was a lot cleaner. Customers still became intoxicated, but most did so indoors. Dubliners' optimism was reflected in the new office buildings and elegant residences either under construction or already completed. In contrast to 1992, Ireland in 1995 seemed a place of peace, growth, and opportunity.

The Irish songwriter Paul Brady and I wrote frequently at his home in Dublin. Though I wouldn't write with Elvis Costello until a few years later, we spent some enjoyable time together. Paul McGuinness, U2's manager, arranged for me to meet Bono, The Edge, Adam, and Larry, and then he set up time for me to write with The Edge and Bono at Hanover Quay, U2's state-of-the-art studio on the Liffey. When the day came, I was so engrossed in trying to figure out how to integrate my style of songwriting with that of these two men with their unique approach to writing, singing, and playing that I remember little about the session. What I do remember is how fearless Bono was in improvising ideas. I had experienced times of being an instrument, but Bono seemed to be one all the time. Music and lyrics poured out of him, for better or worse, with a preponderance of the former. Unfortunately, our song then in progress lies buried beneath my conscious memory. If a tape of our writing session is ever disinterred from U2's studio archives, I would love to hear it.

As a visiting American celebrity I was invited on several occasions to the Phoenix Park residence of my country's then ambassador to Ireland, Jean Kennedy Smith. There John and I mingled with Irish and American luminaries, including Neil Jordan and Jim Sheridan; Jim's brother, the writer and theater director Peter Sheridan, and his wife, Sheila; and actors Sean Penn, Gabriel Byrne, and Lauren Bacall. After dinner the ambassador led us to the salon, where anyone who wished could get up and perform what the Irish call a "party piece." If you guessed that my party piece was "You've Got a Friend," you win the chance to read on.

The morning of March 31, 1995, I received a call from Lorna asking if I wanted to go to London to write with Bob Dylan. I caught the next flight out of Dublin and proceeded to Bob's hotel. Though Bob and I had met previously, this was the first time we had come together with the specific intention of writing a song. In between Bob's random improvisations on guitar and the few chords I essayed on a keyboard in his elegant suite, we spoke about mutual friends, the state of the world, our respective children, and Gerry Goffin, with whom Bob had written several songs. After a couple of hours of more talking than writing, we concluded that no song was likely to emerge that day. I didn't mind. I had thoroughly enjoyed my visit with this intelligent man who'd made musical and political history in a decade in which the answer was blowin' in the wind.

Though we never discussed our common status as celebrities, I came away with the feeling that Bob wasn't comfortable with the fame that followed him everywhere. He had learned to wear it as if it were a coat that hadn't been a good fit in the first place—old, familiar, but never quite right. Exception: when Bob was writing or playing, he didn't seem to notice or need the coat. His music fit him perfectly.

When I stood up and started to walk over to the door to collect my purse and my actual coat, Bob stood up, walked with me, and asked if I'd like to join him onstage that night at Brixton Academy. As if I needed extra persuasion, he said, "Elvis and Chrissie are gonna do it."

"Sure," I said, trying to be matter-of-fact even though I could barely contain my excitement about playing simultaneously with Bob Dylan, Elvis Costello, and Chrissie Hynde. I started to put my coat on but had trouble finding my second sleeve. I busied myself with that while trying to regain my composure and then found both simultaneously. I said, "See you then!" stepped into the hallway, and made my way to the lift.

Bob's set that night included "Rainy Day Women #12 & 35" and "I Shall Be Released." Chrissie Hynde, Elvis Costello, and I sang backup on both songs.

Bob must have had as much fun as we did, because he invited us to sit in with him again for the final performance of his tour at the Point in Dublin on April 11. Chrissie couldn't make it, but Elvis would be there.

Wait, I thought. Let me check my imaginary schedule. Between sitting in with Bob Dylan and Elvis Costello or attending a state dinner with Prime Minister John Major, President Bill Clinton, Queen Elizabeth, and Princess Diana to participate in a conversation in which peace in the former Yugoslavia would be discussed, which would I choose?

I would be offered that choice only in my dreams. Of course I would sit in with Bob in Dublin.

Chapter Ten

They Say That Ev'ry Man Must Fall

*T*he difference between an event and reports of that event reminds me of the game Telephone, in which someone whispers a sentence into another person's ear, who then whispers it into the next person's ear, and on down the line. By the time it gets to the tenth person, "Joey's going to visit his father" has become "Alice was arrested for farming Jonah's goat." Some of the early news reports after Bob's April 11 concert were so far from the truth that they could only have been written by reporters playing Telephone.

Here's what happened.

In Bob's Dublin concert I played piano on "Highway 61 Revisited," "In the Garden," and "Ballad of a Thin Man." I played and sang on "Like a Rolling Stone," "Real Real Gone," and "Rainy Day Women #12 & 35." Then I joined Elvis Costello and Van Morrison in singing backup on "I Shall Be Released."

As usual with Bob, there were multiple encores, each of which elicited wildly enthusiastic chants of "More! More! More! More!" When the show was over I lined up at the front of the stage with Bob and his band and Van and Elvis to take our final band bow.

When the applause and chanting didn't abate, the stage manager signaled for the house lights to be turned on. The band members nearest stage left turned and walked down the stairway on our left. Bob, Van, Elvis, and the band members at center stage turned, walked upstage, and exited down a stairway behind the drums. The primary responsibility of Bob's road crew was to look after Bob, and he was appropriately well attended. Others on the crew were using their flashlights to guide the other artists and band members offstage. The crew must have assumed that I, the only performer in proximity to stage right, was in good hands.

Unfortunately, the only hands around were mine. With John gone to escort Ambassador Smith and her party backstage, and with all the artists, band members, and other responsibilities that Bob's crew had to look after, I literally slipped through the cracks. The stage right black curtain had seemed a logical point of exit for me. I thought it would lead to a stairway on my side of the stage. But when I stepped through the curtain there was nothing under my feet. I felt something strike my head as I fell off the edge of the platform, and then I blacked out. When I came to, I barely had time to notice that I was lying on a pile of black rubber cables before my head began to hurt. I touched the spot where it hurt and felt warm liquid oozing out of my head. I must have been in a mild state of delirium because I began repeating a mantra to reassure myself:

"It's oozing. I must be okay. It's not spurting. That wouldn't be good. It's oozing. Oozing is okay. I'm okay."

Such was my habit: denial of personal pain.

Suddenly people began to converge. Some were wearing armbands with red crosses. They told me I had fallen fifteen feet to the arena floor. My landing had been cushioned by the piles of thick rubber electrical cables on the concrete. EMTs examined my head, stanched the bleeding, then loaded me carefully into an ambulance that would take me to the emergency room at Mater Misericordiae Hospital in North Dublin. When I arrived, the ER staff was occupied with several patients with injuries more serious than mine. Even so, they got to me fairly quickly. After examining my head, one of the doctors determined that my head injury was superficial. While he was treating the wound, he asked a question that earned him an A-plus on my "Diagnosing Patients" test.

"Are you feeling pain anywhere else?"

I was. It turned out that my head wound was the least of my injuries. My right wrist was broken, and I had fractured my left thumb. I would not be playing piano for a while. After X-raying my wrist and thumb, the medical attendants built a cast for my arm and put a splint on my thumb. Everything they needed was right there in the emergency room. Thankfully "everything" included an analgesic to relieve my pain.

Having heard me speak, the staff in the emergency room must have known that I wasn't an Irish citizen. But if they knew that I had been injured in the line of performing with Bob Dylan, they gave no indication. As far as I could tell, they treated all their patients with the same combination of compassion, competence, personal attention, and quality of care. It being Ireland, liberal doses of humor were dispensed along with the health care.

When at last the medical staff informed me that they had done all they could for the time being, I sent John out to ask the head nurse when I could leave the hospital. While I was waiting for an answer someone brought a telephone over to me with a very long cord. It was Bob on the line. He, Van, and Elvis had been whisked out of the venue immediately after the show and hadn't learned about my fall until they were on their way to the after-party. Bob's tour manager had been trying to find out how I was doing, but no one would tell him. The news of my fall had cast a pall over the party. Everyone was imagining the worst. Bob said the crew in particular felt awful. To a man, every crew member blamed himself for not having thought to cover stage right.

Not wanting to ruin Bob's party, I tried to put the best face on the situation.

"I'm doing well, Bob. The doctors are taking good care of me. Everything's under control."

"Are you gonna be okay?"

I assured him that I was. I had suffered no permanent damage, and I wanted him and everyone else to have a good time at the party.

"You know," I said brightly, "you gave a really good performance at the Point tonight. You have every reason to celebrate."

"Are you sure you're okay? Are they givin' you everything you need?"

"They are. Please don't be anxious. I'm fine."

Bob wasn't buying my attempt at a good face. We had come from the same culture in which Jewish mothers famously say, "I'm fine. I'll just sit here in the dark."

Finally, having exhausted all the ways he could tell me how sorry he was, Bob wished me a speedy recovery and put Van on.

Van didn't have a lot to say that night—not that I minded. His words and music over the years have expressed thoughts and emotions familiar to me and pretty much everyone else on the planet. He expressed his sympathy and well-wishes in a few words and then handed the telephone over to Elvis. In contrast to Van, Elvis uses a profusion of words to express whatever he's thinking at the moment, a quality appreciated by fans and friends alike. Elvis's many words that night were as welcome as Van's few.

As I handed the phone back to the attendant, John came in with the verdict from the head nurse. I would be released that night only in Bob's song. The doctors wanted to keep me overnight to make sure I didn't have a concussion. This gave reporters eight more hours to play the Telephone game. The next morning John told me he had received calls from friends and family in the United States who had heard either that Bob had pushed me or that he had hugged me too enthusiastically. The only fact that all the reports had gotten right was that I had fallen off the stage. John had also heard that there had been a flurry of phone calls among Bob's managers, the business people at the Point, and an assortment of lawyers to discuss their concern that I might file a lawsuit, but I would never have done that. Still, the people at the Point and Bob's team went out of their way to make sure I had everything I needed and appropriately offered to reimburse me for medical expenses.

As it turned out, reimbursement wasn't an issue. Ireland had national health care. Every Irish citizen was covered. No one had to forgo seeing a doctor because she or he couldn't afford it. At the Point, in the ambulance, in the emergency room at Mater, and during my overnight stay, I received excellent and efficient care that continued through several follow-up visits, checkups, multiple X-rays, a change of cast, the use of modern equipment, and ongoing medications. When on occasion I had to wait, it was never for more than twenty minutes. I suffered minimally, recovered completely, and for all that I paid a total of twelve Irish pounds—at the time approximately twenty-four dollars. And *I* wasn't even an Irish citizen.

Chapter Eleven

Ireland, Yet Again

After returning to America in 1995, I went back to Ireland in the summer of 1996. Peter Sheridan was directing a production of Neil Simon's *Brighton Beach Memoirs* and wanted me to play the role of Kate. We would open at the Andrews Lane Theatre in Dublin, move to the Theatre Royal in Waterford, then take the show around Ireland. Peter never doubted that the universal humor and familiarity of the interactions among Simon's Jewish characters would resonate with Irish audiences. During rehearsals, when Peter wanted to help me find an emotion, he'd relate an anecdote from among the many he'd accumulated growing up in a large Irish Catholic family in North Dublin. Invariably the story he chose evoked the desired emotion, though I had yet to find exactly where Kate was in me.

As the only Jewish American cast member I became the default dialect coach for the Irish and British actors. My biggest challenge was young Alan King, who eventually overcame his thick North Dublin accent to become entirely convincing as Kate's son Stanley. I consulted my father, then eighty, over the phone about such details as what type of head covering my character should wear while lighting the Sabbath candles. He recommended I go to the Jewish quarter in Dublin. And could he remind me of the melody of the Chanukah prayer? He could and did. At the end of every performance, when my character lit the Chanukah candles, it was I, Carole, who sang the prayer my father had taught me with the tune that he had learned when he was a little boy:

"Baruch atah Adonai, eloheinu melech ha'olam, asher kidishanu b'mitz'votav v'tsivanu l'hadlik neir shel Chanukah. Ah-mein."

In the late twentieth century the melodies of many traditional Jewish prayers were being modernized. I was not a fan of the major-key version of the Chanukah prayer. In 2011, at the suggestion of my daughter Louise, who produced my album *A Holiday Carole*, I recorded the traditional Chanukah prayer with its traditional melody. Louise arranged the prayer into a song form, then she and her son sang it with me. The last vocal we hear on that track is then eight-year-old Hayden singing, *"L'hadlik neir shel Chanukah . . ."* Tears come to my eyes every time I hear the prayer of our ancestors marching forward to future generations through my grandson, my daughter, and me.

Neil Simon's character Kate was around forty. I was then fifty-four, but women of Kate's generation often looked older than their years. In fact, Kate's life experience was not unlike that of my Grandma Sarah. The problem was that I had no personal knowledge of my grandmother at Kate's age as anything but "Grandma." Though Peter's stories had been helpful, I still hadn't found Kate in me. My mother came to the rescue. She traveled to Dublin to celebrate her eightieth birthday with me and coach me in the role. Her gift for directing actors, familiarity with the character, and understanding of how to convey her knowledge to me gave me enough confidence to feel on opening night that I had command of the role. With audience reinforcement, my confidence continued to grow until the night I found myself channeling my grandmother. I had experienced something similar with Mrs. Johnstone, except this character was someone whose genes I carried. When I spoke Kate's lines that night I was deeply affected by my grandmother's frustration. Thankfully, Peter helped me make the distinction between myself as an actor and the emotions of my character. The run lasted nearly three months—long enough for me to explore different facets of Kate, but not so long that I grew weary of playing her.

When the show was over I went to a castle in France to write with other songwriters at a semiannual gathering hosted by Miles Copeland. Miles was known for managing the Police and creating music industry companies with three letters and three periods. The best known was I.R.S. During my week at the castle I again connected with music and established friendships with songwriters that continue to this day. After my return to the United States in the fall of 1996, the rest of that year was not a happy time. John and I saw the end of our relationship approaching, and by the beginning of 1997 it was time. Though an ending had been understood from the beginning, I took it hard. I was stuck in pain, grief, loss, and depression for nearly eight months. It was one of the rare periods in my life when I was too miserable to eat—a diet I do not recommend. I was just beginning to rediscover my happier self and appreciate my status as a free, independent, unattached woman when I met Phil Alden Robinson in October 1997. I was already familiar with his work as the screenwriter of *All of Me* and the screenwriter and director of *Field of Dreams*. I became romantically involved with this kind, intelligent, and gifted man and remained with him for seven years until we realized that his ties to Los Angeles and mine to Idaho made us geographically incompatible.

In 1998, with encouragement from my friend Carole Bayer Sager, I coproduced an album called *Love Makes the World* with

Humberto Gatica, whose collection of Grammys for producing and engineering would require several mantels. Humberto is known for his work with artists whose superior sound is as instantly recognizable as their first names: Céline, Barbra, Bette, Chaka, Mariah, Cher, three Michaels, and three Kennys.[*] Then there are the Latinos: Gloria, Julio, Marc, Ricky, Olga, and two Alejandros.[†]

I lost my father on November 10, 1998. He was eighty-two.

Yizkor elohim et nishmat avi mori . . .

May God remember the soul of my father, my teacher.

---

[*]Michael Bublé, Michael Jackson, Michael McDonald; Kenny Rogers, Kenny Loggins, and Kenny G.

[†]Alejandro Sanz and Alejandro Lerner.

Chapter Twelve

The Towers

After recording all the songs for *Love Makes the World*, Humberto did a final mix on all the tracks, then we worked on a sequence and created a digital master. I had written the title song with Sam Hollander and Dave Schommer, then collectively known as PopRox. I loved the song then, and I still enjoy performing it. The lyric is a positive message with a snippet of attitude and a hint of a love story. The melody has a sexy groove, a syncopated rhythm, and more than a hint of an urban arrangement. "Love Makes the World" is the first track on the CD, followed by the equally positive "You Can Do Anything," written by Carole Bayer Sager, Kenny Edmonds (Babyface), and me.

Lorna helped me form a new label, which I named with an anagram of Carole King: Rockingale Records. Our scheduled release date for both the album and the single was September 11, 2001.

I was in an apartment building more than a hundred blocks north of the World Trade Center when I turned on the TV that morning. When NY1, New York's news channel, came on, I noted the time in the little square on the screen with the time and temperature. It said 9:02. With my mind on other things, I barely registered the import of what the anchor was saying—something about a plane having crashed into a building. I assumed they meant something like a Cessna until they showed the silhouette of the twin towers with smoke coming out of one of the towers. The question "How could a small plane have caused all that smoke?" was just beginning to form in my mind when the digital clock on the nightstand changed to 9:03. I watched in disbelief as the second plane hit and a fireball appeared on the screen. By 9:04 smoke was billowing from both buildings and flames were spreading rapidly.

Clicking to other channels, I saw similar live shots of the Trade Center interspersed with images of journalists trying to understand and explain what was happening. Personal emotions were overcoming the reporters' usual composure as each correspondent endeavored to interpret the events unfolding in real time. Through a south-facing window I could see smoke blackening a corner of the crystal blue sky. At 9:59, when the South Tower collapsed, my first thought was that someone had placed a bomb in the building with a timer set to go off an hour after the plane hit. The images on the TV showed that people were running now, with papers that had been important the day before wafting down all around them. The morning blue sky of daylight downtown was rapidly giving way to the darkness of ash turning everything black. I don't remember if I saw images of people jumping out of the buildings that day, but it was as if I were watching the most horrific disaster movie ever made, except that it was happening to real people. At 10:28, the North Tower collapsed. It was almost as if a movie producer had said, "Make it even more horrific!" When I heard that a third plane had hit the Pentagon, I thought, Holy shit! They're going to destroy every symbolic building in America. Then, when a fourth plane crashed in Pennsylvania, I was convinced that humanity was doomed. I didn't think it was God visiting his or her wrath on humankind, nor did I think it an act of nature. Those acts of destruction were too closely timed. They had to have been planned by human beings trying to wreak as much havoc and create as much fear as possible. My imagination ran wild as I envisioned potential targets all around the United States being blown up in one terrifying act of destruction after another. But there would be no more planes that day.

Remarkably, my landline was still working. Molly, now living in Brooklyn, would have been on her way to work near Grand Central Station when the planes hit. She would normally have taken a different subway line than the one that passed under the Trade Center, but I became anxious when I couldn't reach her. I left a message on her mobile and work voicemails and didn't stop worrying until she called me back. Though Molly was an exceptionally competent young woman who had heard the news and knew exactly what to do, I couldn't stop myself from shifting into Jewish-mother command voice.

"Molly. Walk north and keep walking till you get here!"

"Mom. I know."

All transportation in the city had been suspended. My daughter became part of a massive movement of people traveling north on foot. It took her half an hour to get to my apartment. We joined neighbors in lining up at a nearby hospital to donate blood that, sadly, would never be needed by the victims. The next morning Molly went home to Brooklyn and I began making calls to see how I could help.

It seemed that everyone in New York who wasn't looking for a loved one or working at an essential job was either already helping in the rescue effort or trying to find a way to help. But New Yorkers had organized themselves so efficiently to get food, water, and clean clothing to rescue workers that we were told additional assistance would put well-meaning people in the way. In between calls, the phone rang. It was my friend Carolyn Maloney, U.S. congress-woman from New York's 14th District, calling to ask if I would accompany her on rounds while she answered questions and tried to bring comfort to families with a missing loved one. There was little that Carolyn or I or anyone else could do, but family members wanted someone in authority to hear their story, tell them what was being done to find their family member, and join them in praying that their loved one had somehow escaped and wasn't calling home only because she or he was wandering around the city in a temporary state of amnesia.

Seeing the attacks and the aftereffects of those acts that had been carried out by what we later learned were nineteen human beings with the deliberate intention of hurting as many Americans as possible and disrupting the economic and social fabric of the Western world, it was difficult for me to keep from sinking into despair. I redirected that feeling by resolving to drive myself harder to be a good person and hold on to my belief that love makes the world . . . what? Go around? A better place? Or, perhaps, simply tolerable.

Some people reacted to the attacks with fear and anger. Others responded with an unprecedented outpouring of love. I saw the latter response on the streets of New York in the days after September 11. I saw it in the selflessness of the first responders and the tireless efforts of the rescue workers. I saw it in the generosity and support of people from every walk of life, from every corner of America, and from countries around the world. And I heard the same heartfelt message of solidarity repeated over and over again by people with dissimilar political views:

"Today we are all New Yorkers."

Unfortunately the camaraderie didn't last. People with opposing political views moved apart to stand on opposite sides of a seemingly impassable divide. Fear and anger began to grow along with a sense of hopelessness among those of us who didn't want to live under that kind of emotional siege. Subsequent efforts to obtain funding for medical services for the first responders and rescue workers who had been digging through the pile in the weeks and months after the attack were met with an appalling level of resistance by enough senators and members of Congress to keep them from getting necessary care for their damaged lungs. Solidarity had given way to, "Yes, I know, we were all New Yorkers, but that was yesterday. Today we have a different agenda."

With so many things out of my control, one thought brought comfort: when in doubt, give back.

Chapter Thirteen

Giving Back

*M*y forebears passed on to me a love of learning and a sense of responsibility to leave the world better than I found it. I'm a grateful beneficiary of my mother's intellectual curiosity and my father's compulsion to solve every problem he encountered. But the call to help others is passed on in many cultures. Consider the volunteers who went to New Orleans following Hurricane Katrina in 2005 to help their fellow human beings and rescue animals. In 2006 ordinary citizens from every conceivable background donated more money online than they could probably afford in order to assist with tsunami relief. The earthquake in Haiti in 2010 brought out the best in people from diverse cultures around the world, as did Japan's triple-whammy earthquake, tsunami, and nuclear crisis in 2011. But human generosity doesn't require earth-shaking events. Good people help their neighbors in communities every day. Whether through military service, political activism, volunteering at a school, hospital, or library, or simply through quotidian acts of kindness, each of us has something to contribute to improve another person's life. I'm grateful to live in a world where there are so many people who act on the impulse to be kind and helpful.

Over the seven decades of my life, my acts of giving back have included canvassing for civil rights in the 1960s, flipping burgers at a county fair, reading to children, reporting for a television news program on both the environment and illiteracy, and performing at benefits at locations ranging from grand hotel ballrooms to raise money for worthy causes to playing guitar on a flatbed trailer in a parking lot to raise money for a neighbor burned out of his home. But the project that has occupied literally half my time for over two decades has been educating staff, members of the United States Congress, and the public about the Northern Rockies Ecosystem Protection Act. The story of the passage of NREPA will have to be told another time. Among other reasons, it's waiting for an ending that includes the date the bill was signed into law.

An unexpected bonus from my environmental activism has been the friends I've made among the conservation community, Congress, and its staff. Though my conservationist friends make quite a bit less money than they could be earning in the commercial sector, they do what they do because they have a passion to make the world a better place, and because someone has to do it. "Because someone has to do it" is probably as good a definition of giving back as any.

I'd like to dedicate the rest of this chapter to other friends whose professional lives and charitable work have inspired me. Maybe they've inspired you as well.

I was already a fan of U2 when I learned about Bono's association with Amnesty International in the cause of human rights. When Bono brought his intense focus to cancellation of Third World debt and raising awareness of the AIDS pandemic in Africa and elsewhere, he was an effective advocate. He used his name and fame to make his case directly to heads of state and lawmakers.

When I visited with Bono in Ireland I found him to be impassioned and articulate about issues that affect tremendous numbers of people. But what impresses me most about Bono's activism is not only how relentless he is in pursuit of his mission to alleviate the suffering of so many people, but that he makes it a point to be well informed in great detail. He does his homework.

If Paul Newman's acting career was inspiring, his charitable accomplishments were even more so. The Academy Award–winning actor combined his cooking skills and business acumen with his name recognition to support a number of worthy causes, but the one closest to his heart was the Hole in the Wall Gang Camp in Ashford, Connecticut. Initially funded in part with the profits from Newman's Own food products, Newman founded the original camp with the support of his wife, Academy Award winner Joanne Woodward, and the writer A. E. Hotchner, his longtime friend. Paul's efforts stirred the generosity of so many people that Hole in the Wall Gang Camps sprang up around the world like mushrooms after a spring shower.[*]

The camps are designed to give children with grave illnesses an opportunity to spend time with other children with serious health issues in an environment that takes into account the children's comfort, health, and safety. For two weeks campers leave behind their identity as "the sick child" and experience life as most children do, in the company of other kids like themselves. Special care, equipment, and medication are provided along with the volunteer services of medical professionals, counselors, cooks, housekeepers, maintenance personnel, and all the other people it takes to keep a camp operational. The season lasts from June through the end of August, with sessions scheduled in two-week increments to allow

---

[*]Other Hole in the Wall Gang Camp locations can be found at http://www
.teamholeinthewall.org/.

a maximum number of children to attend. There is also a session for siblings, whose identity as "the healthy child" often puts them later in line for the family's attention. A session gives siblings peer input as well as adult counseling to help them understand that they're neither "bad" nor alone in sometimes feeling resentful of their brother or sister with special medical needs.

As part of the camp's fund-raising effort in 1990, Newman recruited friends from Broadway and other celebrities to participate in the First Annual Fandango Benefit Gala. The gala included a gourmet lunch, a silent auction, a live auction, and a performance with musical parodies loosely based on a script adapted by Hotch. The show featured Paul, Joanne, guest celebrities, and, most important of all, campers who acted, sang, danced, and/or played instruments. The children's disabilities were accommodated in such a way that any child who wished to participate could do so.

I didn't realize when I agreed to participate that I would be embarking on a journey that would compel me back to Ashford almost every September for the next seventeen years. Performing with the children was a heartening and highly entertaining experience. How could I not become a camp regular?

The downside was losing the children. The upside was helping the youngsters bring to fruition dreams they might not otherwise have achieved and bearing witness to the courage, determination, and grace of the children, parents, and siblings. Performers and celebrity counselors over the years have included Julia Roberts, Marisa Tomei, Robin Williams, Nathan Lane, Whoopi Goldberg, Alec Baldwin, Jerry Seinfeld, Jim Naughton, Kristin Chenoweth, and Cy Coleman. Every show closed with the entire cast singing a song Cy wrote with Dorothy Fields called "(If There Were) More People Like You."

If there were more people who cared
There would be fewer people to care for
More people of worth
Good people worth our saying a prayer for

Less people who don't
There would be more people who do
If there were more people like you

In 1998 the children and I sang a song at that year's gala that I wrote with A. E. Hotchner. The song was called "Hope." Hearing Hotch's words sung by the campers made everyone in the theater believe in miracles.

The word is hope
Light as air, you don't care
You can cope if you have . . . hope
You may be down
Things are bleak, you can't speak
Don't you frown, you'll come around
'Cause there is hope

Among my many memories of autumn weekends in Ashford, these three stand out:

1. The hectic scene backstage—if you could call it "backstage." The building was so small that there was no room behind the stage, just a wall. "Backstage" was a passageway in the basement through which offstage performers crossed from stage left to stage right. Off the passageway were a couple of bathrooms that doubled as male and female dressing

rooms. Several other small rooms accommodated volunteer seamstresses working overtime to fit costumes on newly arrived guest performers, adjust previously fitted costumes on campers, and assemble hats, shoes, socks, jewelry, reindeer noses, bunny ears, and other vital costume pieces. Odds were that not everything would be ready by showtime, but everything always was.

Upstairs the director was blocking the movements of the actors and the children onstage. "You! Move over here, please. And you, stand there, please....Leo, can we please run through that last number again?...What? Okay. Everyone needs to leave the stage right now so more lights can be hung....I'm sorry, what? The children need a food break? Okay. Children, line up, please. Hot dogs and other finger foods are available outside...." Twenty minutes later: "The lights are hung? Great! Everyone back on the stage, please....Wait, it's time for the children's scheduled rest period? Can we *please* get all the adults back onstage?" (*Exeunt* the children.)

2. Nathan Lane playing an elderly Sundance Kid opposite Newman's aged Butch Cassidy. Hotch had set the scene in a nursing home in which the two outlaws might have found themselves had they lived into their dotage. As did many of the actors in these shows, Nathan strayed so far from the script (a very loose structure to begin with) that the other actors couldn't say their lines because they were laughing so hard. My daughter Sherry played the attractive nurse who brought meds to the elderly Butch and Sundance. In addition to performing at almost every gala, Sherry volunteered regularly as a counselor. That year she shared counselor duties with the very down-to-earth, hardworking Julia Roberts.

3. Newman playing Sarah Brown in 2006 opposite Bernadette Peters as Sky Masterson in *Guys and Dolls*. Hotch usually cast Newman in opposite-gender roles for the galas. On this occasion, he cast most, though not all, actors across gender. As Benny Southstreet, I traded repartée with Alec Baldwin playing Nathan Detroit. Kyra Sedgwick glowed with femininity as the respiratorially challenged Miss Adelaide, while Paul and Bernadette egged each other on to find yet another improvised comedic moment between them. The audience of extraordinarily generous donors couldn't have been happier. Nor could I.

Paul Newman's turn as Sarah Brown in that show was one of his last performances in a Hole in the Wall Gang Camp gala. This song says it all:

Can do . . . can do . . . This guy says the horse can do . . .

Paul Newman could do.

James Taylor, Bonnie Raitt, Graham Nash, and Jackson Browne are never too busy to perform for a cause, be it a local school, saving the Amazon rain forest, or an effort to bring about world peace. No cause is too big or too small for them to lend their names and voices in support. I consider it an honor to share an occupation and a longtime friendship with each and every one of them.

Sometimes I lose hope that human beings will do right by each other, animals, and the planet. Wars continue to be fought. People continue to commit violence against each other. *Homo sapiens* is the only species I can think of whose behavior includes deliberate cruelty to other beings. This knowledge sorely tests my belief that the human inhabitants of this planet will be able to function as a world community with integrity and compassion.

When I feel this way, it helps to remember my ancestors' journey. My grandparents left their homes and villages and traveled all those miles believing they would find a better world for their children and grandchildren. More than a century later their courage keeps me going. The "you can do anything" message from my father and mother buoys me. Because of all these people, my life really was a tapestry, with each thread leading to a range of possibilities including—knock wood—a wonderful family, good health, great friends, music, peace, joy, love, curiosity, and adventure.

With every sunrise I reaffirm my intention to spend part of that day giving back, be it through a smile, a song, a letter to the editor, a friendly email with compulsively correct spelling and grammar (my father would have it no other way), or simply remembering to say thank you.

With every sunset I'm grateful that I made it through another day, and I hope that my descendants and I are granted enough days to fulfill the promise of my grandparents' journey.

Showtime 2005, continued

Slice is walking rapidly toward me.

"Sorry about that," he says. "Are you ready?"

I barely have time to quip, "I was *born* ready!" before he takes off again.

As I try to keep up I hear my boots clicking noisily on the concrete floor. We approach a door marked "Stage Right." Slice stops, puts up his hand, and says, "Hold up a minute."

I do as he says.

Slice opens the door, pops his head in, and says something I can't hear to several stagehands who, I observe, are in physical positions suggesting inactivity. Despite Slice's relatively small stature, his comment and the manner in which he delivers it causes the stagehands to spring immediately into action. Soon everything is up to Slice's standard of readiness for the entrance of his artist. He pops his head back out and reaches for something in a pocket of his shorts. Indoors or out, no matter how cold it is, I've never known Slice to work in anything but shorts. He brings out a small flashlight and uses it to guide me around a row of tables with computers, stacks of chairs, coiled-up cables, equipment cases, electricians, stagehands, and other potential obstacles. The memory of coiled rubber cables in Dublin flickers in my mind, then just as quickly disappears. Slice is on it. I'm safe.

The rest of my walk through the backstage area is illuminated by Slice's flashlight and minuscule bulbs emitting just enough light that each crew member can see what he or she is doing. On the opposite side of the stage I see "Rasta" Jon Schimke moving faders on the monitor to set the opening levels. The glow from the mixing board illuminates, with a ghostly light, Rasta's face and the dreadlocks he has cultivated over many years. At the top of his list is keeping his eye on me at all times when I'm onstage so he can make an immediate adjustment should I indicate a need using universally understood sign language. If I point to my mouth and then point up, Rasta knows to raise the level of my vocal. And so on. Rasta also watches Rudy and Gary and makes adjustments for them. If we can hear the music in a good balance, it'll feel right when we play it. We don't hear what the audience hears, but their reaction tells us that Christian Walsh's front-of-house mix is everything it needs to be.

Slice delivers me to my holding position and turns off his light. Black curtains intrude just enough on each side of the stage to hide backstage activity from the audience. A scrim hangs at the back of the set to enhance Joe Cardosi's lighting design. There is no front curtain. The set is visible to the audience as they enter. It's an arrangement of furniture softly lit with several lamps. There are several rugs, plants, a couch, a coffee table, photos and books, a grand piano with a small lamp on it, and a wedge monitor to the left of the piano bench. Notwithstanding the presence of a couple of stools, microphones, and wedges for Rudy and Gary, the audience knows that the set is a living room.

From the wings I see people chatting animatedly, visiting, milling around, looking for their seats, and doing what audiences have done before shows since they came to see Ugg wrestle Krog for the tusk of a newly killed mammoth.

It's kind of cool to be invisible, I think as I watch the audience. In less than a minute, they'll be watching me.

"House to half," Slice says to one of the stagehands, who repeats the command into his headset. The house lights dim. Audience members who aren't in their seats quickly scramble to find them. The level of excitement in the audience begins to rise and I suddenly feel an overwhelming rush of responsibility. I've been performing for so long that I should no longer doubt that I'll be able to give everyone in the audience what they came for, yet every night when I hear Slice say, "House to half," I feel the weight of that undertaking. At that moment, the knowledge that I'm the person the crowd has come to see feels a little daunting. That isn't necessarily a bad thing. It gives me an edge, a surge of energy short of butterflies that keeps me from being complacent.

Like a great impresario—which Slice is right now, because he is in total control of the stage—he gives the people in the audience just enough time to get to their seats without letting the excitement lag before giving the command, "House to black."

The stagehand with the headset repeats Slice's command, the house goes dark, and the audience erupts in anticipatory applause. The lamps onstage are now the brightest objects in the room. Slice turns on his flashlight. Then, with the ceremonial air of an Olympian passing the torch, he officially turns control of the stage over to me.

"The stage is yours. Remember to turn on your light, and have fun!"

His light guides me through the darkness until the spotlight finds me. The welcoming roar engulfs me. I wave to the audience, take a deep, appreciative bow, and remind myself that their applause isn't only for me. They're clapping for significant events in their own lives that have little to do with me—falling in love, marching for peace, dancing at friends' weddings, serving in Vietnam or the Peace Corps, losing a parent, conceiving a child, going through a difficult divorce—passages for which my songs happened to be the soundtrack. I'm surprised to see so many audience members in their thirties and forties, but it's my contemporaries who are most enthusiastic in celebration of our shared history and individual survival.

I walk along the proscenium to acknowledge the folks from whose view I'll be hidden by the piano for much of the show. I give one last wave from stage left, then walk to the piano. Per Slice's reminder, I turn on my lamp. Then I sit down on the bench. It is exactly the right height. (Me of little faith.)

I lift my hands to the keys and play the opening C-minor chord of "Beautiful." I hear, "You've got to get up every morning" coming out of my wedge in perfect balance with the piano and smile at Rasta so he knows all is well. I continue through the first chorus. As electric energy begins to pulse through my mind in little bursts of neurons firing, I am reminded of the way in which some Eastern philosophers compare a mind jumping from thought to thought to a monkey leaping from tree to tree. As I sing, my monkey mind wonders where songs come from. God? Which god? Apollo? Adonai? Jesus Christ? Allah? Buddha, Yahweh, or Jehovah?

When I was nineteen I questioned the existence of God. I didn't feel guilty about it because I reasoned that if God had not meant for us to question his or her existence, she or he would not have given us the intelligence to so question. It wasn't until a decade later that I arrived at something resembling faith—a combination of cultural and religious precepts that ended my need to question the existence of a something, a higher power, a whatever you want to call it. I also arrived at the conviction that belief or nonbelief in the existence of God by whatever name is something each of us has to figure out for ourselves.

You're gonna find, yes, you will
That you're beautiful as you feel . . .

The instrumental of "Beautiful" requires more dexterity and occupies more of my attention, but then, after I execute the modulation and begin to sing the last verse, monkey mind wonders why God by whatever name gave human beings the instinct and ability to kill other human beings simply because they define holiness in different ways and have different names for their understanding of God. Or did people learn how to kill each other on their own? If that's the case, is God by whatever name wringing his or her figurative hands?*

As I begin singing the last chorus I wonder how one part of my mind can be thinking about theology while the other part is completely focused on what I'm there to do. But what I'm hearing in the monitor sounds present and joyous, and the audience seems happy, so whatever's happening is probably okay.

You've got to get up every morning with a smile on your face
And show the world all the love in your heart
Then people gonna treat you better
You're gonna find, yes, you will
That you're beautiful . . . you're beautiful
You're beautiful as you feel

The audience applauds with heartfelt appreciation after the last chord. I thank them and reach down to get my water bottle. As I sip, monkey mind comes up with a rapid series of questions. Why have I spent so much of my life pushing away from this thing

---

*Monkey thoughts race through my mind in a lot less time than it takes to write or read.

I do that people seem to enjoy, and that I, too, enjoy, so much? Was it because I wanted to experience other things, other lifestyles, other adventures, other career paths? Are those such bad things to want?

With startling clarity I grasp the answer, and I feel the essential truth of it with every cell of my body.

It's always been important to me to encourage the best in people, and music has been my principal instrument in doing that. And yet I kept pushing music away because I thought it was keeping me from having a normal life.

At this moment I understand that for me, music *is* normal life.

And then I stop thinking. Monkey mind merges into the moment. I set the bottle on the floor, place my hands on the piano, and strike the A-flat major 7th chord that heralds the next song. The applause immediately dies down, and I begin to sing.

> *Music is playing inside my head*
> *Over and over and over again, my friend*
> *There's no end to the music . . .*
>
> *Ah, it's not always easy*
> *But the music keeps playing and won't let the world get me*
> *down*

Afterword

$\mathcal{B}$ecause my father, Sid Klein, died while I was still writing *A Natural Woman*, his passing is included as part of my narrative. I honor my father for his readiness to help others, for teaching me to value excellence in myself and others, and for his role in creating Lake Waubeeka, a community that is still thriving after more than half a century.

My mother, Eugenia Gingold (née Cammer), was ninety-four when I lost her on December 22, 2010. In the summer of her life she helped my father build the aforementioned community and put on shows there. In her autumn years, my mother earned respect in South Florida as an actress, director, and theater critic. I was privileged to bear witness to her acceptance of the winter and the end of her life with courage, grace, and dignity. I honor my mother for her unwavering love and support, for her wisdom, encouragement, editorial comments, and remarkable memory while I was writing this book, and for being an example of how to live life to the fullest.[*]

---

[*] (http://www.miamiherald.com/2011/01/01/1995973/eugenia-gold-carole-kings-mother.html)

Rudy Guess passed away at age fifty-seven on December 31, 2010. No one misses Rudy more than his wife and best friend, but Lorna is not alone in missing him. Whether one met him for a moment, knew him for years, or was lucky enough to play music with him, simply being around Rudy brought joy to everyone.[*]

Don Kirshner was surrounded by his children and grandchildren and his beloved wife, Sheila, when he passed away at age seventy-six on January 17, 2011, in Boca Raton, Florida. Donnie's talent for both music and business redounded to the benefit of many more songwriters and musicians than history may record. I'm thankful that I was one of them.

The seeds of James Taylor's and my 2010 Troubadour Reunion Tour were planted in 2007 when James and I played at the Troubadour club in Los Angeles with our original bandmates. Those shows are memorialized in a CD and DVD, *Carole King/James Taylor—Live at the Troubadour.*

Our reunion with that talented group of musicians and friends recalled for all of us the period of tremendous growth during which we had influenced each other both musically and personally. If you'd like to learn more about James and me and other singer-songwriters and musicians who emerged in California in the early 1970s, documentary filmmaker Morgan Neville captured that period remarkably well in his film *Troubadours: The Rise of the Singer-Songwriter.*

Because there wasn't enough room in this memoir for me to give the 2010 Troubadour Reunion Tour the depth and reflection it deserves, please be assured that it's a subsequent tale that I want very much to tell.

---

[*] (http://www.caroleking.com/rudy/rudy.html)

Acknowledgments

COLLEEN DALY: my first editor—"Just write."

SHERRY KONDOR: bff, manager, and child of mine.

ROBBIE KONDOR, DILLON KONDOR, AND SOPHIE KONDOR: music, love, and laughter.

LOUISE GOFFIN: gifted songwriter and producer, daughter of light and wisdom.

HAYDEN AND ELIJAH WELLS: rhythm and joy.

MOLLY LARKEY: maker of art and LOVE.

LEVI, BENA, AND OCEAN LARKEY: sun beauty rock steady love family hilarious.

LOU ADLER: then, now, and always.

ELISSA KLINE: fine art photographer, archivist, documentarian, and caring friend.

ERIK GILLBERG: "I just call out your name" and there you are.

IAN GILLBERG: the person you get when you teach your children well.

JOY HARRIS: friend and literary agent.

DEB FUTTER: my esteemed editor at Grand Central Publishing.

KRIS ADETOSOYE: for keeping it all together.

ACKNOWLEDGMENTS

KATIE PAGE: for making a good noize better.

ROBIN FORT-LINCKE: 'tis a wondrous web she weaves.

JACK KAUFMAN AND EDITH PREVER: "Always begin with an outline."

MARTY BANDIER AND NEIL LASHER at Sony/ATV Music Publishing.

VERONICA COTA, EVELYN HADDAD, AND RONNY SCHIFF.

JULIE MCDOWELL with Hal Leonard Corporation.

LAURIE SORIANO, JEFF SILBERMAN, SETH MILLER, AND STEVE MILLEMANN: *the* eagles.

DAVID WEISE, BETH SABBAGH, ROB SALZMAN, DINA DEMAS, VIOLETA DAVIDYAN, and everyone at DWA: for care and excellence with numbers.

BRAD SNOW AND TIM ROGERS: for taking care of the "it" we get out amongst.

CAROLYN MALONEY, COLLEEN CORRIGAN, and everyone on the NREPA team: water on a rock.

GRAND CENTRAL PUBLISHING: Chris Barba, Dianne Choie, Jimmy Franco, Tommy Harron, Liz Kessler, Michele McGonigle, Mari Okuda, Martha Otis, Roland Ottewell, Bruce Paonessa, Jamie Raab, Karen Torres, Anne Twomey, and David Young.

JOY HARRIS LITERARY AGENCY: Adam Reed and Sarah Twombly.

Lorna Guess, Ralph and Emily Simon, Gerry and Michele Goffin, Barry Mann, Cynthia Weil, Toni Stern, Carole Bayer Sager, and Sheila Kirshner.

Rudy Guess, Charles Larkey, Danny Kortchmar, Russ Kunkel, Ralph Schuckett, Paul Hipp, and Charlie Macey.

ACKNOWLEDGMENTS

James and Kim Taylor, Paul Simon, and Paul McCartney.

Jerry Wexler, Ahmet Ertegun, Peter Asher, and Hank Cicalo.

Phil Robinson, Beverly Klein, Judith Freeman, Howard Frank, Roy and Mon'nette Reynolds, and Captains Greg Freitas and Barbara Emerson.

Special thanks to Bob DiCorcia, Mary Rohlfing, José Martinez, and all my longtime fans and CK heads: Thank you for your steadfast appreciation of my work and for being cool enough to know "when not to play."

Deepest gratitude to all.

Credits

Page 11

"Twinkle, Twinkle, Little Star"
Lyrics by Jane Taylor from the poem "The Star" (1806); music adapted from the French folk song "Ah! vous dirai-je, Maman" (1761)

Page 13

"Bell Bottom Trousers (Coat of Navy Blue)"
Written by Moe Jaffe and performed by Guy Lombardo and His Royal Canadians (Tony Pastor's Orchestra had the longest- and highest-charting version)

Page 14

"Heart and Soul"
Lyrics by Frank Loesser; music by Hoagy Carmichael

"Chopsticks"
Music by Euphemia Allen, aka Arthur de Lulli

Page 16

Teaching Little Fingers to Play—A Book for the Earliest Beginner
Written by John Thompson

Page 17

"Shoo Fly Pie and Apple Pan Dowdy"
Lyrics by Sammy Gallop; music by Guy Wood

Page 19

The Romance of Helen Trent (soap opera)
Created by Frank and Anne Hummert; various directors and writers

"Dance with a Dolly (With a Hole in Her Stocking)"
Lyrics and Music by Terry Shand, Jimmy Eaton, and Mickey Leader

Page 20

The Shadow (radio drama series)
Adapted by David Chrisman and Bill Sweets; various directors and writers

The Lone Ranger (radio drama series)
Created by Fran Striker (George W. Trendle is disputed); various directors and writers

Inner Sanctum Mysteries (radio drama series)
Created by Himan Brown; various directors and writers

The Green Hornet (radio drama series)
Created by Fran Striker (George W. Trendle is disputed); various directors and writers

Suspense (radio drama series)
Created by producers of the CBS summer series *Forecast*; various directors and writers

Mr. Keen, Tracer of Lost Persons (radio drama series)
Created by Frank and Anne Hummert; various directors and writers

Page 21

I Love Lucy (TV series)
Created by Jess Oppenheimer, Madelyn Davis, Bob Carroll Jr.;
written by Jess Oppenheimer, Madelyn Davis, Bob Carroll Jr., Bob
Schiller, Bob Weiskopf; various directors

Texaco Star Theater (TV variety series)
Various writers including Milton Berle; directed by Edmund
L. Cashman, Greg Garrison, Sid Smith, Milton Berle

The Milton Berle Show (TV variety series)
One season only; see *Texaco Star Theater* above

Page 22

The Horn and Hardart Children's Hour (TV variety series)
Created by Stan Lee Broza; directed by Stan Lee Broza and
various directors

"If I Knew You Were Comin' I'd've Baked a Cake"
Lyrics and music by Al Hoffman, Bob Merrill, and Clem Watts

Page 23

Hit Parader (magazine)
Published by Charlton Publications; edited by various

(Ted Mack's) The Original Amateur Hour (TV variety series)
Written by Jac Hein; directed by Albert Fisher

You Bet Your Life (TV)
Created by John Guedel; directed by Robert Dwan and Bernie
Smith

Page 24

"You Belong to Me"
Lyrics and music by Pee Wee King, Redd Stewart, and Chilton
Price

"The Glow Worm"
English lyrics by Lilla Cayley Robinson, revised by Johnny Mercer; music by Paul Linke

"Wheel of Fortune"
Lyrics and music by Bennie Benjamin and George David Weiss

Page 25
The Man in the Gray Flannel Suit (1956)
Written and directed by Nunnally Johnson, based on the novel by Sloan Wilson

Page 27
"Music! Music! Music!"
Lyrics and music by Bernie Baum and Stephen Weiss

"Rocket 88"
Lyrics and music by Jackie Brenston and performed by Jackie Brenston and His Delta Cats, featuring Ike Turner on piano

"5-10-15 Hours"
Lyrics and music by Rudolph Toombs and performed by Ruth Brown

"(Mama) He Treats Your Daughter Mean"
Lyrics and music by Herb Lance, Charlie Singleton, and John Wallace and performed by Ruth Brown

"Earth Angel"
Authorship has long been disputed but is generally credited to Jesse Belvin, Gaynel Hodge, and Curtis Williams and performed by the Penguins

"Rock Around the Clock"
Lyrics and music by Max C. Freedman and James E. Myers (aka Jimmy De Knight) and performed by Bill Haley and His Comets

Page 28

The Blackboard Jungle (1955)
Written by Richard Brooks, based on the novel by Evan Hunter; directed by Richard Brooks

Page 35

Guys and Dolls
Book by Jo Swerling and Abe Burrows; lyrics and music by Frank Loesser

South Pacific
Book by Joshua Logan and Oscar Hammerstein II, based on *Tales of the South Pacific* by James A. Michener; lyrics by Oscar Hammerstein II; music by Richard Rodgers

Oklahoma!
Book by Oscar Hammerstein II, based on the play *Green Grow the Lilacs* by Lynn Riggs; lyrics by Oscar Hammerstein II; music by Richard Rodgers

The King and I
Book by Oscar Hammerstein II, based on the novel *Anna and the King of Siam* by Margaret Landon; lyrics by Oscar Hammerstein II; music by Richard Rodgers

Carousel
Book by Oscar Hammerstein II based on the play *Liliom* by Ferenc Molnár; lyrics by Oscar Hammerstein II; music by Richard Rodgers

Peter Pan
Book by Sir James M. Barrie; lyrics and music by Mark Charlap and Carolyn Leigh; additional lyrics and music by Jule Styne, Betty Comden, and Adolph Green

CREDITS

My Fair Lady
Book by Alan Jay Lerner, based on the play *Pygmalion* by George Bernard Shaw; lyrics and music by Alan Jay Lerner and Frederick Loewe

West Side Story
Book by Arthur Laurents, based on a conception of Jerome Robbins; lyrics by Stephen Sondheim; music by Leonard Bernstein

Page 39
The Mikado
Book, lyrics, and music by W. S. Gilbert and Arthur Sullivan

Page 40
"Sincerely"
Lyrics and music by Harvey Fuqua and Alan Freed and performed by the Moonglows

Page 42
"Tutti Frutti"
Lyrics and music and performed by Richard Wayne Penniman (Little Richard)

Page 43
Carmen
Composed by Georges Bizet; libretto by Henri Meilhac and Ludovic Halévy, based on a novella by Prosper Mérimée

Surprise Symphony
Composed by Josef Haydn

Peter and the Wolf
Music and text by Sergei Prokofiev

Page 44

"Let the Good Times Roll"

Written by Shirley Goodman and Leonard Lee and performed by Shirley and Lee

"Ain't That a Shame" aka "Ain't It a Shame"

Lyrics and music by Antoine "Fats" Domino and Dave Bartholomew and performed by Fats Domino

Page 46

"No Other Love"

Lyrics by Oscar Hammerstein II; music by Richard Rodgers; and performed by Perry Como

"(How Much Is That) Doggie in the Window?"

Written by Bob Merrill and Ingrid Reuterskiöld and performed by Patti Page

Page 47

"Pledging My Love"

Lyrics and music by Don Robey and Ferdinand Washington and performed by Johnny Ace

Page 53

"Beau Soir"

Music composed by Claude Debussy; lyrics, based on a setting of a poem, *Beau Soir*, by Paul Bourget

Page 55

Rebel Without a Cause (1955)

Written and directed by Nicholas Ray; screenplay by Stewart Stern; adaptation by Irving Shulman

Page 57

Reefer Madness (1938)

Written by Arthur Hoerl (with additional dialogue by Paul

Franklin); original story by Lawrence Meade; directed by Louis J. Gasnier

Page 60

"While I Dream"
Lyrics and music by Neil Sedaka and Howard Greenfield and performed by the Linc-Tones

"I Love My Baby"
Lyrics and music by Neil Sedaka and Howard Greenfield and performed by the Linc-Tones

"Leave, Schkeeve"
Lyrics and music by Carole King, Joel Zwick, Iris Lipnick, and Lenny Pullman

Page 61

"Once in a While"
Lyrics by Bud Green; music by Michael Edwards; and performed by Patti Page

"Young and Foolish"
Lyrics by Arnold B. Horwitt; music by Albert Hague; and performed by Tony Bennett

Page 66

"Diana"
Written and performed by Paul Anka

"(Ghost) Riders in the Sky: A Cowboy Legend"
Lyrics and music by Stan Jones and performed by Vaughn Monroe and His Orchestra

Page 72

"Baby Sittin'"
Lyrics and music by Carole King

"Under the Stars"
Lyrics and music by Carole King

Page 73

"Goin' Wild"
Lyrics and music by Carole King

"The Right Girl"
Lyrics and music by Carole King

Page 78

"Hey Schoolgirl"
Lyrics and music by Paul Simon and performed by Tom and Jerry (Paul Simon and Art Garfunkel)

"Just to Be with You"
Lyrics and music by Marv Kalfin (demo by Paul Simon and Carole King) and performed by the Passions

"The Sound of Silence"
Lyrics and music by Paul Simon and performed by Paul Simon and Art Garfunkel

Page 81

"Love Is Strange"
Lyrics and music by Mickey Baker, Sylvia Robinson, and Ellas McDaniel (music also claimed by Jody Williams)

"The Kid Brother"
Lyrics and music by Gerry Goffin and Carole King

Page 82

"Ooh Sha La La"
Lyrics and music by Neil Sedaka and Howard Greenfield

Page 84

"Stupid Cupid"
Lyrics and music by Neil Sedaka and Howard Greenfield and performed by Connie Francis

"Twilight Time"
Lyrics by Buck Ram; music by Artie Dunn, Morty Nevins, and Al Nevins; and performed by the Platters

Page 91

"Girls Grow Up Faster Than Boys"
Written by Gerry Goffin and Jack Keller and performed by the Cookies

"Don't Say Nothin' Bad About My Baby"
Lyrics and music by Gerry Goffin and Carole King

"Chains"
Lyrics and music by Gerry Goffin and Carole King

Page 94

"Tonight's the Night"
Lyrics and music by Luther Dixon and Shirley Owens and performed by the Shirelles

Page 95

"Will You Love Me Tomorrow"
Lyrics and music by Gerry Goffin and Carole King

"Kansas City"
Lyrics and music by Jerry Leiber and Mike Stoller and performed by Wilbert Harrison

Page 96

"There Goes My Baby"
Lyrics and music by Ben E. King, Lover Patterson, George Treadwell, Jerry Leiber, and Mike Stoller and performed by the Drifters

CREDITS

Page 97

"Who Put the Bomp (in the Bomp, Bomp, Bomp)"
Lyrics and music by Gerry Goffin and Barry Mann and performed by Barry Mann

Page 101

"Child of Mine"
Lyrics and music by Gerry Goffin and Carole King

"Daughter of Light"
Lyrics and music by Gerry Goffin and Carole King

Page 103

"Mashed Potato Time"
Lyrics and music by Robert Bateman, Georgia Dobbins, William E. Garrett, Freddie Gorman, Brian Holland, and Kal Mann

"The Loco-Motion"
Lyrics and music by Gerry Goffin and Carole King

Page 106

"It Might as Well Rain Until September"
Lyrics and music by Gerry Goffin and Carole King

Page 109

"Yes I Will"
Lyrics and music by Gerry Goffin and Russ Titelman

"I'm Into Something Good"
Lyrics and music by Gerry Goffin and Carole King

Page 113

David and Lisa (1962)
Written by Eleanor Perry, based on the novel by Theodore Isaac Rubin; directed by Frank Perry

The Manchurian Candidate (1962)

Written by George Axelrod and John Frankenheimer (uncredited), based on the novel by Richard Condon; directed by John Frankenheimer

To Kill a Mockingbird (1962)

Written by Horton Foote, based on the novel *To Kill a Mockingbird* by Harper Lee; directed by Robert Mulligan

Page 115

"Take Good Care of My Baby"
Lyrics and music by Gerry Goffin and Carole King

"Run to Him"
Lyrics and music by Gerry Goffin and Jack Keller

"Crying in the Rain"
Lyrics and music by Carole King and Howard Greenfield

Page 116

"Bye Bye Love" and "Wake Up Little Susie"
Lyrics and music by Boudleaux Bryant and Felice Bryant

Page 122

"(You Make Me Feel Like A) Natural Woman"
Lyrics and music by Gerry Goffin, Carole King, and Jerry Wexler

Page 129

"Hey Girl"
Lyrics and music by Gerry Goffin and Carole King

Page 130

"The Porpoise Song"
Lyrics and music by Gerry Goffin and Carole King

CREDITS

Page 132

"The Times They Are A-Changin'"
Lyrics and music and performed by Bob Dylan

Page 138

A Patch of Blue (1965)
Written and directed by Guy Green, based on the book *Be Ready with Bells and Drums* by Elizabeth Kata

Doctor Zhivago (1965)
Written by Robert Bolt, based on the novel by Boris Pasternak; directed by David Lean

Thunderball (1965)
Written by Richard Maibaum and John Hopkins; directed by Terence Young; original screenplay by Jack Whittingham; original story by Kevin McClory, Jack Whittingham, and Ian Fleming

The Sound of Music (1965)
Musical book by Howard Lindsay and Russel Crouse; screenplay by Ernest Lehman, based on the Broadway musical *The Sound of Music*; lyrics by Oscar Hammerstein II; music by Richard Rodgers; directed by Robert Wise

Page 139

One Flew Over the Cuckoo's Nest (1975)
Written by Lawrence Hauben and Bo Goldman, based on the novel by Ken Kesey; directed by Milos Forman

Page 141

"California Girls"
Lyrics and music by Brian Wilson and Mike Love and performed by the Beach Boys

"Help Me, Rhonda"
Lyrics and music by Brian Wilson and Mike Love and performed by the Beach Boys

"Good Vibrations"
Lyrics by Brian Wilson and Mike Love; music by Brian Wilson; and performed by the Beach Boys

Page 142
"Shower the People"
Lyrics and music and performed by James Taylor

Page 161
"Our House"
Lyrics and music by Graham Nash and performed by Crosby, Stills, Nash & Young

Page 172
"Lady of the Lake"
Lyrics and music by Carole King and Toni Stern

"Blues for a Young Girl Gone"
Lyrics and music by Carole King and Toni Stern

"It's Going to Take Some Time"
Lyrics and music by Carole King and Toni Stern

"Where You Lead"
Lyrics and music by Carole King and Toni Stern

"It's Too Late"
Lyrics and music by Carole King and Toni Stern

Page 173
"Where You Lead I Will Follow"
Lyrics and music by Carole King and Toni Stern

Page 177

"Rainy Day Man"
Lyrics and music by James Taylor and Zach Wiesner and performed by James Taylor

Page 183

"California Dreamin'"
Lyrics and music by John Phillips and Michelle Phillips and
performed by the Mamas and the Papas

"San Francisco (Be Sure to Wear Some Flowers in Your Hair)"
Lyrics and music by John Phillips and performed by Scott
McKenzie

"Eve of Destruction"
Lyrics and music by P. F. Sloan and performed by Barry
McGuire

Page 184

"My Sweet Home"
Lyrics and music and performed by Margaret Allison

"Snow Queen"
Lyrics and music by Gerry Goffin and Carole King

"Wasn't Born to Follow"
Lyrics and music by Gerry Goffin and Carole King

"A Man Without a Dream"
Lyrics and music by Gerry Goffin and Carole King

"Lady"
Lyrics and music by Gerry Goffin and Carole King

"All My Time"
Lyrics and music by Gerry Goffin and Carole King

"Hi-de-Ho (That Old Sweet Roll)"
Lyrics and music by Gerry Goffin and Carole King

Page 198

"A World Without Love"
Lyrics and music by Paul McCartney and John Lennon and performed by Peter and Gordon

"Nobody I Know"
Lyrics and music by Paul McCartney and John Lennon and performed by Peter and Gordon

"I Go to Pieces"
Lyrics and music by Del Shannon and performed by Peter and Gordon

Page 201

"So Far Away"
Lyrics and music by Carole King

Page 204

"Up on the Roof"
Lyrics and music by Gerry Goffin and Carole King

Page 210

"I Feel the Earth Move"
Lyrics and music by Carole King

"You've Got a Friend"
Lyrics and music by Carole King

Page 213

"How High the Moon"
Lyrics by Nancy Hamilton; music by Morgan Lewis; and performed by Les Paul and Mary Ford

"The World Is Waiting for the Sunrise"
Lyrics by Eugene Lockhart; music by Ernest Seitz (aka Raymond Roberts); and performed by Les Paul and Mary Ford

Page 217
"Tapestry"
Lyrics and music by Carole King

Page 228
"Smackwater Jack"
Lyrics and music by Gerry Goffin and Carole King

Page 236
"Song of Long Ago"
Lyrics and music by Carole King

Page 247
"Jazzman"
Lyrics and music by Carole King and David Palmer

Page 249
"Goodbye Don't Mean I'm Gone"
Lyrics and music by Carole King

"Weekdays"
Lyrics and music by Carole King

Page 254
"An Uncommon Love"
Written by Carole King, Rob Hyman, and Rich Wayland

"Oh No Not My Baby"
Written by Gerry Goffin and Carole King

Page 255
Le Ballon rouge (The Red Balloon) (1956)
Written and directed by Albert Lamorisse

Page 256

"Faithless Love"
Lyrics and music by John David Souther and performed by Linda Ronstadt

Page 270

Taxi Driver (1976)
Written by Paul Schrader; directed by Martin Scorsese

Page 332

"Fire on the Mountain"
Lyrics by Robert Hunter; music by Mickey Hart; and performed by the Grateful Dead

"Don't Think Twice, It's All Right"
Lyrics and music and performed by Bob Dylan

"Mama Don't Let Your Babies Grow Up to Be Cowboys"
Lyrics and music by Ed Bruce and Patsy Bruce and performed by Waylon Jennings and Willie Nelson

"Mama Tried"
Lyrics and music and performed by Merle Haggard

"Crazy"
Lyrics and music by Willie Nelson and performed by Patsy Cline

"Put Another Log on the Fire"
Lyrics and music by Sheldon Allan Silverstein and performed by Tompall Glaser

Page 406

"Sweet Child O' Mine"
Lyrics and music by Steven Adler, Saul (Slash) Hudson, Michael (Duff) McKagan, Axl Rose, and Izzy Stradlin (Guns N' Roses)

CREDITS

Page 407

After Dark, My Sweet (1990)
Directed by James Foley; screenplay by Robert Redlin and James Foley, based on the novel by Jim Thompson; starring Jason Patric, Rachel Ward, and Bruce Dern

State of Grace (1990)
Written by Dennis McIntyre; directed by Phil Joanou; starring Sean Penn, Ed Harris, and Gary Oldman

Let's Get Lost (1988)
Directed by Bruce Weber

"Wishful Thinking"
Lyrics and music by Carole King

A League of Their Own (1992)
Directed by Penny Marshall; story by Kim Wilson and Kelly Candaele; screenplay by Lowell Ganz and Babaloo Mandel

Page 408

"Losing My Religion"
Lyrics and music by Bill Berry, Peter Buck, Mike Mills, and Michael Stipe and performed by R.E.M.

Page 441

"Can do...can do...This guy says the horse can do..."
From "Fugue for Tinhorns" from *Guys and Dolls*; music and lyrics by Frank Loesser; book by Jo Swerling and Abe Burrows

Page 448

"Music"
Lyrics and music by Carole King

Permissions

The author is grateful for permission to quote lyrics from the following songs:

- "Three Little Maids" from *The Mikado*. Written by W. S. Gilbert & Arthur Sullivan.
- "Tutti Frutti." Written by Dorothy LaBostrie/Joe Lubin/ Richard W. Penniman. Copyright © 1955 Sony/ATV Music Publishing LLC. All rights administered by Sony/ATV Music Publishing LLC, 8 Music Square West, Nashville, TN 37203. All rights reserved. Used by permission.
- "Let the Good Times Roll." Words and music by Leonard Lee & Shirley Goodman. Copyright © 1956 (Renewed 1984) Atlantic Music Corp and Primary Wave Pixley International Copyright Secured. All Rights Reserved. Reprinted by Permission of Hal Leonard Corp.
- "Leave, Schkeeve." Written by Carole King, Lenny Pullman, Iris Lipnick, Joel Zwick. Unpublished: Used by permission.
- "Babysittin'." Words and music by Carole King. © 1958 Songs of Universal, Inc. Copyright Renewed. All Rights

Index

Album titles appear in italics; song titles appear in quotation marks; albums by Carole King are followed by the date of release.